Public Health

What It Is and How It Works

Bernard J. Turnock, MD, MPH

Professor and Director
Division of Community Health Sciences
School of Public Health
University of Illinois at Chicago
Chicago, Illinois

AN ASPEN PUBLICATION®
Aspen Publishers, Inc.
Gaithersburg, Maryland
1997

Library of Congress Cataloging-in-Publication Data
Turnock, Bernard J.
Public health : what it is and how it works / Bernard J. Turnock.
p. cm.
Includes bibliographical references and index.
ISBN 0-8342-0898-9
1. Public health—United States. 2. Public health administration—
United States. I. Title.
[DNLM: 1. Public Health—United States. 2. Delivery of Health
Care—United States. WA 540 AA1 T95p 1977]
RA445.T86 1997
362.1'0973—dc21
DNLM/DLC
for Library of Congress
96-39565
CIP

Orders: (800) 638-8437
Customer Service: (800) 234-1660

About Aspen Publishers • For more than 35 years, Aspen has been a leading professional publisher in a variety of disciplines. Aspen's vast information resources are available in both print and electronic formats. We are committed to providing the highest quality information available in the most appropriate format for our customers. Visit Aspen's Internet site for more information resources, directories, articles, and a searchable version of Aspen's full catalog, including the most recent publications: **http://www.aspenpub.com**
Aspen Publishers, Inc. • The hallmark of quality in publishing
Member of the worldwide Wolters Kluwer group.

Editorial Resources: Bill Fogle
Library of Congress Catalog Card Number: 96-39565
ISBN: 0-8342-0898-9

Printed in the United States of America
1 2 3 4 5

To my parents, Jane and Barney Turnock

Table of Contents

Foreword

The public health system in the United States has achieved remarkable successes. Public and private water systems deliver clean water for drinking and bathing to Americans every day. Extensive sewage systems clear our waste without noise or odor. Multiple levels of inspection ensure that our food is safe. Communicable diseases are identified, and their spread is rapidly limited. Immunizations are effective against many life-threatening diseases.

The public health system is built on a strong foundation. The consistent application of public health principles to multiple and varied health risks has been a highly successful strategy. The primary functions of public health include

- assessment of the health of the community
- policy development in the public interest
- assurance of the public's health

Decade after decade in the 20th century, we have relied upon public health to continue to improve the American way of life. We have taken for granted the ability of public health professionals and the public health system to solve most of our bothersome health concerns. We now believe that it is merely a nuisance when a few cases of a communicable disease arise, food poisoning strikes, or drinking water becomes contaminated. We simply expect the public health system to be there when we need it. The system itself remains invisible most of the time.

Faced with a terrifying new infectious disease, beholding an outbreak in another country, or viewing a third world country's daily health challenges, we get a glimpse of the public health system's importance to our daily lives. These events provide a graphic demonstration that an effective public health system is a basic ingredient in a country's economic prosperity. It is dangerous to forget the strength that our public health system provides our country.

New challenges and opportunities face the public health system of the next century. Patterns of disease are changing rapidly. Increases in chronic diseases, new and emerging infections, injuries and violence, and curable genetic diseases are new challenges assigned to the public health agenda.

The medical care system has dominated policy makers' attention and accounts for nearly all of national spending on health care. It has produced remarkable technological achievements at tremendous costs. As we face the next century, Americans are just beginning to wrestle with concerns about prevention of disease, decisions about death and dying, and new strategies to promote health.

Although changing patterns of disease and a reforming medical care system offer the public health system an unprecedented opportunity to assume a leadership role in promoting health, these trends are occuring at a time of erosion of funding for the public health system, inadequate leadership capacity, an enhanced public focus on proven interventions, and few innovations in public health technologies.

The public health professionals of the future will be engaged in ensuring that the human species evolves with hope and promise. In the words of C.E.A. Winslow, public health must "enable every citizen to realize his birthright of health and longevity."[1] The statutory base, structural framework, and capacity for action and leadership in the public health system must be systematically evaluated and enhanced. Public health practice and scholarship must be closely linked to create professionals who are ready for the challenges of the next century.

Public health leaders of the next century will need courage and creativity. They will form new partnerships with public- and private-sector entities committed to improving health. They will aggressively advocate for public policies and resources that lead to improved health outcomes. Most important, they will recognize the power of community action. Public health is about each of us taking responsibility for improving our community's health.

It is hard to imagine a discipline that promises more excitement, more hope, or more possibility than the future for public health! Dr. Bernard Turnock has provided us with a scholarly and visionary bridge for public health into the next century.

Coleen Kivlahan, MD, MSPH
Director, Missouri Department of Health

Preface

Public health remains a generally familiar though somewhat unclear concept both to the general public and to those dedicated to its improvement. This book is written as an attempt to describe simply and clearly what it is, what it does, how it works, and why it is important to all of us.

As someone who has spent 15 years in public health practice and another half-dozen in teaching and researching the field, I have been concerned why something so important and useful is not better understood by those who work in the field and those who benefit from its work. Throughout my career as a public health physician, I have developed a profound respect for the field, the work, and the workers. But I must admit that even while serving as director of a large state health department, I lacked a full understanding and appreciation of this unique enterprise.

What has become clear to me is that the story of public health is not simple to tell. There is no one official at the helm, guiding it through the turbulence that is constantly encountered. There is no clear view of its intended destination and of what work needs to be done by whom to get there. We cannot turn to the deans of our schools of public health, the CEOs of managed-care organizations, or even our federal officials, such as our Surgeon General, for vision and direction. Surely, these people play important roles, but public health is so broadly involved with the biological, environmental, social, cultural, behavioral, and service utilization factors associated with health that no one is accountable for addressing everything. Still, we all share in the successes and failures of our collective decisions and actions, making us all accountable to each other for the results of our efforts. I hope that this book will present a broad view of the public health system and deter current and future public health workers from narrowly defining public health in terms of only what they do.

While there is no dearth of fine books in this field, there is most certainly a shortage of understanding, appreciation, and support for public health and its various manifestations. Many of the current texts on public health attempt to be comprehensive in covering the field without the benefit of conceptual framework understandable to insiders and outsiders alike. The dynamism and complexity of the field suggest that public health texts are likely to become even larger and more comprehensive as the field advances. In contrast, this book aims to present the essentials of public health, with an emphasis on comprehensibility rather than comprehensiveness. It presents fundamental concepts but links those concepts to practice in the real world.

These are essential topics for public health students early in their academic careers, and they are increasingly important for students in the social and political sciences and other health professions as well. But this book is intended as much for public health practitioners as it is for students. It represents the belief that public health cannot be adequately taught through a text, that it needs to be learned through exploration and practice of its concepts and methods. In that light, this book should be viewed as a framework for learning and understanding public health rather than the definitive catalog of its principles and practices.

The first four chapters of the book cover topics of interest to general audiences. Basic concepts underlying public health are presented in Chapter 1; included are definitions, historical highlights, and unique features of public health. This and subsequent chapters focus largely on public health in the United States, although information on public health globally and comparisons among nations appear in Chapters 2 and 3. Health and illness and the various factors that influence health status are discussed in Chapter 2. This chapter also presents data and information on health status and risk factors in the United States and introduces a method for analyzing health problems to identify their precursors. The third chapter addresses the overall health system, with a special emphasis on trends and developments that are important to public health. Interfaces between public health and a rapidly changing health system are highlighted. Chapter 4 examines the organization of public health responsibilities in the United States by reviewing its legal basis and the current structure of public health agencies at the federal, state, and local levels. Together, these four chapters serve as a primer on what public health is and how it relates to health interests in modern America.

The final four chapters flesh out the skeleton of public health introduced in the first half of the book. They examine how public health does what it does, addressing issues of the inner workings of public health that are designed for the more serious students of the field. Chapter 5 reviews the core functions of public health and both how and how well these are being addressed in the mid-1990s. This chapter identifies key processes or practices that operationalize public health's core functions and tools that have been developed to improve public health practice. Chapter 6 builds on the governmental structure of American public health (from Chapter 4) and examines other inputs of the public health system, including human, informational, and fiscal resources. Outputs of the public health system, in the form of programs and services, are the subject of Chapter 7. Population-based community prevention services and clinical preventive services are examined, and an approach to program planning and evaluation for public health interventions is presented. The final chapter looks to the future of public health at the turn of the century. Emerging problems, opportunities afforded by the expansion of managed care, and improving local public health practice are discussed, along with obstacles impeding effective public health responses.

Each chapter includes a variety of figures, tables, and exhibits to illustrate the concepts and provide useful resources for public health practitioners. A glossary of public health terminology is provided for the benefit of those unfamiliar with some of the commonly used terms, as well as to convey the intended meaning for terms that may have several different connotations in practice. At the end of each chapter are discussion questions and exercises that complement the topics presented and provide a framework for thought and discussion. These allow the text to be used more flexibly in public health courses at various levels and with learners at different levels of their training and careers.

Together, the chapters represent a systems approach to public health grounded in a conceptual model that characterizes public health by its mission, functions, inputs, practices, outputs, and outcomes. This model is the unifying construct for this text. It provides a framework for examining and questioning the wisdom of our current investment strategy that directs 100 times more resources toward medical services than it spends for population-based prevention strategies—even though medical services can account for only 5 of the 30 years of increased life expectancy at birth that have been achieved in the United States since 1900.

Whatever wisdom might be found in this book has filtered through to me as a result of my mentors, colleagues, and friends. For those who follow us into this vineyard of challenge and opportunity, this is meant to be a primer on public health in the United States. It is a book that seeks to reduce the vast scope, endless complexities, and ever-expanding agenda to a format simple enough to be understood by first-year students and state health commissioners alike.

REFERENCE

1. Winslow CEA. The untilled field of public health. *Mod Med* 1920; 2:183–191.

Acknowledgments

Many persons have shaped the concepts and insights provided in this text. This book evolved from an introductory course on public health concepts and practice that I have been teaching at the University of Illinois-Chicago School of Public Health since 1991. During that time, more than 1,000 current and aspiring public health professionals have influenced the material included in this book. Their enthusiasm and expectations have challenged me to find ways to make this subject interesting and valuable to learners at all levels of their careers.

Many parts of this book rely heavily on the work of public health practitioners and public health practice organizations. The Public Health Practice Program Office (PHPPO) at the Centers for Disease Control and Prevention deserves special acknowledgment for their contributions, especially those of Ed Baker (Director of PHPPO), Carl Tyler, Bud Nicola, Randy Gordon, Greg Christenson, Ed Vaughn, and Tom Richards. The contributions and collaborations of Bill Dyal, formerly with PHPPO, are readily apparent throughout this text. Other valuable contributions came from the Association of State and Territorial Health Officials, especially three state health commissioners: John Lumpkin, Chris Atchison, and Coleen Kivlahan. The fine work of the National Association of County and City Health Officials (NACCHO) is also evident in this text; NACCHO's Mo Mullett, Mary McGlothlin, Nancy Rawding, and Carol Brown merit acknowledgment. Similarly, the Public Health Foundation, especially Sue Addiss and Ron Bialek, have helped to make this work possible. In several chapters, I have drawn on the work of two public health agencies at which I have worked during my career, the Illinois Department of Public Health and the Chicago Department of Public Health. The influence of four outstanding public health figures who have served as mentors and role models—Jean Pakter, Quentin Young, George Pickett, and C. Arden Miller—is also apparent in this book.

Lloyd Novick provided early encouragement and support for this undertaking, as well as useful suggestions on the scope and focus of this text. Judith Munson worked with me in the early development of the course upon which this book is based; her influence on the administrative law section is greatly appreciated. Critical review and constructive suggestions were provided by Naoko Muramatsu, Julia Simmons, Charles Catania, Jim Masterson, several anonymous reviewers, and especially Arden Handler, my colleague and collaborator on many public health capacity–building projects. I am grateful for the many and varied contributions from all these sources.

CHAPTER 1

What Is Public Health?

Few people would consider 1996 a spectacular year for public health in the United States, even though it was the 200th anniversary of Edward Lister's discoveries that eventually resulted in the global eradication of smallpox. It was also the 50th anniversary of the birth of the Centers for Disease Control and Prevention, one of the most respected public health organizations in the world. Beyond these two events, however, there were no major discoveries or triumphs that would make 1996 stand out from other years in recent memory. Yet on closer examination, maybe there were!

In 1996, there were nearly 900,000 fewer cases of measles reported than in 1941, 200,000 fewer cases of diphtheria than in 1921, more than 250,000 fewer cases of whooping cough than in 1934, and 21,000 fewer cases of polio than in 1951. In 1996, average blood lead levels in children were less than one-third of what they had been in 1976.

As a result of three decades of effort, 1996 witnessed 42 million fewer smokers than would have been expected given trends in tobacco use through 1965. More than 2 million Americans were alive in 1996 who otherwise would have died from heart disease and stroke if it had not been for two decades of effort targeting these killing conditions. More than 80,000 Americans were alive in 1996 as a result of automobile seat belt use. By 1996, protection of the United States blood supply had prevented more than 1.5 million hepatitis B and hepatitis C infections and more than 50,000 HIV infections, as well as more than $3.5 billion in medical costs associated with these three diseases.[1] And this catalog of accomplishments could be expanded many times over.

These results did not occur by themselves. They came about through decisions and actions that represent the efforts of public health practice. It is the story of public health practice, and its current value and importance in our lives, that is the focus of this text. With this impressive litany of accomplishments, it would seem that public health's story would be easily told. For several reasons, however, it is not. As a result, public health remains poorly understood by its prime beneficiaries, the public, as well as many of its dedicated practitioners. Although public health's results, as measured in terms of improved health status, diseases prevented, scarce resources saved, and improved quality of life, are more apparent today then they have ever been, somehow most people fail to link public health with its results. This calls for a more understandable presentation of what public health is and what it does so that its results can be readily traced to their source.

This chapter is an introduction to public health that links basic concepts to practice. It considers three questions:

- What is public health?
- Where did it come from?
- Is it important in modern America?

To address these questions, the chapter begins with a sketch of the historical development of public health activities in the United States. Then it examines several definitions and characterizations of what public health is and explores some of its unique features. Finally, it offers insights into the value of public health in both economic and human terms.

Taken together, the topics in this chapter provide a foundation for understanding what public health is and why it is important. A conceptual framework that approaches public health from a systems perspective is introduced to clarify the dimensions of the public health system and facilitate an understanding of the various images of public health that coexist in modern America. We will see that as in the story of the blind men examining the elephant, the American public has mistaken separate components of the public health system for the whole system. Later chapters will more thoroughly examine and discuss the various components and dimensions of the public health system.

A BRIEF HISTORY OF PUBLIC HEALTH IN THE UNITED STATES

Early Influences on American Public Health

Although the complete history of public health is a fascinating saga in its own right, this section will present only selected highlights. Suffice it to say that when ancient cultures perceived illness as the manifestation of supernatural forces, they also felt that little in the way of either personal or collective action was possible. Diseases, including horrific epidemics of infectious diseases such as the Black Death (plague), leprosy, and cholera, were phenomena that simply had to be accepted. It was not until the so-called Age of Reason and the Enlightenment that scholarly inquiry began seriously to challenge the "givens" or acceptable realities of society. Eventually, the expansion of the science and knowledge base would reap substantial rewards.

With the advent of industrialism and imperialism, the stage was set for epidemic diseases to increase their terrible toll. As populations shifted to urban centers for the purpose of commerce and industry, public health conditions worsened. The mixing of dense populations who lived in unsanitary conditions and worked long hours in unsafe and exploitative industries with wave after wave of cholera, smallpox, typhoid, tuberculosis, yellow fever, and other diseases was a formula for disaster. And disaster struck and struck again across the globe, but most seriously and most often at the industrialized seaport cities that provided the portal of entry for diseases transported as stowaways alongside commercial cargoes.

The British colonies in North America and the fledgling United States certainly bore their share of the burden. American diaries of the 17th and 18th centuries chronicle one infectious disease onslaught after another. These epidemics left their mark on families, communities, and even history. For example, the national capital had to be moved out of Philadelphia due to a devastating yellow fever epidemic in 1793. This epidemic prompted the city to develop its first board of health in that same year.

The formulation of local boards of distinguished citizens, the first boards of health, was one of the earliest responses to epidemics. This response was revealing in that it was an attempt to confront disease collectively. Since science had not yet determined that specific microorganisms were the causes of epidemics, avoidance was the primary tactic used. Avoidance meant evacuating the general location of the epidemic until it subsided or isolating diseased individuals or those recently exposed to diseases on the basis of a mix of fear, tradition, and scientific speculation. Several developments, however, were swinging the pendulum ever closer to more effective counteractions.

The work of public health pioneers such as Edward Jenner, John Snow, and Edwin Chadwick shows the value of public health even when its methods are applied amidst scientific uncertainty. Well before Koch's postulates established scientific methods for linking bacteria with specific diseases and before Pasteur's experiments helped establish the germ theory, both Jenner and Snow used deductive logic and common sense to do battle with smallpox and cholera respectively. In 1996, we celebrated the 200th anniversary of Jenner's successful use of vaccination for a disease that ran rampant through communities across the world. This was the initial shot in a long and arduous campaign that, by the year 1977, had eradicated smallpox totally.

Snow's accomplishments even further advanced the art and science of public health. In 1848, Snow traced an outbreak of cholera to the water of a well drawn from the pump at Broad Street and helped prevent hundreds, perhaps thousands, of cholera cases. In 1854, he demonstrated that another large outbreak could be traced to one particular water company that drew its water from the Thames River downstream from London and that another company that drew its water upstream from London was not linked with cholera cases. In both efforts, Snow's ability to collect and analyze data allowed him to determine causation, which, in turn, allowed him to implement corrective actions that prevented additional cases. All this occurred without benefit of the knowledge that there was an odd-shaped little bacterium that was carried in water and spread from person to person by hand-to-mouth contact!

Chadwick was a more official leader of what has become known as the "sanitary movement" of the latter half of the 19th century. In a variety of official capacities, he played a major part in structuring government's role and responsibilities for protecting the public's health. Due to the growing concern over the social and sanitary conditions in England, a National Vaccination Board was established in 1837. Shortly thereafter, Chadwick's *Report on an Inquiry into the Sanitary Conditions of the Laboring Population of Great Britain* articulated a framework for broad public actions that served as a blueprint for the growing sanitary movement. One result was the establishment in 1848 of a General Board of Health. Interestingly, Chadwick's interest in public health had its roots in Bentham's utilitarian movement.[2] For Chadwick, disease was viewed as causing poverty, and poverty was responsible for the great social ills of the time, including societal disorder and high taxation to provide for the general welfare. Public health efforts were necessary to reduce poverty and its wider social effects. This view recognizes a link between poverty and health that differs somewhat from current views. Today it is more common to consider poor health as a result rather than as a cause of poverty.

Chadwick was also a key participant in the partly scientific, partly political debate that was taking place in British government as to whether deaths should be attributed to clinical conditions and diagnoses or whether the underlying factors, such as hunger and poverty, should be identified. It was Chadwick's view that pathologic, as opposed to less proximal social and behavioral, factors should be the basis for classification of deaths.[2] Chadwick's arguments held sway, although the debate continues to the present day. William Farr, sometimes called "the father of modern vital statistics," championed the opposing view.

In the latter half of the 19th century, as sanitation and environmental engineering methods evolved, more effective interventions became available against epidemics. Further, the scientific advances of this period paved the way for modern disease control efforts targeting specific microorganisms.

The Growth of Local and State and Public Health Activities in the United States

In the United States, Lemuel Shattuck's *Report of the Sanitary Commission of Massachusetts* in 1850 outlined existing and future public health needs for that state and became America's blueprint for development of a public health system. Shattuck called for the establishment of state and local health departments to organize public efforts aimed at sanitary inspections, communicable disease control, food sanitation, vital statistics, and services for infants and children. Although Shattuck's report closely paralleled Chadwick's efforts in Great Britain, acceptance of his recommendations did not occur for several decades. Eventually, in the latter part of the century, his far-sighted and far-reaching recommendations came to be widely implemented. With greater understanding of the value of environmental controls for water and sewage, and the role of specific control measures for specific diseases (including quarantine, isolation, and vaccination), the creation of local health agencies to carry out these activities supplemented, and in some cases supplanted, local boards of health.

These local health departments developed rapidly in the seaport and other industrial urban centers, beginning with a health department in Baltimore in 1798, because this was where the problems were reaching unacceptable levels. An illustration of such local public health efforts is presented in Appendix 1–A, which traces public health activities in Chicago from 1835 to 1961. The history summarized in this appendix parallels that of other American cities through much of the 19th and 20th centuries.

Because infectious and environmental hazards are no respecters of local jurisdictional boundaries, states began to develop their own boards and agencies after 1870. These agencies often had very broad powers to protect the health and lives of state residents, although the clear intent at the time was that these powers be used to battle epidemics of infectious diseases. In later chapters, we will revisit these powers and duties, since they provide the basis for both what is done and what can be done in dealing with contemporary public health issues and problems.

Federal Public Health Activities in the United States

This sketch of the development of public health in the United States would be incomplete without a brief discussion of the roles and powers of the federal government. Federal health powers, at least as enumerated in the U.S. Constitution, are minimal. It is surprising to some to learn that the word *health* does not even appear in the Constitution. As a result of not being a power granted to the federal government (such as defense, foreign diplomacy, international and interstate commerce, or printing money), health became a power to be exercised by states or reserved to the people themselves.

Two sections of the Constitution have been interpreted over time to allow for federal roles in health in concert with the concept of the so-called implied powers necessary to carry out explicit powers. These are the ability to tax in order to provide for the "general welfare" (a phrase appearing in both the preamble and body of the Constitution) and the specific power to regulate commerce, both international and interstate. These openings authorized the federal government to establish a beachhead in health, initially through the Marine Hospital Service (eventually to become the Public Health Service). After the ratification of the Sixteenth Amendment in 1916, allowing for a national income tax, the federal government acquired the ability to raise vast sums of money, which could then be directed toward promoting the general welfare. The specific means to this end were a variety of grants-in-aid to state and local governments. Beginning in the 1960s, federal grant-in-aid programs designed to fill gaps in the medical care system nudged state and local governments further and further into the business of medical service provision. These were soon followed by federal grant programs for other social, substance abuse, mental health, and community prevention services. The expansion of federal involvement into these areas, however, was not accomplished by these means alone.

Prior to 1900, and perhaps not until the Great Depression, Americans did not believe that the federal government should intervene in their social circumstances. Social values shifted dramatically during the Depression, a period of such great social insecurity and need that the federal government was now permitted, indeed expected, to intervene. Later chapters will expand on the growth of the federal government's influence on public health activities and its impact on the activities of state and local governments.

To explain more easily the broad trends of public health in the United States, it is useful to delineate distinct eras in its history. One simple scheme, illustrated in Exhibit 1–1, uses the years 1850 and 1950 as approximate dividers. Prior to 1850, the system was characterized by recurrent epidemics of infectious diseases, with little in the way of collective response possible. During the sanitary movement in the second half of the 19th century and first half of the 20th century, science-based control measures were organized and deployed through a public health infrastructure developing in the form of local and state health departments. After

---

Exhibit 1–1 Major Eras in United States Public Health History

Prior to 1850	Epidemics: avoidance and acceptance
1850–1949	Sanitary reform through state and local infrastructure
1950–present	Gaps in medical care and expanding agenda

1950, gaps in the medical care system and federal grant dollars acted together to increase public provision of a wide range of health services. That increase set the stage for the current reexamination of the links between medical and public health practice. Some retrenchment from the direct service provision role has occurred in the 1990s; whether this represents the beginning of a fourth era for public health is unclear.

IMAGES AND DEFINITIONS OF PUBLIC HEALTH

The historical development of public health activities in the United States provides a basis for understanding what public health is today. Nonetheless, the term *public health* evokes several different images among the general public and those dedicated to its improvement. To some, the term describes a broad social enterprise or system.

To others, the term describes the professionals and work force whose job it is to solve certain important health problems. At a meeting in the early 1980s to plan a communitywide education and outreach campaign to encourage early prenatal care in order to reduce infant mortality, a community relations director of a large television station made some comments that reflected this view. When asked whether his station had been involved in infant mortality reduction efforts in the past, he responded, "If you people in public health had been doing your job properly, we wouldn't be called on to bail you out!" Obviously, this man viewed public health as a group of which he was not a part.

Still another image of public health is that of a body of knowledge and techniques that can be applied to health-related problems. Here public health is seen as what public health does.

Somewhat similarly, many people perceive public health primarily as the activities ascribed to governmental public health agencies. For the majority of the public, this latter image represents public health in the United States, resulting in the common view that public health primarily involves the provision of medical care to indigent populations.

A final image of public health is that of the intended results of these endeavors. In this image, public health is literally the health of the public as measured in terms of health and illness in a population.

In this chapter, we will focus primarily on the first of these images, public health as a social enterprise or system. Later chapters will examine each of the other images of public health. It is important to understand what people mean when they speak of public health. As summarized in Exhibit 1–2, the profession, the methods, the governmental services, the ultimate outcomes, and even the broad social enterprise itself are all commonly encountered images of what public health is today.

Exhibit 1–2 Images of Public Health

- Public Health: The System and Social Enterprise
- Public Health: The Profession
- Public Health: The Methods (Knowledge and Techniques)
- Public Health: Governmental Services (Especially Medical Care for the Poor)
- Public Health: The Health of the Public

With varying images of what public health is, we would expect no shortage of definitions. There have been many, and it serves little purpose to try to catalog all of them here. Three definitions, each separated by a generation, provide important insights into what public health is; these are summarized in Exhibit 1–3.

In 1988, the prestigious Institute of Medicine (IOM) provided a useful definition in its landmark study of public health in the United States entitled *The Future of Public Health*. The IOM report characterized public health's mission as "fulfilling society's interest in assuring conditions in which people can be healthy."[3(p7)] This definition directs our attention to the many conditions that influence health and wellness, underscoring the broad scope of public health and legitimizing its interest in social, economic, political, and medical care factors that affect health and illness. The definition's premise that society has an interest in the health of its members implies that improving conditions and health status for others is acting in our own self-interest. The assertion that improving the health status of others provides benefits to all is a core value of public health.

Another core value of public health is reflected in the IOM definition's use of the term *assuring*. Assuring conditions in which people can be healthy means vigilantly promoting and protecting everyone's interests in health and well-being. This value echoes the wisdom in the often-quoted African aphorism that "it takes a village to raise a child." David Satcher, the first African American to head this country's most respected federal public health agency, the Centers for Disease

---

Exhibit 1–3 Selected Definitions of Public Health

- "the science and art of preventing disease, prolonging life and promoting health and efficiency through organized community effort" (Winslow, 1920)
- "successive re-definings of the unacceptable" (Vickers, 1958)
- "fulfilling society's interest in assuring conditions in which people can be healthy" (IOM report, 1988)

Control and Prevention, once described a visit to Africa in which he met with African teenagers to learn firsthand of their personal health attitudes and behaviors. He was struck by their concerns over the urbanization of the various African nations and the rapid changes that were affecting their culture and sense of community. These young people felt lost and abandoned; they questioned Satcher as to what his agency, the U.S. government, or the world community were willing to do to help them survive these changes. As one young man put it, "Where will we find *our* village?" Public health's role is one of serving us all as our village, whether we are teens in Africa or adults in the United States. The IOM report's characterization of public health advocated for just such a social enterprise and stands as a philosophical statement of mission and purpose.

The IOM report also sought to define the boundaries of public health by identifying three core functions of public health: assessment, policy development, and assurance. In one sense, these functions are comparable to those generally ascribed to the medical care system: diagnosis and treatment. *Assessment* is the analogue of diagnosis except that the diagnosis, or problem identification, is made for a group or population of individuals. Similarly, *assurance* is analogous to treatment and implies that the necessary remedies or interventions are put into place. Finally, *policy development* is an intermediate role of collectively deciding which remedies or interventions are most appropriate for the problems identified (the formulation of a treatment plan is the medical system's analog). These core functions broadly describe what public health does (as opposed to what it is) and will be examined more thoroughly in later chapters.

The concepts embedded in the IOM definition are also reflected in a less abstract definition developed more than 75 years ago by a highly respected public health figure, C.E.A. Winslow. His definition describes both the what and the how of public health. It is a comprehensive definition that has stood the test of time in characterizing public health as

> the science and art of preventing disease, prolonging life and promoting health and efficiency through organized community effort for the sanitation of the environment, the control of communicable infections, the education of the individual in personal hygiene, the organization of medical and nursing services for the early diagnosis and preventive treatment of disease, and for the development of the social machinery to insure everyone a standard of living adequate for the maintenance of health, so organizing these benefits as to enable every citizen to realize his birthright of health and longevity.[4(p183)]

There is much to consider in Winslow's definition. The phrases "science and art," "organized community effort," and "birthright of health and longevity" capture the substance and aims of public health. Winslow's catalog of methods illuminates the scope of the endeavor, embracing public health's initial targeting of infectious and environmental risks as well as current activities related to the organization, financing, and accountability of medical care services. His allusion to the "social machinery necessary to insure everyone a standard of living adequate for maintenance of health" speaks to the relationship between social conditions and health in all societies.

There have been many other attempts to define public health, although these have received less attention than either the Winslow or IOM definitions. Several build on the observation that over time, public health activities reflect the interaction of disease with two other phenomena that can be roughly characterized as science and social values. What do we know, and what do we choose to do with that knowledge?

A prominent British industrialist, Geoffrey Vickers, provided an interesting addition to this mix four decades ago while serving as Secretary of the Medical Research Council. In identifying the forces that set the agenda for public health, Vickers noted, "The landmarks of political, economic and social history are the moments when some condition passed from the category of the given into the category of the intolerable. . . . I believe that the history of public health might well be written as a record of successive re-definings of the unacceptable."[5(p600)]

The usefulness of Vicker's formulation lies in its focus on the delicate and shifting interface between science and social values. Through this lens, we can view a tracing of public health over history, facilitating an understanding of why and how different societies have reacted to health risks differently at various points in time and space. In this light, the history of public health is one of blending knowledge with social values to shape responses to problems that require collective action after they have crossed the boundary from the acceptable to the unacceptable.

Each of these definitions offers important insights into what public health is and what it does. Individually and collectively, they describe a social enterprise that is both important and unique, as we will see in the section that follows.

PUBLIC HEALTH AS A SYSTEM

So what is public health? Maybe no single answer will satisfy everyone. There are in fact several public healths that must be considered when the subject arises. One or more of them may be apparent to the inquirer. The public health described in this chapter is a broad social enterprise, more akin to a movement, that seeks to extend the benefits of current knowledge in ways that will have the maximum impact on the health status of a population. It does so through identifying problems that call for collective action to protect, promote, and improve health, primarily through preventive strategies. This public health is unique in its interdisciplinary approach and methods, its emphasis on preventive strategies, its linkage with government and political decision making, and its dynamic adaptation to new problems placed on its agenda. Above all else, it is a collective effort to identify and address the unacceptable realities that result in preventable and avoidable health outcomes, and it is the composite of efforts and activities that are carried out by people committed to these ends.

With this broad view of public health as a social enterprise, the question shifts from what public health is to what these other images of public health represent and how they relate to each other. To understand these separate images of public health, a conceptual model would be useful. Surprisingly, an understandable and useful framework to tie these pieces together has been lacking. Other enterprises have found ways to describe their complex systems, and from what appears to be an industrial model, we can begin to look at the various components of our public health system.

This framework brings together the mission and functions of public health in relation to the inputs, processes, outputs, and outcomes of the system.[6,7] Exhibit 1–4 provides general descriptions for the terms used in this framework. It is sometimes easier to appreciate this model when a more familiar industry, such as the automobile industry, is used as an example. The mission or purpose might be expressed as meeting the personal transportation needs of the population. This

---

Exhibit 1–4 Components of a Public Health System

- *Inputs or Capacities:* the community leadership, human resources, fiscal and physical resources, information resources, and system organization necessary to carry out the core functions of public health
- *Practices or Processes:* those organizational practices or processes that are necessary and sufficient to ensure that the core functions of public health are being carried out effectively
- *Outputs or Services:* health services intended to prevent death, disease, and disability and to promote the quality of life
- *Outcomes or Results:* indicators of health status, risk reduction, and quality-of-life enhancement

Source: Reprinted from Public Health Practice Program Office, 1990, Centers for Disease Control and Prevention.
Source: Data from Institute of Medicine, National Academy of Sciences, *The Future of Public Health,* © 1988, National Academy Press; C.EA. Winslow, The Untilled Field of Public Health, *Modern Medicine,* Vol. 2, pp. 183–191, © 1920; and G. Vickers, What Sets the Goals of Public Health?, *Lancet,* Vol. 1, pp. 599–604, © 1958.

industry carries out its mission by providing passenger cars to its customers; this characterizes its function. In this light, we can now examine the inputs, processes, outputs, and outcomes of the system set up to carry out this function. Inputs would include steel, rubber, plastic, and so forth, as well as the workers, know-how, technology, facilities, machinery, and support services necessary to allow the raw materials to become automobiles. The key processes necessary to carry out the primary function might be characterized as designing cars, making or acquiring parts, assembling parts into automobiles, moving cars to dealers, and selling and servicing cars after purchase. No doubt this is an incomplete listing of this industry's processes, but it is oversimplified here to make the point. In any event, these processes translate the abstract concept of getting cars to people into the operational steps necessary to carry out this basic function. The outputs of these processes are cars located where people can purchase them. The outcomes include satisfied customers and company profits.

Applying this same general framework to the public health system is also possible but may not be so obvious to the general public. The mission and functions of public health are well described in the IOM report's framework. The core functions of assessment, policy development, and assurance are considerably more abstract functions than making cars but still can be made operational through descriptions of their key steps or practices. The inputs of the public health system include its human, organizational, informational, fiscal, and other resources. These inputs are structured to carry out the core functions through processes that can also be termed *public health practices*. The outputs that result when inputs are subjected to these processes include a variety of activities that could be labeled as *programs* or *services* or perhaps *interventions*. These are intended to produce the desired results, which with public health might well be characterized as *health* or *quality-of-life* outcomes. Figure 1–1 illustrates these relationships.

In this model, not all components are as readily understandable and measurable as others. Several of the inputs are easily counted or measured, including human, fiscal, and organizational resources. Outputs are also generally easy to recognize and count: prenatal care programs, number of immunizations provided, health messages on the dangers of tobacco, and so on. And health outcomes are readily understood in terms of mortality, morbidity, functional disability, time lost from work or school, and even more sophisticated measures like years of potential life lost and quality-of-life years. The elements that are most difficult to understand and visualize are the processes or practices of the public health system. Although this is an evolving field, there have been several recent efforts to characterize these operational aspects of public health. By such efforts, we are better able to understand public health practice, measure it, and relate it to its outputs and outcomes.

Public Health System

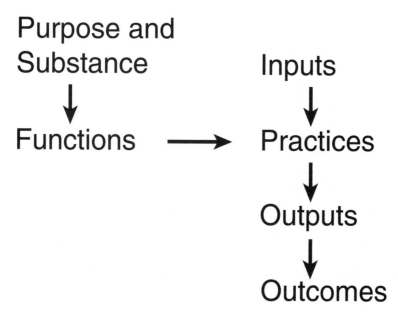

Figure 1–1 A Framework for Examining the Public Health System. *Source:* Data from J.P. Bunker, H.S. Frazier, and F. Mosteller, Improving Health: Measuring Effects of Medical Care, *Milbank Quarterly*, Vol. 72, pp. 225–258, © 1994.

This framework attempts to bridge the gap between what public health is and does (mission and functions on the left side of Figure 1–1) and how it does what it does (through inputs, practices, outputs, and outcomes on the right side of Figure 1–1). It also allows us to examine the various components of the system so that we can better appreciate how the pieces fit together. Later chapters will refer back to this model as the outcomes, outputs, practices, and inputs are presented in greater depth.

Suffice it to say these are concepts that are not readily understandable by many public health professionals and the general public. Partly for that reason, a national work group was assembled by the U.S. Public Health Service in 1994 in an attempt to develop a consensus statement of what public health is and does in language understandable to both those inside and outside the field of public

Exhibit 1–5 Public Health in the U.S.

Vision:
Healthy People in Healthy Communities
Mission:
*Promote Physical and Mental Health
and Prevent Disease, Injury, and Disability*

Public Health
- Prevents epidemics and the spread of disease
- Protects against environmental hazards
- Prevents injuries
- Promotes and encourages healthy behaviors
- Responds to disasters and assists communities in recovery
- Assures the quality and accessibility of health services

Essential Public Health Services
- Monitor health status to identify community health problems
- Diagnose and investigate health problems and health hazards in the community
- Inform, educate, and empower people about health issues
- Mobilize community partnerships to identify and solve health problems
- Develop policies and plans that support individual and community health efforts
- Enforce laws and regulations that protect health and ensure safety
- Link people with needed personal health services and assure the provision of health care when otherwise unavailable
- Assure a competent public health and personal health care workforce
- Evaluate effectiveness, accessibility, and quality of personal and population-based health services
- Research for new insights and innovative solutions to health problems

Source: Reprinted from Public Health Practice Program Office, 1990, Centers for Disease Control.

---

health. Exhibit 1–5 presents the result of that process in a framework often called "The Ten Essential Services of Public Health." There is a high level of consistency between the conceptual framework in Figure 1–1 and the narrative representation in Exhibit 1–5 in terms of the concepts addressed. Both are useful models for looking carefully at the system and how it works, as we will see in later chapters.

UNIQUE FEATURES OF PUBLIC HEALTH

Several unique features of public health individually and collectively serve to make understanding and appreciation of this enterprise difficult (Exhibit 1–6). These include the underlying social justice philosophy of public health; its inher-

Exhibit 1–6 Selected Unique Features of Public Health

- Basis in social justice philosophy
- Inherently political nature
- Dynamic, ever-expanding agenda
- Link with government
- Grounding in the sciences
- Use of prevention as a prime strategy
- Uncommon culture and bond

Source: Reprinted from Essential Public Health Services Working Group of the Core Public Health Functions Steering Committee, 1994, U.S. Public Health Services.

ently political nature; its ever-expanding agenda, with new problems and issues being assigned over time; its link with government; its grounding in a broad base of biological, physical, quantitative, social, and behavioral sciences; its focus on prevention as a prime intervention strategy; and the unique bond and sense of mission that links its proponents.

Social Justice Philosophy

It is vital to recognize the social justice orientation of public health and even more critical to understand the potential for conflict and confrontation it generates. Justice is an abstract concept that determines how each member of a society is allocated his or her fair share of collective burdens and benefits. Societal benefits to be distributed may include happiness, income, or social status. Burdens include restrictions of individual action and taxation. Market justice and social justice represent two forms of modern justice.

Market justice emphasizes personal responsibility as the basis for distributing burdens and benefits. Other than respecting the basic rights of others, individuals are responsible primarily for their own actions and are free from collective obligations. Individual rights are highly valued, while collective responsibilities are minimized. In terms of health, individuals assume primary responsibility for their own health. There is little expectation that society should act to protect or promote the health of its members beyond addressing risks that cannot be controlled though individual action.

Social justice argues that significant factors within the society impede the fair distribution of benefits and burdens.[8] Examples of such impediments include social class distinctions, heredity, racism, and ethnism. Collective action often leading to the assumption of additional burdens is necessary to neutralize or overcome those impediments. In the case of public health, the goal of extending the potential benefits of the physical and behavioral sciences to all groups in the society, especially when the burden of disease and ill health within that society is unequally distributed, is largely based on principles of social justice. It is clear that many modern public health (and other public policy) problems disproportionately affect some groups, generally a minority of the population, more than others. As a result, their resolution requires collective actions in which those less affected take on greater burdens while not commensurately benefiting from those actions. When the necessary collective actions are not taken, even the most important public policy problems remain unsolved despite periodically becoming highly visible.[8] This scenario reflects responses to such intractable American problems as inadequate housing, poor public education systems, unemployment, racial discrimination, and poverty. However, it is also true for public health problems such as tobacco-related illnesses, infant mortality, substance abuse, mental health services, long-term care, and environmental pollution. The failure to effect comprehensive national health reform in 1994 is a recent example of this phenomenon. At that time, middle-class Americans deemed the modest price tag of health reform as excessive, refusing to pay more out of their own pockets when they perceived that their own access and services were not likely to improve.

These and similar examples suggest that a critical challenge for public health as a social enterprise lies in overcoming the social and ethical barriers that prevent us from doing more with the tools already available to us.[8] Extending the frontiers of science and knowledge may not be as useful for improving public health as shifting the collective values of our society to act on what we already know. Recent public health successes such as public attitudes toward smoking in both public and private locations and operating motor vehicles after alcohol consumption provide evidence in support of this assertion. These advances came through changes in social norms rather than bigger and better science.

Inherently Political Nature

The social justice underpinnings of public health serve to stimulate political conflict. Advocating causes and agitating various segments of society to identify and address unacceptable conditions that adversely affect health status often lead to increased expectations and demands on society, generally through government. As a result, public health advocates appear at times as antigovernment and anti-institutional. Governmental public health agencies seeking to serve both the interests of government and public health are frequently caught in the middle. This creates tensions and conflict that can put these agencies at odds with governmental leaders on the one hand and external public health advocates on the other.

Expanding Agenda

A third unique feature of public health is its broad and ever-increasing scope. Traditional domains of public health interest include biology, environment, lifestyle, and health service organization. Within each of these domains are many factors that affect health status; in recent decades, many new public policy problems have been moved onto the public health agenda as their predisposing factors have been identified and found to fall into one or more of these domains.

The assignment of new problems to the public health agenda is an interesting phenomenon. For example, prior to 1900, the primary problems addressed by public health were infectious diseases and related environmental risks. After 1900, the focus expanded to include problems and needs of children and mothers to be addressed through health education and maternal and child health services as public sentiment over the health and safety of children increased. In the middle of the century, chronic disease prevention and medical care fell into public health's realm as an epidemiological revolution began to identify causative agents for chronic diseases and links between use of health services and health outcomes. Later, substance abuse, mental illness, teen pregnancy, long-term care, and other issues fell to public health, as did several emerging problems, most notably the epidemic of violence and HIV infections, including AIDS. The public health agenda is likely to expand even further as a result of the recent national dialogue over health reform and how health services will be organized and managed.

Link with Government

A fourth unique facet of public health is its link with government. Although public health is far more than the activities of federal, state, and local health departments, many people think only of governmental public health agencies when they think of public health. Government does play a unique role in seeing that the key elements are in place and that public health's mission gets addressed. Only government can exercise the enforcement provisions of our public policies that limit the personal and property rights of individuals and corporations in areas such as retail food establishments, proper sewage and water systems, occupational health and safety, consumer product safety, and drug efficacy and safety. Government also can play the convenor and facilitator role for identifying and prioritizing health problems that might be addressed through public resources and actions. Two general strategies are available for governmental efforts to influence public health. At the broadest level, governments can modify public policies that influence health through social and environmental conditions. Policies for education, employment, housing, public safety, child welfare, pollution control, workplace safety, and family support address factors that influence health. In line with the IOM report's definition of public health, these actions seek to ensure conditions in which people can be healthy.

Another strategy of government is to provide directly programs and services that are designed to meet the health needs of the population. It is often easier to garner support for relatively small-scale programs directed toward a specific problem (such as tuberculosis or HIV infections) than to achieve consensus around broader health and social issues. This strategy is basically a "command-and-control" approach, in which government attempts to increase access to and utilization of services largely through deployment of its own resources rather than through working with others.

A variation of this strategy for government is to ensure access to health care services through public financing approaches (Medicare and Medicaid are prime examples) or through specialized delivery systems (such as the Veterans Administration facilities, the Indian Health Service, and federally funded community health centers).

Whereas the United States has generally opted for the latter of these strategies, other countries have acted to place greater emphasis on broader social policies. Both the overall level of investment for and relative emphasis between these strategies contribute to the widely varying results achieved in terms of health status indicators among different nations (to be discussed in Chapter 2).

Many factors dictate the approaches used by a specific government at any point in time. These factors include history, culture, the structure of the government in question, and current social circumstances. There are also several underlying motivations that support government intervention. For paternalistic reasons, governments may act to control or restrict the liberties of individuals in order to benefit a group, whether or not that group seeks these benefits. For utilitarian reasons, governments intervene because of the perception that the state as a whole will benefit in some important way. For equality considerations, governments act to ensure that benefits and burdens are equally distributed among individuals. And for equity considerations, governments justify interventions in order to distribute the benefits of society in proportion to need. These motivations reflect the views of each society as to whether health itself or merely access to health services is to be considered a right of individuals and populations within that society. Many societies, including the United States, act through government to ensure equal access to a broad array of preventive and treatment services. However, equity in health status for all groups within the society may not be an explicit aspiration even where efforts are in place to ensure equality in access. Even more important for achieving equity in health status are concerted efforts to improve health status in population groups with the greatest disadvantage, mechanisms to monitor health status and contributing factors across all population groups, and participation of disadvantaged population groups in the key political decision-making processes within the society.[9] To the extent that equity in health status among all population groups does not guide actions of a society's government, these other elements will be only marginally effective.

As noted previously, the link between government and public health makes for a particularly precarious situation for governmental public health agencies. The conflicting value systems of public health and the wider community generally translate into public health agencies' having to document their failure in order to make progress. It is said that only the squeaky wheel gets the grease; in public health it often takes an outbreak, disaster, or other tragedy to demonstrate public health's value. Since 1985, outbreaks related to bacteria-contaminated milk in Illinois, tainted hamburgers in Washington State, and contaminated public water supplies in Milwaukee were quickly followed by increased funding for basic public health protection programs.

The assumption and delegation of public health responsibilities are quite complex in the United States, with different patterns in each of the 50 states (to be described in Chapter 4). Over the past 25 years, the concept of a governmental presence in health has emerged and gained widespread acceptance within the public health community. This concept characterizes the role of local government, often—but not necessarily always—operating through its official health agencies, which serve as the residual guarantors that needed services will actually be there when needed. In practice, it means that no matter how duties are assigned locally, there is a presence that ensures health needs are identified and considered for collective action. We will return to this concept and how it is operationalized in Chapter 5.

Grounding in Science

One of the most unique aspects of public health, and one that continues to separate public health from many other social movements, is its grounding in the sciences.[10] This relationship is clear for the medical and physical sciences that govern our understanding of the biological aspects of humans, microorganisms, and vectors, as well as the risks present in our physical environments. But it is also true for the social sciences of anthropology, sociology, and psychology that affect our understanding of human culture and behaviors influencing health and illness. The quantitative sciences of epidemiology and biostatistics also remain essential tools and methods of public health practice. Often five basic sciences of public health are identified: epidemiology, biostatistics, environmental science, management sciences, and behavioral sciences. These constitute the core education of public health professionals.

The importance of a solid and diverse scientific base is both a strength and weakness of public health. Surely, there is no substitute for science in the modern world. The public remains curiously attracted to scientific advances, at least in the physical and biological sciences, and this base is important to market and promote public health interventions. In recent decades, knowledge from the social sciences has greatly enriched and supplemented the physical and biological sciences. Yet these are areas less familiar to and perhaps less well appreciated by the public, making it difficult to garner public support for newer, more behaviorally mediated public health interventions. The old image of public health based on the scientific principles of environmental sanitation and communicable disease control is being superseded by a new image of public health approaches more grounded in what the public perceives to be "softer" science. This transition, at least temporarily, threatens to diminish public understanding and confidence in public health and its methods.

Focus on Prevention

If public health professionals were pressed to provide a one-word synonym for *public health*, the most frequent response would probably be "prevention." In general, prevention characterizes actions that are taken to reduce the possibility that something will happen, or in hopes of minimizing the damage that may occur if it does happen. Prevention is a widely appreciated and valued concept that is best understood when its object is identified. Although prevention is considered by many to be the purpose of public health, the specific intentions of prevention can be numerous. Prevention can be aimed at deaths, hospital admissions, days lost from school, consumption of human and fiscal resources, and many other ends. There are as many targets for prevention as there are various health outcomes and effects to be avoided.

Prevention efforts often lack a clear constituency because success results in unseen consequences. Because these consequences are unseen, people are less likely to develop an attachment for or to support the efforts preventing them. Advocates for mental health services, care for individuals with developmental disabilities, organ transplants, and end-stage renal disease often make their presence felt. But few state capitols have seen candlelight demonstrations by thousands of people who did not get diphtheria. This invisible constituency for prevention is partly a result of the interdisciplinary nature of public health. With no predominant discipline, it is even more difficult for people to understand and appreciate the work of public health. Despite its lack of recognition, prevention as a strategy has been remarkably successful and appears to offer great potential for future success as well. Later chapters will explore this potential in greater depth.

Uncommon Culture

The final unique feature of public health to be discussed here appears to be both a strength and a weakness. The tie that binds public health professionals is not a common preparation through education and training. Nor is it a common set of work experiences and work settings. Public health is unique in that the common link is a set of intended outcomes toward which many different sciences, arts, and methods can contribute. As a result, public health professionals include anthropologists, sociologists, psychologists, physicians, nurses, nutritionists, lawyers, economists, political scientists, social workers, laboratorians, managers, sanitarians, engineers, epidemiologists, biostatisticians, gerontologists, disability specialists, and dozens of other professions and disciplines. All are bound to common ends, and all employ somewhat different perspectives from their diverse education, training, and work experiences. "Whatever it takes to get the job done" is the theme, suggesting that the basic task is one of problem solving around health issues. This aspect of public health is the foundation for strategies and methods that rely heavily on collaborations and partnerships.

This multidisciplinary and interdisciplinary approach is unique among professions, calling into question whether public health is really a profession at all. There are several strong arguments that public health is not a profession. There is no minimum credential or training that distinguishes public health professionals from either other professionals or nonprofessionals. Only a tiny proportion of those who work in organizations dedicated to improving the health of the public possess one of the academic public health degrees (the master's of public health degree and several other master's and doctoral degrees granted by schools of public health and other institutions). With the vast majority of public health workers not formally trained in public health, it is difficult to characterize the work force as a profession. In many respects, it is more reasonable to view public health as a movement than as a profession.

THE VALUE OF PUBLIC HEALTH

How can we measure the value of public health efforts? This question is addressed both directly and indirectly throughout this text. Later chapters will examine the dimensions of public health's value in terms of lives saved and diseases prevented, as well as in dollars and cents. Nonetheless, some initial information will set the stage for greater detail later.

Public health's prevention efforts are responsible for 25 years of the nearly 30-year improvement in life expectancy at birth in the United States since 1900 (Figure 1–2). This bold claim is based on evidence that only 5 years of the 30-year improvement are the result of medical care.[11] Of these 5 years, medical treatment accounts for 3.7 years, and clinical preventive services (such as immunizations and screening tests) account for 1.5 years. The remaining 25 years have resulted largely from prevention efforts in the form of social policies, community actions, and personal decisions. These decisions and actions targeted infectious diseases affecting infants and children early in the century. Prevention efforts are also responsible for 4 of the 5 years of additional life expectancy at birth that have been achieved since 1960; this increase, however, has been achieved more

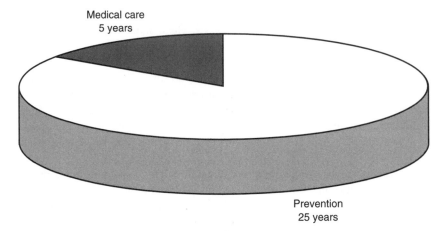

Medical care
5 years

Prevention
25 years

Figure 1–2 Contributions of Prevention and Medical Treatment to the 30 Years of Increased Life Expectancy Achieved since 1900. *Source:* Data from *The State of America's Children, 1991,* 1991, Children's Defense Fund; J.D. Forrest and S. Singh, Public Sector Savings Resulting From Expenditures for Contraceptive Services, *Family Planning Perspectives 1990,* Vol. 22, No. 1, pp. 6–15; Case Prevention and Economic Benefits of STD Program Activities Report, 1993, Sexually Transmitted Disease Section, Illinois Department of Public Health; B. Devaney et al., The Savings in Medicaid Costs for Newborns, 1991, Mathematica Policy Research, Inc.; and C.C. White et al., Benefits, Risks, and Costs of Immunizations for Measles, Mumps and Rubella, *American Journal of Public Health,* Vol. 75, pp. 749–754, © 1985.

---

through reductions in chronic diseases affecting adults than from reductions in conditions affecting children. During the preceding 60 years, only 3 of the 19 years gained have been attributable to declines in adult mortality.

Economic benefits of public health efforts can be measured in several ways. For example, they can be described in terms of treatment cost savings:

- Prevention of one AIDS case can result in savings of $119,379 in treatment costs.[12]
- A six-months' course of tuberculosis prevention therapy can save up to $50,000 in the cost of active disease treatment.[1]
- Each male smoker incurs approximately $11,100 more in health care costs during his lifetime than a male who has never smoked; for females, the additional costs are approximately $13,000.[13]

Savings on a dollar-for-dollar basis are apparent for many public health programs and services, as illustrated in Figure 1–3:

- Every dollar spent on prenatal care saves at least $3.38 in short-term inpatient hospital costs.[14]

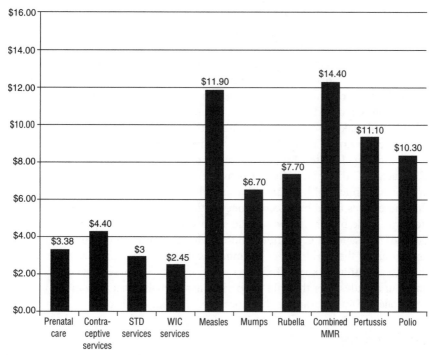

Figure 1–3 Savings per Dollar Spent on Selected Public Health Services.

- Every dollar spent on contraceptive services saves an average of $4.40 in additional public costs for public assistance during the first two years after birth.[15]
- Every dollar spent on sexually transmitted disease (STD) prevention and containment activities results in an estimated savings of $3.00 in health care costs.[16]
- Every dollar spent on the Special Supplemental Nutrition Program for Women, Infants and Children (WIC) saves from $1.77 to $3.13 ($2.45 average) in Medicaid costs.[17]
- Each dose of pertussis vaccine is estimated to save $11.10 in health care costs.[18]
- Each dose of polio vaccine saves $10.30 in health care costs.[18]
- Every dollar spent on measles, mumps, rubella, and the combined vaccine translates into $11.90, $6.70, $7.70, and $14.40, respectively, in savings from future health care costs.[18]

The value of public health in our society can be described in human terms as well as dollars and cents. One particularly good example dates from the 1950s, when the United States was in the midst of a terrorizing polio epidemic. Few communities were spared during the periodic onslaughts of this serious disease during the first half of the 20th century in America. Public fear was so great that public libraries, community swimming pools, and other group activities were closed during the summers when the disease was most feared. But biomedical research had developed a possible weapon against epidemic polio in the form of the Salk vaccine, which was developed in 1954 and licensed for use one year later. A massive and unprecedented campaign to immunize the public was quickly undertaken, setting the stage for a triumph of public health. But the real triumph came not in a way that might not have been expected because soon into the campaign, isolated reports of vaccine-induced polio were identified in Chicago and California. Within two days of the initial case report, action by governmental public health organizations at all levels resulted in the determination that these cases could be traced to one particular manufacturer. This determination was made only hours before the same vaccine was to be provided to hundreds of thousands of California children. The result was prevention of a disaster and rescue of the credibility of an immunization campaign that has virtually cut this disease off at its knees (Exhibit 1–7). The campaign proceeded on schedule, and four decades later the wild polio virus has been eradicated from the western hemisphere. Similar examples have occurred throughout history.

CONCLUSION

Public health evokes different images for different people, and even to the same people it can mean different things in different contexts. The intent of this chapter has been to identify some of the common perceptions of public health in the United States. Is it a complex, dynamic social enterprise, akin to a move-

---

Exhibit 1–7 The Value of Public Health: Fear of Polio, United States, 1950s

"I can remember no experience more horrifying than watching by the bedside of my five-year-old stricken with polio. The disease attacked his right leg, and we watched helplessly as his limb steadily weakened. On the third day, the doctor told us that he would survive and that paralysis was the worst he would suffer. I was grateful, although I continued to agonize about whether my wife and unborn child would be affected. What a blessing that no other parent will have to endure the terror that my wife and I and thousands of others shared that August."—Morton Chapman, Sarasota, Florida

Source: Reprinted from *For a Healthy Nation: Returns on Investment in Public Health*, 1994, U.S. Public Health Service.

ment? Or is it best characterized as a goal, the improved health outcomes and health status that can be achieved by the work of all of us individually and collectively? Or is public health some collection of activities that move us ever closer toward our aspirations? Or is it the profession that includes all those dedicated to its cause? Or is public health merely what we see coming out of our official governmental health agencies—a strange mix of safety-net medical services for the poor and a variety of often invisible community prevention services?

Though it is tempting to consider expunging the phrase *public health* from our vocabularies because of the baggage associated with these various images, this would do little to address the obstacles to accomplishing our central task. For public health encompasses all these images and perhaps more!

Based on principles of social justice, inherently political in its processes, addressing a constantly expanding agenda of problems, inextricably linked with government, grounded in science, emphasizing preventive strategies, and with a work force bound by common aspirations, public health is unique in many ways. Its value, however, transcends its uniqueness. Public health efforts have been major contributors to recent improvements in health status and can contribute even more as we approach a new century with new challenges.

By carefully examining the various dimensions of the public health system in terms of its inputs, practices, outputs, and outcomes, we can gain insights into what it does, how it works, and how it can be improved. Better results do not come from setting new goals; they come from understanding and improving the processes that will then produce better outputs, in turn leading to better outcomes. This theme of understanding the public health system and public health practice as a necessary step toward its improvement will recur throughout this text.

DISCUSSION QUESTIONS AND EXERCISES

1. Which definition of *public health* best describes public health today? Why?
2. To what extent has public health contributed to improvements in health status and health outcomes over history?
3. Is public health's value best expressed in monetary terms? If not, how?
4. What historical phenomena are responsible for the development of public health responses?
5. What are the primary roles of the U.S. federal government in public health? Give examples.
6. Review the selected history of public health in a large urban setting (Appendix 1–A) and describe how public health strategies and interventions have changed over time. What factors have been most respon-

continues

sible for these changes? Does this suggest that public health functions have changed as well?

7. Is public health currently viewed as an ethical enterprise—that is, an agent of social change seeking to make possible the attainment of social goals?

8. Which features make public health different from other fields? Which feature sets it off the most? Which is most important?

REFERENCES

1. *For a Healthy Nation: Returns on Investment in Public Health.* Washington, DC: US Public Health Service; 1994.

2. Hamlin C. Could you starve to death in England in 1839? The Chadwick-Farr controversy and the loss of the "social" in public health. *Am J Public Health.* 1995;85:856–866.

3. Institute of Medicine, National Academy of Sciences. *The Future of Public Health.* Washington, DC: National Academy Press; 1988.

4. Winslow CEA. The untilled field of public health. *Mod Med.* 1920;2:183–191.

5. Vickers G. What sets the goals of public health? *Lancet.* 1958;1:599–604.

6. Baker EL, Melton RJ, Stange PV, et al. Health reform and the health of the public. *JAMA.* 1994;272:1276–1282.

7. Dyal WW. Ten organizational practices of public health: a historical perspective. *Am J Prev Med.* 1995;11(No. 6, suppl):6–8.

8. Beauchamp DE. Public health as social justice. *Inquiry.* 1976;13(No. 1):3–14.

9. Susser M. Health as a human right: an epidemiologist's perspective on public health. *Am J Public Health.* 1993;83:418–426.

10. Afifi AA, Breslow L. The maturing paradigm of public health. *Ann Rev Public Health.* 1994;15:223–235.

11. Bunker JP, Frazier HS, Mosteller F. Improving health: measuring effects of medical care. *Milbank Q.* 1994;72:225–258.

12. Hellinger F. Lifetime cost of treating a person with HIV. *JAMA.* 1993;270:474–478.

13. *The Role of Public Health and Community Prevention under Health Care Reform.* Springfield, Ill: Illinois Public Health Association; 1994.

14. *The State of America's Children, 1991.* Washington, DC: Children's Defense Fund; 1991.

15. Forrest JD, Singh S. Public sector savings resulting from expenditures for contraceptive services. *Fam Plann Perspect.* 1990;22(No. 1):6–15.

16. *Case Prevention and Economic Benefits of STD Program Activities Report.* Springfield, Ill: Illinois Dept of Public Health, Sexually Transmitted Disease Section; 1993.

17. Devaney B, Bilheimer L, Schore J. *The Savings in Medicaid Costs for Newborns.* Princeton, NJ: Mathematica Policy Research Inc; 1991.

18. White CC, Kaplan JP, Orenstein WA. Benefits, risks, and costs of immunization for measles, mumps and rubella. *Am J Public Health.* 1985;75:749–754.

Appendix 1–A

Selected Highlights in the History of Public Health, Chicago, 1835–1961

1835   The Chicago Board of Health is established by the state legislature to secure the general health of the inhabitants because of the threat of cholera epidemic. Chicago, at this point a town, has an estimated 3,265 residents.

1837   Chicago is incorporated as a city of 4,170 residents. Three health commissioners and a health officer are named to inspect marketplaces, prepare death certificates, construct a pesthouse, visit persons suffering from infectious diseases in their homes, and board vessels in the harbor to check on the health of crews.

1841   Vital statistics start in a limited way with collection of data (age, sex, disease) related to deaths.

1848   The first cooperative effort of the medical profession and city officials is undertaken to prevent the spread of smallpox as physicians volunteer to vaccinate the poor without charge.

1849   Cholera is brought to Chicago by the emigrant boat *John Drew* from New Orleans, killing 1 in 36 of the entire population. A district health officer is appointed for each city block.

1855   The quarantine placard is introduced, with signs reading "Smallpox Here" after 30 die of the disease.

1857   A new, permanent city hospital is completed at a cost of $75,000 (later taken over by Cook County Hospital as one of its earlier buildings).

1868   Meat inspection is initiated at Union Stock Yards.

1870   The first milk ordinance is passed, making it illegal to sell skim milk unless so labeled.

Source: Adapted from *150 Years of Municipal Health Care in the City of Chicago: Board of Health, Department of Health, 1835–1985,* 1985, Chicago Department of Health.

1871   Help is given to refugees of the Chicago Fire, camps of the homeless are inspected, and controls are initiated for food supply and epidemic prevention. Birth and death records are lost in the fire.

1872   In the aftermath of the Great Fire, the death rate increases 32.6 percent to 27.6 deaths per 1,000 persons. Smallpox attacks 2,382 and kills 655. Fatalities among children under five are the highest ever recorded. (For the period 1843 to 1872, children under five account for half of all deaths occurring in the city.)

1889   Drainage and plumbing regulations are issued, and five women inspectors of tenements are appointed.

1892   Full milk inspection starts.

1893   A bacteriological laboratory opens to conduct microscopic examinations of milk samples and examine throat cultures for diphtheria. A "Boil the Water" crusade against typhoid is conducted.

1893–94 The last smallpox epidemic to cause great loss of life takes place (1,033 die in its second year). Vigorous vaccination efforts (1,084,500 given) result in a reduction of cases to 7 in 1897. During this period, the department is the first to proclaim the superiority of hermetically sealed glycerinated vaccine. Circulars are distributed on hot-weather care of infants in one of the first public education efforts.

1895   The first diphtheria antitoxin is issued, and a corps of antitoxin administrators are appointed. Daily analysis of water supply is inaugurated.

1896   Medical school inspections are inaugurated—Chicago is the second city in the United States to do this.

1899   A campaign against infant mortality enlists support of a voluntary corps of 73 physicians.

1900   The department publishes a study reporting that the average span of life in Chicago has more than doubled in a generation.

1901   An ordinance is passed prohibiting spitting in public places.

1902   Fourth of July "Don'ts" are first promulgated to prevent accidents.

1905   The 39th Street intercepting sewer opens, resulting in a marked decrease in typhoid deaths.

1908   A full communicable disease program is inaugurated, and 100 physicians are sent to congested districts during July and August to instruct mothers in infant care. Forty nurses are loaned to the department by the Visiting Nurses Association of Chicago to help in a scarlet fever epidemic. They are so effective that the City Council appropriates funds to hire the department's first nurses to work in maternal and child welfare and communicable and venereal diseases.

1909   Chicago becomes the first city in the United States to adopt a compulsory milk pasteurization ordinance.

1910	The Municipal Social Hygiene Clinic is established, and dispensaries are required to report venereal diseases. New milk standards are applied to ice cream.
1911	Common drinking cups and common roller towels are prohibited by ordinance.
1912	Sterilization of Chicago's water begins, and within four years the entire supply is being treated, causing a dramatic decline in the city's typhoid fever rate—from second highest among the 20 largest U.S. cities in 1881 to the lowest by 1917.
1915	Dental services are provided in Chicago public schools following a three-year introductory pilot program funded by philanthropist Julius Rosenwald.
1916	A policy is initiated to hospitalize all cases of infantile paralysis (polio) after 34 patients die out of 254 afflicted.
1917	The Municipal Contagious Disease Hospital is established. New health ordinances range from requiring the reporting and treatment of venereal diseases to requiring the screening of residences, stables, and barns against fleas. Immunization against diphtheria with von Behring's toxin-antitoxin starts in public schools and institutions.
1918	Influenza becomes a reportable disease, with the pandemic of influenza reaching Chicago to cause 381 deaths on one day (October 17) alone.
1919	The department wins its first case in the prosecution of landlords for failure to provide sufficient heat to tenants.
1920	The right of the department to quarantine carriers of contagion is upheld in the Superior Court of Cook County.
1923	A committee is appointed on prenatal care in the first concerted effort to coordinate the activities of all agencies doing prenatal work in the city. Inspection of summer camps for children is inaugurated.
1925	The department institutes a regular schedule of home visits by nurses during the first six months of an infant's life. Conferences are inaugurated for care of preschool children. Installation of sanitary types of drinking fountains is ordered.
1930	An intensive campaign against diphtheria results in 400,219 injections being given in three months.
1932	A staff of 300 nurses are carried throughout the city on buses to give diphtheria inoculations. Physicians are sent to the homes of mothers unable to take children to welfare stations for shots. After the campaign, cases drop to 154 with 9 deaths, compared to 1,266 cases with 68 deaths the previous year.
1933	An outbreak of amebic dysentery occurs among out-of-town guests who came to the Century of Progress (1,409 cases and 98 deaths scat-

tered in 43 states, the Territory of Hawaii, and three Canadian provinces) in the first recognized water-borne epidemic of the disease in a civilian population. The cause is traced to water contamination through faulty plumbing.

1934   A plumbing survey for cross-connections in hotels and mercantile buildings is begun to prevent future amebic dysentery outbreaks. As a result of drinking from a contaminated water supply at the Union Stock Yards fire on May 19, 69 persons contract typhoid fever, 11 of whom die.

1935   An ordinance is passed requiring that only Grade A milk and milk products be sold in Chicago. A premature-infant welfare program is initiated. A mother's milk station starts operating to supply breast milk to premature, sick, or debilitated infants whose parents cannot afford this expense.

1936   Summer brings 210 deaths from sunstroke and exhaustion, compared to 11 from the same cause in 1935. With 1,000 premature infants under supervision, two additional premature stations open, making 31 conferences available each week.

1937   Chicago public schools open three weeks late because of a polio scare. The Chicago Syphilis Control Project is established, with the emphasis on breaking the chain of infection.

1942   The Chicago Intensive Treatment Center for venereal disease launches an effort so successful that it wins a War Department commendation in 1943 and records a declining VD rate following World War II demobilization, in contrast to soaring rates in other large cities.

1948   A federal grant of $46,270 is made available through the state to subsidize a psychiatric program. A comprehensive food ordinance is adopted by the City Council.

1952   Chicago counts 1,203 cases of polio, including 82 deaths and hundreds of persons with paralysis. Frightened parents keep their youngsters out of movies and swimming pools. Beaches close. An insect and rodent control program starts.

1955   Chicago is one of the first cities in the United States to introduce the Salk vaccine after it is pronounced safe and effective against the polio virus on April 12.

1956   With warning signs of an approaching polio epidemic, mass inoculations of Salk vaccine are given in all parts of the city, with department staff working in vacant stores, in garages, on street corners, from the backs of trucks, and in park fieldhouses. Chicago takes the lead among major American cities in introducing a water fluoridation program, which reduces tooth decay among children.

1957   A Nursing Home Section and Hospital Inspection Unit is initiated.

1958   A section for chronic illness is activated, with mental health as one of its activities.

1959   The first community mental health center is started on South Side.

1960   The Bureau of Institutional Care consolidates nursing home and hospital inspection services.

1961   The Division of Adult Health and Aging begins consolidating activities of chronic diseases, cardiovascular diseases, diabetes, cervical cancer, rheumatic heart fever, and nutrition. A lead poison survey begins on Chicago's West Side.

4

CHAPTER 2

Health Measures
and Health Status

Public health differs from other systems in one important respect: its outcomes. In many enterprises called the "bottom line," outcomes often consist of profits, consumer satisfaction, and the like. For public health, the bottom line is improved health status in the population.

Enterprises can best direct their efforts toward certain outcomes and track their progress by ensuring that these outcomes are clearly defined and measurable. In public health, this means that we must clarify definitions and measures of health in populations. That task is the focus of this chapter. Key questions to be addressed are:

- What is health?
- What factors influence health and illness?
- How can health status be measured?
- How can this information be used to develop effective interventions?
- What do current measures of health tell us about the health status of the United States in the 1990s?

Interest in these questions is reflected in a recent development in public health practice. In mid-1996, public health surveillance in the United States took a historic step reflecting a shift in national morbidity and mortality patterns as well as in the ability to identify specific factors that result in disease and injury. Exhibit 2–1 reprints the important announcement appearing in the Centers for Disease Control and Prevention's (CDC) *Morbidity and Mortality Weekly Report (MMWR)* that adds prevalence of cigarette smoking to the list of diseases and conditions to be reported by states to CDC.[1] As the first-ever reportable health-related behavior, this was a ground-breaking step for surveillance efforts. How the focus of public health efforts shifted from conventional disease outcomes to

33

Exhibit 2–1 First Reportable Underlying Cause of Death: Addition of Prevalence of Cigarette Smoking as a Nationally Notifiable Condition (June 1996)

On June 6, 1996, by a unanimous vote, the Council of State and Territorial Epidemiologists (CSTE) added *prevalence of cigarette smoking* to the list of conditions designated as reportable by states to CDC. The addition of prevalence of cigarette smoking marks the first time a behavior, rather than a disease or illness, has been considered nationally reportable.

Goals of smoking prevalence surveillance identified by CSTE include monitoring trends in tobacco use, guiding allocation of tobacco-use prevention resources, and evaluating public health interventions to reduce smoking. Given these goals, CSTE selected population sampling as the appropriate surveillance methodology and designated the Behavioral Risk Factor Surveillance System (BRFSS) as the preferred data source. CSTE and CDC are developing the format to regularly present this information in national disease reporting statistics. The addition of cigarette smoking prevalence brings to 56 the number of diseases and conditions designated by CSTE as reportable by states to CDC.

Source: Reprinted from First Reportable Underlying Cause of Death, *MMWR*, Vol. 45, p. 537, 1996, Centers for Disease Control and Prevention.

reporting on underlying causes amenable to public health intervention is part of the story told in this chapter.

HEALTH, ILLNESS, AND DISEASE

Before attempting to describe Americans' health status in the late 1990s, we must understand what we will be measuring. Health is difficult to define and more difficult yet to measure. For much of history, the notion of health has been negative. This was due in part to the continuous onslaught of epidemic diseases. With disease a frequent visitor, "health" became the disease-free state. One was healthy by exclusion.

However, as knowledge of disease increased and methods of prevention and control improved, it became possible to consider health from a positive perspective. The World Health Organization (WHO) seized this opportunity in its 1946 constitution, defining health as not merely the absence of disease but a state of complete physical, mental, and social well-being.[2] This definition of health underscores that there are different, complexly related kinds of wellness and illness and suggests that a wide range of factors can influence the health of individuals and groups. It also suggests that health is not an absolute concept.

Although *health* and *well-being* may be synonyms, *health* and *disease* are not necessarily opposites. Most people continue to view health and illness as existing along a continuum and as opposite and mutually exclusive states. However, this simplistic unidimensional model of health and illness does not comport very well with the real world. A person can have a disease or injury and still be healthy or at least feel well. There are many examples, but certainly Olympic wheelchair racers would fit into this category! It is also possible for someone without a specific disease or injury to feel ill or not well. If health and illness are not mutually exclusive, then they exist in separate dimensions, with wellness and illness in one dimension and the presence or absence of disease or injury in another.

These distinctions are important because disease is a relatively objective, pathologic phenomenon, whereas wellness and illness represent subjective experiences. This allows for several different states to exist: wellness without disease or injury, wellness with disease or injury, illness with disease or injury, and illness without physical disease or injury. This multidimensional view of health states is consistent with WHO's delineation of physical, mental, and social dimensions of health or well-being. Health or wellness is more than the absence of disease alone. Furthermore, one can be physically but not mentally and socially well.

With different dimensions of health states, the question arises as to whether there is some maximum or optimal end point of health or well-being or whether health or well-being can always be improved through changes in its physical, mental, and social facets. The latter alternative would suggest that some minimal acceptable level of health should be our aim rather than a more absolute and complete state. With that in mind, WHO revised its definition in 1978, calling for a level of health that will permit people to lead a socially and economically productive life.[3] Despite these considerations, measuring illness remains a simpler task than measuring health.

In attempting to measure health, both quantity and quality become important considerations. But it is not always easy to answer the questions "How much?" and "Compared to what?" For example, physical health for a 10-year-old child carries a much different expectation than physical health for an 80-year-old. It is reasonable to conclude that the natural process of aging leads to gradual diminution of functional reserve capacity and that this is normal and not easily prevented. Thus perceptions of normal functioning are largely determined by social and cultural factors.

In conceptions of health as existing along a continuum, disease or injury tend to be viewed as phenomena that may lead to significant loss or disability in social functioning, making one unable to carry out one's main personal or social functions in life, such as parenting, schooling, or employment. In this model, health is equivalent to the absence of disability; individuals able to carry out their basic functions in life are healthy. This characterization of health as the absence of significant functional disabilities is perhaps the most widely held and common one for this highly sought state. Still, this definition is negative in that it defines one thing (health) as the absence of another (disability). The concept of well-being advanced in the WHO definition goes beyond the physical aspects of health that are usually the focus of measurements and comparisons. Including the mental and social aspects of well-being or health legitimizes the examination of factors that affect mental and social health. These themes suggest that we need to consider carefully what we are measuring in order to understand what these measures are telling us about health, illness, and disease states in a population and the factors that influence these outcomes.

INFLUENCES ON HEALTH

Risk Factors

Many factors directly or indirectly influence the level of a health outcome. For example, greater per capita tobacco use in a population is associated with higher rates of heart disease and lung cancer, and lower rates of early prenatal care are associated with higher infant mortality rates. Since these factors are part of the chain of causation for health outcomes, tracking their levels provides an early indication as to the direction in which the health outcome is likely to change. These factors increase the likelihood or risk of particular health outcomes occurring and can be characterized broadly as *risk factors*.

The types and number of risk factors are as varied as the influences themselves. Depending on how these factors are lumped or split, traditional categories include biological factors (from genetic endowment to aging), environmental factors (from food, air, and water to communicable diseases), lifestyle factors (from diet to injury avoidance and sexual behaviors), psychosocial factors (from poverty to stress, personality, and cultural factors), and use of and access to health-related services. Some recent refinements of this framework differentiate several outcomes of interest—disease, functional capacity, and well-being—that are affected by various risk factors. They argue that these various components are often interrelated (e.g., stress, a social environmental factor, may stimulate individual responses like tobacco or illicit drug use, which in turn influence the likelihood of disease, functional capacity, and well-being). In addition, variations in one outcome, such as disease, may influence variations in another, such as well-being, depending on the mix of other factors present. In any event, this model emphasizes general factors that can result in many diseases rather than focusing on specific factors that contribute little to populationwide health outcomes.

Though many factors are causally related to health outcomes, some are more direct and proximal causes than others. Specific risk factors have been clearly linked to specific adverse health states through epidemiologic studies. For example, numerous studies have linked unintentional injuries with a variety of risk factors, including the accessibility to firearms and the use of alcohol, tobacco, and seat belts. For heart disease, tobacco, hypertension, overnutrition, and diabetes are well-known risk factors. Epidemiological research and studies over the past 50 years have identified behavioral risk factors for many common diseases and conditions,[4] as shown in Table 2–1. Ongoing behavioral risk factor surveys through phone interviews are conducted by governmental public health agencies to track trends in the prevalence of these behaviors within the population. These surveys document that the health-related behaviors of tens of millions of Americans place them at risk of developing chronic disease and injuries.

With the current attention to behavioral factors, risk factors in the physical environment can be overlooked when hazards are catalogued and examined. For example, air pollution is directly related to a wide range of diseases, including lung cancer, pulmonary emphysema, chronic bronchitis, and bronchial asthma.[5] Other health consequences of air pollution include eye irritation and premature lung tissue aging. The annual health costs associated with the most serious air pollutants are estimated to exceed $50 million.[6] National standards exist for many of the most important air pollutants[7] and are tracked to determine the extent of these risks in the general population. Health risks and contributing sources for six important air pollutants are included in Table 2–2. The proportion of the U.S. population residing in counties that have exceeded national standards for these pollutants are provided in Figure 2–1. These data suggest that air pollution risks, like behavioral risks, affect tens of millions of Americans.

Behavioral and environmental risk factors are clearly germane to public health interest and efforts. Focusing on these factors presents a different perspective of the enemies of personal and public health than is conveyed by mortality data. Such a focus also promotes a more rational framework for policy development and intervention.

Which of these underlying factors are most important? The answer depends on the specific outcomes in question. At a population level, for example, a study using 1980 data found somewhat different groupings of underlying factors for deaths before age 65 and years of potential life lost (YPLL) before age 65, as demonstrated in Figure 2–2.[8] For deaths before age 65, tobacco, hypertension, and overnutrition accounted for about three-fourths of such premature deaths. For YPLL before age 65, injury risks, alcohol, tobacco, and gaps in primary prevention accounted for three-fourths of these years of life lost.[8]

Individual risk factors may result in several different health outcomes, as illustrated in Figure 2–3. Alcohol is linked with motor vehicle injuries, other injuries, cancer, and cirrhosis. Tobacco use can result in heart disease, stroke, ulcers, fire and burn injuries, and low birth weight as well as cancer.[8]

Table 2–1 Selected Behavioral Risk Factors Related to Leading Causes of Deaths in the United States, 1990

Cause of Death and % of all deaths	Smoking	High Fat/ Low Fiber	Sedentary Lifestyle	High Blood Pressure	Elevated Cholesterol	Obesity	Diabetes	Alcohol Use
Heart disease (32%)	X	X	X	X	X	X	X	X
Cancer (24%)	X	X	X			X		X
Stroke (7%)	X	X		X	X	X		
Chronic lung disease (5%)	X							
Unintentional injuries (4%)	X							X
Pneumonia and influenza (4%)	X							
Diabetes (3%)		X	X			X	X	
HIV infection (2%)								X
Suicide (1%)								X
Chronic liver disease (1%)								X
Atherosclerosis (1%)	X	X	X		X		X	

Source: Data from *Health United States 1995*, 1996, National Center for Health Statistics, Public Health Service; R.C. Brownson et al., Chronic Disease Epidemiology and Control, © 1993, American Public Health Association; and the Surgeon General's *Report on Nutrition and Health*, 1988.

Table 2–2 Selected Air Pollutants, Health Risks, and Sources

Pollutants	Health Risks	Contributing Sources
Ozone (O₃)	Asthma, reduced respiratory function, eye irritation	Cars, refineries, dry cleaners
Particulate matter (PM-10)	Bronchitis, cancer, lung damage	Dust, pesticides
Carbon monoxide (CO)	Blood oxygen carrying capacity reduction, cardiovascular and nervous system impairments	Cars, power plants, wood stoves
Sulfur dioxide (SO₂)	Respiratory tract impairment, destruction of lung tissue	Power plants, paper mills
Lead (Pb)	Retardation and brain damage, especially for children	Cars, nonferrous smelters, battery plants
Nitrogen dioxide (NO₂)	Lung damage and respiratory illness	Power plants, cars, trucks

Source: Reprinted from *Environmental Progress and Challenges: EPA's Update*, 1988, U.S. Environmental Protection Agency, Washington, DC.

A more recent examination[9] corroborates these findings, relating tobacco, alcohol, and diet to about one-half of all U.S. deaths in 1990. Table 2–3 presents this well-known comparison of 1990 deaths by their listed causes of death as given by the National Center for Health Statistics (NCHS)[10] and their actual causes (major risk factors). The actual causes clearly present a different picture as to the major health problems and needs of the U.S. population.

Social and Cultural Influences

Despite the importance and scope of environmental and behavioral risk factors, socioeconomic and sociocultural risk factors cut across the various categories and affect health in a variety of ways. Socioeconomic status and poverty are two such factors that reflect position in society. There is considerable evidence that social position is an over-arching determinant of health status, even though the indicators used to measure social standing are imprecise at best.

Social class affects lifestyle, environment, and the utilization of services; it remains an important predictor of good and poor health in our society. Social

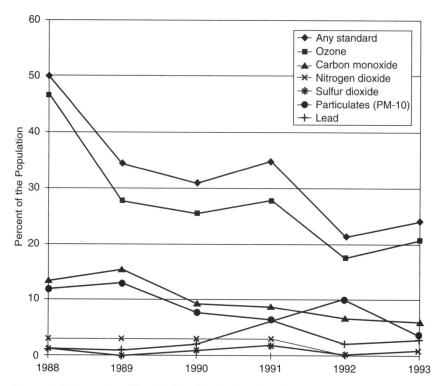

Figure 2–1 Proportion of People Who Live in Counties That Exceeded National Ambient Air Quality Standards in the Previous 12 Months, United States, 1988–1993. *Source:* Reprinted from the Environmental Protection Agency.

class differences in mortality have long been recognized around the world. In 1842, Chadwick reported that the average ages at death for occupationally stratified groups in England were as follows: "gentlemen and persons engaged in the professions, . . . 45 years; tradesmen and their families, . . . 26 years; mechanics, servants and laborers, and their families, . . .16 years."[11] Life expectancies and other health indicators have improved considerably in England and elsewhere since 1842, but differences in mortality rates among the various social classes persist to the present day.

Both Great Britain and the United States have identifiable social strata that permit comparisons of health status by social class. Britain even maintains an ongoing analysis of socioeconomic differences according to the Registrar General's Social Class categorizations based on general social standing within the community. For the United States, educational status, race, and family income are

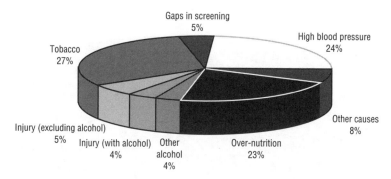

Figure 2–2a Percentage of Deaths in the United States in 1980 before Age 65, by Risk Factor. *Source:* Reprinted from R.W. Amler and D.L. Eddins, Cross-Sectional Analysis: Precursors of Premature Death in the U.S., *Closing the Gap,* Carter Center, 1985, Centers for Disease Control and Prevention.

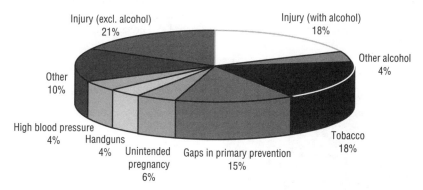

Figure 2–2b Percentage of Years of Life Lost in the United States in 1980 before Age 65, by Risk Factor. *Source:* Reprinted from R.W. Amler and D.L. Eddins, Cross-Sectional Analysis: Precursors of Premature Death in the U.S., *Closing the Gap,* Carter Center, 1985, Centers for Disease Control and Prevention.

often used as indirect or proxy measures of social class. Despite the differences in approaches and indicators, there is little evidence of any real difference between Britain and the United States in terms of what is being measured. In both countries, explanations for the differences in mortality appear to relate primarily to inequalities in material resources, although the use of educational status as a proxy for social standing may also reflect differences in nonmaterial resources such as norms, values, and access to information and services.

In the United States, epidemiologists have studied socioeconomic differences in mortality risk since the early 1900s. Infant mortality has been the subject of many studies that have consistently documented the effects of poverty. Findings from the

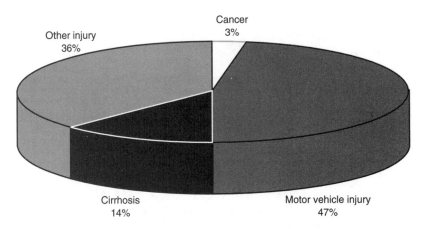

Figure 2–3a Percentage of Alcohol-Related Years of Life Lost in the United States in 1980 before Age 65, by Cause of Death. *Source:* Reprinted from R.W. Amler and D.L. Eddins, Cross-Sectional Analysis: Precursors of Premature Death in the U.S., *Closing the Gap,* Carter Center, 1985, Centers for Disease Control and Prevention.

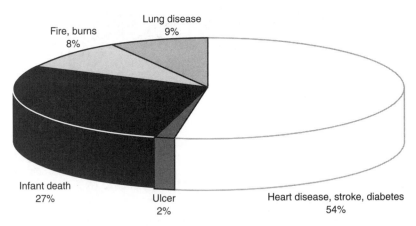

Figure 2–3b Percentage of Tobacco-Related Years of Life Lost in the United States in 1980 before Age 65, by Cause of Death. *Source:* Reprinted from R.W. Amler and D.L. Eddins, Cross-Sectional Analysis: Precursors of Premature Death in the U.S., *Closing the Gap,* Carter Center, 1985, Centers for Disease Control and Prevention.

1988 National Maternal and Infant Health Survey, for example, demonstrated that the effects of poverty were greater for infants born to mothers with no other risk factors than for infants born to high-risk mothers.[12] Poverty status was associated with a 60 percent higher rate of neonatal mortality and a 200 percent higher rate for postneonatal mortality than for those infants of higher-income mothers.

Table 2–3 Listed and Actual Causes of Death, United States, 1990

10 Leading Causes of Death	Number	Actual Causes of Death	Number
Heart disease	720,058	Tobacco	400,000
Cancer	505,322	Diet/activity patterns	300,000
Cerebrovascular disease	144,088	Alcohol	100,000
Unintentional injuries	91,983	Certain infections	90,000
Chronic lung disease	86,679	Toxic agents	60,000
Pneumonia and influenza	79,513	Firearms	35,000
Diabetes	47,664	Sexual behavior	30,000
Suicide	30,906	Motor vehicles	25,000
Chronic liver disease	28,815	Drug use	20,000
HIV infection	25,188		
Total	1,757,216	Total	1,060,000

Source: Data from the National Center for Health Statistics and J.M. McGinnis and W. Foege, Actual Causes of Death in the United States, *Journal of the American Medical Association,* Vol. 270, pp. 2207–2212, © 1993, American Medical Association.

Poverty affects many health outcomes, as illustrated in Table 2–4. Low-income families in the United States have an increased likelihood (or relative risk) for a variety of adverse health outcomes, often two to five times greater than that of higher income families.[13]

If relative social disadvantage results in differences in outcomes, then it should be possible to demonstrate differences even among relatively affluent subgroups of the same population. Such a study based on 1971 British census follow-up data found that a nonmanual, home-owning group with two cars had a lower mortality risk than a similar relatively privileged group with only one car.[14] These findings in an explicitly stratified society have important implications for populations without such clearly defined categories of social class, such as the United States. They suggest that studies need to pay attention to how and how well social class is categorized and measured. Imprecise measures may understate the actual differences due to socioeconomic position in society. Importantly, if racial or ethnic differences are simply attributed to social class differences, factors that operate through race and ethnicity, like racism or ethnism, will be overlooked. These additional factors also affect the difference between the social position one has and the position one would have attained were it not for one's race or ethnicity.

Studies of the effect of socioeconomic factors on health status across nations add some interesting insights. In general, health appears to be closely associated with income differentials within countries, but there is only a weak link between national mortality rates and average income among the developed countries.[15] This pattern suggests that health is affected less by changes in absolute material standards across affluent populations than by relative income differences and the

Table 2-4 Selected Outcomes and Relative Risk for Low-Income Families as Compared with High-Income Families

Outcome	Relative Risk
Child neglect	9
Child abuse	4.5
Iron-deficiency anemia	3–4
Childhood mortality	>3
Fair or poor health	3
Fatal injuries	2–3
Growth retardation	2.5
Severe asthma	2
Pneumonia	1.6
Infant mortality	1.3–1.5
Low birth weight	1.2–2.2
Extreme behavioral problems	1.3

Source: Data from P.L. Geltman et al., Welfare Reform and Children's Health, *Health Policy and Child Health,* Vol. 3, No. 2, pp. 1–5, © 1996.

resulting disadvantage in each country. It is not the richest countries that have the greatest life expectancy. Rather, it is those nations with the narrowest income differentials between rich and poor. This finding argues that health in the developed world is less a matter of a population's absolute material wealth than of how their circumstances compare with those of other members of their society.

The effects of culture on health and illness are also becoming better understood. To medical anthropologists, diseases are not purely independent phenomena. Rather, they are to be viewed and understood in relation to ecology and culture. Certainly the type and severity of disease varies by age, sex, social class, and ethnic group. The different distributions and social patterns of diseases reveal differences in culture-mediated behaviors. Such insights are essential to developing successful prevention and control programs. Culture serves to shape health-related behaviors as well as human responses to diseases, including changes in the environment, which, in turn, affect health. As an adaptive mechanism to the environment, culture has great potential for both positively and negatively affecting health.

There is evidence that different societies shape the ways in which diseases are experienced and that social patterns of disease persist even after risk factors are identified and effective interventions become available.[16–18] For example, the link between poverty and various outcomes has been well established; yet even after advances in medicine and public health and significant improvement in general living and working conditions, the association persists. One explanation is that as some risks were addressed, others developed, such as health-related behaviors including violent behavior and alcohol, tobacco, and drug use. In this way, societies create and shape the diseases they experience. This makes sense especially if we view diseases as phenomena that befall individuals in their communities, where both individuals and communities react to and live with disease on a continuous basis. In this light, the social and cultural influences on health and illness are easily appreciated.

If these themes of social and cultural influences are on target, they place the study of health disparities near the top of the public health agenda. They also argue that health should be viewed as a social phenomenon. Rather than attempting to identify each and every risk factor that contributes to only marginally disparate health outcomes of the lower social classes, a more effective approach would directly address the broader social policies (distribution of wealth, education, employment, and the like) that foster the social disparities that cause the observed differences in health outcomes. This broad view of health and its determinants is critical to understanding and improving health status in the United States as well as internationally.

Global Health Influences

Considerable variation exists among the world's nations on virtually every measure of health and illness currently in use. The principal factors responsible for observed trends and obvious inequities across the globe fall into the general categories of the social and physical environment, personal behavior, and health services. Given the considerable variation in social, economic, and health status among the developed, developing, and underdeveloped nations, it is naive to make broad generalizations. Countries with favorable health status indicators, however, generally have a well-developed health infrastructure, ample opportunities for education and training, relatively high status for women, and economic development that counterbalances population growth.[3] Nonetheless, countries at all levels of development share some problems, including the escalating costs involved in providing a broad range of health, social, and economic development services to disadvantaged subgroups within the population.[3] Social and cultural upheaval associated with urbanization is another problem common to countries at all levels of development. During the course of the 20th century, the proportion of the world's population living in urban areas will have nearly tripled to about 40 percent by the year 2000.

The principal environmental hazards in the world today appear to be those associated with poverty. This is true for developed as well as developing and underdeveloped countries. Some international epidemiologists argue, however, that as the next century approaches, it is likely that poverty will be joined by the effects of overpopulation and production of greenhouse gases as major threats to global health. These factors represent human effects on the world's climate and resources and are easily remembered as the "3 Ps" of global health (pollution, population, and poverty):

- *pollution* of the atmosphere by greenhouse gases, which will result in significant global warming, affecting both climate and the occurrence of disease
- worldwide *population* growth, which will result in a population of 10 to 12 billion people within the next century
- *poverty,* which is always associated with ill health and disease[19,20]

It may surprise many Americans to see population listed as a major concern for health. Birthrates vary inversely with the level of economic development and the status of women among the nations of the world. Continuing high birthrates and declining death rates will mean even more rapid growth in population in developing countries. It has taken all of history to reach our current world population, but it will take less than half a century to double that. Many factors have influenced this growth, including public health, which has increased the chances of conception by improving the health status of adults, increasing infant and child survival, preventing premature deaths of adults in the most fertile age groups, and reducing the number of marriages dissolved by one partner's death.

In general, public health approaches to dealing with world health problems must overcome formidable obstacles, including the unequal and inefficient distribution of health services, lack of appropriate technology, poor management, poverty, and inadequate or inappropriate government programs to finance needed services. The toll for failure to overcome these obstacles can be immense, as evidenced by WHO's 1995 estimates of mortality and morbidity of water-related diseases worldwide (Table 2–5).

Much of the preventable disease in the world is concentrated in the developing and underdeveloped countries, where the most profound differences can be found in terms of social and economic influences. Underdevelopment is related to many factors, including economic stagnation; cultural patterns unfavorable to development; lack of adequate agricultural and other employment opportunities; poor quality of life due to scarcities of basic essentials; an unfavorable environment predisposing to communicable disease and malnutrition; inadequate health facilities and lack of sanitation; poor educational opportunities; social injustices, including land tenure systems, rigid hierarchies, and class systems; inadequate representation and influence in decision making; suppression of women; and inequities based on race, ethnic background, and/or religion.[3,21]

Though many of these factors appear to stem from low levels of national wealth, the link between national health status and national wealth is not as firm as one might expect. As a result, comparisons across nations are not nearly as

Table 2-5 World Health Organization (WHO) Estimates of Morbidity and Mortality of Water-Related Diseases, Worldwide, 1995

Disease	Morbidity (Episodes per Year)	Mortality (Deaths per Year)	Relationship to Water Supply, Sanitation
Diarrheal (drinking)	1 billion	3.3 million	Unsanitary excreta disposal, poor personal and domestic hygiene, unsafe water
Infection with intestinal helminths	1.5 billion[a]	100,000	Unsanitary excreta disposal, poor personal and domestic hygiene
Schistosomiasis	200 million[a]	200,000	Unsanitary excreta disposal and absence of nearby sources of safe water
Dracunuliasis	100,000[a,b]	—	Unsafe drinking water
Trachoma	150 million[c]	—	Lack of face washing, often due to absence of nearby sources of safe water
Malaria	400 million	1.5 million	Poor water management and storage, poor operation of water points and drainage
Dengue fever	1.75 million	20,000	Poor solid wastes management, water storage, and operation of water points and drainage
Poliomyelitis (drinking)	114,000	—	Unsanitary excreta disposal, poor personal and domestic hygiene, unsafe water
Trypanosomiasis	275,000	130,000	Absence of nearby sources of safe water
Bancroftian filariasis	72.8 million[a]	—	Poor water management and storage, poor operation of water points and drainage
Onchocerciasis	17.7 million[a,d]	40,000	Poor water management and large-scale projects

[a]People currently infected.
[b]Excluding Sudan.
[c]Case of active disease. Approximately 5.9 million cases of blindness or severe complications of trachoma occur annually.
[d]Includes an estimated 270,000 blind.

Source: Reprinted from WHO Warns of Inadequate Communicable Disease Prevention, *Prevention Health Reports*, Vol. 111, pp. 296–297, 1996, US Public Health Service.

straightforward as they might seem. Changes in standards of living, advances in literacy, education and welfare policies, and changes in the politics of human relations generally have more to do with improved health status as measured by current indicators than with specific preventive interventions. The complexities involved in identifying and understanding these forces and their interrelationships often confound comparisons in health status between the United States and other nations.

ANALYZING HEALTH PROBLEMS FOR RISK FACTORS

The ability to identify risk factors and pathways for causation is essential for rational public health decisions and actions to address important health problems in a population. First, however, it is necessary to define what is meant by *health problem*. Here, *health problem* means a condition of humans that can be represented in terms of measurable health status or quality-of-life indicators. In later chapters, additional dimensions will be added to this basic definition for the purposes of community problem solving and the development of interventions. This characterization of a health problem as something measured only in terms of outcomes is difficult for some to accept. They point to important factors such as access to care or poverty itself and feel that these should rightfully be considered as health problems. Important problems they may be, but if truly important in the causation of some unacceptable health outcome, they can be dealt with as related factors rather than health problems.

The factors linked with specific health problems are often generically termed *risk factors* and can exist at one of three levels. Those risk factors most closely associated with the health outcome in question are often termed *determinants*. Risk factors that play a role further back the chain of causation are called *direct* and *indirect contributing factors*. Risk factors can be described at either an individual or a population level. For example, tobacco use for an individual increases the chances of developing heart disease or lung cancer, and an increased prevalence of tobacco use in a population increases that population's incidence of (and mortality rates from) these conditions.

Determinants are scientifically established factors that relate directly to the level of a health problem. As the level of the determinant changes, the level of the health outcome changes. Determinants are the most proximal risk factors through which other levels of risk factors act. The link between the determinant and the health outcome should be well established through scientific or epidemiological studies. For example, for neonatal mortality rates, two well-established determinants are the low–birth weight rate (the number of infants born weighing less than 2,500 grams, or about 5.5 pounds, per 100 live births) and weight-specific mortality rates. Improvement in the neonatal mortality rate cannot occur unless one of these determinants improves. Health outcomes can have one or many determinants.

Direct contributing factors are scientifically established factors that directly affect the level of a determinant. Again, there should be solid evidence that the level of the direct determinant affects the level of the determinant. For the neonatal mortality rate example, the prevalence of tobacco use among pregnant women has been associated with the risk of low birth weight. A determinant can have many direct contributing factors. For low birth weight, other direct contributing factors include low maternal weight gain and inadequate prenatal care.

Indirect contributing factors affect the level of the direct contributing factors. Though less proximal to the health outcome in question, these factors are often proximal enough to be modified. The indirect contributing factor affects the level of the direct contributing factor, which, in turn, affects the level of the determinant. The level of the determinant then affects the level of the health outcome. Many indirect contributing factors can exist for each direct contributing factor. For prevalence of tobacco use among pregnant women, indirect contributing factors might include easy access to tobacco products for young women, lack of health education, and lack of smoking-cessation programs.

The health problem analysis framework begins with the identification of a health problem (defined in terms of health status indicators) and proceeds to establish one or more determinants; for each determinant, one or more direct contributing factors; and for each direct contributing factor, one or more indirect contributing factors. Intervention strategies at the community level generally involve addressing these indirect contributing factors. When completed, an analysis identifies as many of the causal pathways as possible in order to determine which contributing factors exist in the setting in which an intervention strategy is planned. The framework for this approach is presented in Table 2–6 and Figure 2–4. This framework forms the basis for developing meaningful interventions; it is used in several of the processes and instruments to assess community health needs that are currently in wide use at the local level. Community needs assessment processes and tools will be further described in Chapter 5.

Although this framework is useful, it does not fully account for the relationships among the various levels of risk factors. Some direct contributing factors may affect more than one determinant, and some indirect contributing factors may influence more than one direct contributing factor. For example, illicit drug use during pregnancy influences both the likelihood of low birth weight and birth weight–specific survival rates. To account fully for these interactions, some direct and indirect contributing factors may need to be included in several different locations on the worksheet.

MEASURING HEALTH

The availability of health outcome and risk factor information should simplify the task of measuring the health status of populations. However, although often

Table 2–6 Risk Factors

Determinant	Scientifically established factor that relates directly to the level of the health problem. A health problem may have any number of determinants identified for it.	Example: Low birth weight is a prime determinant for the health problem of neonatal mortality.
Direct contributing factor	Scientifically established factor that directly affects the level of the determinant.	Example: Use of prenatal care is one factor that affects the low–birth weight rate.
Indirect contributing factor	Community-specific factor that affects the level of a direct contributing factor. Such factors can vary considerably from one community to another.	Example: Availability of day care or transportation services within the community may affect the use of prenatal care services.

Source: Data from Centers for Disease Control and Prevention Public Health Practice Program Office.

---

interesting and sometimes even dramatic, the commonly used measures of health status fail to paint a complete picture of health. Many of the reasons are obvious. The commonly used measures actually reflect disease and mortality rather than health itself. The long-standing misperception that health is the absence of disease is reinforced by the relative ease of measuring disease states in comparison to states of health. Actually, the most commonly used indicators focus on a state that is not really either health or disease—namely death.

Despite the many problems with using mortality as a proxy for health, mortality data are generally available and widely used to describe the health status of populations. This is ironic because such data only indirectly describe the health status of living populations. Unfortunately, data on morbidity (illnesses, injuries, and functional limitations of the population) are neither as available nor as readily understood as mortality data. This situation is improving, however, as new forms and sources of information on health conditions become more available. Sources for information on morbidities and disabilities now include medical records from hospitals, managed-care organizations, and other providers, as well

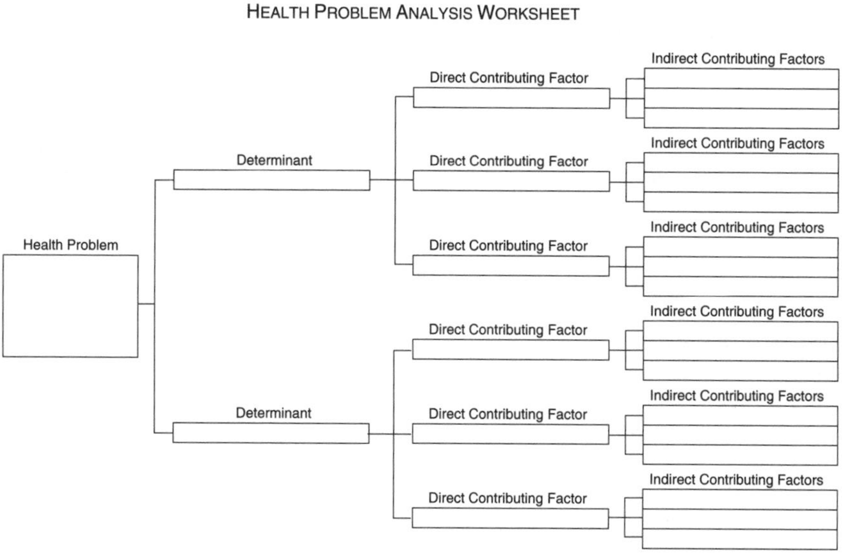

HEALTH PROBLEM ANALYSIS WORKSHEET

Figure 2–4 Health Problem Analysis Worksheet. *Source:* Reprinted from CDC Public Health Practice Program Office, 1991.

as information derived from surveys, businesses, schools, and other sources. Assessments of the health status of populations are increasingly utilizing measures from these sources. Chapter 6 will further describe data and information sources for use in public health. An excellent compilation of data and information on both health status and health services is published annually by the National Center for Health Statistics. For both consistency and ease in referencing, this text presents data from the most recent edition available (*Health United States 1995*)[10] unless noted otherwise.

Mortality-Based Indicators

Although mortality-based indicators of health status are both widely used and useful, there are some important differences in their use and interpretation. The most commonly used are crude mortality, age-specific and age-adjusted mortality, life expectancy, and YPLL. Though all are based on the same events, each provides somewhat different information as to the health status of a population.

Crude mortality rates count deaths within the entire population and are not sensitive to differences in the age distribution of different populations. The mortality comparisons included in Table 2–7 illustrate the use of crude death rates in

Table 2-7 Crude and Cause-Specific Mortality Rates and Rankings, United States, 1900 and 1994

Cause of Death	Crude Mortality Rate in 1900	Crude Mortality Rate in 1994	Ranking of Cause in 1900	Ranking of Cause in 1994
All causes	1719.1	876.9		
Influenza and pneumonia	202.2	31.5	1	6
Tuberculosis, all forms	194.4	NA	2	NA
Gastroenteritis	142.7	NA	3	NA
Diseases of the heart	137.4	281.6	4	1
Cerebrovascular disease	106.9	59.2	5	3
Chronic nephritis	81.0	9.1	6	12
Accidents and adverse effects	72.3	34.6	7	5
Malignant neoplasms	64.0	206.0	8	2
Certain diseases of infancy	62.6	5.4	9	15
Diphtheria	40.3	NA	10	NA

Note: Rates are per 100,000 population. Some categories are not strictly comparable due to changes in classification. NA = no longer listed among the top 15 causes of death.

Source: Reprinted from *Health United States 1995*, 1996, National Center for Health Statistics, Public Health Service, Hyattsville, MD.

comparing the mortality experience of the U.S. population in 1994 with that of the year 1900. On the basis of these data, we might conclude that mortality rates in the United States had declined about 50 percent since 1900. But since there was a greater proportion of the 1994 population in the higher age categories, these may not be truly comparable populations. The 50 percent reduction may actually understate the differences in mortality experience between 1900 and 1994. Since differences in the age characteristics of the two populations are a primary concern, we look for methods to correct or adjust for the age factor. Age-specific and age-adjusted rates do just that.

Age-specific mortality rates relate the number of deaths to the number of persons in a specific age group. Infant mortality rates are probably the best known example, describing the number of deaths of live-born infants occurring in the first year of life per 1,000 live births. Public health studies often use *age-adjusted mortality rates* to compensate for different mixes of age groups within a population—for example, a high proportion of children or elderly. Age-adjusted rates are calculated by applying age-specific rates to a standard population (often the 1940 U.S. population). This adjustment permits more meaningful comparisons of mortality experience between two populations with different age distribution patterns. Figure 2–5 tracks crude and age-adjusted mortality rates for the United States from 1950 through 1993. Crude mortality rates declined, but not as much as age-adjusted rates, from 1950 to 1993. The explanation is simply that the 1993 population had a greater proportion of persons in older age groups than the 1950 population. Using crude rates, the improvement was about 10 percent; age-adjusted rates showed a 40 percent improvement.

Life expectancy, also based on the mortality experience of a population, is a computation of the number of years between any given age (e.g., birth or age 45) and the average age of death for that population. Together with infant mortality rates, life expectancies are commonly used in comparisons of health status among nations. These two mortality-based indicators are often perceived as general indicators of the overall health status of a population. As illustrated in Figure 2–6, infant mortality and life expectancy indicators for the United States do not fare well in comparison to those of other developed nations.

YPLL is a mortality-based indicator that places greater weight on deaths that occur at younger ages. Years of life lost before some arbitrary age (often age 65 or 75) are computed and used to measure the relative impact on society of different causes of deaths. If age 65 is used as the threshold for calculating YPLL, an infant death would contribute 65 YPLL, and a homicide at age 25 would contribute 40 YPLL. A death due to stroke at age 70 would contribute no years of life

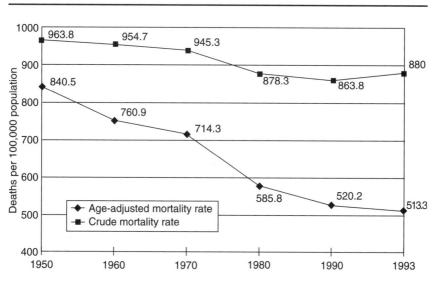

Figure 2–5 Crude and Age-Adjusted Mortality Rates, United States, 1950–1993. *Source:* Reprinted from *Health United States 1995*, 1996, National Center for Health Statistics, Public Health Service, Hyattsville, MD.

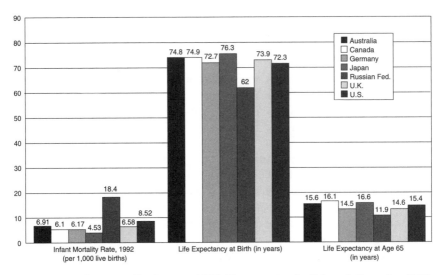

Figure 2–6 Infant Mortality Rates and Life Expectancies for Selected Countries, 1992. *Source:* Reprinted from *Health United States 1995*, 1996, National Center for Health Statistics, Public Health Service, Hyattsville, MD.

lost before age 65, and so on. Until relatively recently, age 65 was widely used as the threshold age. With life expectancies now exceeding 75 years at birth, YPLL calculations using age 75 as the threshold have become more common. Table 2–8 presents data on YPLL before age 65, illustrating the usefulness of this approach in providing a different perspective on which problems are most important in terms of their magnitude and impact. The use of YPLL ranks HIV/AIDS and various forms of injuries and infant deaths higher than the use of crude numbers or rates does. Conversely, the use of crude rates ranks heart disease, stroke, pneumonia, diabetes, and chronic lung disease higher than the use of YPLL does.

Each of these mortality indicators can be examined for different racial and ethnic subpopulations to identify disparities among these groups. For example, age-adjusted rates of YPLL before age 75 for 1993 ranged from 7,114 per 100,000 population for Hispanics to 15,468 per 100,000 for blacks. The rate for all groups was 8,384 per 100,000. The large disparity for blacks is attributable primarily to differences in infant mortality, homicide, and HIV infection deaths.

Mortality indicators can also be combined with other health indicators that describe quality considerations to provide a measure of the *span of healthy life*. This indicator can be an especially meaningful measure of health status in a population. Span-of-healthy-life indicators combine mortality data with self-reported health status and activity limitation data acquired through the National Health

Table 2–8 Years of Potential Life Lost (YPLL) before Age 65 by Cause of Death
and Ranks for YPLL and Number of Deaths, United States, 1990

Cause of Death	YPLL	Rank by YPLL	Rank by No. of Deaths
Unintentional injuries	2,148,660	1	4
Cancer	1,840,455	2	2
Intentional injuries (homicide/suicide)	1,518,230	3	8
Heart disease	1,356,095	4	1
Birth defects	690,855	5	x
HIV/AIDS	648,730	6	10
Prematurity	417,315	7	x
Sudden infant death syndrome	348,945	8	x
Stroke	244,730	8	3
Liver disease and cirrhosis	214,545	10	9
Pneumonia and influenza	168,905	11	6
Diabetes	143,110	12	7
Chronic obstructive pulmonary disease	127,130	13	5

Note: x indicates cause of death is not one of the 15 highest-ranked causes of death.
Source: Reprinted from *Health United States 1995*, 1996, National Center for Health Statistics, Public Health Service, Hyattsville, MD.

Interview Survey. In 1990, an average of about 11 years of life (when life expectancy was 75.4 years at birth) involved limitations of major life activities such as self-care (bathing, grooming, cooking, etc.), recreation, work, and school. The 64-year span of healthy life presents a better, although not precise, picture of health status and quality of life. This indicator is illustrated in Figure 2–7, with 1990 data identifying disparities among blacks, whites, and Hispanics in both the number of healthy years of life and the percentage of healthy years in comparison to life expectancy.[22] Hispanics had the greatest life expectancy at 79.1 years, of which 64.8 (82 percent) were years of healthy life. In contrast, blacks had 10 fewer years in life expectancy (69.1 years), of which 56 years (81 percent) were healthy years. Life expectancy for whites was 76.1 years, with 65 years of healthy life (85 percent). The differences between blacks and both whites and Hispanics is due to both the higher mortality and the greater prevalence of morbidity among the black population. Among the mortality-related measures discussed here, span of healthy life comes closest to measuring health in terms of the ability to function normally.

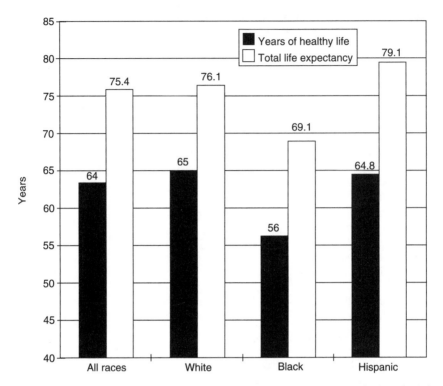

Figure 2–7 Total Life Expectancy and Years of Healthy Life by Race and Hispanic Origin, United States, 1990. *Source:* Reprinted from P. Erickson, R. Wilson, and I. Shannon, Years of Healthy Life, *Healthy People Statistical Notes*, Number 7, 1995, NCHS.

Morbidity and Disability Measures

Though less frequently encountered, indicators of morbidity and disability are also quite useful in measuring health status. Figure 2–8 presents information on both morbidity and disability for children in terms of the prevalence of specific childhood diseases (here the percentage of children 0 to 17 years old who have ever had these conditions) and the relationship between these conditions and self-reported health and activity status (a measure of disability).[23] Both prevalence (the number or rate of cases at a specific point or period in time) and incidence (the number or rate of new cases occurring during a specific period) are widely used measures of morbidity.

One of the oldest systems for reporting on diseases of public health significance is the national notifiable disease–reporting system for specific diseases.

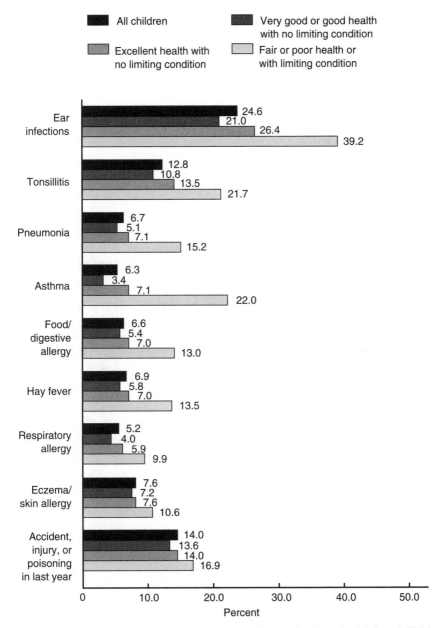

Figure 2–8 Percentage of Children 0 to 17 Years of Age Who Have Had Selected Childhood Diseases, by Child's Health and Limitation Status, United States, 1988. *Source:* Reprinted from M.J. Coiro, N. Zill, and B. Bloom, Health of Our Nation's Children, *Vital Health Statistics*, Vol. 10, No. 191, 1994, National Center for Health Statistics.

This system operates through the collaboration of local, state, and federal health agencies. Although initially developed to track the incidence of communicable diseases, this system has steadily moved toward collecting information on noninfectious conditions as well as important risk factors (refer back to Exhibit 2–1). The evolution of this reporting system over its 50-year history is summarized in Exhibit 2–2.

Exhibit 2–2 National Disease Surveillance and Notifiable Disease Statistics— United States, June 1946 and June 1996

National surveillance for infectious diseases is used to document the morbidity and impact associated with these conditions in the United States. This report includes morbidity data for the weeks ending June 8, 1946, and June 22, 1996, and describes changes since 1946 both in the procedures for conducting surveillance and in the incidence of selected diseases.

Surveillance Notes

The history of the reporting and tracking of diseases that could pose a risk to public health in the United States dates back more than a century. In 1878, Congress authorized the U.S. Marine Hospital Service (the forerunner of todays Public Health Service [PHS]) to collect morbidity reports on cholera, smallpox, plague, and yellow fever from U.S. consuls overseas; this information was used to institute quarantine measures to prevent the introduction and spread of these diseases into the United States. In 1879, a specific Congressional appropriation was made for collecting and publishing reports of these notifiable diseases. The authority for weekly reporting and publication was expanded by Congress in 1893 to include data from states and municipal authorities. By 1928, all states, the District of Columbia, Hawaii, and Puerto Rico were reporting 29 infectious diseases to the Surgeon General.

Fifty years ago, morbidity statistics published each week were accompanied by the statement "No health department, state or local, can effectively prevent or control disease without knowledge of when, where, and under what conditions cases are occurring." These statistics appeared under the heading "Prevalence of Disease—United States" in each issue of *Public Health Reports* printed by PHS, Office of the Surgeon General (Division of Public Health Methods). In 1949, the collection, compilation, and publication of these morbidity statistics was transferred to the National Office of Vital Statistics, which produced the *Weekly Morbidity Report*. In 1952, the publication was renamed *Morbidity and Mortality Weekly Report*, and the responsibility for the publication was transferred to CDC in 1961.

continues

Exhibit 2–2 continued

In 1946, reports of notifiable diseases consisted of summary statistics, transmitted by telegram each week by all state and some city health officers. The numbers were tabulated and sent immediately by letter to each site for verification. Data published in the June 28, 1946, issue of Public Health Reports were for the week ending June 8, 1946. Today for most diseases, each state health department enters individual case reports (rather than summary numbers) into a computer for transmission to CDC through the National Electronic Telecommunications System for Surveillance; data published in this issue of *MMWR* represent cumulative totals reported through June 22, 1996. Except for New York City and Washington, DC, morbidity data from individual cities are no longer published weekly.

Because the reporting frequency varied for different conditions (i.e., weekly, monthly, or annually), the precise number of conditions considered nationally reportable in 1946 is unclear. The first list of 41 infectious diseases that all states agreed should be nationally notifiable to PHS was developed at the first conference of state and territorial epidemiologists in 1951. This group was the forerunner of the Council of State and Territorial Epidemiologists (CSTE), now CDC's primary collaborator for determining what is nationally reportable. In 1951, as now, because reporting can be mandated only at the state level, reporting to CDC by the states was voluntary. Today 52 infectious diseases are notifiable nationally; in addition, at the 1995 CSTE meeting, the first noninfectious condition—elevated blood levels—was added to the list of conditions designated at the national level. On June 6, 1996, CSTE added silicosis and acute pesticide poisoning/injuries to the list of nationally reportable conditions. Also on June 6, CSTE unanimously agreed to include prevalence of cigarette smoking in the list of conditions designated as reportable by states to CDC; this is the first time tobacco has been included and the first time a risk behavior, rather than a disease or illness, has been included.

Disease Notes

Comparing reports of notifiable conditions during June 1946 and June 1996 highlights some of the differences in the prevalent or common diseases. For example, 50 years ago, in the fundamentally prevaccine era, for the week ending June 8, 1946, health departments reported 161 cases of poliomyelitis, 229 cases of diphtheria, 1,886 cases of pertussis, and 25,041 cases of measles. Through the week ending June 22, 1996, a cumulative total of no confirmed cases of polio, one case of diphtheria, 1,419 cases of pertussis, and 263 cases of measles have been reported for 1996. Since 1946, vaccines have been licensed for all four of these conditions: diphtheria and tetanus toxoids and pertussis vaccine in 1949, inactivated polio vaccine in 1955 and live attenuated vaccine in 1961, and measles vaccine in 1963. Because of the advent of these and other disease-control strategies, during the past decade public health authorities have established as targets for the year 2000 eradication of polio globally and measles elimination in the Americas. Four

continues

Exhibit 2–2 continued

cases of another vaccine-preventable disease, smallpox, were reported for the week ending June 8, 1946, and a total of 337 cases for the entire year of 1946; the last documented cases of smallpox in the United States occurred 3 years later, in 1949. In 1958, the World Health Organization targeted smallpox for global eradication, a campaign that was declared successful in 1980.

Among the 10 nationally notifiable infectious diseases that are most commonly reportable today, several were unknown in June 1946. The 10 most frequent nationally reportable infectious conditions in 1994 were, in descending order, gonorrhea, acquired immunodeficiency syndrome (AIDS), salmonellosis, shigellosis, hepatitis A, tuberculosis, primary and secondary syphilis, Lyme disease, hepatitis B, and pertussis. Fifty years ago, AIDS and Lyme disease were unknown. "Infectious hepatitis" (subsequently identified as hepatitis A) had just been identified, and morbidity reports for this condition first appeared in 1947. In 1953, serum hepatitis (subsequently named hepatitis B) was recognized as a separate entity, although it was included in the general category of hepatitis until 1966, when infectious and serum hepatitis began to be reported separately. Other diseases reported on a weekly basis during 1946 included amebiasis, murine typhus fever, and tularemia; during the past 10 years, these three conditions were deleted from the nationally notifiable disease list and are no longer routinely reported to CDC.

Because of the acknowledged underreporting of most diseases (particularly those typically characterized by clinically mild illness) to this passive surveillance system, the National Notifiable Disease Surveillance System (NNDSS) does not capture all cases of disease nationwide. However, these data are essential for monitoring disease trends and for determining relative disease burdens. In addition, this same NNDSS—with origins dating more than a century ago—continues to be used for monitoring the decline in incidence of vaccine-preventable and other diseases and to detect and document the appearance of new public health problems.

Source: Reprinted from *MMWR*, Vol. 45, pp. 530–536, 1996, CDC.

Placing a Value on Health Outcomes

The ability to measure and quantify outcomes and risks is essential for rational decisions and actions. Specific indicators as well as methods of economic analysis are available to provide both objective and subjective valuations. Several health indicators attempt to value differentially health status outcomes, including age-adjusted rates, span of healthy life, and YPLL. For example, YPLL represents a method of weighting or valuing health outcomes by placing a higher value on deaths that occur at earlier ages. Years of life lost thus become a common denominator or, in one sense, a common currency. Health outcomes can be translated into this currency or into an actual currency such as dollars. This translation allows for comparisons to be made among outcomes in terms of which costs more per person, per episode, or per another reference point. Cost comparisons of health outcomes and health events have become common in public health. Approaches include cost benefit, cost-effectiveness, and cost utility studies.

Cost benefit analyses provide comprehensive information on both the costs and the benefits of an intervention. All health outcomes and other relevant impacts are included in the determination of benefits. The results are expressed in terms of net dollars, such as the $10.30 savings for every dollar spent for pertussis immunizations described in Chapter 1. This provides a framework for comparing disparate interventions, such as those included in Figure 1–1. When comprehensively performed, cost benefit analyses are considered the gold standard of economic evaluations.

Cost-effectiveness analyses focus on one outcome to determine the most cost-effective intervention when several options are possible. Cost-effectiveness examines a specific option's costs to achieve a particular outcome. Results are often specified as the cost per case prevented or cost per life saved. For example, screening an entire town for a specific disease might identify cases at a cost of $150 per new case, whereas a screening program directed only at high-risk groups within that town might identify cases at a cost of $50 per new case. Though useful for evaluating different strategies for achieving the same result, cost-effectiveness approaches are not very helpful in evaluating interventions intended for different health conditions.

Cost utility analyses are similar to cost-effectiveness studies except that the results are characterized as cost per quality-adjusted life years. These are most useful when the intervention affects both morbidity and mortality and there are a wide range of possible outcomes that include quality of life.

These approaches are especially important for interventions based on preventive strategies. The argument is frequently made that "an ounce of prevention is worth a pound of cure." If this wisdom is true, preventive interventions should result in savings equal to 16 times their actual cost. Not all preventive interventions measure up to this standard, but even crude information on the costs of many health outcomes suggests that prevention can save dollars as well as people. Table 2–9 presents information from *Healthy People 2000*[24] regarding the economics of prevention for a number of common diseases and conditions; for each, the potential savings represents an enormous sum. Figure 2–9 illustrates that the impacts of disease and injuries can be many in terms of medical care costs for treatment in outpatient, emergency department, and hospital settings.[25] The U.S. Public Health Service has estimated that as much as 11 percent of projected health expenditures for the year 2000 can be averted through investments in public health for six conditions: motor vehicle injuries, occupationally related

Table 2-9 The Economics of Prevention

Condition	Overall Magnitude	Avoidable Intervention[a]	Cost/Patient[b]
Heart disease	7 million with coronary artery disease 500,000 deaths/year 284,000 bypass procedures/year	Coronary bypass surgery	$30,000
Cancer	1 million new cases/year 510,000 deaths/year	Lung cancer treatment Cervical cancer treatment	$29,000 $28,000
Stroke	600,000 strokes/year 150,000 deaths/year	Hemiplegia treatment and rehabilitation	$22,000
Injuries	2.3 million hospitalizations per year 142,500 deaths/year 177,000 persons with spinal cord injuries in the United States	Quadriplegia treatment and rehabilitation Hip fracture treatment and rehabilitation Severe head injury treatment and rehabilitation	$570,000 (lifetime) $40,000 $310,000
HIV infection	1–1.5 million infected 118,000 AIDS cases (as of Jan. 1990)	AIDS treatment	$75,000 (lifetime)
Alcoholism	18.5 million abuse alcohol 105,000 alcohol-related deaths/year	Liver transplant	$250,000
Drug abuse	Regular users: 1–3 million cocaine 900,000 IV drugs 500,000 heroin Drug-exposed infants: 375,000	Treatment of cocaine-exposed infant	$66,000 (5 years)
Low–birth weight infants	260,000 LBW infants/year 23,000 deaths/year	Neonatal intensive care for LBW infant	$10,000
Inadequate immunization	Lacking basic immunization series: 20%–30% aged 2 and younger 3% aged 6 and older	Congenital rubella syndrome treatment	$354,000 (lifetime)

[a]Interventions represent examples (other interventions may apply).
[b]Representative first-year costs, except as noted. Not indicated are nonmedical costs, such as lost productivity to society.
Source: Reprinted from *Healthy People 2000*, 1990, U.S. Public Health Service, Washington, DC.

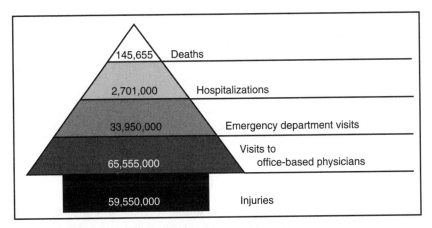

Figure 2–9 Health Impacts of Injuries. *Source:* Reprinted from C.W. Burt, Injury-Related Visits to Hospital Emergency Departments, *Advance Data 1995*, No. 261, 1992, NCHS.

injuries, stroke, coronary heart disease, firearms-related injuries, and low–birth weight infants.[26] Beyond the direct medical effects, there are often nonmedical costs related to lost wages, taxes, and productivity.

Economists assert that the future costs for care and services that result from prevention of mortality must be considered a negative benefit of prevention. For example, the costs of preventing a death due to motor vehicle injuries should include all subsequent medical care costs for that individual over his or her lifetime, since these costs would not have occurred otherwise. They also argue that it is unfair to compare future savings to the costs of current prevention programs and that those savings must be discounted to their current value. If a preventive program will save $10 million 20 years from now, that $10 million must be translated into its current value in computing cost benefits, cost-effectiveness, or cost utility. It may be that the value of $10 million 20 years from now is only $4 million now. If the program cost $1 million, its benefit-to-cost ratio would be 4 to 1 instead of 10 to 1 before we even added any additional costs associated with medical care for the lives that were saved. These economic considerations contribute to the difficulty of marketing preventive interventions.

Two additional economic considerations are important for public health policy and practice. The first of these is what economists term *opportunity costs*. These represent the costs involved in choosing one course of action over another. Resources spent for one purpose are not available to be spent for another. As a result, there is a need to consider the costs of not realizing the benefits or gains from paths not chosen. A second economic consideration important for public health is related to the heavy emphasis of public health on preventive strategies. The savings or gains from successful prevention efforts are generally not reinvested in public health or even other health purposes. These savings or gains from investments in prevention are lost. Maybe this is proper, since the overall benefits accrue more broadly to society, and public health remains, above all else, a social enterprise. But imagine the situation for American industry and businesses if they could not reinvest their gains to grow their businesses. This is often the situation faced by public health, further exacerbating the difficulty of arguing for and securing needed resources.

HEALTH IN THE UNITED STATES: 1900–1995

Several important indicators of U.S. health status have improved considerably over the past century, although there is ample evidence that health status could be even better than it is. At the turn of the century, about 2 percent of the U.S. population died each year. The crude mortality rate in 1900 was about 1,700 deaths per 100,000 population, with the leading causes of death as follows: influenza and pneumonia; tuberculosis; diarrhea and related diseases; heart disease; stroke; chronic nephritis; accidents; cancer; perinatal conditions; and diphtheria. Life expectancy at birth was 47 years. Additional life expectancy at age 45 was another 24 years. Medicine and health care were largely proprietary in 1900 and of questionable benefit to health. More extensive information on the health status of the population at that time would be useful, but very little exists.

Indicators of health status improved in the United States throughout the 20th century. By 1994, the crude mortality rate (not adjusted for differences in the population's age distribution between 1900 and 1994) had decreased by about 50 percent. On an age-adjusted basis, improvements were even more impressive. Age-adjusted mortality fell about 75 percent between 1900 and 1994 to about 500 per 100,000 (it was 840 in 1950). (Refer back to Figure 2–5.) Infant and child mortality rates fell 95 percent, adolescent and young adult mortality rates dropped 80 percent, rates for adults aged 25 to 64 fell 60 percent, and even the rate for older adults (over age 65) declined 35 percent.

The leading causes of death also changed dramatically between 1900 and 1994, as demonstrated in Table 2–7. Tuberculosis, diarrheal diseases, and diphtheria had dropped off the list of the top 15 killers. These infectious disease processes were superseded by diseases of aging and other chronic conditions, even though a new infectious disease (HIV infections) emerged as a major cause of death during the 1980s. Changes in the age structure of the population, especially the increase of persons over age 65, resulted in increases in the overall rates for heart disease and cancer and in the emergence of chronic obstructive lung disease and diabetes as leading causes of death.

Due to lower age-adjusted mortality rates, life expectancy in 1994 was nearly 76 years. Life expectancy at age 45 was another 34 years. Gains for adult age groups in recent decades have outstripped those for younger age groups, a trend that began about 1960 as progress accelerated toward reduction of mortality from injuries and certain major chronic diseases that largely affected adults (earlier reductions for children also left little room for further improvements). Table 2–10 demonstrates more recent changes in the age-adjusted frequency of the major causes of death. Recent reductions in the rates for heart disease, stroke, and unintentional injuries have been partly offset by increased rates for HIV infections, diabetes, and pneumonia and influenza.

This same table also demonstrates some of the considerable disparities that exist in the United States for virtually all mortality indicators. Differences among races are most notable, but there are also significant differences by gender for the various causes of death. These disparities have emerged as the greatest challenges to the health system in the United States. The differences are often dramatic and in all cases disconcerting. They run from top to bottom through the chain of causation and are found not only in indicators of poor health outcomes like mortality but also in the levels of risk factors in the population groups most severely affected. A closer examination of these disparities paints a vivid picture of health

Table 2–10 Age-Adjusted Death Rates from 10 Leading Causes for 1993, with Percentage Change from 1979 to 1993 and Ratio by Sex and Race, United States

Rank	Cause of Death	1993 Rate	1979–1993 % Change	Ratio: Male to Female	Ratio: Black to White
1	Diseases of the heart	145.3	−27.2	1.9	1.5
2	Malignant neoplasms	132.6	1.4	1.5	1.4
3	Cerebrovascular disease	26.5	−36.3	1.2	1.8
4	Chronic lung disease	21.4	46.6	1.6	0.8
5	Accidents and adverse effects	30.3	−29.4	2.6	1.3
	Motor vehicle accidents	16.0	−31.0	2.3	1.0
	All other accidents	14.4	−26.5	2.9	1.6
6	Pneumonia and influenza	13.5	20.5	1.6	1.4
7	Diabetes	12.4	26.5	1.2	2.4
8	HIV infections	13.8	NA	6.3	4.0
9	Suicide	11.3	−3.4	4.4	0.6
10	Homicide	10.7	4.9	3.8	6.8

Note: Rates per 100,000 population age adjusted to the 1940 U.S. population.
Source: Reprinted from *Health United States 1995*, 1996, National Center for Health Statistics, Public Health Service, Hyattsville, MD.

status in modern America. Many different indicators provide the colors for this picture. For example, about three-fourths of the U.S. population resides in counties that meet national ambient air quality standards. However, as demonstrated in Figure 2–10, substantial differences exist among the various racial and ethnic groups even for these environmental risks.

A sampling of health indicators derived from *Health United States 1994*[27] and *Health United States 1995*[10] highlight key aspects of the health disparities facing the nation.

- In 1994, overall life expectancy at birth was 75.6 years, near the record high set in 1992. Life expectancy at birth was about 8 years longer for white males than for black males and 6 years longer for white females than for black females (Figure 2–11).
- The difference in life expectancy between white females and black males is 15 years: an alarming gap.
- The leading causes of YPLL in 1993 were unintentional injuries for white males, homicide for black males, and malignant neoplasms for white females and black females. By 1993, HIV infection was the eighth leading

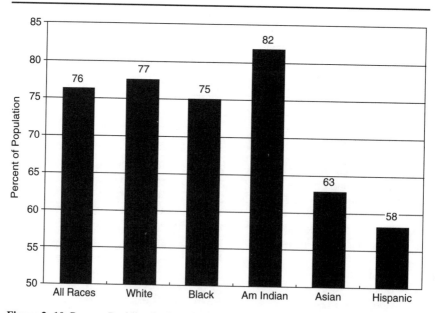

Figure 2–10 Persons Residing in Counties That Met National Ambient Air Quality Standards, by Race and Hispanic Origin, United States, 1993. *Source:* Reprinted from the Environmental Protection Agency.

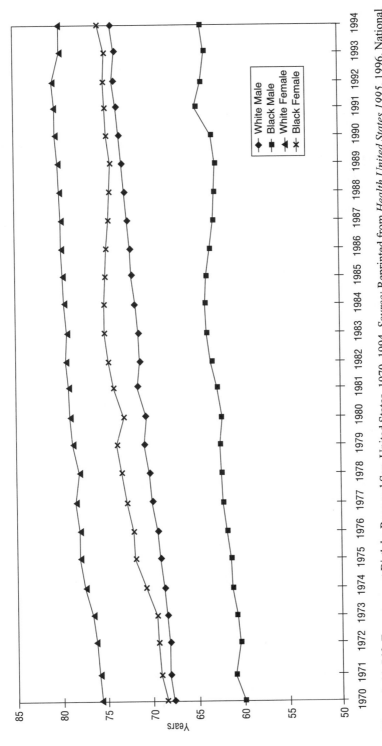

Figure 2–11 Life Expectancy at Birth by Race and Sex, United States, 1970–1994. *Source:* Reprinted from *Health United States 1995*, 1996, National Center for Health Statistics, Public Health Service, Hyattsville, MD.

cause of death for all persons and the leading cause of death at ages 25 to 44 years. In terms of YPLL, however, HIV infection was the fourth leading contributor to YPLL for all persons (behind injuries, cancer, and heart disease). For black males, it ranked as the second leading contributor to YPLL; for black females, it was fourth.

- Educational attainment is inversely associated with mortality. Between 1990 and 1993, the educational gradient in mortality for persons 25 to 64 years of age widened due to increases in the age-adjusted death rates for persons with a high school education or less and decreases in the death rates for persons with more than a high school education. The ratio of the age-adjusted death rate for persons 25 to 64 years of age with less than a high school education was more than double the rate for those with more than a high school education.

- In 1993, the death rate for Hispanic white males 15 to 24 years of age was 53 percent greater than for non-Hispanic white males. Death rates for Hispanic white males 25 to 44 years of age were 30 percent greater than for non-Hispanic white males of similar age.

- Between 1980 and 1993, the age-adjusted death rates for heart disease and stroke, the first and third leading causes of death for men and women, declined by approximately one-third, continuing the downward trend of the 1970s. Stroke mortality for the black population is two to three times greater than for any other racial or ethnic group. The age-adjusted death rate for stroke for black women is about two times that for women in other racial and ethnic groups.

- Between 1980 and 1993, the age-adjusted death rate for breast cancer increased 14 percent for black women and decreased 7 percent for white women. In 1993, the age-adjusted death rate for breast cancer for black women was 28 percent higher than the rate for white women.

- In 1994, the overall proportion of the population experiencing limitations of major activities was 10 percent, but the rate varied greatly among racial and ethnic groups. The rate for low-income populations was two times greater, at 19.6 percent. The rate for blacks was 13.8 percent. The age-adjusted percentage of blacks reporting fair or poor health was nearly double that of whites.

- In 1994, the infant mortality rate was 7.9 deaths per 1,000 live births, a record low. In the mid-1960s, rates began a steady decline that slowed somewhat during the 1980s (Figure 2–12). Nearly two-thirds of infant deaths occur during the first 27 days of life (neonatal deaths). Between 1980 and 1993, the infant mortality rate for white infants declined 38 percent while mortality for black infants declined 26 percent, resulting in a widening gap in infant mortality between the two races. In 1993, the infant mortality rate for black infants was 2.4 times that for white infants. Compared with whites,

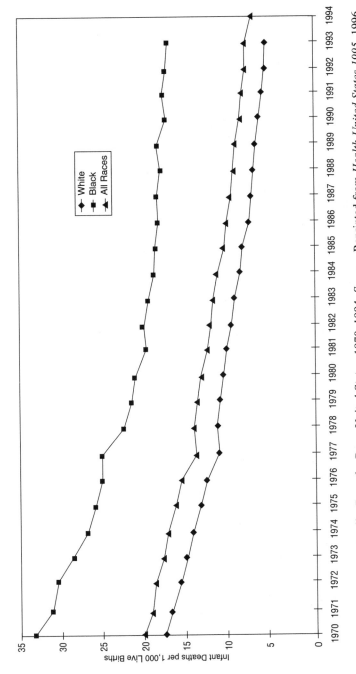

Figure 2–12 Infant Mortality Rates by Race, United States, 1970–1994. *Source:* Reprinted from *Health United States 1995*, 1996, National Center for Health Statistics, Public Health Service, Hyattsville, MD.

infant mortality rates were about 73 percent higher for American Indian infants, 42 percent higher for Puerto Rican infants, 23 percent higher for Hawaiian infants, and 27 to 30 percent lower for Japanese and Chinese infants in the United States. Compared with rates from other countries, the 1992 U.S. rate was 88 percent higher than in Japan and 40 percent higher than in Canada. The combined fetal and infant mortality rate in the U.S. was 58 percent higher than in Japan and 28 percent higher than in Canada.

- Low birth weight (LBW) is associated with increased risk of death and disability in infants. In 1993, the incidence of LBW (less than 2,500 grams) among live-born infants was 7.2 percent, up slightly from 6.8 percent in 1980. Between 1980 and 1993, the incidence of very low birth weight (VLBW, less than 1,500 grams) increased 19 percent among black infants, to 3.0 percent, and 7 percent among white infants, to 1.0 percent. Mortality for LBW infants is more than 20 times and for VLBW infants is more than 85 times that for infants of normal weight.

- In 1993, the proportion of mothers beginning prenatal care in the first trimester of pregnancy rose noticeably, to 79 percent. Although early initiation of prenatal care increased for all racial and ethnic groups, large disparities remain. Only 63 to 71 percent of American Indian, Mexican American, non-Hispanic black, Central and South American, Puerto Rican, and Hawaiian mothers initiated prenatal care in the first trimester. In contrast, 81 to 88 percent of non-Hispanic white, Chinese, Cuban, and Japanese mothers received early prenatal care in 1993.

- The poverty rate increased between 1989 and 1994 from 13 to 15 percent for all persons and from 19 to 22 percent for all persons under 18 years of age. The poverty rates among Mexican American children (40 percent), black children (46 percent), and Puerto Rican children (54 percent) were two to three times that for white children (17 percent). In 1994, a total of 38 million persons lived in poverty, including nearly 15 million children.

- Health status is strongly associated with family income. In 1993, the age-adjusted percentage of persons with low family income (less than $14,000) who reported fair or poor health was 5.5 times that for persons with a high income of $50,000 or more. Similarly, the age-adjusted percentage of low-income persons who were unable to carry on their major activity due to a chronic health condition was seven times the level for high-income persons.

In sum, U.S. health indicators tell two very different tales. By many measures, the American population has never been healthier. By others, much more needs to be done for specific racial, ethnic, and gender groups. The improvement in many health indicators over the past 50 years has not been shared equally by all subgroups of the population. In fact, relative differences have been increasing. This widening gap in health status creates a dilemma for future health improvement efforts. The greatest gains can be made through closing these gaps and equalizing health status within the population. Yet the burden of greater risk and poorer health status resides in a relatively small part of the total population, calling for efforts that target those minorities with increased resources. An alternative approach is to continue current strategies and resource deployment levels. Although this may continue the steady overall improvement among all groups in the population, it is likely to continue or worsen existing gaps. At some point in time, these disparities will become the major health status issue in the United States, challenging the nation's commitment to its principles of equality for all.

These data only broadly describe disparities in health status in the United States in the mid-1990s. Several common themes emerge, however, that form the basis for national health objectives focusing on the year 2000. This national health agenda for prevention and health promotion is presented in *Healthy People 2000*,[24] including three major goals:

1. Increase the span of healthy life for Americans.
2. Reduce health disparities among Americans.
3. Achieve access to preventive health services for all Americans.

The year 2000 objectives build on the nation's experience with similar health objectives established for the year 1990. The earlier effort was initially generated in the late 1970s through the efforts of Surgeon General Julius Richmond and coordinated by the Office of Disease Prevention and Health Promotion within the Office of the Assistant Secretary for Health. The year 2000 national health objectives include 300 specific objectives addressing health status measures, risk factor prevalence, and use of preventive health services. These 300 objectives fall into 22 priority categories (Exhibit 2–3). To assist communities in assessing community health status, a minimum set of key indicators was established in 1991 (Exhibit 2–4). These indicators include a mixture of mortality, morbidity, and risk factor measures. Although a useful starting point, these indicators are not sufficient to adequately assess community health status. Additional measures of morbidity, disability, and important risk factors are sorely needed.

Progress toward achievement of the year 2000 national health objectives was assessed in 1995. The status of each objective was reviewed and classified as moving in the right direction, moving in the wrong direction, showing no change, or unable to be tracked. The midcourse review found that about half the overall objectives were moving in the right direction, 18 percent were moving in the wrong direction, 3 percent showed no change, and 29 percent could not be tracked.[28] A substantially higher proportion of the objectives targeting special populations, especially blacks and American Indians, were found to be moving in

Exhibit 2–3 Healthy People 2000 Goals

Goal 1   Increase the span of healthy life.
Goal 2   Reduce health disparities.
Goal 3   Increase access to preventive services.
Health Promotion
   1. Physical activity and fitness
   2. Nutrition
   3. Tobacco
   4. Alcohol and other drugs
   5. Family planning
   6. Mental health and mental disorders
   7. Violence and abusive behavior
   8. Educational and community-based programs
Health Protection
   9. Unintentional injuries
 10. Occupational safety and health
 11. Environmental health
 12. Food and drug safety
 13. Oral health
 14. Maternal and infant health
 15. Heart disease and stroke
 16. Cancer
 17. Diabetes and chronic disabling conditions
 18. HIV infections
 19. Sexually transmitted diseases
 20. Immunization and infectious diseases
 21. Clinical preventive services
Surveillance and Data Systems
 22. Surveillance and data systems

Source: Reprinted from *Healthy People 2000*, 1990, U.S. Public Health Service, Washington, DC.

the wrong direction (Figure 2–13). These findings raise concerns that disparities are persisting, if not increasing, in the United States.

CONCLUSION

The health status of a population is influenced by many factors drawn from biology, behavior, the environment, and the use of health services. Social and cultural factors also play an important role in the disease patterns experienced by different populations, as well as in the responses of these populations to disease

Exhibit 2–4 Consensus Set of Health Status Indicators for the General Assessment of Community Health Status, 1991

Indicators of health status outcome
- Race/ethnicity-specific infant mortality, as measured by the rate (per 1,000 live births) of death among infants less than one year of age

Death rates (per 100,000 population, age adjusted to the 1940 standard population) for
- Motor vehicle crashes
- Work-related injury
- Suicide
- Lung cancer
- Breast cancer
- Cardiovascular disease
- Homicide
- All causes

Reported incidence (per 100,000 population) of
- Acquired immunodeficiency syndrome
- Measles
- Tuberculosis
- Primary and secondary syphilis

Indicators of risk factors
- Prevalence of low birth weight, as measured by percentage of total number of live-born infants weighing less than 2,500 grams at birth
- Births to adolescents (females aged 10–17 years) as a percentage of total live births
- Prenatal care, as measured by the percentage of mothers delivering live infants who did not receive care during the first trimester of pregnancy
- Childhood poverty, as measured by the proportion of children under 15 years of age living in families at or below the poverty level
- Proportion of persons living in counties exceeding U.S. Environmental Protection Agency standards for air quality during the previous year

Note: Position of indicator does not imply priority.
Source: Reprinted from Centers for Disease Control and Prevention, 1991.

and illness. Globally, risks associated with population growth, pollution, and poverty result in mortality and morbidity that are still associated with infectious disease processes. In the United States, behaviorally mediated risks, including tobacco, diet, alcohol, and injury risks, rather than infectious disease processes, are the major contributors to health status, and the considerable gap between low-income minority populations and other Americans continues to widen. Reduction of the disparities in health status among population groups has emerged as a

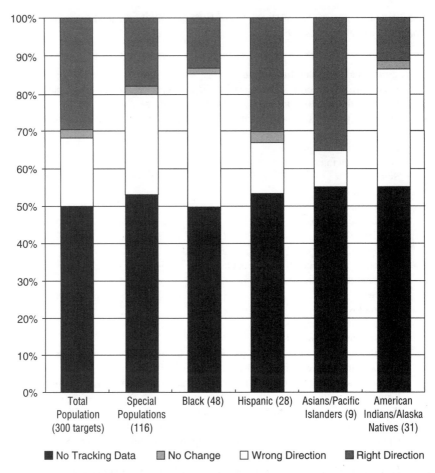

Figure 2–13 Progress on Racial and Ethnic Minority Objectives for the Year 2000 as of 1995. *Source:* Reprinted from *Prevention Report,* 1995, U.S. Public Health Service, Washington, DC.

national health goal for the year 2000. With the increasing availability of data on health status as well as on determinants and contributing factors, the potential for more rational policies and interventions has increased. The challenge now is to turn data into information that will guide more effective individual and collective actions.

DISCUSSION QUESTIONS AND EXERCISES

1. What are the major social and political factors that influence health today?
2. Are the factors that influence health the same for the United States as for the rest of the world?
3. Is social class a significant determinant of health? If so, how?
4. What are the major environmental factors that influence health in the United States today?
5. What are the major lifestyle factors that influence health in the United States today?
6. What are the major biological factors that influence health in the United States today?
7. What are the "3 Ps" of global health, and why are they important?
8. Review the evolution of a national system of notifiable conditions (Exhibit 2–2) and describe changes over its 50-year history in terms of its usefulness as an information source for assessing the health status of the population.
9. Select a health outcome from the information presented in this chapter as it relates to a particular age, racial, or ethnic group, and identify at least two major determinants for that problem. For each determinant, identify at least two contributing factors, and for each contributing factor, identify at least two indirect contributing factors.

REFERENCES

1. Centers for Disease Control and Prevention. First reportable underlying cause of death. *MMWR.* 1996;45:537.
2. Constitution of World Health Organization. In: *Chronicle of World Health Organization.* Geneva, Switzerland: World Health Organization; 1947;1:29–43.
3. Whaley RF, Hashim TJ. *A Textbook of World Health.* New York, NY: Parthenon; 1995.
4. Brownson RC, Remington PL, Davis JR, eds. *Chronic Disease Epidemiology and Control.* Washington, DC: American Public Health Association; 1993.
5. *Environmental Progress and Challenges: EPA's Update.* Washington, DC: Environmental Protection Agency; 1988.
6. *Health Care Costs of Air Pollution.* New York, NY: American Lung Association; 1990.
7. Seitz F, Plepys C. Monitoring air quality in healthy people 2000. *Healthy people 2000 statistical notes.* Hyattsville, Md: National Center for Health Statistics; 1995:No. 9.
8. Amler RW, Eddins DL. Cross-sectional analysis: Precursors of premature death in the U.S. In Amler RW and Dull DL, eds. *Closing the Gap.* Atlanta, Ga: Carter Center; 1985:181–187.

9. McGinnis JM, Foege W. Actual causes of death in the United States. *JAMA*. 1993;270:2207–2212.

10. National Center for Health Statistics. *Health United States 1995*. Hyattsville, Md: US Public Health Service; 1996.

11. Chadwick E. *Report on the Sanitary Conditions of the Labouring Population of Great Britain 1842*. Edinburgh, Scotland: Edinburgh University Press; 1965.

12. Centers for Disease Control and Prevention. Poverty and infant mortality: United States, 1988. *MMWR*. 1996;44:922–927.

13. Geltman PL, Meyers AF, Greenberg J, Zuckerman B. Welfare reform and children's health. *Health Policy and Child Health*. 1996;3(No. 2):1–5.

14. Smith GD, Egger M. Socioeconomic differences in mortality in Britain and the United States. *Am J Public Health*. 1992;82:1079–1081.

15. Wilkenson RG. National mortality rates: the impact of inequality. *Am J Public Health*. 1992; 82:1082–1084.

16. Sargent CF, Johnson TM, eds. *Medical Anthropology: Contemporary Theory and Method*. Rev ed. Westport, Ct: Praeger Publishers; 1996.

17. Susser M, Watson W, Hopper K. *Sociology in Medicine*. New York, NY: Oxford Press; 1985.

18. Link BG, Phelan JC. Understanding sociodemographic differences in health: the role of fundamental social causes. *Am J Public Health*. 1996;86:471–473.

19. Doll R. Health and the environment in the 1990s. *Am J Public Health*. 1992;82:933–941.

20. Winkelstein W. Determinants of worldwide health. *Am J Public Health*. 1992;82:931–932.

21. Pickett G, Hanlon JJ. *Public Health Administration and Practice*. 9th ed. St. Louis, Mo; Times-Mirror Mosby; 1990.

22. Erickson P, Wilson R, Shannon I. Years of healthy life. *Healthy People 2000 Stat. Notes*. 1995:7.

23. Coiro MJ, Zill N, Bloom B. Health of our nation's children. *Vital Health Stat*. 1994;10(191).

24. *Healthy People 2000*. Washington, DC: US Public Health Service; 1990.

25. Burt CW. *Injury-Related Visits to Hospital Emergency Departments, U.S., 1992*. Hyattsville, Md: US Public Health Service; 1995:261.

26. *For a Healthy Nation: Return on Investments in Public Health*. Washington, DC: US Public Health Service; 1994.

27. National Center for Health Statistics. *Health United States 1994*. Hyattsville, Md: US Public Health Service; 1995.

28. *Prevention Report*. Washington, DC: US Public Health Service; Fall 1995.

CHAPTER 3

Health and the
Health System

In 1993, an unprecedented campaign to reform the American health care system was initiated. The ensuing dialogue and debate served to focus national attention on both what is right and what is wrong with the health system in the United States. That campaign quite properly identified cost and access as important problems threatening both personal security and the national economic interest. But there was another important theme that was not addressed in this campaign, certainly not to the extent that cost and access were. That forgotten theme was health, something that many consider to be the ultimate aim of any health system. Why was health reform so preoccupied with cost and access? Have these now become the new bottom lines of our health system? Aren't these secondary to a greater end—improved health status? At times, it appears that our health system views health as a byproduct rather than its primary product.

This chapter picks up where Chapter 2 left off—with influences on health. The influences to be examined here, however, relate to the utilization of services available through our health system.

The sheer size and scope of the American health system make it a force to be reckoned with, engendering comparisons with a similar force that existed in the United States in the 1950s and 1960s. At that time, and as he left office, President Eisenhower warned the nation of the potentially dangerous influence of the nation's "military industrial complex." His observations were both ominous and insightful as he decried a powerful industry whose self-interest was coloring the nation's view of other countries and their people. The plight of the American health system raises the specter of a 1990s analogue in a "medical industrial complex." One danger posed by these complexes is their ability to influence the way we address (or even think about) a major public policy problem or issue. This occurs through interpreting and recasting the issues involved, sometimes even to the extent of altering public perceptions as to what is occurring and why.

Public understanding of the meaning of the terms *health reform* and *health care* is a case in point. Although as a society we have come to substitute the term *health care* for what is really medical or treatment care, these are simply not the same. The health status of a population is largely determined by a different set of considerations as discussed in Chapter 2. Those considerations are very much the focus of the public health system. If the ultimate goal is a healthier population, and more specifically the prevention of disease and disability, the national health system must aggressively balance treatment with population- and community-based prevention strategies.

Some argue that this is merely semantics. After all, the argument goes, health reform will reduce waste, freeing up resources that can be used to increase access to and utilization of medical services for those without adequate access. This will mean more services for more people and result in improved health for those individuals and the population as a whole. Although this sounds logical, the reasoning is sadly mistaken. It is based on some fundamental assumptions and myths that many Americans have come to accept as truth, partly because they have been continuously reinforced by the medical care interests in this country.

The most basic of these myths is that access to and use of medical services are directly related to—and the best approach for improving—the health status of a population. More and better medical care means healthier people. The fallacy here is that the services that we Americans call health care are only indirectly related to health. Rather, they are directed toward disease (or ill health) and relate to health only to the extent that they can restore persons to health and normal functioning. There are services that directly address health in that they seek to promote and protect health. These include many of the communitywide efforts to protect food and water supplies, control communicable diseases, and otherwise reduce the behaviors and risk factors that can result in disease and injury. For poorly understood reasons, however, these are not widely considered "health services," whereas treatment and rehabilitation activities are.

To the surprise of those who believe in and perpetuate this myth, the evidence convincingly shows that community and public health activities have been most responsible for the increased life expectancy of Americans from 47 years in 1900 to over 75 years today.[1] Even more recently, community and public health approaches have been primarily responsible for the 67 percent reduction in stroke mortality, 49 percent decline in cardiovascular disease death rate, and 28 percent reduction in mortality due to motor vehicle crashes experienced between 1960 and 1993.[2,3]

These are spectacular successes when you consider that less than 1 percent of our current health expenditures supports these truly health-oriented services. If we look at the major causes of death, illness, or injury today, it is apparent that illness care will be of limited value in dealing with conditions caused by tobacco, diet and activity patterns, alcohol, toxic agents, firearms, sexual behavior, motor vehicles, and illicit drug use. These are the factors accounting for the majority of deaths in the United States in the 1990s. The evidence from both history and the factors responsible for our current major health problems argues that preventive strategies, including communitywide public health services, have been and are likely to continue to be more effective than medical care in improving health status. The modern medical care system does not reflect these values, however, and has lost sight of its purpose and primary goal, health. In losing its way, the system stands on the brink of disaster in terms of its affordability and return on investment.

There is a term for what happens when an organization finds that it is unable to achieve its primary objectives and outcomes (bottom line) and then justifies its existence in terms of how well it does the things it is doing. *Outcome displacement* is that term; it means that the original outcome (here, improved health status) has been displaced by a focus on how well the means to that end (the organization, provision, and financing of services) are being addressed. These then become the new purpose or mission for that system. Instead of "doing the right things" to affect health status, the system focuses on "doing things right" (regardless of whether they maximally affect health). It is possible to have the best medical care services in the world but still have an inadequate health system.

When bottom lines are not attended to in the private sector, changes are made or companies do not survive. For the American health system—a mosaic of public and private components—the lack of attention to the original bottom line and the preoccupation with the processes of organizing, financing, and providing service delivery have resulted in what we have today: an incredibly expensive and complex system that does not improve our health status as much as it could and should.

This chapter will examine the U.S. health system from a perspective that considers the public health implications of costs and affordability as well as other important public policy and public health questions that are often overlooked:

- Does the United States have a rational strategy for investing its resources to maintain and improve people's health?
- Is the current strategy excessive in ways that inequitably limit access to and benefit from needed services?
- Is the health system accountable to its end-users and ultimate payers for the quality and results of its services?

It is these issues of health, excess, access, accountability, and quality that make the health system a public health concern.

PUBLIC HEALTH AND THE HEALTH SYSTEM

The relationship between public health and the overall health system has never been clear, but in recent years it has become even less well defined. Some of the lack of clarity may be due to the several different images of public health described in Chapter 1, but certainly not all. Not only does the U.S. health system remain poorly understood by the public, but there are different views among health professionals and policy makers as to whether public health is part of the health system or the health system is part of the public health enterprise. In this text, the term *health system* will refer to all aspects of the organization, financing, and provision of programs and services for the prevention and treatment of illness and injury. The public health system is a component of this larger health system. This view conflicts with the image most people have of our health system; commonly, the public perceives the health system to include only the medical care and treatment aspects of the overall system. Though it is likely to confuse some, both public health and the overall health sector will be referred to as "systems," with the understanding that the public health system is part of the larger health system.

Systems are defined by their mission and purpose. Arguably, the health system in the United States focuses on two forms of outcomes: health outcomes and corporate outcomes (such as profits and jobs). The public health system maintains a strong interest in the first of these bottom lines while certainly recognizing the importance of the second.

Although their relationships remain unclear, there is ample cause for public health interest in the health system. Perhaps most compelling is the sheer size and scope of the U.S. health system, characteristics that have made the health system an ethical issue. More than 10 million workers and $1 trillion in resources are devoted to health-related purposes.[3] But this huge investment in fiscal and human resources is not accomplishing what it can and should in terms of health outcomes. Lack of access to needed health services for an increasing number of Americans and inconsistencies in quality contribute to these poor health outcomes. Though access and quality have long been public health concerns, the excess capacity of the health system is a relatively new issue for public health. This excess capacity of our current system, however, creates many of the problems in access and quality.

The following sections examine various aspects of the complex set of interactions of public health within the U.S. health system, initially by reviewing a simple framework for linking various health strategies and activities to their strategic intent, level of prevention, relationship to medical and public health practice, and community or individual focus. Key economic, demographic, and resource trends will then be briefly presented from a public health perspective as a prelude to understanding important themes and emerging paradigm shifts. New opportunities afforded by sweeping changes in the health system, many of which are related to managed care, will be apparent in the review of these issues. A more focused examination of the interfaces between public health and managed care appears in Chapter 8.

HEALTH AND HEALTH SERVICES

The health system influences health status through its various intervention strategies and services.[4] The relationships among health, illness, and various interventions intended to maintain or restore health are summarily presented in Table 3–1. As discussed previously, health and illness are dynamic states that are influenced by a wide variety of biological, environmental, behavioral, social, and health service factors. The complex interaction of these factors results in the presence or absence of disease or injury, which, in turn, contributes to the health status of individuals and populations. Several different intervention points are possible, including two general strategies that seek to maintain health by intervening prior to the development of disease or injury.[4] These are health promotion and specific protection strategies. Both involve activities that alter the interaction of the various health-influencing factors in ways that contribute either to averting or to altering the likelihood of occurrence of disease or injury.

Table 3–1 Health Strategies, Prevention Levels, Practice Domains, and Targets

Strategy	State Addressed	Prevention Level	Practice Domain	Target
Health promotion	Health	Primary	Public health	Community
Specific protection	Health	Primary	Public health	Community or risk group
Early case finding and prompt treatment	Illness	Secondary	Public health and primary medical care	Individual
Disability limitation	Illness	Tertiary	Secondary/ tertiary medical care	Individual
Rehabilitation	Illness	Tertiary	Long-term care	Individual and group

Source: Data from H.R. Leavell and E.G. Clark, *Preventive Medicine for the Doctor in His Community, Third Edition,* © 1965, McGraw-Hill.

Health Promotion and Specific Protection

Health promotion activities attempt to modify human behaviors to reduce those known to affect adversely the ability to resist disease or injury-inducing factors, thereby eliminating exposures to harmful factors. Examples of health promotion activities include interventions such as nutritional counseling, genetic counseling, family counseling, and the myriad activities that constitute health education. But health promotion also properly includes the provision of adequate housing, employment, and recreational conditions, as well as other forms of community development activities. What is clear from these examples is that many fall outside the common public understanding of what constitutes health care. Several of these are viewed as the duty or responsibility of other societal institutions, including public safety, housing, education, and even industry. It is somewhat ironic that activities that focus on the state of health and that seek to maintain and promote health are not commonly perceived to be "health services." To some extent, this is also true for the other category of health-maintaining strategies, specific protection activities.

Specific protection activities provide individuals with resistance to factors (such as microorganisms like viruses and bacteria) or modify environments to decrease potentially harmful interactions of health-influencing factors (such as toxic exposures in the workplace). Examples of specific protection includes activities directed toward specific risks (e.g., the use of protective equipment for asbestos removal), immunizations, occupational and environmental engineering, and regulatory controls and activities to protect individuals from environmental carcinogens (such as exposure to sidestream smoke) and toxins. Several of these are often identified with settings other than traditional health care settings. Many are implemented and enforced through governmental agencies.

Early Case Finding and Prompt Treatment, Disability Limitation, and Rehabilitation

Although health promotion and specific protection both focus on the healthy state and seek to prevent disease, a different set of strategies and activities is necessary if the interaction of factors results in disease or injury. When disease occurs, the strategies that become necessary are those that facilitate early detection, rapid control, or rehabilitation, depending on the stage of development of the disease.

In general, early detection and prompt treatment reduce individual pain and suffering and are less costly to both the individual and society than treatment initiated only after a condition has reached a more advanced state. Interventions to achieve early detection and prompt treatment include screening tests, case-finding efforts, and periodic physical exams. Screening tests are increasingly available to detect illnesses before they become symptomatic. Case-finding efforts for both infectious and noninfectious conditions are directed at populations at greater risk for the condition on the basis of criteria appropriate for that condition. Periodic physical exams, such as those mentioned in the age-specific recommendations of the U.S. Preventive Health Services Task Force, incorporate these practices and are best provided through an effective primary medical care system. Primary care providers who are sensitive to disease patterns and predisposing factors can play substantial roles in the early identification and management of most medical conditions.

Another strategy targeting disease is disability limitation through effective and complete treatment. It is this set of activities that most Americans equate with the term *health care,* largely because this strategy constitutes the lion's share of the U.S. health system in terms of resource deployment. Quite appropriately, these efforts largely aim to arrest or eradicate disease or limit disability and prevent death. The final intervention strategy focusing on disease, rehabilitation, is designed to return individuals who have experienced a condition to the maximum level of function consistent with their capacities.

Links with Prevention

There are several useful aspects of this framework. It emphasizes the potential for prevention inherent in each of the five health service strategies. Prevention can be categorized in several ways. The best known approach classifies prevention in relation to the stage of the disease or condition.

Preventive intervention strategies are considered primary, secondary, or tertiary. *Primary prevention* involves prevention of the disease or injury itself, generally through reducing exposure or risk factor levels. *Secondary prevention* attempts to identify and control disease processes in their early stages, often before signs and symptoms become apparent. *Tertiary prevention* seeks to prevent disability through restoring individuals to their optimal level of functioning after damage is done. The selection of an intervention point at the primary, secondary, or tertiary level is a function of knowledge, resources, acceptability, effectiveness, and efficiency, among other considerations.

The relationship of health promotion and specific protection to these levels of prevention is also presented in Table 3–1. Health promotion and specific protection are primary prevention strategies seeking to prevent the development of disease. Early case finding and prompt treatment represent secondary prevention, as they seek to interrupt the disease process before it becomes symptomatic. Both disability limitation and rehabilitation are considered tertiary-level prevention in that they seek to prevent or reduce disability associated with disease or injury.

Although these are considered tertiary prevention, they receive primary attention under current policy and resource deployment.

Figure 3–1 illustrates each of the three levels of prevention strategies in relation to the population's disease status and their effects on disease incidence and prevalence. The various potential benefits from the three intervention levels derive from the basic epidemiological concepts of incidence and prevalence.[5] Prevalence (the number of existing cases of illness, injury, or a health event) is a function of both incidence (the number of new cases) and duration. Prevalence can be reduced by lessening either component. Primary prevention aims to reduce the incidence of conditions, whereas secondary and tertiary prevention seek to reduce prevalence by shortening duration and minimizing the effects of disease or injury. It should be apparent that there is a finite limit to how much a condition's duration can be reduced. As a result, approaches emphasizing primary prevention have greater potential benefit than approaches emphasizing other levels of prevention. This basis for understanding the differential impact of prevention and treatment approaches to a particular health problem or condition cannot be overstated.

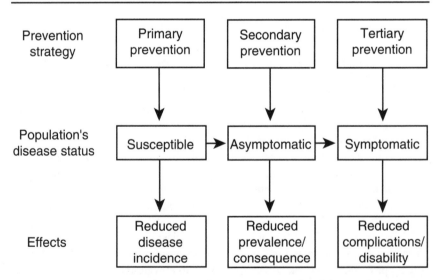

Figure 3–1 Levels of Prevention with Effects. *Source:* Reprinted from R.C. Brownson, P.L. Remington, and J.R. Davis, Chronic Disease Epidemiology and Control, © 1993, American Public Health. *Source: From Chronic Disease Epidemiology and Control.* Copyright 1993 by the American Public Health Association. Reprinted with permission.

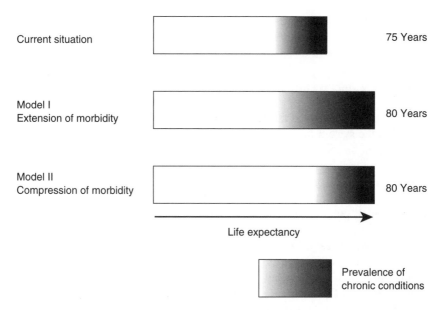

Figure 3–2 Alternative Models of Extension or Compression of Morbidity as Life Expectancy is Extended. *Source:* Reprinted from R.C. Brownson, P.L. Remington, and J.R. Davis, Chronic Disease Epidemiology and Control, © 1993, American Public Health Association, Washington, DC. *Source:* From *Chronic Disease Epidemiology and Control.* Copyright 1993 by the American Public Health Association. Reprinted with permission.

These same considerations are pertinent to the idea of postponement of morbidity as a prevention strategy, as illustrated in Figure 3–2. As demonstrated in Model I, increased life expectancy without postponement of morbidity may actually increase the burden of illness within a population, as measured by prevalence. However, postponement may result in the development of a condition so late in life that it results in either no or less disability in functioning.

Another approach to classifying prevention efforts groups interventions by the nature of the intervention into clinical, behavioral, or environmental categories. Clinical interventions are provided to individuals, while environmental interventions are organized for populations or groups. Behavioral interventions can be provided either for individuals or for populations including subgroups identified as being at higher risk for a particular condition.

Within this framework for considering intervention strategies aimed at health or illness, the potential for prevention as an element of all strategies is clear. There are substantial opportunities to use primary and secondary prevention strategies to improve health in general and reduce the burden of illness for individuals and for society. As noted in Chapter 2, reducing the burden of illness carries the potential for substantial cost savings. These concepts serve to promote a more rational intervention and investment strategy for the U.S. health system.

Links with Public Health and Medical Practice

Another useful aspect of this framework is the overall allocation of responsibility within the system for carrying out the various interventions. These practice domains can be roughly delineated as three—public health practice, medical practice, and long-term care practice.[4] Public health practice incorporates health promotion, specific protection, and a good share of early case finding. This is a broad definition of public health practice that accommodates the activities carried out by all public health professionals and workers, not only public health physicians or public health agencies. Although many of these activities are carried out in public health agencies of the federal, state, or local government, many are not. Public health practice occurs in voluntary health agencies, as well as in settings such as schools, social service agencies, industry, and even traditional medical care settings. In terms of prevention, public health practice embraces all of the primary prevention activities in the model, as well as some of the activities for early diagnosis and prompt treatment.

The demarcations between public health and medical practice are neither clear nor absolute. Traditionally, public health practice has been extensively involved in screening while also serving as a major source of primary medical care for populations with diminished access to care. Medical practice has also been extensively involved with early case finding while traditionally providing the major share of primary care services to most segments of the population.

Medical practice, meaning those services usually provided by or under the supervision of a physician or other traditional health care provider, can be viewed as including three levels of services[6] (Exhibit 3–1). Primary medical care has been variously defined but generally focuses on the health needs of individuals and families. It is first-contact health care in the view of the patient; provides at least 80 percent of necessary care; includes a comprehensive array of services, on site or through referral, including health promotion and disease prevention as well as curative services; and is accessible and acceptable to the patient population. This description of primary care differs substantially from what is commonly considered primary care in the U.S. health system. Especially lacking from current so-called primary care services are those activities relating to health promotion and disease prevention.

Beyond primary care are two more specialized types of care that are often termed *secondary* and *tertiary care*. Secondary care is specialized care serving the major share of the remaining 20 percent of the need that lies beyond the scope

Exhibit 3–1 Health Care Pyramid Levels

- Tertiary Medical Care
  Subspecialty referral care requiring highly specialized personnel and facilities
- Secondary Medical Care
  Specialized attention and ongoing management for common and less frequently encountered medical conditions, including support services for people with special challenges due to chronic or long-term conditions
- Primary Medical Care
  Clinical preventive services, first-contact treatment services, and ongoing care for commonly encountered medical conditions
- Population-Based Public Health Services
  Interventions aimed at disease prevention and health promotion that shape a community's overall health profile

Source: U.S. Public Health Service, 1994.[6]

---

of primary care. Secondary care is generally provided by physicians or hospitals, ideally upon referral from a primary care source. Tertiary medical care is even more highly specialized and technologically sophisticated medical and surgical care for those with unusual or complex conditions (generally no more than a few percent of the need in any service category). Tertiary care is almost always provided in large medical centers or academic health centers. Long-term care is appropriately classified separately because of the special needs of the population requiring such services and the specialized settings where many of these services are offered. This, too, is changing as specialized long-term care services increasingly move out of long-term care facilities and into home settings.

Within the health services pyramid presented in Figure 3–3, primary prevention activities are largely associated with population-based public health services at the base of the pyramid, although some primary prevention in the form of clinical preventative services is also associated with primary medical care services. Secondary prevention activities are split somewhat more evenly between the population-based public health services and primary medical care. Tertiary prevention activities fall largely in the secondary and tertiary medical care components of the pyramid. The use of a pyramid to represent health services implies that each level serves a different proportion of the total population. Everyone should be served by populationwide public health services, and nearly everyone should be served by primary medical care. But increasingly smaller proportions of the total population require secondary- and tertiary-level medical care services. In any event, the system should be built from the bottom up. It would not be rational to build such a system from the top down; there might not be enough

Health Services Pyramid

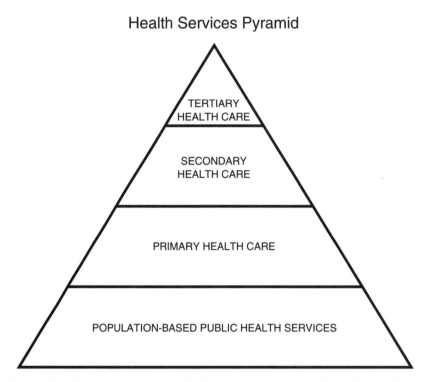

TERTIARY
HEALTH CARE

SECONDARY
HEALTH CARE

PRIMARY HEALTH CARE

POPULATION-BASED PUBLIC HEALTH SERVICES

Figure 3–3 Health Services Pyramid. *Source:* Reprinted from *For a Healthy Nation: Return on Investments in Public Health*, 1994, Public Health Service, Washington, DC.

resources to address the lower levels that served as the foundation for the system. Nonetheless, we will see in later sections of this chapter that this is exactly what has occurred with the U.S. health system.

Targets of Health Service Strategies

A final facet of this model characterizes the targets for the strategies and activities. Generally, primary preventive services are community based and are targeted toward populations or groups rather than individuals. Early case-finding activities can be directed toward groups or toward individuals. For example, many screening activities target groups at higher risk when these are provided through public health agencies. The same screening activities can also be provided for individuals through physicians' offices and hospital outpatient departments. Much of primary and virtually all of secondary and tertiary medical care is appropriately individually oriented. It should be noted that there is a concept termed *community-oriented primary care* in which primary care providers assume responsibility for all the individuals in a community rather than only those who seek out care from the provider. Even in this model, however, care is provided on an individual basis. Long-term care involves elements of both community-based service and individually oriented service. These services are tailored for individuals, but often in a group setting or as part of a package of services for a defined number of recipients, as in a long-term care facility.

Public Health and Medical Practice Interfaces

This framework also sheds light on the potential conflicts between public health and medical practice. Though the two are presented as separate domains of practice, there are many interfaces that provide a template for either collaboration or conflict. Both paths have been taken over the past century. Public health practitioners have traditionally deferred to medical practitioners for providing the broad spectrum of services for disease and injuries in individuals. Medical practitioners have generally acknowledged the need for public health practice for health promotion and specific protection strategies. The interfaces raise difficult issues. For example, for one specific protection activity, childhood immunizations, it can be argued that the extensive role of public health practice has served to fragment health services for children. It would be logical to provide these services within a well-functioning primary care system where they could be better integrated with other services for this population. Despite occasional differences as to roles, in most circumstances, medical practice has supported the role of public health to serve as the provider of last resort in ensuring medical care for persons who lack financial access to private health care. This, too, has varied over time and from place to place.

Some of the most serious conflicts have come in the area of primary care services, including early case-finding activities. Because of the increased yield of screening tests when these are applied to groups at higher risk, public health practice has sought to deploy more widely risk group or community case-finding methods (including outreach and linkage activities). This has at times been perceived by medical practitioners as encroachment on their practice domain for certain primary care services such as prenatal care. Although there has been no rule that public health practice could not be provided within the medical practice domain and vice versa, the perception that these are separate, but perhaps unequal, territories has been widely held by both groups.

It is important to note that this territoriality is not based only on turf issues. There are significant differences in the worldviews and approaches of these two domains. Medical practice quite properly seeks to produce the best possible outcome through the development and execution of individualized treatment plans. Seeking the best possible outcome for an individual suggests that decisions are made primarily for the benefit of that individual. Costs and resource availability are secondary considerations. Public health practice, on the other hand, seeks to deploy its limited resources to avoid the worst outcomes (at the level of the group). Some level of risk is tolerated at the collective level to prevent an unacceptable level of adverse outcomes from occurring. These are quite different approaches to practice: maximizing individual positive outcomes as opposed to minimizing adverse collective outcomes. As a result, differences in perspective and philosophy often underlie differences in approaches that initially appear to be concerns over territoriality.

A recent example that illustrates these differences is apparent in approaches to widespread use of HIV antibody testing in the mid- and late 1980s. Medical practitioners perceived that HIV antibody testing would be very useful in clinical practice and that its widespread use would enhance case finding. As a result, medical practitioners generally opposed restrictions on use of these tests, such as specific written informed consent and additional confidentiality provisions. Public health practitioners perceived that widespread use of the test without safeguards and protections would actually result in fewer persons at risk being tested and decreased case finding in the community. With both groups focusing on the same science in terms of the accuracy of the specific testing regimen, these differences in practice approaches may be difficult to understand. However, in view of their ultimate aims and concerns as to individual versus collective outcomes, the conflict is more understandable.

Perspectives and roles may differ for public health and medical practice, but both are important and necessary. The real question is what blending of these approaches will be most successful in improving health status throughout the population. There is sufficient cause to question current policy and investment strategies. Table 3–2 examines the potential contributions of various strategies (personal responsibility, health care services, community action, and social policies) toward reducing the impact of the actual causes of death identified in Chapter 2. This table suggests that more medical care services are not as likely to reduce the toll from these causes as public health approaches (community action and social policies). Yet there are opportunities available through the current system and perhaps even greater opportunities in the near term as the system seeks to address the serious problems that have brought it to the brink of major reform.

THE HEALTH SYSTEM IN THE UNITED STATES

There are many sources of more complete information on the health system in the United States than will be provided in this chapter. Here the intent is to exam-

Table 3–2 Actual Causes of Death in the United States and Potential Contribution to Reduction

Causes	Deaths Estimated No.	%	Personal	Health Care System	Community Action	Social Policy
Tobacco	400,000	19	++++	+	+	++
Diet/activity patterns	300,000	14	+++	+	+	++
Alcohol	100,000	5	+++	+	+	+
Microbial agents	90,000	4	+	++	++	++
Toxic agents	60,000	3	+	+	++	++++
Firearms	35,000	2	++	+	+++	+++
Sexual behavior	30,000	1	++++	+	+	+
Motor vehicles	25,000	1	++	+	+	++
Illicit use of drugs	20,000	<1	+++	+	++	++

Columns under *Potential Contribution to Reduction*[a]

[a]Plus sign indicates relative magnitude (4+ scale).
Source: Reprinted with permission from Fielding and Halfon, *JAMA* 272:1292–1296, © 1995, American Medical Association.

ine those aspects of the health industry and health system that interface with public health or raise issues of public health significance. There is no shortage of either. This section will examine some of the issues facing the health system in the United States, with a special focus on the problems of the system that are fueling reform and change. Interfaces with public health will be identified and discussed, as well as possible effects of these changes on the various images of public health. Throughout these sections, data from *Health United States 1995*[3] will be used to describe the economic, demographic, and resources aspects of the American health system.

Economic Dimensions

The health system in the United States is immense and still growing rapidly. It is naive to consider the possible public health interfaces with the health system in the United States without understanding the context in which they take place: the health sector of modern America. The 1980s and 1990s were decades that brought the U.S. economy the longest peacetime expansion in its history. During this period, economic growth was strong and employment grew steadily. The health care sector grew as well and assumed a powerful position in the overall U.S. economy. By 1996, the health care sector produced some $1 trillion in goods and services (nearly $4,000 per capita), representing one-seventh of our total gross domestic product (GDP). Total health expenditures in the United States grew by a factor of 40 between 1960 and 1996. Expenditures quadrupled between 1980 and 1996 and doubled between 1987 and 1996, as demonstrated in Figure 3–4. About one-half of the increase since 1960 can be traced to medical practice in terms of medical inflation and greater intensity of services. Population growth accounts for only 10 percent of the increase, and general inflation is responsible for about 40 percent of the increase.

The health sector's 14 percent proportion of the total GDP is two and a half times what it was in 1965. Even after inflation and medical care costs were under somewhat better control after about 1990, the rate of increase for health care costs has been twice the rate of the overall cost of living. The United States spends a greater share of its GDP on health care services than any other industrialized nation. Figure 3–5 traces the growth in health expenditures for the United States and five other developed countries. These other nations spend less than half the U.S. proportion, and Canada, the country with the second highest health share of GDP, spends 25 percent less than the United States. The same picture exists for per capita health expenditures for these six countries. The United States spends twice as much as the average for Australia, Canada, Germany, Japan, and the United Kingdom, as shown in Figure 3–6. By 1996, the United States was spending about $4,000 per person on health services. At least three factors sug-

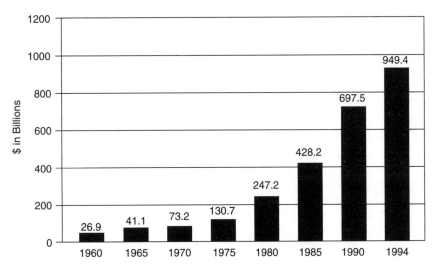

Figure 3–4 National Health Expenditures, United States, 1960–1994. *Source:* Reprinted from *Health United States 1995*, 1996, National Center for Health Statistics, Hyattsville, MD.

gest this is too much: the current system is reaching the point of no longer being affordable; the U.S. population is no healthier than other nations that spend far less; and the opportunity costs are considerable.

There are three general sources of this $1 trillion: about one-third of the costs is paid directly by households; approximately 28 percent is paid by businesses; and about 35 percent is paid by local, state, and federal governments. The rapidly increasing costs for health services have hit all three sources in their pocketbooks, and each is reaching the point where further increases may not be affordable. Personal health care expenditures make up the bulk of all health-related expenditures. For personal health care expenditures (about 90 percent of total health expenditures), one-fifth is paid out of pocket, one-third by private health insurance (using resources derived from households and businesses), one-third by the federal government, and one-tenth by state or local government (Figure 3–7). Between 1990 and 1994, the federal share has increased by 5 percent, while the other sources have declined slightly.

Out-of-pocket expenses of families have been steadily increasing in recent years. The average family now spends more than 13 percent of its income for health care, as compared with 9 percent in 1980. By the year 2000, family out-of-pocket payments for health care will rise to 16 percent of family income. In terms

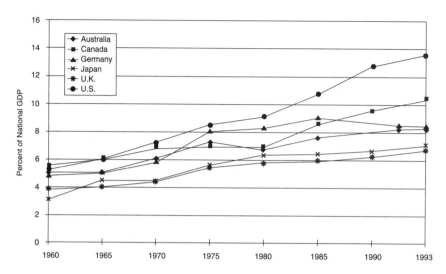

Figure 3–5 Total Health Expenditures as a Percentage of Gross Domestic Product, Selected Countries, 1960–1993. *Source:* Reprinted from *Health United States 1995*, 1996, National Center for Health Statistics, Hyattsville, MD.

of actual dollars, family out-of-pocket expenses grew from $1,700 in 1980 to $4,300 in 1991 and are expected to grow to $9,400 in the year 2000.

Business costs for health care will have mushroomed by some 700 percent between 1980 and 2000. The costs per employee hour worked reached $1.14 per hour in 1994. Costs per employee hour worked are greater for large businesses than for small employers, a sign that smaller employers are dropping or reducing their role in providing health insurance for employees and dependents. In 1980, the health care costs of businesses were 41 percent of business profits. By 1991, health care costs equaled after-tax profits. Profitability and survival of many businesses, especially small businesses, are closely linked with ever-increasing health care costs.

The largest single purchaser of health care in the United States remains the federal government, although its spending on health care represents only a fraction of the total federal budget. Health expenditures constituted 19 percent of total federal expenditures in 1994, up from 15 percent in 1990, 12 percent in 1980, and only 4 percent in 1965 (Figure 3–8). Health expenditures have constituted 13 to 14 percent of state and local government expenditures since 1990. Escalating costs for health care services seriously constrain efforts to reduce the federal budget deficit, and there is little public or political support for additional

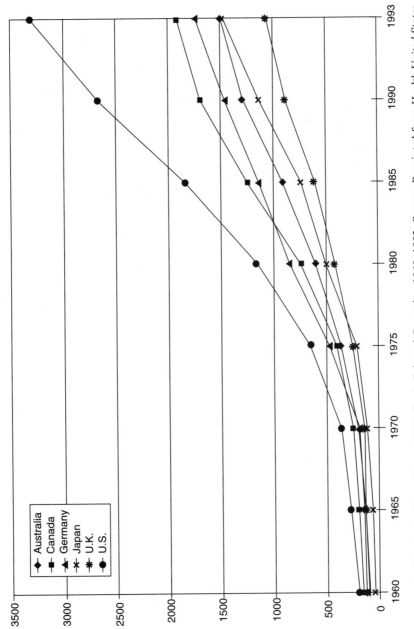

Figure 3–6 Per Capita Expenditures (in Dollars), Selected Countries, 1960–1993. *Source:* Reprinted from *Health United States 1995*, 1996, National Center for Health Statistics, Hyattsville, MD.

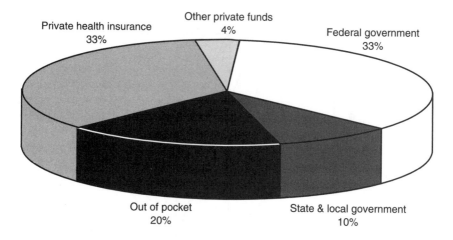

Private health insurance 33% — Other private funds 4% — Federal government 33% — State & local government 10% — Out of pocket 20%

Figure 3–7 Sources for Medical Expenditures, United States, 1993. *Source:* Reprinted from *Health United States 1995*, 1996, National Center for Health Statistics, Hyattsville, MD.

taxes for health purposes. As a result, the federal government has been forced to bring health costs under control.

The two most important public financing programs for health are Medicare and Medicaid, both established in 1965 through amendments to the Social Security Act. Each is projected to double in cost between the years 1993 and 2000. Medicare expenditures in 1994 amounted to $165 billion, providing services for some 37 million enrollees. Medicaid represents a joint federal and state-funded program that offers access to specific low-income individuals who lack other health insurance coverage. In 1994, 35 million Medicaid recipients used medical services costing $108 billion. From 1993 to 1994, the ratio of Medicaid recipients to persons below the poverty level varied from 59 per 100 in Nevada to 168 per 100 in Vermont. Medicaid costs have been increasing at an annual rate of 16 percent, while the number of recipients has been increasing at an annual rate of 8 percent. Children under the age of 21 years constituted 49 percent of Medicaid recipients in 1994, although they accounted for only 16 percent of expenditures (Figure 3–9). The major share of Medicaid resources supports services to the elderly (largely for long-term care services) and disabled populations. These two groups account for fully 70 percent of Medicaid expenditures. As a result, there is only limited potential for realizing substantial savings through enrollment of mothers and children into managed-care arrangements, a trend that reached most states by the mid-1990s. Ultimately, taxpayers end up paying either for Medicaid

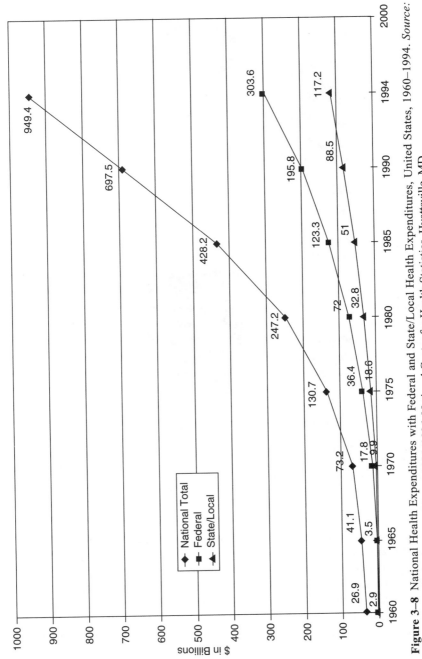

Figure 3–8 National Health Expenditures with Federal and State/Local Health Expenditures, United States, 1960–1994. *Source:* Reprinted from *Health United States 1995, 1996*, National Center for Health Statistics, Hyattsville, MD.

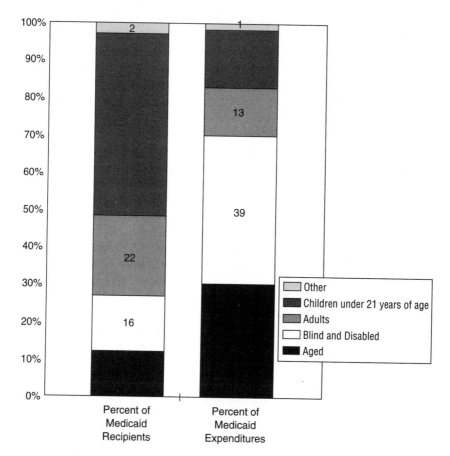

Figure 3–9 Medicaid Recipients and Expenditures by Basis of Eligibility, United States, Fiscal Year 1994. *Source:* Reprinted from *Health United States 1995*, 1996, National Center for Health Statistics, Hyattsville, MD.

coverage or for hospital subsidies to provide acute care for the uninsured. The push toward various forms of welfare reform in 1996 is expected to provide states with greater control over their Medicaid programs. The effects of these policy changes on access to and use of health services by low-income populations will be important public health issues for state and local governments as well as for the citizen-taxpayers they represent.

Only limited information is available on expenditures for prevention and population-based services. A study using 1988 data estimated that total national expenditures for all forms of health-related prevention (including clinical preventive services provided to individuals and the population-based public health programs including environmental protection) amounted to $33 billion.[7] The intent was to include all activities directed toward health promotion, health protection, disease screening, and counseling. As a result, the $33 billion figure approximates expenditures for primary and secondary prevention efforts. Of this total, about $14 billion was expended for activities not included in the calculation of national health expenditures (such as sewage systems, water purification, and air traffic safety). The remaining $18 billion in prevention-related health expenditures for that year represented only 3.4 percent of all national health expenditures (Figure 3–10a).

Nearly one-half (48 percent) of the health-related prevention resources came from the federal government; another 31 percent represented expenditures for clinical preventive services, often paid out of pocket by individuals.[7] As shown in Figure 3–10b, preventive health services were the largest category of health-related prevention expenditures (35 percent), although health protection and health promotion services each made up about one-fourth of prevention-related expenditures. The share of these expenditures that represent population-based services cannot be directly determined from this study. However, it appears that population-based services constitute $6 to $7 billion in view of the prominence of health protection and health promotion services.

As part of the development of a national health reform proposal in 1994, federal officials developed the first estimate of national health expenditures for

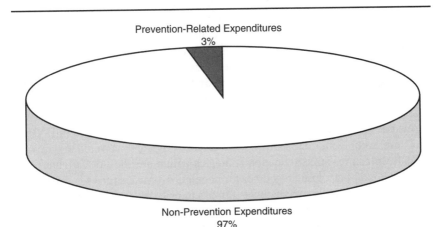

Prevention-Related Expenditures
3%

Non-Prevention Expenditures
97%

Figure 3–10a Health-Related Prevention Expenditures within Total National Health Expenditures, United States, 1988. *Source:* Reprinted from R.E. Brown et al., National Expenditures for Health Promotion and Disease Prevention Activities in the United States, Medical Technology Assessment and Policy Research Center and Centers for Disease Control and Prevention, 1991, Washington, D.C.

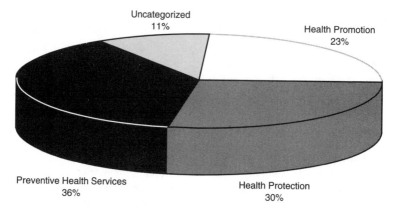

Figure 3–10b Health-Related Prevention Expenditures by Category of Programs and Services, United States, 1988. *Source:* Reprinted from R.E. Brown et al., National Expenditures for Health Promotion and Disease Prevention Activities in the United States, Medical Technology Assessment and Policy Research Center and Centers for Disease Control and Prevention, 1991, Washington, D.C.

population-based services.[8] On the basis of expenditures in 1992, this study concluded that less than 1 percent of all national health expenditures ($8.4 billion) supported population-based programs and services. Because expenditures for personal health care services have been increasing more rapidly than expenditures for population-based services, the proportion of all health expenditures attributed to population-based services declined from 1.2 percent in 1980 to 0.9 percent a decade later (Table 3–3). U.S. Public Health Service (PHS) agencies spent $4.3 billion for population-based services in 1993, and state and local health agencies spent another $4.1 billion. In that same year, PHS agencies spent a total of $8 billion on both population-based and clinical preventive services. PHS estimates of resource requirements for levels of population-based services defined as "essential" call for doubling 1993 expenditure levels. A "fully effective" level would require tripling of 1993 levels. Although this would require only a small shift in resource allocation strategies within a trillion-dollar enterprise, the likelihood of increased resources for population-based services is small.

Assuming that the U.S. economy continues to grow moderately, projections are that by the year 2000 an estimated $1.5 trillion (16 percent of the GDP) will be spent on the health system. This projection suggests that the health sector will become an even more important factor in the overall U.S. economy as it continues to grow more rapidly than the nonhealth sector. Certain categories of health expenditures are likely to grow more rapidly than others, although it is unlikely that population-based services will grow as rapidly as other services. Future trends for clinical preventive services are more difficult to predict, as these

Table 3–3 Population-Based Public Health Expenditures[a] by Source of Funds, Selected Years 1981–1993

	Expenditures (in Billions)				"Essential"	"Fully Effective"
	1981	1985	1989	1993		
Public Health Service agency expenditures (excluding federal grants to health departments)	$1.4	$1.3	$1.9	$3.0	$5.4	$8.5
State and local health dept. expenditures						
Federal grants to health departments[b]	$0.4	$0.5	$0.7	$1.3[c]	$5.9	$12.4
State Funds	$1.1	$1.6	$2.2	$2.5[c]		
Local Funds	$0.6	$0.7	$0.9	$1.6[c]	$4.1	$4.1
Total	$3.5	$4.1	$5.7	$8.4	$15.4	$25.0
Population-based expenditures as percentage of total national health expenditures	1.2%	1.0%	0.9%	0.9%	1.7%	2.7%

[a]Expenditures for services to individuals have been excluded. For state and local health departments, the exclusion totals 58.6% of total expenditures.
[b]Excluding the Special Supplemental Nutrition Program for Woman, Infants and Children (WIC).
[c]Estimated based on preliminary reported figures.
Source: Reprinted from *Health Care Reform and Public Health: A Paper Based on Population-Based Core Functions*, 1993, The Core Functions Project, U.S. Public Health Service, Office of Disease Prevention and Health Promotion, Washington, DC.

depend in part on whether managed-care organizations vigorously pursue prevention as a long-term cost-control strategy.

The postindustrial U.S. economy, despite ever tighter public budgets under pressure from increasing health expenditures, has come to look to the health sector for economic leadership. With a trillion dollars or more at stake, there will be growing interest in health services and how they are organized, financed, and provided. This interest will be manifest in government offices, corporate boardrooms, and financial institutions, as well as in hospitals and physicians' offices. Nonetheless, these economic trends tell only part of the story. The disparities between rich and poor in the United States are also growing, leaving an increasing number of Americans without financial access to many health care services. These and other important aspects will be examined as we review the demands on and resources of the U.S. health system.

Demographic and Utilization Trends

Several important demographic trends affect the U.S. health care system. These include the slowing population growth rate, the shift toward an older population, the increasing diversity of the population, changes in family structure, and persistent lack of access to needed health services for too many Americans. The growing impact of HIV infections and other similar increases in the relative prevalence of particular diseases is another demographic phenomenon but will not be addressed here.

Census studies document that the growth of the U.S. population has been slowing, a trend that would be expected to restrain future growth in demand for health care services. However, this must be viewed in light of projected changes in the age distribution of the U.S. population that document that the age distribution of the U.S. population is expected to change considerably. Between 1990 and 2025, all of the older age brackets will have experienced substantial increases in numbers (nearly doubling), whereas the younger age groups will grow little, if at all.

Utilization of health care services in general is closely correlated with the age distribution of the population. For example, adults 75 years and older see physicians three to four times as frequently as children under the age of 17. Since older persons utilize more health care services than younger people, their expenditures are higher. Also, the percentage of their total annual expenses that are devoted to health care is higher. Obvious reasons for the higher utilization of health care resources by the elderly include the high prevalence of chronic conditions, such as arteriosclerosis, cerebrovascular disease, diabetes, senility, arthritis, and mental disorders. As the population ages, it is expected that the prevalence of chronic disorders and the treatment costs associated with them will also increase. This could be minimized through prevention efforts that either avert or postpone the onset of these chronic diseases. Nonetheless, these important demographic shifts portend greater use of health care services in the future by both males and females, with a slightly greater increase in overall utilization by males. This is largely due to the shifting age distribution patterns noted earlier, since females tend to utilize more health care services at younger age levels than males do.

Another important demographic trend is the increasing diversity of the population. The nonwhite population is growing three times faster than the white population, and the Hispanic population is increasing at five times the rate for the entire U.S. population. These trends will mean that the proportion of nonwhites and Hispanics among all persons served by the health care system will increase. These changes will disproportionately affect the younger age groups, suggesting that services for mothers and children will face considerable challenges in their ability to provide culturally sensitive and acceptable services. At the same time, the considerably less diverse baby boom generation will be increasing its ability to affect public policy decisions and resource allocations into the next century.

Changes in family structure also represent a significant demographic trend in the United States. There is only a 50 percent chance that married partners will reach their 25th anniversary. One in three children spend part of their lives in a one-parent household; for African American children, the chances are two in three. Labor force participation for women more than doubled from under 25 percent in 1950 to 54 percent by 1985. Even more indicative of gender changes in the labor market, the proportion of married women in the work force with children under age five grew from 44 percent in 1975 to 64 percent in 1987. Many American households have maintained their economic status over the past two decades with the second paychecks from women in the work force. As the nature of families change, so do their needs for access, availability, and even types of services (such as substance abuse, family violence, and child welfare services).

Intermingled with many of these trends are the persistent inequalities in access to services for low-income populations, including blacks and Hispanics. For example, despite higher rates of self-reported fair or poor health, and greater utilization of hospital inpatient services, low-income persons are 50 percent more likely to report no physician contacts within the past two years than persons in high-income households. Figure 3–11 demonstrates that nonpoor individuals in fair or poor health have 50 to 100 percent more physician contacts each year than poor or near-poor individuals of similar health status. Differences in the use of clinical preventive services also mirror this picture. Only 66 to 67 percent of black and Hispanic mothers initiated prenatal care in the first trimester in 1993, compared with 81 percent of white mothers (Figure 3–12). Black and Hispanic mothers were more than twice as likely as white mothers to have waited until the third trimester to initiate prenatal care (9 percent vs. 4 percent). Only 65 percent of poor children, but 69 percent of nonpoor children, 19 to 35 months of age were

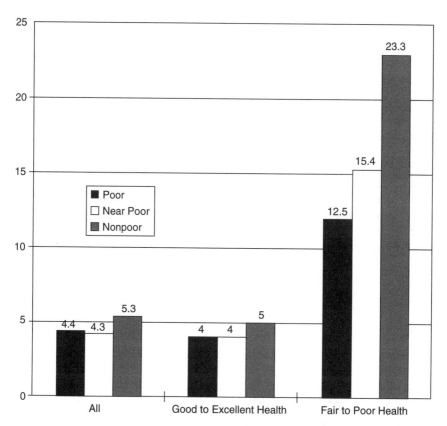

Figure 3–11 Physician Contacts by Health Status and Poverty Status for Children under 15 Years of Age, United States, 1992–1994. *Source:* Reprinted from *Health United States 1995*, 1996, National Center for Health Statistics, Hyattsville, MD.

up to date with their immunizations in 1994 (Figure 3–13). Public programs to fill the gaps created by lack of financial access to health services have been variably successful, as evidenced in these three exhibits. Greater success is apparent for immunization status and prenatal care than for equalizing access to medical care.

Despite outspending other developed countries on health services, the United States leads other industrialized nations by a wide margin in the rate of its citizens who lack health insurance coverage. Health insurance coverage of the population has been declining since 1980 for all age groups except those under age five, whose access was improved through Medicaid eligibility changes in the late 1980s even though the percentage of children covered through employer-based

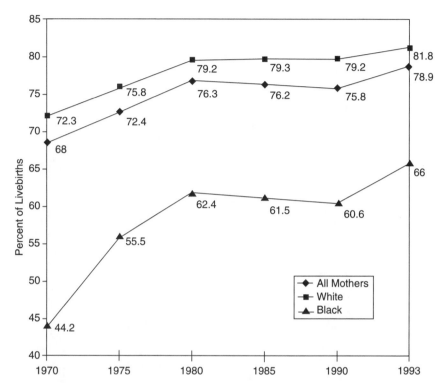

Figure 3–12 Mothers Initiating Prenatal Care in the First Trimester by Race of Mother, United States, 1970–1993. *Source:* Reprinted from *Health United States 1995*, 1996, National Center for Health Statistics, Hyattsville, MD.

insurance programs was declining (Figure 3–14). The age-adjusted percentage of persons under the age of 65 who were not covered by health insurance increased from 12 percent in 1980 to 18 percent in 1994. Young adults 15 to 44 years of age were most likely to be uninsured (22 percent) in 1993. The percentage of this age group uncovered increased by more than 50 percent since 1980.

Blacks were about 25 percent more likely than whites, and Hispanics were twice as likely as whites, to be uninsured in 1994. Individuals in households earning less than $14,000 per year were about five times more likely to be uninsured than persons living in households earning $35,000 or more (Figure 3–15). Still, of the 40 million uninsured people under the age of 65, about two-thirds are 15 to 44 years of age, three-fourths are white, and one-third live in families earning $25,000 or more. Lack of insurance coverage may disproportionately affect minority low-income individuals, but its growth in recent years has affected individuals in almost all

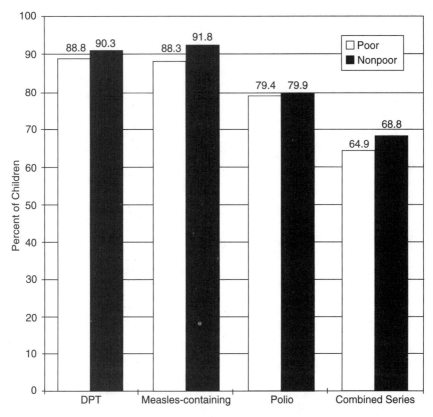

Figure 3–13 Vaccination of Children 19 to 35 Months of Age for Selected Diseases by Poverty Status, United States, 1994. *Source:* Reprinted from *Health United States 1995*, 1996, National Center for Health Statistics, Hyattsville, MD.

groups. About two-thirds of uninsured individuals in the United States are either employed or are dependents of an employed family member.

Health Care Resources

The supply of health care resources is another key component of the health care system. During the past quarter-century, the number of active U.S. physicians increased by more than two-thirds, with even greater increases among women physicians and international medical graduates. The specialty composition of the physician population also changed during this period as a result of many factors, including changing employment opportunities, advances in med-

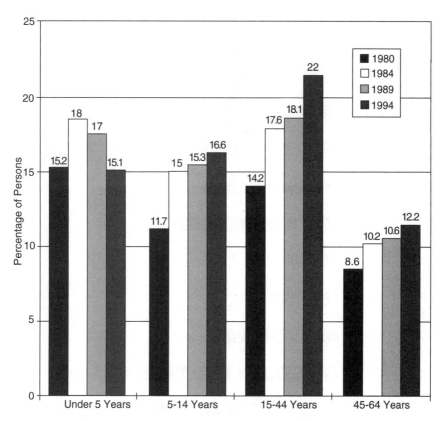

Figure 3–14 Percentage of Persons under 65 Years of Age Who Are Uninsured, by Age, in Selected Years, United States, 1980–1994. *Source:* Reprinted from *Health United States 1995*, 1996, National Center for Health Statistics, Hyattsville, MD.

ical technology, and the availability of residency positions. Suffice it to say that medical and surgical subspecialties grew more rapidly than the primary care specialties. Recent projections suggest that by the year 2000, there will be a substantial surplus of physicians, primarily among those trained in the surgical and medical specialties. The rate of increase for women physicians will greatly exceed that for male physicians. By the year 2010, it is expected that almost 30 percent (or about 200,000) of the total supply of physicians will be women.

As would be expected with the supply of physicians increasing faster than the population and insurance coverage declining, the average number of patient visits per physician per week has been falling. This includes visits in offices, emergency departments, outpatient clinics, and all other locations, including hospital

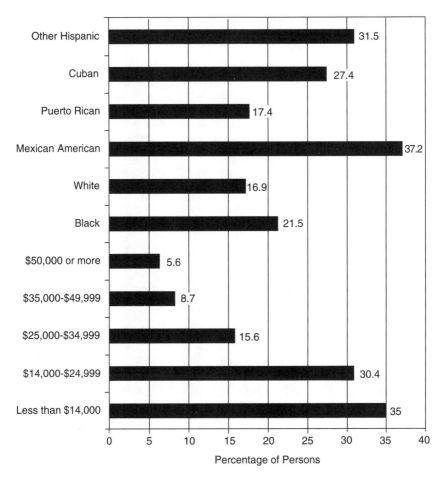

Figure 3–15 Percentage of Persons under 65 Years of Age Who Are Uninsured, by Family Income, Race, and Hispanic Origin, United States, 1994. *Source:* Reprinted from *Health United States 1995*, 1996, National Center for Health Statistics, Hyattsville, MD.

rounds. The sharp decline in office and hospital visits was offset, to some extent, by visits in other settings such as emergency rooms and outpatient clinics, but the average number of overall contacts with physicians has changed little in the 1990s.

The supply of health resources is also determined by the number of nonphysician health care personnel. Job growth in the health care sector generally is among the fastest in the U.S. economy. From 1980 to 1994, employment in the health industry increased by 44 percent, as compared with a 24 percent increase in total civilian employment. Since 1980, the health work force grew by more than 3 million; since 1990, more than 1 million new jobs have appeared.

Another trend in the delivery of health care resources relates to the numbers and types of health care delivery systems. For example, the supply of hospital resources has been changing in recent years. Since the mid-1970s, the number of community hospitals has decreased, and the number of admissions, days of care, average occupancy rates, and average length of stay have all declined as well. On the other hand, the number of hospital employees per 100 average daily patients has continued to increase. Since 1980, this number has increased about 4 percent each year. Hospital outpatient visits have also been increasing since the mid-1970s.

The supply of physicians and hospitals influences practice patterns and the use of health services. In fact, these resource factors have more to do with observed variation in rates of hospitalizations and surgeries than differences in the health of patient populations. Several studies have related physician and hospital bed availability to practice patterns, finding little difference in outcomes but considerable difference in costs and use of procedures. Across urban areas of the United States, two- to threefold differences exist in terms of hospital beds per 1,000 population, physicians per 100,000 population, and Medicare payments per enrollee, without appreciable differences in outcome.[9] Findings such as these suggest that excess capacity within the health system contributes significantly to its overall costs.

The growth in the number and types of health care delivery systems in recent years is one reflection of a rapidly changing health care environment. Increasing competition, combined with cost containment initiatives, has led to the proliferation of group medical practices, health maintenance organizations, preferred provider organizations, ambulatory surgery centers, and emergency centers. Common to many of these delivery systems since the early 1990s have been managed-care strategies and methods that seek to control the utilization of services. Managed care represents a system of administrative controls intended to reduce costs through managing the utilization of services. Elements of managed-care strategies generally include some combination of the following:

- risk sharing with providers to discourage the provision of unnecessary diagnostic and treatment services and, to some degree, to encourage preventive measures
- to attract specific groups, designing of tailored benefit packages that include the most important (but not necessarily all) services for that group; cost sharing for some services through deductibles and copayments can be built into these packages

- case management, especially for high-cost conditions, to encourage seeking out of less expensive treatments or settings
- primary care gatekeepers, generally the enrollee's primary care physician, who control referrals to specialists
- second opinions as to the need for expensive diagnostic or elective invasive procedures
- review and certification for hospitalizations in general and hospital admissions through the emergency department in particular
- continued-stay review for hospitalized patients as they reach the expected number of days for their illness (as determined by diagnostic related groupings)
- discharge planning to move patients out of hospitals to less expensive care settings as quickly as possible

The growth and expansion of these delivery systems has significant implications for the cost of, access to, and quality of health care. By the mid-1990s, more than half the U.S. population was being served through a managed-care organization. Within the next decade, managed care will capture 80 to 90 percent of the market. The growth of managed care also has significant implications for both the population-based services of governmental public health agencies and the clinical services that have been provided in the public sector. Chapter 8 will examine some of these emerging and future issues as public health and managed care seek to coexist peacefully with each other in a rapidly changing health sector.

The dramatic growth in the number of health maintenance organizations (HMOs) during the early and mid-1980s was followed by a period of slower growth and consolidations and mergers. Rapid growth resumed in the 1990s, and by 1995 more than 16 percent of the U.S. population (46 million Americans) were enrolled in HMOs, up from only 2 percent in 1980. Considerable variation is apparent across regions of the country, ranging from 29 percent of the population in the West to 11 percent in the South. The structure of HMOs varies as well, with about one-third of enrollees found in independent practice, group, and mixed-model HMOs, as illustrated in Figure 3–16. Recent growth has come largely in the form of the mixed-model HMOs, which include aspects of both the staff and independent models. In general, cost-control measures are more effectively implemented through staff-model HMOs.

CHANGING ROLES, THEMES, AND PARADIGMS IN THE HEALTH SYSTEM

Not even a cursory review of the health sector would be complete without an examination of the key participants or key players in the health industry. The list

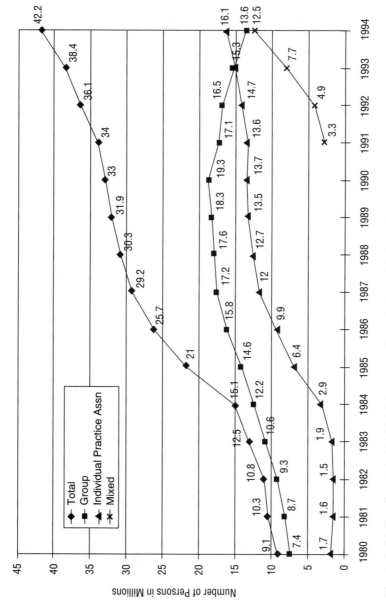

Figure 3–16 Enrollment in Health Maintenance Organizations by Type of Plan, United States, 1980–1994. *Source:* Reprinted from *Health United States 1995*, 1996, National Center for Health Statistics, Hyattsville, MD.

of major stakeholders has been expanding as the system has grown and now includes government, business, third-party payers, health care providers, drug companies, and labor, as well as consumers. The federal government has grown to become the largest purchaser of health care and, along with business, has attempted to become a more prudent buyer by exerting more control over payments for services. Government seeks to reduce rising costs by altering the economic performance of the health sector through stimulation of a more competitive health care market. Still, budget problems at all levels make it increasingly difficult for government to fulfill commitments to provide health care services to the poor, the disadvantaged, and the elderly. Over recent years, new and expensive medical technology, inflation, and unexpected increases in utilization forced third parties to pay out more for health care than they anticipated when premiums were determined. As a result, insurers have joined government in becoming more aggressive in efforts to contain health care costs. Many commercial carriers are exploring methods to anticipate utilization more accurately and to control outlays through managed-care strategies. Business, labor, patients, hospitals, and professional organizations are all trying to restrain costs while maintaining access to health services.

As these stakeholders search for methods to reduce costs and as competition intensifies, efforts to preserve the quality of health care will become increasingly important. Public debate will continue to focus on how to define and measure quality. Despite the difficulty in measuring quality of medical care, it is likely that quality measurement systems will increase substantially. Dialogue and debate among the major stakeholders in the health system will be influenced by the tension between cost containment and regulation; the interdependence of access, quality, and costs; the call for greater accountability; and the slow but steady acceptance of the need for health reform.

From this brief review of selected issues confronting the health system, several general themes or conclusions can be drawn. The first is that cost pressures will continue to be the principal driving force underlying change in the health system; any of the current trends can be traced, either directly or indirectly, to the cost issue. It is likely that rapid environmental change in the health system will persist until the cost issue is resolved in some manner. It is not at all clear which approaches will preserve the most crucial features of the current delivery system and also contain costs. The growing proportion of the GDP allocated to the health system means that its economic efficiency will continue to be scrutinized and that proposals to alter the economic performance of the sector will continue to emerge. It is likely that the growing federal deficit will place added emphasis on the development of methods to contain federal health care costs. Reducing the national deficit and balancing the federal budget will look in part to proposals that will control costs within Medicare and Medicaid as well as in discretionary federal health programs. Except for Medicare, these recommendations are likely to be politically popular, even though the public has little understanding of the federal budget. For example, a 1994 poll[10] found that Americans believe health care costs constitute 5 percent of the federal budget, although these costs actually constitute 16 percent. At the same time, Americans believe that foreign aid and welfare constitute 27 and 19 percent respectively of the federal budget, when in fact they constitute only 2 and 3 percent respectively. When the time comes to balance the federal budget and reduce the national deficit, the American public will face difficult choices as to which programs can be reduced. Public health programs, largely discretionary spending, may not fare well in this scenario.

Governmental initiatives are likely to continue to be a major source of change in the health system. The combination of governmental concern over rising health care costs and governmental power to alter the health care financing and delivery systems through legislation and regulation portend a significant role for government, with or without enactment of national health reform.

Advances in biotechnology and medical technology will also continue to strongly influence the health system. Changes in technology represent a powerful long-range force for change as more effective methods of diagnosis and treatment of disease are developed and deployed. Advances will provide relief to many patients whose conditions would otherwise have been hopeless. Technological innovations may be increasingly scrutinized from a cost benefit standpoint by third-party payers and others.

As cost containment pressures continue to grow, pressures will mount to develop effective methods for evaluating and ensuring the quality of health care. Methods of reimbursing providers may alter traditional relationships between these providers and patients. Recent changes and current proposals to alter the way providers are reimbursed under the Medicare program, as well as which providers can be reimbursed, could affect the quality of care delivered to Medicare recipients. The federal government can be expected to continue to intervene in the health care system. Some of this intervention will be perceived as increased interference by health professionals, including physicians and possibly nurses. Business and labor will continue to be concerned about the cost of care. Health care practice data may be scrutinized by groups that never before expressed interest in such information. New types of relationships are likely to develop between providers and business/labor communities. Third parties may attempt to influence excessively how health care is delivered through reimbursement mechanisms as well as changes in the settings in which certain services are delivered. A consistent theme throughout these cost and access issues is that providers and professionals are likely to perceive many of these changes as interference.

As previously described, fundamental shifts in the demographic characteristics of the U.S. population will have a major effect on the long-range demand for health care services. The changing demographic characteristics will place added emphasis on treating the health problems of the elderly population. Consequently, treatment of chronic conditions will gain added emphasis. The shifting age composition of the population is likely to create shifts in the demand for professional services such as geriatrics, rheumatology, obstetrics, pediatrics, and AIDS services. The migration patterns of the U.S. population suggest that the growth in demand for services is likely to vary substantially from area to area. In general, states in the South and West will experience rapid growth, whereas states in the Northeast and Midwest will experience a slower growth in demand.

The supply of physicians will continue to increase at a faster rate than the U.S. population overall. The increasing supply of physicians should serve to increase access to medical care and allow physicians more time to spend with each patient, perhaps to enhance preventive guidance and services. As specialists continue to locate in nonmetropolitan areas and small cities, referral patterns for specialized care may change. The growing supply of physicians and the shifting specialty composition are likely to raise concerns about the mechanisms that influence the specialty mix of physicians. Limitations on the number of medical graduates or on the availability of residency positions in some specialties will be considered more frequently than in the past.

Almost certainly, health policy issues will become increasingly politicized. The debate on health care issues will continue to expand beyond the health care community. Many health policy issues may no longer be determined by sound science and practice considerations but rather by political factors. Changes in the health sector may lead to unexpected divisions and alliances on health policy issues. The intensity of economic competition in the health sector is likely to continue to increase because of the increasing supply of health care personnel and because of the changes in the financing of care. Increased competition is likely to cause realignments among key participants in the health care sector, often depending upon the particular issue involved.

The failure of health reform at the national policy level in 1994 did not preclude the implementation of significant improvements in either the public or the private components of the health sector. With or without changes in national health policies, the health system in the United States is clearly reforming itself. With the persistence of cost and access as the system's twin critical problems, new approaches and models were both needed and expected. The federal as well as state governments have moved to control the costs of Medicaid services, primarily through attempts to enroll nondisabled Medicaid populations (largely mothers and children) into capitated managed-care programs. The rapid conversion of Medicaid services to managed-care operations and the growth of private managed-care organizations pose new issues for the delivery of clinical preventive and public health services. Though it is anticipated that these changes will result in fewer clinical preventive and treatment services being provided through public health agencies, both the extent and impact of these shifts remain unclear. Chapter 8 will present and discuss these issues in greater depth.

In any event, the underlying investment strategy of the U.S. health system appears to remain unchanged, with 97 percent of the available resources allocated for treatment services, approximately 2 percent for clinical preventive services, and 1 percent for population-based public health services. Without at least some additional investment in prevention and public health approaches, the long-term prospects for controlling costs within the U.S. health system are bleak. In the meantime, some 35 to 40 million Americans remain outside the system and will continue to incur excessive costs when they inappropriately access needed services. Universal access is a prerequisite for eventual control of costs. However, it is not clear how true reform can be effected without reform of *both* our medical care and public health subsystems.

Though progress along this road has been painfully slow, there is evidence that a paradigm shift is already underway. The Pew Health Professions Commission argues that by the end of the century, the characteristics of the American health care system will be quite different from those that have dominated the health system prior to 1990.[11] The health system of the year 2000 and beyond will be

- more managed, with better integration of services and financing
- more accountable to those who purchase and use health services
- more aware of and responsive to the needs of enrolled populations
- more able to use fewer resources more effectively
- more innovative and diverse in how it provides for health
- more inclusive in how it defines health
- less focused on treatment and more concerned with education, prevention, and care management
- more oriented to improving the health of the entire population
- more reliant on outcomes data and evidence

These gains, however, are likely to be accompanied by pain. The number of hospitals may decline by as much as 50 percent and the number of hospital beds by 60 percent or more. There will be continued massive expansion of primary care in community and other ambulatory settings; this will foster replication of services in different settings, a development likely to confuse consumers. These forces also suggest major traumas for the health professions, with projected surpluses of physicians, nurses, and pharmacists.[11] An estimated 100,000 to 150,000 excess physicians, mainly specialists, will be joined by 200,000 to 300,000 excess nurses as hospitals close, and as many as 40,000 excess pharmacists as drug dispensing is automated and centralized. The massive fragmentation among 200 or more allied health fields will cause consolidation into multiskilled professions to meet the changing needs of hospitals and other care settings. One of the few professions likely to flourish in this environment will be public health, with its focus on populations, information-driven planning, collaborative responses, and broad definition of health and health services.

Where these forces will move the health system is not yet known. To blend better the contributions of preventive and treatment-based approaches, several important changes are needed. There must be a new and more rational understanding of what is meant by "health services." This understanding must include a broad view of health promotion and health protection strategies and provide these equal standing with treatment-based strategies. Once and for all, health services must be seen to include services that focus on health as well as those that focus on ill health. This should result in support for a more comprehensive approach to defining a basic benefit package that would be provided to all Americans. A second and companion change needed is to finance this enhanced basic benefit package from the same source, rather than funding public health and most prevention from one source (government resources) and treatment and the remaining prevention activities from private sources (business, individuals, insurance). With these changes, a gradual reallocation of resources can move the system toward a more rational and effective investment strategy.

CONCLUSION

Every day in America, decisions are made that influence the health status of individuals and groups of individuals. The aggregate of these decisions and the activities necessary to carry them out constitute our health system. It is important to view interventions as linked with health and illness states as well as with the dynamic processes and multiple factors that move an individual from one state to another. Preventive interventions act at various points and through various means to prevent the development of a disease state or, if it occurs, to minimize its effects to the extent possible. These interventions differ in their linkages with public health practice, medical practice, and long-term care, as well as in their focus on individuals or groups. The framework represents a rational one, reflecting known facts concerning each of its aspects and their relationships with each other.

As this chapter has described, current health policy in the United States reflects a different view of the factors incorporated in the model. Current policy focuses unduly on disease states and strategies for restoring as opposed to promoting or protecting health. It directs the vast majority of human, physical, and financial resources to tertiary prevention, and particularly to acute treatment. It focuses disproportionately on individually oriented secondary and tertiary medical care. In so doing, it raises questions as to whether these policies are effective and ethical.

Characterized in the past largely by federalism, pluralism, and incrementalism, the health sector in the United States is undergoing fundamental change, primarily in response to economic realities that have invested a trillion dollars in a model that equates medical care with health care. We are now realizing that this investment strategy is not producing results commensurate with its resource consumption. Health indicators, including those characterizing large disparities in outcomes and access among important minority groups, are not responding to more resources being deployed in the usual ways. The major problems have been widely characterized as cost and access, with the former being considered a cause of the latter. How to fix the cost question without aggravating the access issue has yet to be addressed, although managed-care approaches are serving to place some controls on the utilization of specific services. A better representation of the twin problems facing the U.S. health sector might be excess and access, suggesting a return to the strategic drawing boards for approaches that reduce and redeploy resources rather than only reducing them. Within this reexamination of purpose and strategies for the health sector, the need to address health as well as disease, and prevention as well as treatment should be apparent. To accomplish these aims, there must be consensus that basic health services include population-based public health services and clinical preventive services as well as diagnostic and treatment services. To facilitate rational policy making and investment decisions, these services should be funded from a common source. This may require that health insurance premiums replace governmental appropriations as the source of funding for public sector activities. It is to be hoped that these realizations will take place before the health sector reaches its meltdown point.

DISCUSSION QUESTIONS AND EXERCISES

1. What are the critical problems facing the health care system in the United States today?
2. What forces are most likely to fuel the current movement toward major health care reform in America?
3. What role will public health and prevention play in a reformed American health care system?
4. What changes will most affect health care providers?
5. What changes will most affect consumers of health care services?
6. What are the advantages of projected surpluses for physicians, nurses, and other health professions? What are the disadvantages?
7. If problems within the health system prompted calls for reform in 1994, why is there less concern over national policy solutions today?

continues

8. Is an ounce of prevention still worth a pound of cure in the United States? If not, what is the relative value of prevention in comparison with treatment?
9. Exhibit 3–2 lists organizations, agencies, and institutions that might be considered part of an overall national prevention effort. Identify those that you would include if you had the task of quantifying the scope and cost of all health-related prevention activities and expenditures in the United States. Which would you choose to leave off the list? Why?

Exhibit 3–2 Health-Related Prevention Organizations, Agencies, and Institutions

Instructions:

Review the following catalog of organizations, agencies, and institutions, and identify those elements that should be included in a compilation of health-related prevention efforts. On the basis of what you know of these agencies, which of their programs or services should be included? Explain why in terms of categories of prevention activities (e.g., health promotion, health protection, clinical preventative services).

Federal Agencies

Department of Agriculture
Department of Transportation
Department of Energy
Department of Health and Human Services
Department of Labor
Department of Education
Department of Justice
Department of the Interior
Department of Veterans Administration
Department of Commerce
Department of Treasury
Department of Housing and Urban Development
Environmental Protection Agency
Consumer Product Safety Commission
Federal Aviation Administration
Federal Mine Safety and Health Commission
National Transportation Safety Board
Nuclear Regulatory Commission
Occupational Safety and Health Review Commission
Federal Emergency Management Agency

continues

Exhibit 3–2 continued

State Agencies (different agency names in different states)

Aging
Agriculture
Alcoholism and Substance Abuse
Children and Family Services
Council on Health and Fitness
Emergency Services and Disaster Agency
Energy and Natural Resources
Environmental Protection Agency
Guardianship and Advocacy Commission
Health Care Cost Containment Agency
Health Facilities Planning Board and Agency
Mental Health and Developmental Disabilities
Nuclear Safety
Pollution Control Board
Professional Regulation Agency
Public Aid
Public Health
Rehabilitation Services
State Fire Marshall
State Board of Education
State Board of Higher Education
Veterans Affairs

Miscellaneous Organizations and Sites

Foundations
Corporations
Voluntary Health Associations
United Way of America
Physician Office Visits
HMO Visits
Dental Visits

Source: Reprinted from *Health Care Reform and Public Health: A Paper Based on Population-Based Core Functions*, 1993, The Core Functions Project, U.S. Public Health Service, Office of Disease Prevention and Health Promotion, Washington, DC.

REFERENCES

1. Bunker JP, Frazier HS, Mosteller F. Improving health: measuring effects of medical care. *Milbank Q.* 1994;72:225–258.

2. National Heart, Lung and Blood Institute. *The Fifth Report of the Joint Committee on Detection, Evaluation and Treatment of High Blood Pressure*. Hyattsville, Md: US Public Health Service; 1994.

3. National Center for Health Statistics. *Health United States, 1995*. Hyattsville, Md; US Public Health Service; 1996.

4. Leavell HR, Clark EG. *Preventive Medicine for the Doctor in His Community*. 3rd ed. New York, NY: McGraw-Hill Book Co.; 1965.

5. Brownson RC, Remington PL, Davis JR, eds. *Chronic Disease Epidemiology and Control*. Washington, DC: American Public Health Association; 1993.

6. *For a Healthy Nation: Return on Investments in Public Health*. Washington, DC: US Public Health Service; 1994.

7. Brown RE, Elixhauser A, Corea J, Luce BR, Sheingold S. *National Expenditures for Health Promotion and Disease Prevention Activities in the United States*. Washington, DC: Medical Technology Assessment and Policy Research Center; 1991.

8. Core Functions Project, US Public Health Service, Office of Disease Prevention and Health Promotion. *Health Care Reform and Public Health: A Paper Based on Population-Based Core Functions*. Washington, DC: US Public Health Service; 1993.

9. Wennberg JE, ed. *Dartmouth Atlas of Health Care in the United States*. American Hospital Publishing; 1996.

10. Blendon RJ. *Kaisar/Harvard/KRC National Election Night Survey*. Menlo Park, Calif: Henry J. Kaisar Family Foundation; 1994.

11. Pew Health Professions Commission. *Critical Challenges: Revitalizing the Health Professions for the Twenty-First Century*. San Francisco, Calif: University of California, San Francisco, Center for Health Professions; 1995.

CHAPTER 4

The Organization of Public Health in the United States

Public health is not limited to what is done by or through governmental public health agencies. Nonetheless, this is the most prevalent misperception held by those inside as well as outside the field. Still, particular aspects of public health rely on government. For example, the enforcement of laws remains one of those governmental responsibilities important to the public's health and public health practice. Yet the law and the legal system are important for public health purposes above and beyond law enforcement. Laws at all levels of government bestow the basic powers of government and distribute these powers among various agencies, including public health agencies. These laws represent governmental decisions as well as collective social values and provide the basis for actions that influence the health of the public.

It is important to remember that decisions and actions that take place outside the sphere of government also influence the health of the public, perhaps even more than those made by our elected officials and administrative agencies. Private-sector and voluntary organizations play key roles in identifying factors important for health and promoting actions to promote and protect health for individuals and groups. Since public health represents collective decisions and actions rather than purely personal ones, however, it is often governmental forums that raise issues, make decisions, and establish priorities for action. Many governmental actions reflect the dual roles of government often seen on official governmental seals or, even more commonly, on the vehicles of local police agencies: to protect and to serve. As they relate to health, the genesis of these two roles lies in separate, often conflicting, philosophies and legacies of government. This chapter will examine how these roles are organized in the United States. This examination particularly emphasizes the relationships among law, government, and public health, seeking answers to the following questions:

- What role does government have in serving the public's health?
- What is the legal basis for public health in the United States?
- How are public health responsibilities and roles structured at the federal, state, and local levels?

To review the organization and structure of governmental public health, this chapter, unlike the history of U.S. public health briefly traced in Chapter 1, will begin with federal public health roles and activities, to be followed in turn by those at the state and local levels. The focus will be primarily on form and structure rather than function, which will be addressed in Chapter 5. In most circumstances, it is logical for form to follow function. Here, however, it is necessary to understand the legal and organizational framework of governmental public health in order to appreciate its functions. The structure established through the law and these governmental agencies is a key element of the public health's infrastructure and one of the basic building blocks of our public health system. Other key inputs, including human, informational, fiscal, and other aspects of organizational resources, will be examined in Chapter 6. The topics in this chapter have been separated from other public health system inputs somewhat arbitrarily. However, the legal basis of public health and the governmental agencies that have been created to serve the public health are basic and important concepts in their own right. This structure itself is a product of our uniquely American approach to government.

AMERICAN GOVERNMENT AND PUBLIC HEALTH

A former speaker of the U.S. House of Representatives, Tip O'Neil, observed quite correctly that "all politics is local." If all politics is local, then public health must be considered primarily a local phenomenon as well because politics is embedded in public health processes. After all, public health represents collective decisions as to which health outcomes are unacceptable, which factors contribute to those outcomes, which unacceptable problems will be addressed in view of resource limitations, and which participants need to be involved in addressing the problems. These are political processes, with different viewpoints and values being brought together to determine which collective decisions will be made. All too often, politics carries a very different connotation, one frequently associated with overtones of partisan politics. But politics is a necessary and productive process, perhaps the best one devised by humans to meet our collective needs.

The political system in the United States is a product of many forces that have shaped governmental roles in health. The framers of the U.S. Constitution did not plan for the federal government to deal directly with health or, for that matter, many other important issues. The word *health* does not even appear in that famous document, relegating health to the group of powers reserved to the states or the people. The Constitution explicitly authorized the federal government to promote and provide for the general welfare (in the Preamble and Article I, Section 8) and to regulate commerce (also in Article I, Section 8). Federal powers evolved slowly in the area of health on the basis of these explicit powers and subsequent U.S. Supreme Court decisions that broadened federal authority by determining that additional powers are implied in the explicit language of the Constitution.

The initial duties to regulate international affairs and interstate commerce led the federal government to concentrate its efforts on preventing the importation of epidemics and assisting states and localities upon request with their periodic needs for communicable disease control. The earliest federal health unit, the Marine Hospital Service, was established in 1798 partly to serve merchant seamen and partly to prevent the spread of epidemic diseases; it grew over time into what is now the U.S. Public Health Service.

But the power to promote health and welfare did not always translate into the ability to act. The federal government acquired the ability to raise significant financial resources only with the authority to levy a federal tax on income, provided by the Sixteenth Amendment in the early 20th century. The capacity to raise vast sums generated the capacity to address health problems and needs through transferring resources to state and local governments in various forms of grants-in-aid. Despite its powers to provide for the general welfare and regulate commerce, the federal government could not act directly in health matters; it could only act through states as the primary delivery system. After 1935, the power and influence of the federal government grew rapidly through its financial influence over state and local programs and, after 1965, through its emergence as a major purchaser of health care through Medicare and Medicaid. As for a public health presence at the federal level, the best known and most widely respected federal public health agency, now known as the Centers for Disease Control and Prevention (CDC), was not established until 1946. Exhibit 4–1 provides a 50-year history of CDC that describes the expansion of the federal presence in both traditional and emerging public health practice.[1]

The emergence of the federal government as a major influence in the health system displaced states from a position they had held since the middle of the 19th century. States themselves had moved slowly to assume health powers during the course of the 19th century. Without much direction from the U.S. Constitution, state powers emanated from two general sources. First, they derived from the so-called police powers of states, which provide the basis for government to limit the actions of individuals in order to control and abate nuisances. A second source for state health powers lay in the expectation for government to serve those individuals who were not able to provide for themselves. This expectation had its roots in the Elizabethan Poor Laws and carried over to states in the new American

Exhibit 4–1 History of CDC

CDC, An institution synonymous around the world with public health, was 50 years old on July 1, 1996. The Communicable Disease Center was organized in Atlanta, Georgia, on July 1, 1946; its founder, Dr. Joseph W. Mountin, was a visionary public health leader who had high hopes for this small and comparatively insignificant branch of the Public Health Service (PHS). It occupied only one floor of the Volunteer Building on Peachtree Street and had fewer than 400 employees, most of whom were engineers and entomologists. Until the previous day, they had worked for Malaria Control in War Areas, the predecessor of CDC, which had successfully kept the southeastern states of Malaria-free during World War II and, for approximately 1 year, from murine typhus fever. The new institution would expand its interests to include all communicable diseases and would be the servant of the states, providing practical help whenever called.

Distinguished scientists soon filled CDC's laboratories, and many states and foreign countries sent their public health staffs to Atlanta for training. Any tropical disease with an insect vector and all those of zoological origin came within its purview. Dr. Mountin was not satisfied with this progress, and he impatiently pushed the staff to do more. He reminded them that except for tuberculosis and venereal disease, which had separate units in Washington, DC, CDC was responsible for any communicable disease. To survive, it had to become a center for epidemiology.

Medical epidiomologists were scarce, and it was not until 1949 that Dr. Alexander Langmuir arrived to head the epidemiology branch. Within months, he launched the first-ever disease surveillance program, which confirmed his suspicion that malaria, on which CDC spent the largest portion of its budget, had long since disappeared. Subsequently, disease surveillance became the cornerstone on which CDC's mission of service to the states was built and, in time, changed the practice of public health.

The outbreak of the Korean War in 1950 was the impetus for creating CDC's Epidemiologic Intelligence Service (EIS). The threat of biological warfare loomed, and Dr. Langmuir, the most knowledgeable person in PHS about this arcane subject, saw an opportunity to train epidemiologists who would guard against ordinary threats to public health while watching out for alien germs. The first class EIS offcers arrived in Atlant for training in 1951 and pledged to go wherever they were called for the next 2 years. These "disease detectives" quickly gained fame for "shoe-leather epidemiology" through which they ferreted out the cause of disease outbreaks.

The survival of CDC as an institution was not at all certain in th 1950s. In 1947, Emory University gave land on Clifton Road for a headquarters, but construction did not begin for more than a decade. PHS was so intent on research and the rapid growth of the National Institutes of Health that it showed little interest in what hap-

continues

Exhibit 4–1 continued

pened in Atlanta. Congress, despite the long delay in appropriating money for new buildings, was much more receptive to CDC's pleas for support than either PHS or the Bureau of the Budget.

Two major health crises in the mid-1950s established CDC's credibility and ensured its survival. In 1955, when poliomyelitis appeared in children who had received the recently approved Salk vaccine, the national inoculation program was stopped. The cases were traced to contaminated vaccine from a laboratory in California; the problem was corrected, and the inoculation program, at least for first and second graders, was resumed. The resistance of these 6- and 7-year-olds to polio, compared with that of older children, proved the effectiveness of the vaccine. Two years later, surveillance was used again to trace the course of a massive influenza epidemic. From the data gathered in 1957 and subsequent years, the national guidelines for infulenza vaccine were developed.

CDC grew by acquisition. The venereal disease program came to Atlanta in 1957 and with it the first Public Health Advisors, non-science college graduates destined to play an important role in making CDC's disease-control programs work. The tuberculosis program moved in 1960, immunization practices and the *Morbidity and Mortality Weekly Report* in 1961. The Foreign Quarantine Service, one of the oldest and most prestigious units of PHS, came in 1967; many of its positions were switched to other uses as better ways of doing the work of quarantine, primarily through overseas surveillance, were developed. The long-established nutrition program also moved to CDC, as well as the National Institute for Occupational Safety and Health, and work of already established units increased. Immunization tackled measles and rubella control; epidemiology added family planning and surveillance of chronic diseases. When CDC joined the international malaria-eradication program and accepted responsibility for protecting the earth from moon germs and vice vers, CDC's mission stretched overseas and into space.

CDC played a key role in one of the greatest triumphs of public health, the eradication of smallpox. In 1962 it established a smallpox surveillance unit, and a year later tested a newly developed jet gun and vaccine in the Pacific island nation of Tonga. After refining vaccination techniques in Brazil, CDC began work in Central and West Africa in 1966. When millions of people there had been vaccinated, CDC used surveillance to speed the work along. The World Health Organization used this "eradication escalation" technique elsewhere with such success that global eradication of smallpox was achieved in 1977. The United States spent only $32 million on the project, about the cost of keeping smallpox at bay for 2.5 months.

CDC also achieved notable success at home tracking new and mysterious disease outbreaks. In the mid-1970s and early 1980s, it found the cause of Legionnaires disease and toxic-shock syndrome. A fatal disease, subsequently named

continues

Exhibit 4–1 continued

acquired immunodeficiency syndrome (AIDS), was first mentioned in the June 5, 1981, issue of *MMWR*. Since then, *MMWR* has published numerous follow-up articles about AIDS, and one of the larges portion of CDC's budget and staff is assigned to address this disease.

Although CDC succeeded more often than it failed, it did not escape criticism. For example, television and press reports about the Tuskegee study on long-term effects of untreated syphilis in black men created a storm of protest in 1972. This study had been initiated by PHS and other organizations in 1932 and was transferred to CDC in 1957. Although the effectiveness of penicillin as a therapy for syphilis had been established during the late 1940s, participants in this study remained untreated until the study was brought to public attention. CDC was also criticized because of the 1976 effort to vaccinate the U.S. population against swine flu, the infamous killer of 1918–19. When some vaccinees developed Guillain-Barre syndrome, the campaign was stopped immediately; the epidemic never occurred.

As the scope of CDC's activities expanded far beyond communicable diseases, its name had to be changed. In 1970 it became the Center for Disease Control and in 1981, after extensive reorganization, Center became Centers. The words "and Prevention" were added in 1992, but, by law, the well-known three-letter acronym was retained. In health emergencies CDC means an answer to SOS calls from anywhere in the world, such as the recent one from Zaire where Ebola fever raged.

Fifty years ago CDC's agenda was non-controversial (hardly anyone objected to the pursuit of germs), and Atlanta was a backwater. In 1996, CDC's programs are often tied to economic, political, and social issues, and Atlanta is as near Washington as the tap of a keyboard.

Source: Reprinted from History of CDC, *MMWR,* Vol 45, pp. 526–528, 1996, Centers for Disease Control and Prevention.

form of government. Despite this common heritage, states assumed these roles quite differently and at different points in time, since the evolution of states during the 19th century took place unevenly.

States developed the structure and organizations needed to use their police powers to protect citizens from communicable diseases and environmental hazards, primarily from wastes, water, and food. State health agencies developed first in Massachusetts and then across the country during the latter half of the 19th century. When federal grants became available, especially after 1935, states eagerly sought out federal funding for maternal and child health services, public health laboratories, and other basic public health programs. In so doing, states surrendered some of their autonomy over health issues. Priorities increasingly were dictated by federal grants tied to specific programs and services. It is fair to say that the grantor-grantee arrangement has never been fully satisfactory to either party, and the results in terms of health, welfare, education, and environmental policy suggest that better frameworks may be possible.

States possess the ultimate authority to create the political subunits that provide various services to the residents of a particular jurisdiction. In this manner, counties, cities, and other forms of municipalities, townships, boroughs, parishes, and the like were established. Special-purpose districts for every conceivable purpose from library service to mosquito control to emergency medical services to education have also abounded. The powers delegated to or authorized for all these local jurisdictions were established by state legislatures for health and other purposes. Although many big-city health departments were established prior to the establishment of their respective state health agencies, states began to establish new frameworks for the creation of additional local public health units. Because most states used the county form of subdividing the state, counties became the primary local governmental jurisdictions with health roles after 1900.

State constitutions and statutes impart the authority for county governments to influence health. This authority comes in two forms: those responsibilities of the state delegated to counties and additional authorities allowed through home rule powers. Home rule options permit counties to enact a local constitution and take on additional authority and powers, such as the ability to levy taxes for local public health services and activities. More than two-thirds of U.S. counties have a county commission form of government with anywhere from 2 to 50 elected county commissioners.[2] These commissions carry out both legislative and executive branch functions, although they share administrative authority with other elected officials such as county clerks, assessors, treasurers, prosecuting attorneys, sheriffs, and coroners. Some counties, generally the more populous ones, have a county administrator accountable to elected commissioners, and a small number of counties (less than 5 percent) have an elected county executive. Elected county executives often have veto power over the county legislative body; home rule jurisdictions are more likely to have an elected county executive than other counties.

Local governments in U.S. cities were first on the scene in terms of public health activities, as noted in Chapter 1. But after states became more extensively involved after about 1875, the relative role of local government began to erode. Both local and state governments were overwhelmed by the availability of federal funding in comparison to their own resources; they found it easier to take what they could get from the federal government than to generate their own revenue to finance needed services.

Many forces have been at work to alter the initial relationships among the three levels of government for health roles. These include

- gradual expansion and maturation of the federal government
- staggered addition of new states and variability in the maturation of state governments
- population growth and shifts over time
- ability of the various levels of government to raise revenues commensurate with their expanding needs
- growth of science and technology as tools for addressing public health and medical care needs
- rapid growth of the U.S. economy
- societal needs for services
- expectations of American society for various services from their government[3,4]

The last of these factors is perhaps the most important. For the first 150 years of U.S. history, there was little expectation that the federal government should intervene in the health and welfare needs of its citizenry. The massive need and economic turmoil of the Great Depression years quickly altered this long-standing value as Americans began to turn to government to help deal with current needs and future uncertainties.

The complex public health network that exists today evolved slowly, with many different shifts in relative roles and influence. Economic considerations and societal expectations, both reaching a critical point in the 1930s, set the tone for the rest of the 20th century. In general, power and influence were initially greatest at the local level, residing there until states began to develop their own machinery to carry out their police power and welfare roles. States then served as the primary locus for these health roles until the federal government began to use its vast resource potential to meet changing public expectations in the 1930s. State actions were soon driven by federal grant programs for public health and eventually personal health care service programs, especially by federal actions in the 1960s. It was then that several new federal health and social service programs were targeted directly to local governments, bypassing states. At the same time, a new federal-state partnership for the medically indigent (Medicaid) was established to address the national policy concern over the plight of the medically indigent.

There is evidence, however, that political and philosophical shifts since about 1980 are altering roles once again.[3] Debates over federal versus state roles continued throughout the 1980s and 1990s, although current indications suggest that some diminution of federal influence and enhancement of state influence is likely to persist for the near term. Still, the federal government has considerable ability to influence the health system through its fiscal muscle power as well as its research, regulatory, technical assistance, and training roles.

LAW AND PUBLIC HEALTH

One of the chief organizing forces for public health lies in the system of law. Unfortunately, the American system of law has become so complex that few people feel capable of dealing with legal principles and concepts. To protect our interests, we rely upon lawyers. Whether the law is as complex as most of us believe it to be is arguable, but the net effect is the same: we tend to think of the law as some mysterious set of concepts and practices rather than something that is based on the ordinary facts and occurrences of everyday life. But if law is even just partly as common and practical as this second interpretation suggests, then it is both useful and possible for nonlawyers to understand it. This section examines how law affects the public health system.

Laws have many purposes in the modern world, and many of these are evident in public health laws. Unfortunately, there is no one repository where the body of law, even the body of public health law, can be found. This has occurred because laws are products of the legal system, which in the United States includes our federal system and 50 different state legal systems. All of these developed at somewhat different times in response to somewhat different circumstances and issues. Common to each is some form of a state constitution, a considerable amount of legislation, and a substantial body of judicial decisions. If there is any road map through this maze, it lies in the federal and state constitutions, which establish the basic framework dividing governmental powers among the three branches of government in ways that allow each to create its own laws.

As a result, four different types of law can be distinguished by virtue of their form or authority: (1) constitutionally based law, (2) legislatively based law, (3) administratively based law, and (4) judicially based law. This framework still allows latitude for judicial interpretation and oversight. A brief description of each of these forms of law follows.

Types of Law

Constitutionally based law is ultimately derived from the U.S. Constitution, the legal foundation of the nation, in which the powers, duties, and limits of the federal government are established. States basically gave up certain powers (defense, foreign diplomacy, printing money, etc.), ceding these to the federal government while retaining all other powers and duties. Health was not one of those powers explicitly bestowed upon the federal government. The federal constitution also included a Bill of Rights intended to protect the rights of individuals from abuses by their government. States, in turn, have developed their own state constitutions, often patterned after the federal framework, although state constitutions tend to be more clear and specific in their language, leaving less room and need for judicial interpretation. These provide the broad framework from which states determine which activities will be undertaken and how those activities will be organized and funded. These decisions and actions come in the form of state statutes.

Statutory-based law includes all the acts and statutes enacted by Congress and the various state and local legislative bodies. This collection of law represents a wide range of governmental policy choices, including

- simple expressions of preferences in favor of a particular policy or service (such as the value of home visits by public health nurses)
- authorizations for specific programs (such as the authority for local governments to license restaurants)
- mandates or requirements for an activity to occur or, alternatively, to be prohibited (such as requiring all newborns to be screened for specific metabolic diseases or prohibiting smoking in public places)
- providing resources for specific purposes (such as the distribution of medications to AIDS patients)

If the legislative intent is for something to occur, the most effective approaches are generally to require or prohibit an activity.

The basic requirement for statutory-based laws is that they must be consistent with the U.S. Constitution and, for state and local statutes, with state constitutions as well. State laws also establish the various subunits of the state and delineate their responsibilities for carrying out state mandates as well as the limits of what they can do. At the local level, ordinances and statutes are also enacted by the legislative bodies of these subunits (e.g., city councils and county boards), setting forth the duties and authorizations of local government and its agencies. Laws affecting public health are created at all levels in this hierarchy, but especially at the state and local levels. Among other purposes, these laws establish state and local boards of health and health departments, delineate the responsibilities of these agencies, including their programs and budgets, and establish health-related laws and requirements. Many of these laws are enforced by governmental agencies.

Administrative law is law promulgated by administrative agencies within the executive branch of government. Rather than enact statutes that include extensive details of a professional or technical nature, and to allow greater flexibility in their design and subsequent revision, administrative agencies are provided with the authority to establish law through rule-making processes. These rules, administrative law, carry the force of law and represent a unique situation in which legislative, judicial, and executive powers are carried out by one agency. Administrative agencies include cabinet-level departments as well as other boards, commissions, and the like that are granted this power through an enactment of the legislative body. Because of its importance and pervasiveness for public health actions, administrative law will be described in greater detail in a subsequent section of this chapter.

The fourth type of law is judicial law, also known as common law. This includes a wide range of tradition, legal custom, and previous decisions of federal and state courts. To ensure fairness and consistency, previous decisions are used to guide judgments on similar disputes. This form of law becomes especially important in areas in which laws have not been codified by legislative bodies. In public health, nuisances (unsanitary, noxious, or otherwise potentially dangerous circumstances) are one such area in which few legislative bodies have specified exactly what does and what does not constitute a public health nuisance. In this situation, the common law for nuisances is derived from previous judicial decisions. These determine under what circumstances and for what specific conditions a public health official can take action, as well as the actions that can be taken.

Purposes of Public Health Law

Two broad purposes for public health law can be described: (1) protecting and promoting health and (2) ensuring the protection of rights of individuals in the processes used by public health. Public health powers ultimately derive from the U.S. Constitution, which bestows the authority to regulate commerce and provide for the general welfare, and from the various state constitutions, which often provide clear but broad authorities based largely on the police power of the state. States often have reasonably well-defined public health codes. But there is considerable diversity in their content and scope despite similarities in their basic sources of power and authority.

Many public health laws are enacted and enforced under what is known as the state's "police power." This is a broad concept that encompasses the functions historically undertaken by governments in protecting the health, safety, welfare, and general well-being of their citizens. A wide variety of laws derive from the police power of the state, a power that is considered one of the least limitable of all governmental powers. The police power of the state can be vested in an administrative agency, such as a state health agency, which becomes accountable for the manner in which these responsibilities are executed. In these circumstances, its use is a duty rather than a matter of choice, although its form is left to the discretion of the user.

Even laws that appear to limit severely or restrict the rights of individuals have been upheld by the courts if these were found to be reasonable attempts to accomplish a government's ends and not arbitrary and capricious efforts. The state's police power is not unlimited, however. Interference with individual liberties and the taking of personal property are considerations that must be balanced on a case-by-case basis. Public health laws requiring vaccinations or immunizations to protect the community have generally withstood legal challenges that they infringed upon the rights of individuals to make their own health decisions. A precedent-setting judicial opinion[5] upheld a Massachusetts ordinance authorizing local boards of health to require vaccinations for smallpox to be administered to residents if deemed necessary by the local boards. Such decisions argue that society can be governed by laws that place the common good ahead of the competing rights of individuals. Similarly, courts have weighed the power of the state to appropriate an individual's property or limit the individual's use of it if the best interests of the community makes such an action desirable. In some circumstances, equitable compensation must be provided. Issues of community interest and fair compensation are commonly encountered in dealing with public health nuisances in which an individual's private property can be found to be harmful to others.

The various forms of law and the changing nature of the relationships among the three levels of government have created a patchwork of public health laws. Despite its relatively limited constitutionally based powers, the federal government can preempt state and local government action in key areas of public health regulation involving commerce and aspects of communicable disease control. States also have authority to preempt local government actions in virtually all areas of public health activity. Although this legal framework allows for a clear and rational delineation of authorities and responsibilities, a quite variable set of arrangements has arisen. Often the higher level of government chooses not to exercise its full authority and shifts that authority to a lower level of government. This can be accomplished in some instances by delegating or requiring, and in other instances by authorizing (with incentives), the lower level of government to exercise authorities of the higher level. This has made for a complex set of relationships among the three levels of government and for 50 variations of the theme to be played in the 50 states. These relationships and their impact on the form and structure of governmental public health agencies will be evident in subsequent sections of this chapter.

There have been many critiques of the statutory basis of public health in the United States. A common one is that public health law, not unlike law affecting other areas of society, simply has not kept pace with the rapid and extensive changes in technology affecting health. Laws have been enacted at different points in time in response to different conditions and circumstances. These laws have often been enacted with little consideration as to their consistency with previous statutes and their overall impact on the body of public health law. For example, many states have different statutes and legal frameworks for general communicable diseases, sexually transmitted diseases, and human immunodeficiency virus (HIV) infections. In view of such inconsistencies, recommendations have been advanced calling for a complete overhaul and recodification of public health law. Recommendations for improvement of the public health codes often call for

- a uniform structure for similar programs and services
- varying levels of confidentiality provisions to be reviewed and made more consistent
- clarification of police power responsibilities to deal with unusual health risks and threats and to ensure that the least restrictive means (intermediate sanctions) are used first to achieve results and that greater compulsion should require the demonstration of necessity and benefits

Although these recommendations have been advanced for several decades, very little progress has been made at either the federal or state level. At times, states have sought to recodify public health statutes by relocating their placement in the statute books rather than dealing with the more basic issues of reviewing the scope and allocation of their public health responsibilities so that these are clearly presented and assigned among the various levels of government.

Administrative Law

This section on administrative law was inspired by a public health lawyer and colleague, Judith Munson, JD, who has convinced me that administrative law is both critically important to and poorly understood by public health practitioners and students alike. This section attempts to capture its revelance for public health practice.

The most frequently encountered legal interactions for most people, affecting both health professionals and consumers, are not associated with constitutional, judicial, or even statutory laws. Rather they occur through the subsystem of administrative law, which develops and enforces rules and regulations through an administrative agency. Administrative law affects people in their daily lives in many ways. It affects people personally (even in very intimate ways) through such requirements as up-to-date immunizations before entering school or identification of sexual contacts of persons with certain sexually transmitted diseases. Administrative law also affects our property: for example, specific requirements for septic fields can prevent us from building our dream vacation home on the perfect lakefront lot. It also affects many of us professionally, most notably in the licensing of health and other professions. These are but a few examples of how pervasive administrative law has become in modern American society.

At first glance, it appears that administrative law violates, or at least circumvents, one of the most fundamental principles of American government: the separation of powers among the legislative, executive, and judicial branches, with its elaborate system of checks and balances. The development and promulgation of administrative law represents the legislative function. The enforcement of the law, through inspections and other means, represents the executive function. Finally, the determination of compliance, often involving hearings and appeals within the agency before a final decision is rendered by the agency, represents the judicial function. Although the life cycle of administrative rules can be complex, it presents an interesting picture of governmental processes in public health.

The process begins with the enactment of a statute, which provides the administrative agency with the authority to develop rules and regulations to implement the intent of the newly enacted law. This authority may be limited to specific aspects of the statute, or the law may only broadly declare the legislative intent, leaving the agency considerable latitude in terms of the scope and content of rule making needed for implementation. The agency then initiates its rule-making processes, which involve technical experts from the field or program affected by the statute and legal staff from the agency or from the legal office of government (such as the attorney general's office at the state level, state's attorney office of the county, or corporation counsel office of the city). Increasingly, agency staff involved in intergovernmental affairs participate in this process, since rule making requires collaboration with the legislative branch. Interested parties, especially those organizations or industries likely to be affected by the law and regulations, may be involved in early stages of drafting rules and regulations through either standing boards, advisory bodies, or ad hoc groups brought together to gain different perspectives. Draft rules are developed and submitted as proposed rules.

There may be public hearings held on the proposals or a specific period in which interested parties and the public can comment on the proposed rules. The agency then must formally respond to public comments and indicate why proposed rules were or were not changed in response to those comments. Revisions are made to the rules, and, depending on the requirements of that level of government, the revised rules are submitted to a legislative oversight commission or committee, which then has its opportunity to comment on whether the proposed rules are consistent with the intent of the legislative body and whether the scope of the rules exceeds the authority conferred in the statute. The oversight commission also reviews the agency's response to the comments received. This presents another opportunity for interest groups and affected constituencies to influence the shape of the final regulations. After the legislative oversight comments and objections are made, the agency finalizes the rules and begins enforcement. If the agency chooses not to make changes suggested by the legislative oversight body, it faces the possibility of more specifically worded amendments to the statute or an adversarial relationship between the agency and the legislature. When final rules are adopted, they are widely circulated to the affected groups, and enforcement begins as specified in the new rules. These can be lengthy processes, taking 6 to 18 months (or longer) after enactment of a statute.

Implementation and enforcement of rules often rest with specific program staff of the agency. For licensing programs, these staff may be surveyors or inspectors. For other programs, they may be professional or administrative personnel. For many licensing programs, evidence of compliance with statutory and regulatory requirements is compiled through routine or complaint-related inspections. Based on the seriousness and, to a lesser extent, on the number of violations, a determination of noncompliance may lead to demands that specific actions take place to correct violations and that specific sanctions (as provided in the law or rules) be imposed. There is generally the opportunity for these decisions and actions to be challenged before they become final. If they are challenged, a hearing is held before a hearing officer within the administrative agency, and testimony and evidence are presented. The legal staff of the agency (or of that level of government) serve as the prosecutors. Program staff, some of whom may have been involved with the development of the rules in question, serve as witnesses. A formal record is compiled, and the hearing officer makes a recommendation to the agency head, who issues the final decision.

Several factors justify the circumvention of the principle of separation of powers (Exhibit 4–2). The basic rationale for permitting one agency to carry out these functions is that these agencies often operate in a narrow and discrete area that requires a high level of technical expertise to ensure that the intent of the legislative body is fulfilled. With the rapid expansion of science and technology in many areas, and certainly in the health system, there is an increasing need for technological and professional expertise to develop and apply the details needed to implement the legislative intent. The growth of regulatory responsibilities for government has also served to expand the need for administrative law, as it is becoming increasingly unwise for legislative bodies to attempt to put extensive details into statutes. Often these details reflect technical or practice standards that are updated or revised periodically, otherwise necessitating revisions and amend-

---

Exhibit 4–2 Factors Influencing the Need for Administrative Law

- Need for technological and professional expertise in applying the statute
- Flexibility for future changes of laws
- Increasing regulatory role for government

ments to existing laws. All of these reasons relate to the growing complexity of society and the need for special expertise to be applied in narrow discrete areas in a timely and professional manner.

But administrative law is not completely free from the system of checks and balances, as illustrated in Figure 4–1. Control points exist both for the rule-making process and for judicial review of final administrative decisions. In general, the development and promulgation of rules is overseen by a committee or commission of legislators to ensure that the legislative intent is being addressed and that the agency is not going beyond the authority provided to it in the statute. This oversight often includes provisions for public notice as to proposed rules and regulations and for written agency responses to public comments received as a result of hearings or public postings of proposed rules. Proposed rules can then be modified or withdrawn if needed. The legislative oversight also serves to alert the agency that actual or perceived transgressions may be met with more explicit statutes that would limit the agency's autonomy in developing rules and regulations in a particular area.

The second control point involves judicial review of final agency decisions. Any decision of the agency that adversely affects a party can be challenged through judicial review. This brings the agency's actions and decisions into the formal court system, where administrative actions, including fines and other sanctions, are either upheld or overturned by the courts and appeals are possible to even higher levels of review. These proceedings generally focus on procedural as opposed to evidentiary issues, relying on the record of facts and findings from the agency adjudication process. Most challenges brought for judicial review argue that the agency did not properly follow its own rules. There are instances in which judicial review is sought to require the agency to make a decision when it has not done so. However, these claims are more difficult to sustain unless the agency has completely failed to act in a situation specifically mandated by the legislative body. Agencies are granted considerable discretion in determining when and where to exercise their authorities and responsibilities, and courts are reluctant to step in and second-guess the experts. The net result is that the courts often presume that the agency's actions are proper and prefer to focus instead on issues of procedural propriety. This suggests that those involved with compliance decisions, from inspectors to administrative hearing officers, must be as concerned over procedural matters as they are with factual issues of health and safety. After the initial judicial review makes its determination, appeals and higher appeals can bring these issues to state and federal supreme courts.

The intricacies of administrative law help outsiders understand the inner workings of federal, state, and local public health agencies. We will now turn to the form and structure of these agencies.

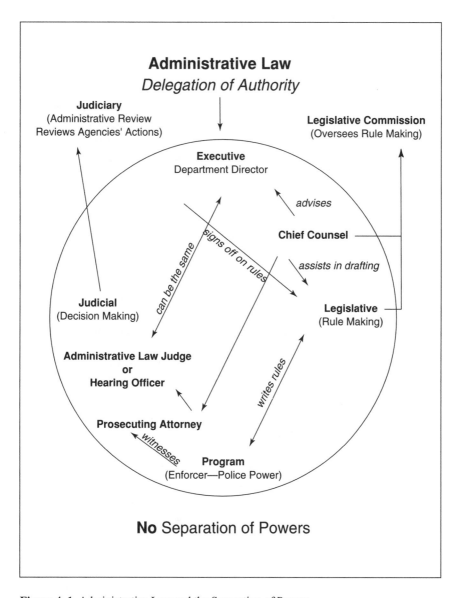

Figure 4–1 Administrative Law and the Separation of Powers.

GOVERNMENTAL PUBLIC HEALTH

Federal Health Agencies

The U.S. Public Health Service (PHS) serves as the focal point for health concerns at the national level. Although there have been frequent reorganizations affecting the structure of PHS and its placement within the massive Department of Health and Human Services (DHHS), the restructuring completed in early 1996 was the most significant in recent years. The changes were undertaken as part of the federal Reinvention of Government Initiative to bring expertise in public health and science closer to the Secretary of DHHS. In the restructuring, the line authority of the Assistant Secretary for Health over the various agencies within PHS was abolished, with those agencies now reporting directly to the Secretary of Health and Human Services, as illustrated in Exhibit 4–3. The Assistant Secretary for Health became the head of a new Office of Public Health and Science (OPHS), a new division reporting to the Secretary that also includes the Office of the Surgeon General. Each of the former PHS agencies became a full HHS operating division. These eight operating agencies, the OPHS, and the regional health administrators for the 10 federal regions of the country now constitute the U.S. Public Health Service. In effect, PHS has become a functional rather than an organizational unit of DHHS.

The PHS agencies address a wide range of public health activities, from research and training to primary care and health protection, as described in Table 4–1. The key PHS agencies are

- Health Resources and Services Administration (HRSA)
- Indian Health Service (IHS)
- Centers for Disease Control and Prevention (CDC)
- National Institutes of Health (NIH)
- Food and Drug Administration (FDA)
- Substance Abuse and Mental Health Services Administration (SAMHSA)
- Agency for Toxic Substances and Disease Registry (ATSDR)
- Agency for Health Care Policy and Research (AHCPR)

PHS agencies actually represent only a small part of DHHS. Other important operating divisions within DHHS include the Administration for Children and Families, the Health Care Financing Administration, and the Office of the Assistant Secretary for Aging. In addition, there are several administrative and support units within DHHS for management and the budget, intergovernmental affairs, legal counsel, civil rights, the inspector general, departmental appeals, public affairs, legislation, and planning and evaluation.

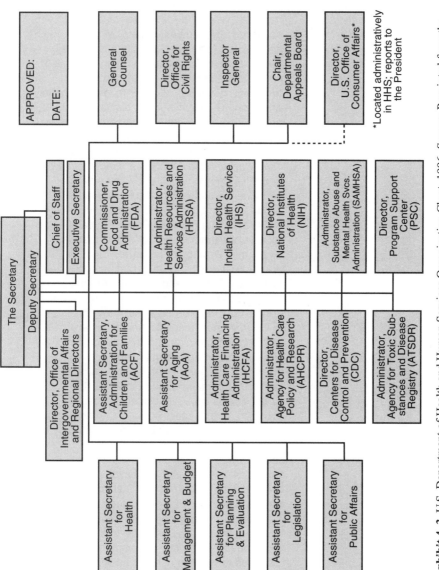

Exhibit 4-3 U.S. Department of Health and Human Services Organization Chart, 1996. *Source:* Reprinted from the U.S. Department of Health and Human Services, 1996.

Table 4–1 U.S. Public Health Service Agencies

Agency	Remarks
Health Resources and Services Administration (HRSA)	HRSA has leadership responsibility for general health services and resources related to access, equity, quality, and cost of care. Major issues addressed by the agency include rural health needs, care for populations with special health needs, maternal and child health, organ transplant resources, care for federal prisoners and Coast Guard personnel, distribution of health professionals, and the training of minorities in health professions. Bureau personnel work through three bureaus. The Bureau of Health Care Delivery and Assistance directs resources and personnel to health-underserved areas. Many health professionals have served in community and migrant health centers through its National Health Services Corps Program. The Bureau of Maternal and Child Health and Resources Development awards funds to states and special groups for maternal and child health promotion. The Bureau of Health Professions monitors the training, supply, distribution, and conduct of health professionals.
Indian Health Service (IHS)	The IHS operates hospitals, health centers, and satellite health clinics, mostly west of the Mississippi, for American Indians and Alaska Natives. Thousands of physicians, nurses, dentists, pharmacists, and other health professionals work alongside local health providers at IHS sites. Some of the facilities are tribally operated; others are administered by the IHS.
Centers for Disease Control and Prevention (CDC)	Headquartered in Atlanta, Georgia, the CDC conducts research and epidemiology throughout the world. Within the United States, most of the agency's employees work in state and local health departments, doing field research and lab analysis. In recent years, CDC has broadened its focus beyond the study of communicable diseases to work on noncommunicable diseases and occupational health concerns, such as studies of workers exposed to toxic materials. The agency's Epidemiological Intelligence Service (EIS) is the backbone for many of these

continues

Table 4–1 continued

Agency	Remarks
	activities. For health professionals interested in epidemiology, the EIS offers a two-year training program.
National Institutes of Health (NIH)	The NIH devotes billions to research funding each year for work that could forever change the world's battle against cancer, heart disease, AIDS, and other important diseases. NIH-funded projects are carried out in every state and almost every major university. Though most of NIH's resources sponsor external research, there is also a large in-house research program.
Food and Drug Administration (FDA)	Often in the public eye, the FDA plays a major role in regulating over one-fourth of all goods and services bought and sold in the United States. Years before products are brought to market, FDA researchers are evaluating their claims and testing their consequences. Working with other PHS scientists in the NIH and CDC, FDA researchers have also aided the development of drugs, vaccines, and essential medical equipment. Under the FDA's regulatory microscope are experimental drugs, cosmetics, food additives, radiation-emitting products, and new medical devices.
Substance Abuse and Mental Health Services Administration (SAMHSA)	SAMHSA organizes and supports a wide range of services for the prevention and treatment of substance abuse and mental impairments. The agency functions through three centers: the Center for Mental Health Services, the Center for Substance Abuse Prevention, and the Center for Substance Abuse Treatment.
Agency for Toxic Substances and Disease Registry (ATSDR)	This agency, closely associated administratively with CDC, probes the toxic effects of over 60,000 chemicals. The agency is working to develop more advanced testing methods to coordinate research and testing efforts among PHS agencies and to publicize its findings among government, industry, labor, environmental, and public interest groups.
Agency for Health Care Policy and Research (AHCPR)	As the federal government's primary focus for health services research, AHCPR has assumed and broadened the responsibilities of its predecessor agency, the National Center for

continues

Agency	Remarks
	Health Services Research and Health Care Technology Assessment. AHCPR's mission is to enhance the quality, appropriateness, and effectiveness of health services and to improve access to those services. It supports research into health services delivery, medical effectiveness, and health outcomes. The agency also sponsors the development of clinical practice guidelines.

Beyond DHHS, health responsibilities have been allocated to several other federal agencies, including the federal Environmental Protection Agency (EPA) and the Departments of Education, Agriculture, and Transportation, just to name a few. The importance of some of these other federal agencies should not be underestimated in terms of the level and proportion of their resources devoted to health purposes. Health-specific agencies at the federal level are a relatively new phenomenon. PHS itself remained a unit of the Treasury Department until 1944, and the first cabinet-level federal human services agency of any kind was the Federal Security Agency in 1939. This historical trivia demonstrates that federal powers and authority in health and public health are a relatively recent phenomenon in U.S. history. The CDC history included in Exhibit 4–1 further documents this claim.

It is no simple task to describe the federal budget development and approval process that determines funding levels for federal health programs. The current process is a complex one that establishes ceilings for broad categories of expenditures and then reconciles individual programs and funding levels within those ceilings. The result is a mixture of substantive decisions as to which programs will be authorized and what they will be authorized to do, together with budget decisions as to the level of resources to be made available in omnibus budget reconciliation acts.

The organization of federal health responsibilities within DHHS is quite complex fiscally and operationally. In federal fiscal year 1997, the overall DHHS budget of about $350 billion was targeted toward five general program areas: Medicare (54 percent), Medicaid (30 percent), discretionary programs largely in the PHS agencies (9 percent), family support programs (5 percent), and other entitlements (2 percent).[6] These funding allocations are illustrated in Figure 4–2.

Within the $32 billion allocated for discretionary programs about 70 percent funds PHS agency efforts. More than half of all PHS funds support NIH research activities ($12 billion), and another $10 billion supports the remaining PHS agencies approximately as follows: HRSA ($3 billion); CDC, SAMHSA, and IHS ($2

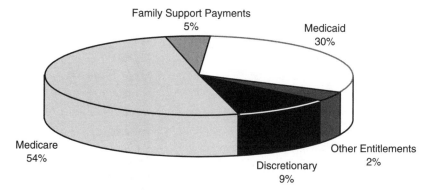

Figure 4–2 Fiscal Year 1997 Distribution of U.S. Department of Health and Human Services Outlays ($354 Billion Total). *Source:* Reprinted from *The Fiscal Year 1997 Budget,* March, 1996, U.S. Department of Health and Human Services, Washington, DC.

billion each); FDA ($0.9 billion); and AHCPR ($0.1 billion). As a result, the best known public health agencies in the federal government (CDC, HRSA, FDA) each expend less than 1 percent of total DHHS resources, and collectively they constitute only about 2 percent of the DHHS total (Figure 4–3).

Since the late 1970s, the Office of Health Promotion and Disease Prevention within the Office of the Assistant Secretary for Health has coordinated the development of a national agenda for public health and prevention efforts. Results of these efforts are apparent in the establishment of national health objectives that targeted the years 1990 and 2000 (see Chapter 2). Among the year 2000 National Health Objectives is one that relates directly to the public health system in the United States (Objective 8.14). This objective calls for increasing to at least 90 percent the proportion of people who are served by a local health department (LHD) that is effectively carrying out the core functions of public health.[7] Approximately 94 percent of the U.S. population is currently served by an LHD functioning at some level of capability. Baseline data on how many local agencies are effectively carrying out the core functions were not available when this objective was established; however, surveillance suggests that core function–related performance in the mid-1990s was not optimal and that the nation was less than halfway toward meeting the year 2000 target. Chapter 5 will describe core functions and performance measures used in these assessments and identify some of the issues that impede progress toward this important national objective.

Another recently proposed federal health initiative is the development of Federal Partnership Performance Grants for key federal health programs, including immunizations, tuberculosis control, sexually transmitted diseases, substance

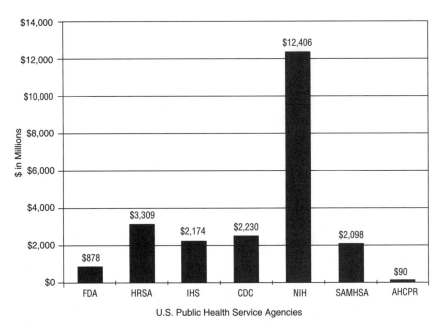

Figure 4–3 Fiscal Year 1997 U.S. Public Health Service Budget Requests. *Source:* Reprinted from *The Fiscal Year 1997 Budget,* March, 1996, U.S. Department of Health and Human Services, Washington, DC.

abuse, and mental health services. As has been described, federal grants-in-aid have become the prime strategy and mechanism by which the federal government generates state and local action toward important health problems. A variety of approaches to grant making have been used over recent decades. These can be categorized by the extent of restrictions or flexibility imparted to grantees. The greatest flexibility and lack of requirements are associated with revenue-sharing grants. Block grants, including those initiated in the early 1980s, consolidate previously categorical grant programs into a block that generally comes with fewer restrictions than the previous collection of categorical grants. Formula grants are awarded on the basis of some predetermined formula, often based at least partly on need, that determines the level of funding for each grantee. Project grants are more limited in availability and are generally intended for a specific demonstration program or project.

The Federal Partnership Performance Grants propose to address some of the shortcomings attributed to block grants implemented in the early 1980s. At that time, restrictions were relaxed for the categorical programs folded into the block grants, including the Maternal and Child Health (MCH) Block Grant and the Prevention Block Grant. Lessons learned from the previous experience suggest the need for a cautious approach to new federal block grant proposals. In the 1980s, the new block grants indeed came with fewer strings attached. However, they also came at funding levels that were reduced about 25 percent from the previous arrangement. The blocking of several categorical programs into one mega-grant also served to dissipate the constituencies for the categorical programs. Without active and visible constituencies advocating for programs, restoration or even maintenance of previous funding levels proved difficult, as demonstrated for the MCH Block Grant[8] in Figure 4–4. In addition, the reduction in reporting requirements made it more difficult to justify budget requests. The success of the Federal Performance Partnership Grants in overcoming these obstacles will be watched closely by advocates as well as state and local public health officials.

In addition to being a prime strategy to influence services at the state and local level, federal grants are also a mechanism to redistribute resources to compensate for inequalities in the ability of states to fund and operate basic health services. They have also served as a useful approach to promoting minimum standards for specific programs and services. For example, federal grants for maternal and child health promoted personnel standards in state and local agencies that fostered the growth of civil service systems across the country. Other effects on state and local health agencies will be apparent as these are examined in the following sections.

State Health Agencies

Several factors have placed states at center stage when it comes to health. The Constitution gives states primacy in safeguarding the health of their citizens. From the mid-19th century until the 1930s, states largely exercised that leadership role with little competition from the federal government and only occasional conflict with the larger cities. Federal funds turned the tables on states after 1935, reaching their peak influence in the 1960s and 1970s. At that time, a number of federal health and human service initiatives (such as model cities, community health centers, and community mental health services) were funded directly to local governments and even to community-based organizations. This practice became a source of concern in the various state capitals and served to damage tenuous relationships among the three levels of government. The relative influence of states began to grow once again after 1980, with both increasing rhetoric and actions restoring some powers and resources to states and their state health agencies. Though states were finding it increasingly difficult to finance public health and medical service programs, they demanded more autonomy and control over the programs they managed, some of them in partnership with the federal

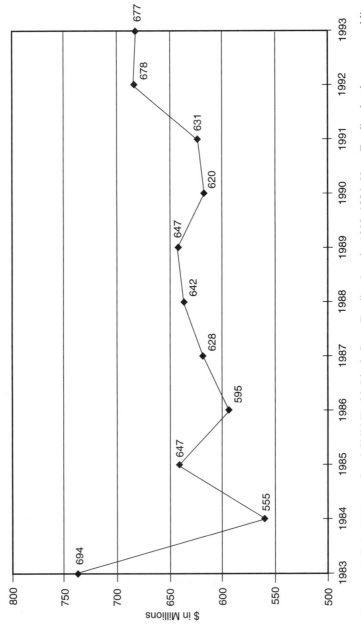

Figure 4–4 Federal Maternal and Child Health Block Grant Funding Levels, 1983–1994. *Note:* Funding levels represent obligated funds in constant 1994 dollars. *Source:* Data from C. Hayes and A. Donnegar, Rethinking Block Grants, *The Finance Project,* © 1995, Washington, D.C.

government. At the same time, local governments were making demands on state governments similar to those that states were making on the federal government. States have found themselves uncomfortably in the middle between federal and local government. At the same time, they are one step removed from both the resources needed to address the needs of their citizens and the demands and expectations of the local citizenry. For health issues, especially those affecting oversight and regulation of health services and providers, states often appear unduly influenced by large, politically active lobbies representing various aspects of the health system.

States carry out their health responsibilities through many different state agencies, although each state has an identifiable lead agency for health. These official health agencies are often freestanding departments reporting to the governor of the state. In some states, the state health agency reports to a state board of health, although this pattern is becoming increasingly rare. Another approach to the organizational placement of state health agencies finds them within a multipurpose human service agency, often with the state's social services and substance abuse responsibilities. This approach has waxed and waned in popularity, although in the mid-1990s it appears to be making a comeback with the hope of fostering better integration of community services across the spectrum of health and social services. As illustrated in Figure 4–5, state health agencies are freestanding agencies in about two-thirds of the states and are part of multipurpose health and/or human services agencies in about one-third of the states. The range of responsibilities varies greatly even within these categories.

The overall constellation of health programs and services within all of state government is more alike than it is different from state to state. Exhibit 4–4 outlines more than two dozen state agencies that carry out health responsibilities or activities in a typical state. The specific programs and services of the official state health agency, however, vary considerably. Information on the resources and programs of state health agencies has been available since the 1970s from the Association of State and Territorial Health Officials (ASTHO) and the Public Health Foundation; the data presented on state health agencies in this chapter are derived from the most recent compilation available[9] unless referenced otherwise. Figure 4–6 illustrates the variability in state health agencies' responsibilities for programs. For example, in 1991, 88 percent of states ran the state program for Children with Special Health Care Needs (a federally supported program in the MCH Block Grant), whereas only about one-sixth (16 percent) were responsible for the state Medicaid program. Just over one-third (38 percent) directed alcohol, substance abuse, or mental health services; one-third operated state institutions; and only one in eight were the lead environmental agency in the state.

Among specific environmental health responsibilities of state health agencies, the most frequent were safe drinking water (62 percent), food and drugs (52 per-

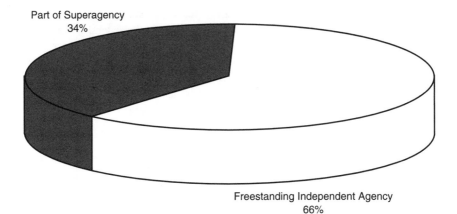

Part of Superagency
34%

Freestanding Independent Agency
66%

Figure 4–5 State Health Agency Organizational Structures, 1995. *Source:* Reprinted from *Public Health Macroview,* Vol. 7, No. 1, 1995, Public Health Foundation.

cent), and consumer product safety (42 percent). Fewer than one-fourth of the state health agencies had responsibility for clean air, resource conservation, clean water, superfund sites, toxic substance control, hazardous substances, or occupational health and safety. Staffing levels and patterns also show a wide range, reflecting the diversity in agency responsibilities.

Expenditures of state health agencies in 1991 were $11.3 billion, more than double the level of expenditures in 1982. The 1991 total included $9.3 billion in direct expenditures and $1.9 billion in transfers to LHDs (Figure 4–7). Total state and local health department (combined) expenditures were $14 billion in 1991. LHDs expended $2.7 billion directly and another $1.9 in transfers from states, for a total of $4.6 billion. For comparison purposes, total health expenditures in the United States for 1991 were $752 billion. Expenditures by state health agencies and LHDs in that year represented only 1.9 percent of all health spending. This reflects a declining proportion of all health expenditures nationally. In 1978, 2.6 percent of all health spending was attributed to state and local health departments.

As documented in Figure 4–8, sources of the $14 billion expended by state and local health agencies combined were state funds (41 percent), federal funds (32 percent), local funds (12 percent), and fees and reimbursements (10 percent). Sources for the share of these expended by state health agencies only were state funds (55 percent), federal WIC funds (20 percent), federal MCH Block Grant funds (5 percent), and other federal sources (5 percent). Excluding WIC funding,

Exhibit 4–4 Typical State Agencies with Health Roles (Names Vary from State to State)

- Official State Health Agency (Department of Health/Public Health)
- Department of Aging
- Department of Agriculture
- Department of Alcoholism and Substance Abuse
- Asbestos Abatement Authority
- Department of Children and Family Services
- Department of Emergency and Disaster Services
- Department of Energy and Natural Resources
- Environmental Protection Agencies
- Guardianship and Advocacy Commissions
- Health and Fitness Council
- Health Care Cost Containment Council
- Health Facilities Authority
- Health Facilities Planning Board
- Department of Mental Health and Developmental Disabilities
- Department of Mines and Minerals
- Department of Nuclear Safety
- Pollution Control Board
- Department of Professional Regulation
- Department of Public Aid
- Department of Rehabilitation Services
- Rural Affair Council
- State Board of Education
- State Fire Marshall
- Department of Transportation
- State University System
- Department of Veterans Affairs

the remaining resources are 69 percent state, 6 percent MCH, and 13 percent other federal funds.

More than one-half (60 percent) of the state health agency resources were expended for noninstitutional personal health care services, including WIC and maternal and child health services. The remaining resources were directed toward state health agency–operated institutions (15 percent), health planning and regulation (9 percent), environmental health (6 percent), general administration (6 percent), and laboratory services (3 percent).

With public health responsibilities allocated differently in each state, the data on state health agency expenditures are incomplete in several important aspects. These data do not allow for meaningful comparison across states because of the

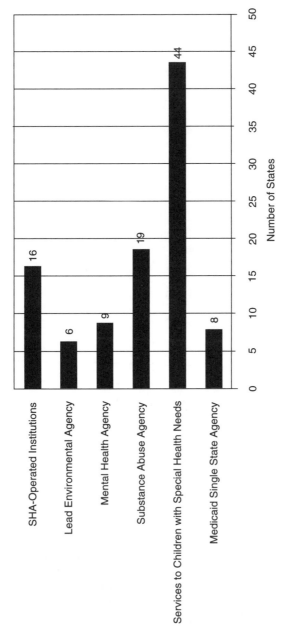

Figure 4–6 Organizational Responsibilities Delegated to State Health Agencies, 1995. *Source:* Reprinted from *Public Health Macroview,* Vol. 7, No. 1, 1995, Public Health Foundation.

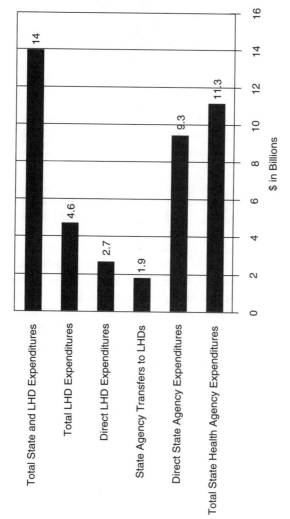

Figure 4–7 Expenditures of State and Local Health Departments, United States, 1991. *Source* Reprinted from *Public Health Macroview,* Vol. 7, No. 1, 1995, Public Health Foundation.

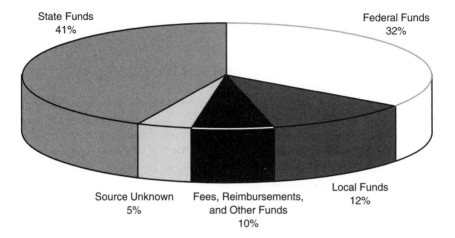

Figure 4–8 Sources of Funds for State and Local Health Departments, 1991. *Source:* Reprinted from *Public Health Macroview,* Vol. 7, No. 1, 1995, Public Health Foundation.

variation in responsibilities assigned to the official state health agency and those assigned to other state agencies. Also lacking is a composite picture of resource allocations for important public health purposes across the state and local agencies with various health roles. To address this latter concern, a recent study sought to capture expenditures in eight states for major public health activities provided through state substance abuse, mental health, and environmental health agencies in addition to state and local public health agencies.[10] The focus of this examination was on core public health functions, which will be defined more specifically in Chapter 5. In characterizing the health-related expenditures of these agencies, however, core public health functions, as opposed to personal health services that are treatment oriented, seek to prevent disease and disability (and include some personal health services that are prevention oriented). This latter category of personal health services and all population-based prevention activities were considered to represent core public health function expenditures.

The findings from this examination are presented in Figures 4–9 and 4–10. Nearly half (46 percent) of the resources from these health, substance abuse, mental health, and environmental agencies supported personal health services, 27 percent supported core public health functions, 8 percent supported WIC services, 8 percent supported other environmental services, and 11 percent supported other activities of these agencies. The study concluded that nationally an estimated total of $11.4 billion, or $44 per capita, was spent on core public health

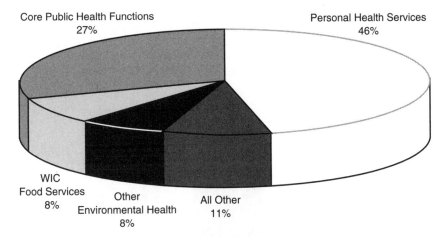

Figure 4–9 State Health, Substance Abuse, Mental Health, and Environmental Agency Expenditures for Selected Functions and Services, 1993. *Source:* Reprinted from *Measuring State Expenditures for Core Public Health Functions,* 1994, Public Health Foundation, Washington, DC.

functions in 1993[10]. Of this amount, the proportions spent on various core functions were as follows:

- protection of environment, housing, food, water, and the workplace (33 percent)
- leadership, planning, policy development, and administration (3 percent)
- public information, education, and community mobilization (12 percent)
- investigation and control of diseases, injuries, and response to natural disasters (10 percent)
- immunization, family planning, STD, and TB clinical services (5 percent)
- accountability and quality assurance (5 percent)
- laboratory services (6 percent)
- health-related data, surveillance, and outcome monitoring (17 percent)
- training and education (9 percent)

One-third of total core public health function expenditures of state health, substance abuse, mental heath, and environmental agencies (which excludes much of their personal health services expenditures) supports environmental health activities. But even this figure understates the overall environmental health and protection efforts of states. This is due to the considerable complexity and diversifica-

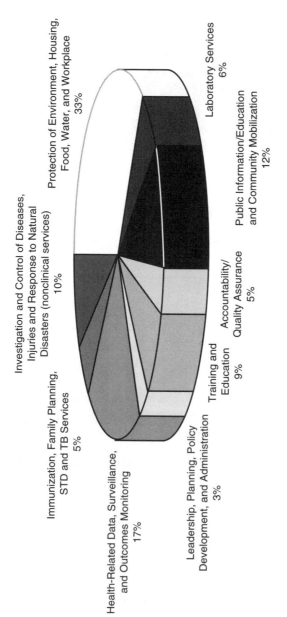

Figure 4–10 State Health, Substance Abuse, Mental Health, and Environmental Agency Expenditures by Core Public Health Function, 1993. *Source:* Reprinted from *Measuring State Expenditures for Core Public Health Functions*, 1994, Public Health Foundation, Washington, DC.

tion of environmental responsibilities at all levels of government, beginning with the federal government.

At the federal level, more than a dozen federal departments, agencies, and commissions (Transportation, Labor, Health and Human Services, Commerce, Energy, Defense, Environmental Protection Agency, Interior, Consumer Product Safety Commission, Agriculture, Nuclear Regulatory Commission, and Housing and Urban Development) have environmental health roles. State and local governments have largely replicated this web of environmental responsibility, creating a confusing and diverse system for the private sector and general public. Federal statutes have driven the organization of state responsibilities. Key federal environmental statutes include

- Clean Air Act (CAA)
- Clean Water Act (CWA)
- Comprehensive Environmental Response, Competition and Liability Act (CERCLA) and Superfund Amendments and Reauthorization Act (SARA)
- Federal Insecticide, Fungicide, and Rodenticide Act (FIFRA)
- Resource Conservation and Recovery Act (RCRA)
- Safe Drinking Water Act (SDWA)
- Toxic Substance Control Act (TCSA)
- Food, Drug, and Cosmetic Act (FDCA)
- Federal Mine Safety and Health Act (MSHA)
- Occupational Safety and Health Act (OSHA)

States, however, have responded in no consistent manner in assigning implementation of federal statutes among various state agencies. The focus of federal statutes on specific environmental media (water, air, waste) has fostered the assignment of environmental responsibilities to state agencies other than official state health agencies, as demonstrated in Table 4–2. The implications of this diversification are important for public health agencies. State health agencies are becoming less involved in environmental health programs; only a handful of states utilize their state health agency as the state's lead agency for environmental concerns. This role has shifted to state environmental agencies, although many other state agencies are also involved. Still, the primary strategy has shifted from a health-oriented approach to a regulatory approach. Despite their diminished role in environmental concerns, state health agencies continue to address a very diverse set of environmental health issues and maintain epidemiologic and quantitative risk assessment capabilities not available in other state agencies. Linking this important expertise to the workings of other state agencies is a particularly challenging task, and there are other implications of this scenario as well.

The shift toward regulatory strategies is clearly reflected in resource allocation at the state level. Nearly $6 billion is spent on environmental health and regula-

Table 4–2 Number and Type of State Agencies Responsible for Implementation of Federal Environmental Statutes

Statute	Agriculture	Environment	Health	Labor	Total
Clean Air Act	0	41	10	1	52
Clean Water Act	1	41	11	1	54
CERCLA (Superfund) Act	3	38	25	1	67
Federal Insecticide, Fungicide, and Rodenticide Act	0	41	11	2	54
Resource Conservation and Recovery Act	0	36	33	3	72
Safe Drinking Water Act	0	12	23	3	38
Toxic Substance Control Act	37	4	5	0	46
Food, Drug and Cosmetic Act	1	1	15	39	56
Federal Mine Safety and Health Act	0	0	0	12	12
Occupational Safety and Health Act	15	1	13	0	29

Source: Reprinted from Health Resources and Services Administration, *Environmental Web: Impact of Federal Statutes on State Environmental Health and Protection—Services, Structure and Funding,* 1995, Rockville, Maryland.

tion by states, with only about $1 billion of that total for environmental health (as opposed to environmental regulation) activities.[11] Public health considerations often take a back seat to regulatory concerns when budget decisions are made. In addition, the fact that many environmental health specialists are working in non-health agencies poses special problems for both their training and their practice performance.

In sum, state health agencies face many challenges related to the fragmentation of health roles and responsibilities among various state agencies. Central to these are two related challenges: (1) how to coordinate public health's core functions effectively and (2) how to leverage changes within the health system to instill greater emphasis on clinical prevention and population-based services. As the various chapters of this text suggest, these are related aims.

Local Public Health Organizations

In the overall structuring of governmental public health responsibilities, local health departments (LHDs) are where the rubber meets the road. These agencies have been established to carry out the critical public health responsibilities embodied in state laws and local ordinances and to meet other needs and expectations of their communities. But LHDs cannot be considered separately from the state network in which they operate. It is important to remember that states, through their state legislative and executive branches, establish the categories of local governmental units that can exist in that state. In this arrangement, the state and its local subunits (however defined) share responsibilities for health and other state functions. How health duties are shared in any given state is dependent on a complex set of factors that include state and local statutes, history, need, and expectations.

LHDs are established by governmental units, including counties, cities, towns, townships, and special districts, by one of two general methods. The legislative body may create an LHD through enactment of a resolution, or the citizens of the jurisdiction may create a local board and agency through a referendum. Both patterns are common. Resolution health agencies are often funded from the general funds of the jurisdiction, whereas referendum health agencies often have a specific tax levy available to them. There are advantages and disadvantages to either approach. Resolution health agencies are simpler to establish and may develop close working relationships with the local legislative bodies which create them. Referendum agencies reflect the support of the local electorate and may have access to specific tax levies that avoid the need to compete with other local government funding sources.

Counties represent the most common form of subdividing states. In general, counties are geopolitical subunits of states that carry out various state responsibilities such as law enforcement (sheriffs and states attorneys) and public health. Counties largely function as agents of the state and carry out responsibilities delegated or assigned to them. In contrast, cities are not established as agents of the state. Instead, they have considerable discretion through home rule powers to take on functions that are not prohibited to them by state law. Cities can choose to have a health department or to rely on the state or their county for public health services. City health departments often have a wider array of programs and services because of this autonomy. As described previously, the earliest public health agencies developed in large urban centers prior to the development of either state heath agencies or county-based LHDs. This status also contributes to their sense of autonomy. These considerations, as well as the increased demands and expectations to meet the needs of the medically indigent, have made many city-based, especially big city–based, LHDs qualitatively different from other LHDs.

Both cities and counties have resource and political bases. Both rely heavily on property and sales taxes to finance health and other services, and both are struggling with the limitations of these funding sources. Political concerns over increasing property taxes are the major limitation for both. Relatively few counties and cities have imposed income taxes, the form of taxation relied upon by federal and state governments. But both generally have strong political bases, although cities generally are more likely than counties to be at odds with state government on key issues.

Counties play a critical role in the public sector, the extent and importance of which is often overlooked. About three-quarters of LHDs are organized at the county level, serving a single county, a city-county, or several counties. As a result, counties provide a substantial portion of the community prevention and clinical preventive services offered in the United States. Counties provide care for 37 to 41 million persons who access LHDs and other facilities; they spend more than $30 billion of their local tax revenues on health and hospital services annually through some 4,500 sites that include hospitals, nursing homes, clinics, health departments, and mental health facilities. Counties play an explicit role in treatment and are legally responsible for indigent health care in over 30 states and pay a portion of the nonfederal share of Medicaid in about 20 states. In addition, counties purchase health care for more than 2 million employees.[12] Public health activities of LHDs are tracked by the National Association of County and City Health Officials (NACCHO). Profiles of LHDs have been completed twice between 1990 and 1995; a third update is expected to be available in 1997. Unless noted otherwise, the data on LHDs in this section are derived from NACCHO's 1992–1993 profile of local health departments.[13]

One limitation of information on LHDs is that there is neither a functional nor a clear definition of what constitutes an LHD. The most widely used definitions call for an administrative and service unit of local government, concerned with health, employing at least one full-time person, and carrying responsibility for health of a jurisdiction smaller than the state. By this definition, more than 3,200 local health agencies operate in 3,042 U.S. counties[13] (Figure 4–11).

More than half (56 percent) are single-county health agencies, and fully 80 percent operate out of a county base (single county, multicounty, or city-county; see Figure 4–12). The remaining LHDs function at the city level (7 percent), town or township level (11 percent), or other (primarily state) levels. Although the precise number is uncertain, it appears that the number has been increasing, from about 1,300 in 1947 to about 2,000 in the mid-1970s to somewhere over 3,000 in the mid-1990s. At the same time, however, there has been some progress toward consolidation and merger of small LHDs into larger units.

Local boards of health are associated with more than two-thirds of U.S. LHDs. Virtually all these boards establish local health policies, fees, ordinances, and

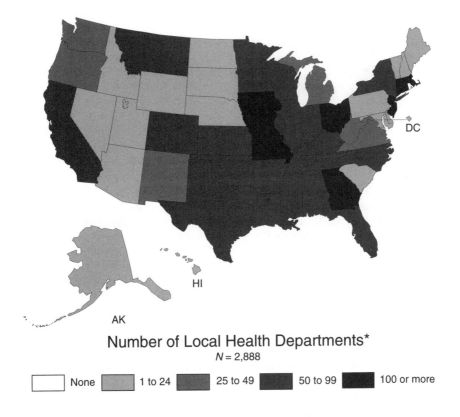

Figure 4–11 Number of Local Health Departments by State, 1992–1993. *Source:* Reprinted from National Association of County and City Health Officials and Centers for Disease Control and Prevention, *Profile of Local Health Departments, 1992-1993,* 1995, Washington, D.C.

regulations. Most also recommend and/or approve budgets, establish community health priorities, and hire the director of the local health agency.

Several reports going back more than 50 years have proposed extensive consolidation of small LHDs because of perceived lack of efficiency and coordination of services, inconsistent administration of public health laws, and inability of small LHDs to raise adequate resources to carry out their prime functions effectively. Consolidations at the county level would appear to be the most rational approach, but only limited progress has been achieved in recent decades.

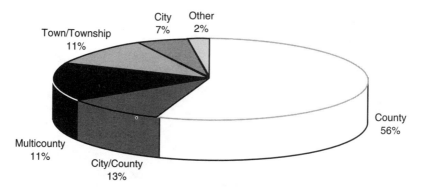

Figure 4–12 Local Health Departments by Type of Jurisdiction, 1992–1993. *Source:* Reprinted from National Association of County and City Health Officials and Centers for Disease Control and Prevention, *Profile of Local Health Departments, 1992-1993,* 1995, Washington, D.C.

States relate to their local health agencies in one of four general forms:

- centralized (the local health agencies are directly operated by the state)
- decentralized (the locals are formed and managed by local government)
- shared (the state has some control over the LHD, such as appointing the health officer or requiring a budget or plan to be submitted annually)
- mixed (both centralized and decentralized—the state serves as the local where none exists; this generally happens where local government chooses not to form a local health agency and the state must provide services)[4]

Most LHDs are relatively small organizations, as documented in Figure 4–13. Among LHDs, two-thirds (66 percent) serve populations of 50,000 or less, whereas only one in five (18 percent) serves a population of 100,000 or more. Only 4 percent of LHDs serve populations of 1 million or more residents.

Some states set qualifications for local health officers. About four-fifths of LHDs employ a full-time health officer. Health officers have a mean tenure of about eight years and a median tenure of about six years. Approximately one-half of all local health officers are physicians, about 15 percent are MD-MPHs, and less than one-fourth have graduate degrees in public health. LHDs serving larger populations are more likely to have full-time health officers than smaller LHDs.

In 1991, LHDs expended $4.6 billion derived from multiple funding sources, often including many different categorical grants from state health agencies (Figure 4–14). LHDs derived their funding from the following sources: local funds (34 percent), the state (40 percent, including federal funds passing through the state), direct federal funds (6 percent), fees and reimbursements (17 percent), and other (3 percent).

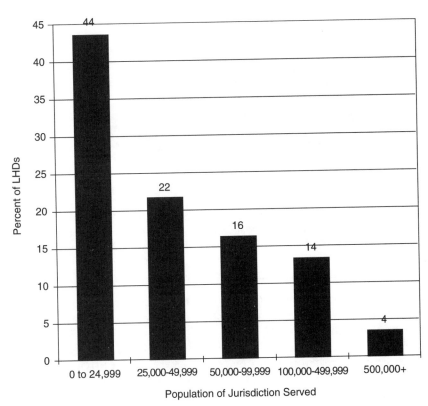

Figure 4–13 Population of Jurisdictions Served by Local Health Departments, 1992–1993. *Source:* Reprinted from National Association of County and City Health Officials and Centers for Disease Control and Prevention, *Profile of Local Health Departments, 1992-1993,* 1995, Washington, D.C.

In 1991, only one-third (34 percent) of LHDs had budgets of $1,000,000 or more, and 13 percent had budgets under $100,000. Figure 4–15 describes various levels of LHD expenditures. In addition, 16 percent had budgets of $500,000 to $999,999, 18 percent had budgets of $250,000 to $500,000, and 19 percent had budgets of $100,000 to $250,000. Expenditures and fee revenues, including Medicaid, all increase with size of population.

The number of full-time employees also increases with the size of the population served (Figure 4–16). Only 9 percent of LHDs employ 100 or more persons, 24 percent have 25 to 99 employees, 25 percent have 10 to 24 employees, 20 percent have 5 to 9 employees, and 22 percent have 4 or fewer employees. The number of employees and the number of different disciplines and professions are

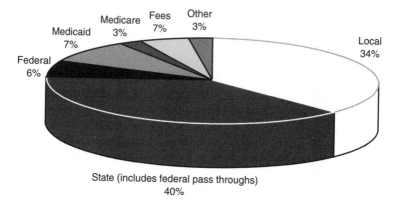

Figure 4–14 Local Health Department Funds by Source, 1992–1993. *Source:* Reprinted from National Association of County and City Health Officials and Centers for Disease Control and Prevention, *Profile of Local Health Departments, 1992-1993,* 1995, Washington, D.C.

---

related to LHD population size. Clerical staff, nurses, sanitarians, physicians, and nutritionists are the most common disciplines (in that order), and are all found in more than one-half of all LHDs.

There is considerable variety in the services provided by LHDs. Later chapters will examine in greater detail the functions and services of LHDs, but several general categories of services and their frequency among LHDs are provided below:

- 92 percent conduct surveillance for communicable diseases, but only 33 percent perform behavioral risk factor surveillance
- 59 percent enforce health codes, and 52 percent conduct priority setting
- over 70 percent carry out health education, environmental health enforcement, food/milk control programs, and 22 percent license health facilities
- over 75 percent operate sewage and water programs, but only 20 percent carry out noise, radiation, and occupational health programs
- over 80 percent have immunization, child health, and TB programs, but very few operate institutional care, emergency medical service, substance abuse, and alcohol programs

Intergovernmental Relationships

The relationships between and among the three levels of government have changed considerably over time in terms of their relative importance and influence in the health sector. This is especially true for the federal and local roles.

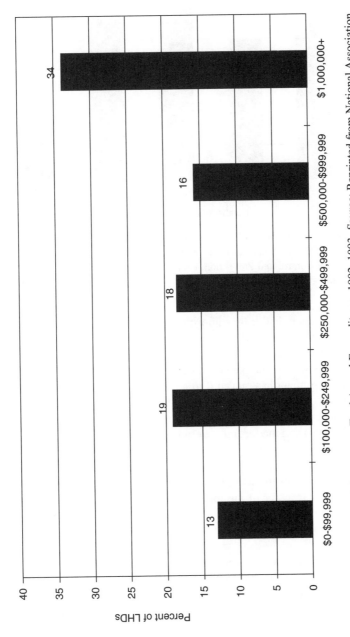

Figure 4–15 Local Health Department Total Annual Expenditures, 1992–1993. *Source:* Reprinted from National Association of County and City Health Officials and Centers for Disease Control and Prevention, *Profile of Local Health Departments, 1992–1993,* 1995, Washington, D.C.

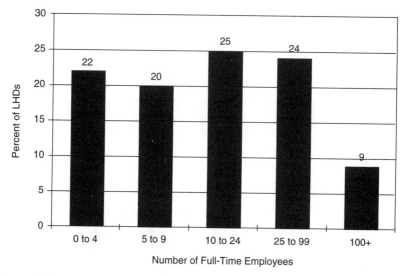

Figure 4–16 Number of Full-Time Employees of Local Health Departments, 1992–1993. *Source:* Reprinted from National Association of County and City Health Officials and Centers for Disease Control and Prevention, *Profile of Local Health Departments, 1992-1993,* 1995, Washington, D.C.

The federal government had little authority and little ability to influence health priorities and interventions until after 1930. Since that time, it has exercised its influence primarily through financial leverage on both state and local government, as well as on the private medical care system. The massive financing role of the federal government has moved it to a position of preeminence among the various levels of government in actual ability to influence health affairs. This is evident in the federal share of total national health expenditures (approximately $300 billion in 1996) and the federal government's substantial support of prevention activities.

There have been recent political initiatives to diminish the powerful federal role and return some of its influence back to the states during the 1990s. But little in the form of true transfer of authority or resource control has taken place through 1996. It is likely that the federal government's fiscal firepower will enable it to continue its current dominant role in its relationships with state and local government.

Local government has experienced the greatest and most disconcerting change in relative influence over the 20th century. Prior to 1900, local government was the primary locus of action, with the development of both population-based interventions for communicable disease control and environmental sanitation and locally provided charity care for the poor. But the massive problems related to simultaneous urbanization and povertization of the big cities spawned needs that could not be met with local resources alone. Outside the large cities, local government responses generally took the form of LHDs organized at the county level at the behest of state governments. This was viewed by states as the most efficient manner of executing their broad health powers. States often viewed local governments in general and LHDs in particular as their delivery system for important programs and services. In any event, the power of states and the growing influence of financial incentives through grant programs of both federal and state government acted to greatly influence local priorities. Priorities were being established by higher levels of government more often than through local determinations of needs. Although the demands and expectations were being directed at local governments, key decisions were being made in state capitals and Washington, D.C. Unfortunately, there are signs that local governments across the country are looking for opportunities to reduce their health roles for both clinical services and population-based interventions where they can. The perception is that the responsibility for clinical services lies with federal and state government or the private sector and that even traditional public health services can be effectively outsourced. How these actions will comport with the widespread belief that services are best provided at the local level raises serious questions regarding new roles of oversight and accountability that are not easily answered. Local governments have lost control over priorities and policies; they bridle under the regulations and grant conditions imposed by state and federal funding sources. As costs increase, grant awards fail to keep pace. However, the growing number of wholly or partly uninsured individuals continue to look to local government for services. These rising expectations and increasing costs are occurring at a time when local governments are unable and unwilling to seek additional tax revenues. The complexities of organizing and coordinating communitywide responses to modern public health problems and risks also push local government to look elsewhere for solutions.

States were slow to assume their extensive powers in the health sector but have been major players since the latter half of the 19th century. Although the growing influence of the federal government since 1930 displaced states as the most important level of government, their relative role has been strengthened since about 1980. Still, states have become secondary players in the health sector. Most states lack the means, political as well as statutory, to intervene effectively in the portion of the health sector located within their jurisdictional boundaries. This is further complicated by their tradition of imitating the federal health bureaucracy whenever possible through the decentralization of health roles and responsibilities throughout dozens of administrative agencies. Coordination of programs, policies, and priorities has become exceedingly difficult within state government.

Outside of state government, it has become virtually impossible. Still, the widely disparate circumstances from state to state make for laboratories of opportunity in which innovative approaches can be developed and evaluated.

The relationship between state and local government in public health has traditionally been tenuous and difficult. Just as the federal government views the states, states themselves have come to view local governments as just another way to get things done. As a result, states have turned to other parties, such as community-based organizations, and have begun to deal directly with them, leaving local government on the sidelines. This undervaluing of LHDs, when coupled with the declining appreciation among local governments for their health agencies, presents major challenges for the future of public health services in the United States. Instead of becoming stronger allies, these forces are working to pull apart the fabric of the national public health network.

These ever-changing and evolving relationships call into question whether the governmental public health network can be strengthened through a more centralized approach involving greater federal leadership and direction. In decentralized approaches, some states may truly be laboratories of innovation and provide better services than can be achieved through a centralized approach. There are many examples of creative policies and programs at the state level, but there are also many examples of state creativity being stifled by the federal government. The recent history of state requests for waivers of Medicaid requirements is a case in point. Many states waited two or more years for federal approval of the waivers necessary to begin innovative programs, and some of the more creative proposals were actually rejected. Still, it can be argued that state political processes are more reflective of the different political values that must be reconciled for progressive policies to develop.

CONCLUSION

The structural framework for public health in the United States includes a network of state and local public health agencies working in partnership with the federal government. This framework is precariously balanced on a legal foundation that gives primacy for health concerns to states, a financial foundation that allows the federal government to promote equality and minimum standards across 50 diverse states, and a practical foundation of local public health agencies serving as the point of contact between communities and their three-tiered government. Over time, the relative influence of these partners has shifted dramatically because of changes in needs, resources, and public expectations. The challenges to this organizational structure are many. Those related to the core functions of public health are addressed in the next chapter, and those emerging from the rapid changes within the health system are addressed in Chapters 3 and

8 of this text. In any event, it is clear that the organizational structure of public health—its form—intimately reflects the structure of government in the United States. As a result, the success or failure of these public health organizations will be determined by our success in governing ourselves.

DISCUSSION QUESTIONS AND EXERCISES

1. What is the legal basis for public health in the United States, and what impact has that had on the public health powers of federal, state, and local governments?
2. How extensive is administrative law in public health, and how does it work?
3. How can the control of nuisances work for as well as against public health agencies?
4. What is meant by a state's police power, and how is that used in public health?
5. What is the basis for the historical tension between the powers of the federal government and the powers of states in public health matters?
6. What are some of the differences in independence and autonomy between cities, counties, and special districts in the United States?
7. Describe the basic structure of a typical LHD in the United States in terms of type and size of jurisdiction served, budget, staff, and agency head.
8. What are some of the current problems related to the organization and delegation of public health responsibilities between state and local public health agencies?
9. What are the primary federal roles and responsibilities for public health in the United States?
10. Review both Exhibit 1–2 (from Chapter 1) and Exhibit 4–1. Describe how the evolution of the local and federal public health agencies described in these materials has taken parallel pathways. How has their development differed in terms of roles and responsibilities? What are the implications of these similarities and differences for public health problems that require more than one level of government?

REFERENCES

1. Centers for Disease Control and Prevention. History of CDC. *MMWR*. 1996;45:526–528.
2. *Profile of State and Local Public Health Systems, 1990*. Atlanta, Ga: Centers for Disease Control and Prevention; 1991.

3. Shonick W. *Government and Health Services: Government's Role in the Development of the U.S. Health Services 1930–1980*. New York, NY: Oxford Press; 1995.

4. Pickett G, Hanlon JJ. *Public Health Administration and Practice*. 9th ed. St. Louis, Mo: Times-Mirror Mosby; 1990.

5. *Jacobson v Massachusetts*, 197 US 11 (1905).

6. *The Fiscal Year 1997 Budget*. Washington, DC: US Dept of Health and Human Services; 1996.

7. *Healthy People 2000*. Washington, DC: US Public Health Service; 1990.

8. George Washington University Health Policy Research Center. Devolving responsibility: proposed block grants affect children's programs. *Health Policy Child Health*. 1995;2(No. 2):1–6.

9. Public Health Foundation. *Public Health Macroview*. 1995;7(1):1–8.

10. *Measuring State Expenditures for Core Public Health Functions*. Washington, DC: Public Health Foundation; 1994.

11. *Environmental Web: Impact of Federal Statutes on State Environmental Health and Protection—Services, Structure and Funding*. Rockville, Md: Health Resources and Services Administration; 1995.

12. *Fact Sheet*. Washington, DC: National Association of County and City Health Officials; 1991.

13. *Profile of Local Health Departments 1992–1993*. Washington, DC: National Association of County and City Health Officials; 1995.

CHAPTER 5

Public Health Functions and Practices

The Institute of Medicine's (IOM) landmark report in 1988[1] initiated important changes in the U.S. public health system. The report rearticulated the mission, substance, and core functions of public health and reenergized a public health community that has widely embraced these concepts over the past decade. Important and achievable national health objectives were established for the year 2000, with nearly every state formally signing onto the process. Exciting opportunities afforded by better integration of public health and medical care activities have emerged rapidly. Amid these changes, new approaches for improving results throughout the public health system have also gained momentum.

There is little doubt that these developments have had a significant impact on both the public health system and public health practice over the past decade. There is greater uncertainty, however, as to whether these developments have improved public health practice and, even more important, the results of the public health system—health outcomes. This chapter will examine the linkage between public health's functions and public health practice. Various understandings as to what has constituted public health functions since 1900 will be traced, as will efforts to measure these functions in practice. These tracings help us understand whether public health is addressing its main functions and the aspects that might need improvement. Key questions to be addressed in this chapter are:

- What are public health's core functions?
- How are these functions translated into practice?
- How well are these functions being carried out by the public health system?
- How can public health practice performance be improved?

IMPROVING PUBLIC HEALTH PRACTICE

Continuous quality management (CQM) principles have been widely adopted by corporate America, including a variety of organizations within the health system. Many of these concepts and practices have also found their way into the public sector, including public health organizations, over the past decade. One of the most useful notions of the CQM movement is that results reflect the systems that produce them. In other words, every system is designed to achieve the results it gets. This somewhat elliptical wisdom identifies a major challenge confronting efforts to improve the results of public health practice: improving health outcomes calls for improving the basic processes of public health practice. But as some additional reasoning from the CQM movement warns, in order to improve something, we must be able to control it; to control it, we must be able to understand it; and to understand it, we must be able to measure it. Public health professionals would be quick to add an even more basic need: before we measure something, we must be able to define it operationally. Defining, measuring, understanding, and controlling the processes that constitute public health practice are essential elements of the improvement agenda for the public health system.

For more than 80 years, the public health community has been grappling with this agenda, with only limited success along the way. For much of this period, an adequate conceptual framework for defining the public health system was lacking. As a result, past efforts generally focused on measuring aspects of the public health system that only indirectly or partially characterized the functions embodied in public health practice. This greatly limited opportunities for understanding, controlling, and improving public health practice and health outcomes. Nonetheless, these efforts set the stage for developments since the 1988 IOM report and the even greater opportunities that lie ahead.

MEASURING PUBLIC HEALTH PRACTICE THROUGH SERVICES

Over much of this century, the mission and purpose of public health (what it is) and its functions (how it addresses its mission) were viewed as synonymous with the provision of specific services in the community. In fact, these services were frequently characterized as public health's functions. Public health, like many other enterprises, became known more by its deeds than its intent. As a result, early efforts to describe and measure public health practice focused primarily on measuring services, both quantity and quality.

The earliest efforts to characterize and measure public health practice in the United States date back more than 80 years. One might speculate that the focus of early efforts would be primarily on counting services and resources. But surprisingly, a substantial emphasis was on measuring performance relative to expected results. Local public health practice was the target of most efforts prior to 1990, although the earliest attempt in 1914 targeted state health departments. At that time, a survey of state health agencies catalogued their various services as well as their roles in fostering the development of local health departments. This study concluded that even though public health agencies were carrying out a wide variety of programs and services, they were missing their mark. Much of what was being done through public health agencies had little effect on community health status, and there was actually much that these agencies could have been doing that would have reduced mortality and morbidity.[2] Health agencies were evaluated using a scoring system that placed greater weight on some public health activities and services than on others, allowing a basis for comparisons across agencies. Key elements of this approach were soon incorporated into local public health practice appraisal initiatives orchestrated by the American Public Health Association (APHA).

In 1921, the first report of APHA's Committee on Municipal Health Department Practice called for the systematic collection and analysis of information on local public health practice to support the development of standards of organization and achievement for local health departments (LHDs) serving the nation's largest municipalities. The committee had determined that LHDs and the communities they served would benefit from standards that would ensure a consistent level of public health services from jurisdiction to jurisdiction. The committee also sought to identify characteristics of LHD practice that fostered the most satisfactory results. An elaborate survey instrument and process were established; more than 80 big-city health departments were reviewed in the initial effort.

The need to examine public health practice outside the nation's large cities, and especially in the growing number of county-based LHDs, was quickly apparent to the committee. In 1925, the committee was reconstituted as APHA's Committee on Administrative Practice to assess more broadly the status of public health practice in the United States. The new committee developed the first version of an "Appraisal Form" designed specifically to provide a complete picture of the public health services performed in each local jurisdiction. The focus was not to be on resources (such as expenditures or personnel levels) or on mortality rates. Even in the 1920s, it was apparent that health outcomes were affected by a wide variety of social, behavioral, environmental, and service utilization factors that would confound comparisons across jurisdictions. Instead, the intent was to measure the immediate results attained from these public health services. Examples of these immediate results included

- birth and death records adequately catalogued and analyzed
- various forms of vaccinations provided for specific age groups
- health problems in school-aged children identified and treated

- tuberculosis cases hospitalized and treated
- laboratory tests performed[3]

The committee believed that tracking these immediate results was appropriate because their performance would eventually lead to improved health status in the community.

The Appraisal Form was designed for use as a self-assessment tool by local health officers to examine public health practice both inside and outside their own agencies. The intent was to capture the results of all organizations and agencies working in the community, not only those of the official governmental agencies. Successive iterations of the Appraisal Form appeared throughout the 1920s and 1930s. The process was well received by LHDs, although there were occasional concerns that quantity was being emphasized over quality.

One particularly useful feature of this process was the ability of local health officers to compare their ratings with those of other public health agencies. The basis for comparison was a numerical rating score based on aggregated points awarded across key administrative and service areas. These ratings were to serve several important purposes. They could be used to improve health programs, advocate for resources, summarize health agency activities in annual reports, and engage other health interests in the community. Agency ratings often attracted considerable public interest, resulting in both good and bad publicity for local agencies. In many communities, the local media took considerable interest in the results. Even at the national level, magazines interested in the public health field commented extensively on the results of local appraisals. More important still, local jurisdictions began to take steps to make the improvements needed. Despite the initial intent to emphasize immediate results, however, the major focus of the ratings remained on measuring the more concrete aspects of public health practice, such as staff, financial resources, and clinic sites.

In 1943, the Appraisal Form was replaced by a new, and still voluntary, instrument, the "Evaluation Schedule," which was scored centrally by the APHA Committee on Administrative Practice rather than through a self-assessment process. The new process was even more explicit in its intent to focus on results rather than activities, to relate local services to local results, to broaden the unit of analysis from the health department to the community as a whole. Information was collected on local health problems and needs, the resources available to address those needs, and the degree to which the local jurisdiction was successful in applying appropriate resources to those various needs. The scores for health agencies of varying size and type were widely disseminated so that individual LHDs could directly compare their performance in meeting community needs with that of their peers. Exhibit 5–1 illustrates some of the key performance measures found in the 1947 version of the Evaluation Schedule.[4]

Exhibit 5–1 Public Health Practice Performance Measures from 1947 Evaluation Schedule

1. Hospital beds: percentage in approved hospitals
2. Practicing physicians: population per physician
3. Practicing dentists: population per dentist
4. Water: percentage of population in communities over 2,500 served with approved water
5. Sewerage: percentage of population in communities over 2,500 served with approved sewerage systems
6. Water: percentage of rural school children served with approved water supplies
7. Excreta disposal: Percentage of rural school children served with approved means of excreta disposal
8. Food: percentage of food-handlers reached by group instruction program
9. Food: percentage of restaurants and lunch counters with satisfactory facilities
10. Milk: percentage of bottled milk pasteurized
11. Diphtheria: percentage of children under 2 years given immunizing agent
12. Smallpox: percentage of children under 2 years given immunizing agent
13. Whooping cough: percentage of children under 2 years given immunizing agent
14. Tuberculosis: newly reported cases per death, 5-year period
15. Tuberculosis: deaths per 100,000 population, 5-year period
16. Tuberculosis: percentage of cases reported by death certificate
17. Syphilis: percentage of cases reported in primary, secondary, and early latent stage
18. Syphilis: percentage of reported contacts examined
19. Maternal: puerperal deaths per 1,000 total births, 5-year rate
20. Maternal: percentage of antepartum cases under medical supervision seen before 6th month
21. Maternal: percentage of women delivered at home under postpartum nursing supervision
22. Maternal: percentage of births in hospital
23. Infant: deaths under 1 year of age per 1,000 live births, 5-year rate
24. Infant: deaths from diarrhea and enteritis under 1 year per 1,000 live births, 2-year rate
25. Infant: percentage of infants under nursing supervision before 1 month
26. Schocl: percentage of elementary children with dental work neglected
27. Accidents: deaths from motor accidents per 100,000 population, 5-year rate
28. Health department budget: cents per capita spent by health department

Source: Data from American Public Health Association, Committee on Administrative Practice, *Evaluation Schedule for Use in the Study and Appraisal of Community Health Programs,* 1947, New York, New York.

To develop a blueprint for a national network of local public health departments that would provide every American with coverage by an LHD, the Committee on Administrative Practice established a Subcommittee on Local Health Units. The subcommittee's major report (also widely known as the Emerson Report) in 1945 served as a landmark for recommendations regarding local public health practice. The Emerson Report was virtually the postwar plan for public health in the United States. The report's far-reaching recommendations called for a minimum population base of 50,000 people for each LHD and included state-by-state proposals for networks of LHDs that would cover all Americans while reducing the number of LHDs by about 50 percent.[5]

The Emerson Report gave increased prominence to six basic services believed to represent local government's public health responsibilities to its citizens: vital statistics, environmental sanitation, communicable disease control, maternal and child health services, public health education, and public health laboratory services.[5] This was in no way a new formulation of local public health services. Rather, it was essentially the same package of services that had been considered the standard of practice among LHDs for several decades and that had been assessed since the early years of the Appraisal Form. Over time, these services had become widely known as the "Basic Six" functions of LHDs; Exhibit 5–2 presents a description of these services. With the added impetus of the Emerson Report, however, they became the cornerstone for restructuring local public

---

Exhibit 5–2 Basic Six Services of Local Public Health

1. Vital statistics—collection and interpretation
2. Sanitation
3. Communicable disease control, including immunization, quarantine, and other measures such as identifying communicable disease carriers and distributing vaccines to physicians as well as doing immunizations directly
4. Maternal and child health, consisting of prenatal and postpartum care for mothers and babies and supervision of the health of schoolchildren; in some places, immunization of children was handled by the MCH program
5. Health education, including instruction in personal and family hygiene, sanitation, and nutrition, given in schools, at neighborhood health center classes, and in home visits
6. Laboratory services to physicians, sanitarians, and other interested parties

Source: Data from W. Shonick, *Government and Health Services: Government's Role in the Development of US Health Services 1930–1980,* © 1995, Oxford Press.

health agencies. Although the report's extensive recommendations never became national public policy, they served to stimulate change in many states. As for the report's most controversial recommendation, there has never been any definitive evidence that would support or refute the assertion that a minimum population base of 50,000 is needed to support a local public health agency.

The APHA Committee on Administrative Practice stimulated considerable interest in local public health practice. After about 1950 and continuing into the 1980s, there were repeated efforts to reexamine and redefine the parameters of local public health practice. This search for mission redefinition is evident in a series of APHA policy statements from 1950 to 1970.[6] In a 1950 APHA statement on LHD services and responsibilities, the Basic Six were presented as desirable minimal services, and a new list of "optimal" responsibilities was unveiled: recording and analysis of health data, health education and information, supervision and regulation, provision of direct environmental health services, administration of personal health services, and coordination of activities and services within the community. Another APHA policy statement in 1963 added seventh and eighth services to the Basic Six: operation of health facilities and areawide planning and coordination. And in 1970, APHA adopted yet another policy statement expanding on these concepts and calling for increased involvement of state and local health departments in coordinating, monitoring, and assessing the adequacy of health services in their jurisdictions. The expansion of these various characterizations of public health practice is illustrated in Exhibit 5–3.

After World War II, some important new expectations for local public health practice emerged. Lack of medical care was becoming increasingly identified as a significant impediment to promoting and improving community health. This resulted in LHDs being increasingly called upon to fill a safety-net function. This expanded direct service provision role moved LHDs into new territory beyond the boundaries of the traditional Basic Six model. There was considerable debate as to whether this new role was appropriate, as well as whether LHDs were truly emerging as leaders within their communities in integrating medical and community health services. The movement into medical care was controversial from its inception. Hanlon, in examining the future of LHDs in 1973, called for official public health agencies to withdraw from the business of providing personal health services (whether preventive or therapeutic) and instead to "concentrate upon [their] important and unique potential as community health conscience and leader"[7(p901)] in promoting the establishment of sound social policy. Despite these admonitions, direct medical care services increased among LHDs throughout the 1960s, 1970s, and 1980s as a result of new federal and state grant programs. LHDs were becoming a significant provider of safety-net medical services, joining public hospitals and community health centers in this important role.

Exhibit 5–3 Expansion of the Basic Six Public Health Services, 1920–1980

Initial "Basic Six"
 • Vital statistics
 • Sanitation
 • Communicable disease control
 • Maternal and child health
 • Health education
 • Laboratory services

"Optimal" Services in 1950s
 • Basic Six as minimal level
 • Analysis and recording of health data
 • Health education and information
 • Supervision and regulation
 • Provision of direct environmental health services
 • Administration of personal health services
 • Coordination of activities and services within the community

Added in 1960s
 • Operation of health facilities
 • Areawide planning and coordination

Added in the 1970s
 • Coordinating, monitoring, and assessing the adequacy of health services

Source: Data from W. Shonick, *Government and Health Services: Government's Role in the Development of US Health Services 1930–1980,* © 1995, Oxford Press.

GOVERNMENTAL PRESENCE IN HEALTH

Slowly evolving through these developments was a unique concept that began to shift the emphasis away from specific services and back to mission and functions. This concept, often characterized as "a governmental presence at the local level" (AGPALL),[8] emerged in the process of fashioning a "model standards" framework for communities to participate in achievement of the 1990 national health objectives (Exhibit 5–4). The basis for AGPALL is that local government acting through various means is ultimately responsible and accountable for ensuring that minimum standards are met in every community. Every locality is served by a unit of government that has responsibility for the health of that locality and population. This responsibility can be executed through an organization other than the official public health agency, but government, through its presence in

Exhibit 5–4 Governmental Presence at the Local Level

This concept is based upon a multi-faceted, multi-tiered governmental responsibility for ensuring that standards are met—a responsibility that often involves agencies in addition to the public health agency at any particular level. Regardless of the structure, every community must be served by a governmental entity charged with that responsibility, and general-purpose government must assign and coordinate responsibility for providing and assuring public health and safety services. Where services in any area covered by standards are readily available, government may also (but need not) be involved in delivery of such services. Conversely, where there is a gap in service availability, it is the responsibility of government to have, or to develop, the capacity to deliver such services. Where county and municipal responsibilities overlap, agreements on division of responsibility are necessary.

In summary, government at the local level has the responsibility for ensuring that a health problem is monitored and that services to correct that problem are available. The State government must monitor the effectiveness of local efforts to control health problems and act as a residual guarantor of services where community resources are inadequate, recognizing of course, that State resources are also limited.

Source: Reprinted from Preamble to Original Model Standards, US Public Health Service.

---

health, is responsible to see that necessary, agreed-upon services are available, accessible, acceptable, and of good quality in every community.

The leadership and change-agent nature of community public health practice are well expressed in this concept. But exercising leadership to serve the community's health is not always straightforward. The complexities of the health problems and their contributing factors call for collaborative and cooperative rather than command-and-control solutions. Other skills needed were the ability to deal with diverse interests and organizations in efforts to identify and solve community health problems and the ability to find support and build constituencies for these efforts. The exercise of the governmental presence in health role suggests that public health practice goes well beyond the provision of services. This broader view of public health's functions was soon provided in the IOM report.

PUBLIC HEALTH CORE FUNCTIONS

The picture of the state of the public health system painted in the 1988 IOM report[1] was more dismal than many had expected. After all, the infrastructure of the national public health system had grown substantially throughout the century, especially in terms of LHD coverage of the population. There was widespread acceptance that appropriate community services should include chronic disease prevention and medical care in addition to the Basic Six. And, more important, health status had never been better. Yet the AIDS epidemic had appeared, and there was no shortage of intractable health and social issues now being placed on the public health agenda. Resources to meet these challenges were greatly limited, due in part to the insatiable appetite of the medical care delivery system for every available health dollar. Somehow these forces had acted together to dissipate public appreciation and support for public health, and the IOM feared that public health would not be able to meet these challenges without a new vision that would engender the support of the public, policy makers, the media, the medical establishment, and other key stakeholders.

The vision articulated in the IOM report was founded in a broader view of public health functions than had existed in the past. Throughout earlier decades, the services provided by public health agencies had come to be viewed by many as public health's "functions." In characterizing three core functions, the IOM report suggested that the function "to serve"—whether described in terms of specific services or assurance or something else—is an inadequate characterization of the unique role of public health in our society. The "functions" of public health need not change whenever the system responds to changing conditions with a revised battery of interventions. Rather, services should be viewed as the output of carrying out public health's core functions rather than as the "functions" themselves. When the focus shifts from services to functions, greater attention can be directed to the operational aspects of those functions in ways that allow for their performance to be improved. As a result, it becomes possible to measure inputs (e.g., budgets, staff) and operational aspects of the core functions themselves (practices or processes) and to relate these to the outputs (e.g., services) provided and ultimately to health status in the community. Figure 1–3 (from Chapter 1) demonstrates this framework for describing and measuring these key aspects of the public health system.

The IOM examination[1] described public health core functions as three: (1) assessment, (2) policy development, and (3) assurance.

Assessment calls for public health agencies

> to regularly and systematically collect, assemble, analyze, and make available information on the health of the community, including statistics on health status, community health needs and epidemiologic and other studies of health problems. Not every agency is large enough to conduct these activities directly; inter-governmental and interagency cooperation is essential. Nevertheless each agency bears the responsibility for seeing that the assessment function is fulfilled. This basic function of public health cannot be delegated.[1(p7)]

Policy development calls for public health agencies

> to serve the public interest in the development of comprehensive public health policies by promoting the use of the scientific knowledge base in decision-making about public health and by leading in developing public health policy. Agencies must take a strategic approach, developed on the basis of a positive appreciation for the democratic political process.[1(p8)]

Assurance calls for public health agencies

> to assure their constituents that services necessary to achieve agreed upon goals are provided, either by encouraging actions by other entities (private or public), by requiring such action through regulation, or by providing services directly . . . . Each public health agency is to involve key policy makers and the general public in determining a set of high-priority personal and community wide health services that government will guarantee to every member of the community. This guarantee should include subsidization or direct provision of high-priority personal health services for those unable to afford them.[1(p8)]

ASSESSMENT, POLICY DEVELOPMENT, AND ASSURANCE PRACTICES IN PUBLIC HEALTH

The concepts of assessment, policy development, and assurance are unquestionably useful. Still, they remain somewhat abstract notions that require more understandable, operational descriptions. Ten public health practices (Exhibit 5–5) were developed to serve this purpose: three for the assessment function, three for the policy development function, and four for the assurance function. Developed in 1990 through a work group representing the national public health organizations, these practices provide a framework for both measuring and improving public health practice.

Assessment in Public Health

Assessing the health needs of the community is the process of systematically describing the prevailing health status and needs of a community. This practice includes the collection, assembly, and dissemination of data and information to the community. Often this can take the form of community needs assessments, which are intended to assist the community in adapting and responding to important health problems and risks. In this context, *community* refers to an aggregate of persons with common characteristics. This practice provides the structure and

Exhibit 5–5 Core Function–Related Practices

ASSESSMENT

1. Assess the health needs of the community by establishing a systematic needs assessment process that periodically provides information on the health status and health needs of the community.
2. Investigate the occurrence of adverse health effects and health hazards in the community by conducting timely investigations that identify the magnitude of health problems, duration, trends, location, and populations at risk.
3. Analyze the determinants of identified health needs in order to identify etiologic and contributing factors that place certain segments of the population at risk for adverse health outcomes.

POLICY DEVELOPMENT

4. Advocate for public health, build constituencies, and identify resources in the community by generating supportive and collaborative relationships with public and private agencies and constituency groups for the effective planning, implementation, and management of public health activities.
5. Set priorities among health needs based on the size and seriousness of the problems, the acceptability, economic feasibility and effectiveness of interventions.
6. Develop plans and policies to address priority health needs by establishing goals and objectives to be achieved through a systematic course of action that focuses on local community needs and equitable distributions of resources, and involves the participation of constituents and other related governmental agencies.

ASSURANCE

7. Manage resources and develop organizational structure through the acquisition, allocation, and control of human, physical, and fiscal resources, and maximize the operational functions of the local public health system through coordination of community agencies' efforts and avoidance of duplication of services.
8. Implement programs and other arrangements ensuring or providing direct services for priority health needs identified in the community by taking actions that translate plans and policies into services.
9. Evaluate programs and provide quality assurance in accordance with applicable professional and regulatory standards to ensure that programs are consistent with plans and policies, and provide feedback on inadequacies and changes needed to redirect programs and resources.
10. Inform and educate the public on public health issues of concern in the community, promoting an awareness about public health services availability and promoting health education initiatives that contribute to individual and collective changes in health knowledge, attitudes, and practices toward a healthier community.

Source: Adapted from Organizational Practice Definitions, 1991, CDC Public Health Practice Program Office.

---

coordination to collect, transmit, and make available information from both internal and external sources. Depending on the setting, this could include information from vital records (births, deaths, etc.), disease-reporting information (communicable disease, cancer registries, etc.), other morbidity data (hospital discharge information, school attendance, etc.), risk factor information (behavioral risk factor data, local surveys, etc.) as well as information on specific services offered by community providers and organizations participating in the assessment of health needs. These sources inform the process of identifying health needs, as well as several subsequent processes.

A second assessment practice is investigation of the occurrence of health effects and health hazards in the community. Investigation is the initiation of a systematic approach to obtaining information regarding health effects, acute and chronic disease, premature death, disability, and environmental hazards. The intent is to develop more detailed information on specific health effects in order to determine whether a problem exists and how best to prevent or control it. Investigations seek to identify problems as well as to provide the basis for intervention, strategies. Investigations vary in scope depending on mission, priorities, resources, opportunities for intervention, and perceived threat to the community. Surveillance systems, active investigations, and response protocols represent various manifestations of this practice.

A third assessment practice is the analysis of identified community health needs in order to identify their determinants and contributing factors. Analysis advances the assessment of data and information to another level by examining those factors that precede and consequently contribute to specific health problems of the community. Data are the facts concerning community health effects that provide a foundation for comparison and conceptualization of information to be used in decision making and subsequent actions. Determinants and contributing factors are etiologic factors that are linked with specific health problems in the community. Identifying determinants and contributing factors facilitates planning interventions. This process involves is the systematic examination of data to determine magnitude, temporal trends, location, affected populations, and causes. Synthesis, interpretation, and presentation of findings are made so that appropriate health policy, plans, and programs can be developed.

Policy Development for Public Health

The assessment function and its related practices provide the foundation for problem solving through the policy development function. One policy development practice involves advocating for public health, building constituencies, and identifying resources in the community. Advocating for public health is the process of generating support among constituent groups that address community health needs and issues. It includes supporting and defending collaborative relationships and policies. Community resource identification and constituency building call for establishing collaborative relationships between a public health agency and the public it serves, the government body it represents, and other health-related organizations in the community. Community resource identification serves to clarify community health status, determine what health care is currently delivered, and help determine what is necessary to solve community health problems. Advocates and supporters result from the constituency building and are critical to setting priorities, developing plans, managing resources, and implementing public health programs. This practice includes the coordination and direction of agency actions to identify where constituent support will be solicited, to identify where support and opposition coexist within the community, to design methods to promote community support and resource development, to establish and utilize networks and communication channels, and to facilitate and empower the community to act on its own behalf. Constituent support is critical to the success of public health organizations.

A second policy development practice is setting priorities among health needs. Priority setting is the process of listing, ordering, and classifying community health problems on the basis of the size and seriousness of the problem and the acceptability, economic feasibility, and effectiveness of interventions. It represents the ability to rank health needs according to their importance and to rate health needs on the basis of their magnitude, the seriousness of their consequences, and the feasibility of available prevention or control strategies. Through this practice, a decision-making structure is provided to direct and select methods and participants who will implement the priority-setting process and establish the rank order of the health needs. In this way an organization arrives at decisions that direct its efforts to plan and implement effective interventions.

A third policy development practice is actually developing the plans and policies that address priority health needs. The development of public health plans and policies is the process in which health agencies, working together with their constituents and other groups, formulate goals and objectives to meet the priority health needs of the community and identify a course of action to achieve those goals and objectives. Plans, policies, goals, and objectives reflect a systematic course of action that fosters community involvement and a sense of ownership, is equitable in the distribution of resources, is responsive to community health needs, ensures healthy conditions, and fulfills the mission of the organization. Goals and objectives are the milestones and steps to be followed. A *goal* defines a desired change in the status of a priority health need, and the *objectives* state what will be accomplished in changing the status of a priority health need. The course of action specifies how the goals and objectives will be achieved, what resources will be required, and how responsibility for achieving objectives will be assigned. This practice serves to establish strategic, managerial, and programmatic direction and links these three different levels in accomplishment of the agency's mission. This practice also provides coordination and control over the preparation, review, approval, integration, and implementation of strategic, managerial, and programmatic direction for a public health agency. In addition, it directs the practices of constituency development, managing resources, and implementing public health programs.

Assurance of the Public's Health

While assessment and policy development set interventions into motion, the assurance function keeps them on track. One assurance practice is managing resources and developing organizational structure. This is the process of acquiring, allocating, and controlling resources, both human and fiscal. By doing so, a public health agency is able to improve its leadership, work force, and operational systems in order to respond to both current and future community health needs. *Managing resources* refers to the ability of health agencies to acquire, allocate, and control their human, organizational, informational, and fiscal resources of people, facilities, and capital and to organize those resources to improve and respond to current and projected health conditions of the community. This involves working with other community organizations to avoid unnecessary duplication and to plan how best to meet community priority health needs. Public health systems must have a clear organizational focal point for public health responsibility. The organizational focal point establishes a balance between state and local level responsibilities, provides for the granting of authority and the delegation of responsibility, establishes standards for public health functions, identifies services to be offered, and defines how services are to be financed. *Developing organizational structure* refers to the ability of health agencies to divide their labor into distinct tasks and achieve coordination among them. This practice links agency direction as established in plan and policy development to the implementation of programs and ties decision-making activities of resource acquisition and utilization and the delegation of organizational responsibility to the accomplishment of public health objectives. Development of organizational structure relies on principles of sound financial management, organizational management, human resources development, and organizational development.

A second assurance practice is implementing programs. This refers to the process of taking action on plans and policies to accomplish the community's public health objectives. Implementation requires that agencies gain acceptance of health programs, assign tasks, acquire resources, manage the programs, and apply interventions that promote health conditions within the community. It seeks to utilize the delivery of services and practices to accomplish a community's public health objectives. This practice uses internal and external resources to translate policy and plans into services.

A third assurance practice is evaluating programs and providing quality assurance. This is the process of continuous inquiry to determine the efficiency and effectiveness of organizational management and program services for the purpose of providing feedback to the organization so that corrections can be made to improve activities and outcomes. Evaluation is often classified as process or outcome. *Process evaluation* is intended to determine the extent to which a program is executed so as to reach a desired goal. *Outcome evaluation* considers the extent to which goals and objectives of a program are reached. Effective quality assurance results in community confidence in public health programs. Quality assurance activities ensure that all program efforts are consistent with recognized policies and procedures of the agency and the needs of the community. The process of continuous inquiry includes the development of objectives about what is expected from evaluation; defines the information needed for the evaluation and the standards to be used for comparison; measures and collects the needed information; analyzes the collected data; reports the results of the analysis, including conclusions as to the success or failure of the program; and makes recommendations as to whether any changes are needed. Performance of this practice provides coordination and direction within the agency to examine, monitor, and improve management and system services, the quality of patient/client and community service, and impact and outcome of services delivered. It directs the establishment of standards for operation and service performance, selects evaluation and monitoring methods, and employs those methods in analysis and interpretation of findings and recommendations for improvement of system performance.

A final assurance-related practice is informing and educating the public. Informing and educating is the process of influencing behaviors by increasing knowledge, shaping attitudes, and developing skills and health practices through informed individual and collective choice and support systems within the community. The community must be informed as to the availability of public health services and provided information that gains the attention of individuals, high-risk groups, and constituents concerning public health issues. Individual behavior and social norms are important factors for some diseases. Many behavioral factors associated with unnecessary loss of health or life are modifiable. Health education can help develop beliefs, attitudes, and skills conducive to good individual and community health. Performance of this practice provides coordination and direction in identifying the role of information and education in addressing community health risks, problems, or issues; directing communications to constituent groups; managing information and education interventions; and utilizing community resources to support information and education of the public. It relies on community outreach public relations, information dissemination, and community and patient education principles to increase awareness, shape attitudes, and develop skills and health practices. Through this practice, constituency development and program implementation are supported.

POST–IOM REPORT INITIATIVES

In addition to this formulation of 10 public health practices, other important initiatives followed the IOM report and served to facilitate operationalization of the core function framework. Most of these focused on the assessment and policy development functions. New national health objectives were established for the year 2000, based on a decade's experience with the year 1990 national health objectives. Broader participation in their design and better tools for their implementation in community settings distinguished the year 2000 objectives from the earlier effort. An updated version of the Model Standards document[8] was created with the specific aim of linking it with the year 2000 health objectives. Several community needs assessment instruments—all using the same basic steps and fostering community participation—were promoted by various health organizations. The national public health organizations developed understandable guidance to facilitate the use of these tools as a means of operationalizing public health's core functions within the community.

In addition, for the first time ever, a national health objective for coverage of the population by an effective local public health presence was developed. Objective 8.14 called for 90 percent of the population, by the year 2000, to be served by an LHD that was effectively carrying out public health's core functions in that community. The Public Health Practice Program Office of the Centers for Disease Control and Prevention (CDC) stimulated several research activities related to this objective. These projects sought to design and test public health practice performance measures related to the core functions of public health both for measuring progress toward Objective 8.14 and for assessing the operational aspects of the core functions (practices). A framework using the 10 public health practices (described in the previous section) as operational definitions for the three core functions was used to evaluate local public health performance; assess LHD practice performance patterns in six states, as well as in a national sample of LHDs to benchmark progress toward Objective 8.14; and relate LHD personnel expenditures to core functions.

The findings from these various studies provide little comfort to the public health community as to the adequacy of the public health system in addressing its core functions. One study[9] conducted in 1993 found that 89 percent of the staff hours of one large LHD were expended in carrying out practices related to the assurance function. Nine percent of the total manpower hours were devoted to the assessment function, and only two percent were devoted to policy development. When the various practices and functions were related to specific programs and services, primary care and communicable disease programs consumed three-fourths of the LHD's resources.

In separate studies that used panels of similar measures of core function–related practice performance, mean LHD performance scores (the percentage of practice performance measures fulfilled) were examined. In one study[10] of a national sample of 208 LHDs in 1993, the mean performance score on a panel of 10 measures was 50 percent. In another 1993 study of 370 LHDs in six states,[11] the mean performance score was 56 percent for a panel of 26 items. The use of this same 26-item panel on a group of 14 LHDs that had been longitudinally followed since the 1970s produced similar performance patterns.[12] These findings are consistent with results from the 1992–1993 profile of LHDs conducted by the National Association of County and City Health Officials (NACCHO), which found similar levels of performance, using questions that were comparable to many of those used in these various studies.[13]

In 1995, a panel of 20 core function–related public health practice performance measures was developed from measures previously used by CDC-supported research projects (Exhibit 5–6). When these measures were applied to a national sample of LHDs, mean performance scores were 55 to 58 percent for practice measures associated with each of the three core functions and overall (Figure 5–1). Larger LHDs (serving populations of 50,000 or more) reported higher mean performance scores than smaller LHDs. The group of LHDs that were not organized at the city or county level but were linked with town, township, and other health districts scored substantially lower than all other LHD types (Figure 5–2).

When the populations served by LHDs of various type and size are considered, these studies indicate that less than 40 percent of the U.S. population in the early and mid-1990s was served by an LHD effectively addressing public health's core functions. To reach the national goal for the year 2000 (90 percent of the population), considerable capacity-building and practice improvement efforts will be necessary. During this same period, however, several important capacity-building strategies and tools were being developed and implemented.

Assessment Protocol for Excellence in Public Health (APEXPH)

One of the most important of these new initiatives was the development of the Assessment Protocol for Excellence in Public Health (APEXPH) by the NACCHO in collaboration with other national public health organizations.[14] APEXPH provided a tool for organizational self-assessment and improvement for LHDs, as well as a simple and effective community needs assessment process. Since its appearance in 1990, APEXPH has been well accepted among LHDs, with nearly one-half of all LHDs having utilized it as of mid-1996. Use of the APEXPH framework has been credited with significant change in LHD practice patterns in Illinois, Washington State, and elsewhere.

APEXPH provides a means for LHDs to enhance their organizational capacity and strengthen their leadership role in their community. APEXPH guides health

Exhibit 5–6 Core Function–Related Practice Performance Measures, 1995

ASSESSMENT

1. For the jurisdiction served by your local health department, is there a community needs assessment process that systematically describes the prevailing health status in the community?
2. In the past three years in your jurisdiction, has the local public health agency surveyed the population for behavioral risk factors?
3. For the jurisdiction served by your local health agency, are timely investigations of adverse health events, including communicable disease outbreaks and environmental health hazards, conducted on an ongoing basis?
4. Are the necessary laboratory services available to the local public health agency to support investigations of adverse health events and meet routine diagnostic and surveillance needs?
5. For the jurisdiction served by your local public health agency, has an analysis been completed of the determinants and contributing factors of priority health needs, adequacy of existing health resources, and the population groups most impacted?
6. In the past three years in your jurisdiction, has the local public health agency conducted an analysis of age-specific participation in preventive and screening services?

POLICY DEVELOPMENT

7. For the jurisdiction served by your local public health agency, is there a network of support and communication relationships that includes health-related organizations, the media, and the general public?
8. In the past year in your jurisdiction, has there been a formal attempt by the local public health agency at informing elected officials about the potential public health impact of decisions under their consideration?
9. For the jurisdiction served by your local public health agency, has there been a prioritization of the community health needs that have been identified from a community needs assessment?
10. In the past three years in your jurisdiction, has the local public health agency implemented community health initiatives consistent with established priorities?
11. For the jurisdiction served by your local public health agency, has a community health action plan been developed with community participation to address priority community health needs?
12. During the past three years in your jurisdiction, has the local public health agency developed plans to allocate resources in a manner consistent with the community health action plan?

---

continues

Exhibit 5–6 continued

ASSURANCE

13. For the jurisdiction served by your local public health agency, have resources been deployed as necessary to address the priority health needs identified in the community health needs assessment?

14. In the past three years in your jurisdiction, has the local public health agency conducted an organizational self-assessment?

15. For the jurisdiction served by your local public health agency, are age-specific priority health needs effectively addressed through the provision of or linkage to appropriate services?

16. In the past three years in your jurisdiction, has there been an instance in which the local public health agency has failed to implement a mandated program or service?

17. For the jurisdiction served by your local public health agency, have there been regular evaluations of the effect that public health services have on community health status?

18. In the past three years in your jurisdiction, has the local public health agency used professionally recognized process and outcome measures to monitor programs and to redirect resources as appropriate?

19. For the jurisdiction served by your local public health agency, is the public regularly provided with information about current health status, health care needs, positive health behaviors, and health care policy issues?

20. In the past year in your jurisdiction, has the local public health agency provided reports to the media on a regular basis?

---

department officials in two principal areas of activity: (1) assessing and improving the organizational capacity of the agency and (2) working with the local community to improve the health status of its citizens. There are three principal parts to this process:

1. *Organizational Capacity Assessment*—a self-assessment of indicators that focus on authority to operate, community relations, community health assessment, public policy development, assurance of public health services, financial management, personnel management, and program management, resulting in an organizational action plan that sets priorities for correcting perceived weaknesses. Exhibits 5–7 and 5–8 present the steps associated with the organizational self-assessment and examples of capacity indicators that can be used in this process.

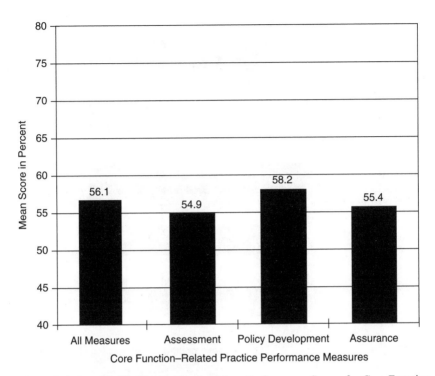

Figure 5–1 Local Public Health Practice Mean Performance Scores for Core Function–Related Performance Measures by Core Function ($N = 298$), 1995.

2. *Community Process*—guides formation of a community advisory committee that identifies health problems requiring priority attention and then sets health status goals and programmatic objectives. The aim is to mobilize community resources in pursuit of locally relevant public health objectives consistent with the Healthy People 2000 objectives. Exhibit 5–9 outlines the basic steps involved in the community needs assessment process included in APEXPH.

3. *Completing the Cycle*—ensures that the activities from the organizational and community processes are effectively carried out and that they accomplish the desired results through policy development, assurance, monitoring, and evaluation activities.

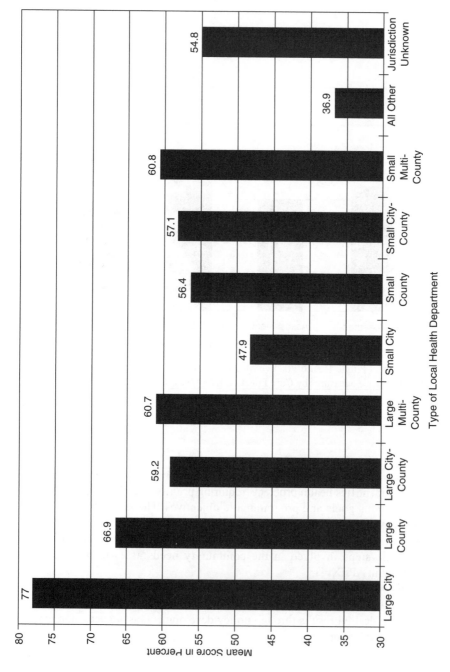

Figure 5–2 Local Public Health Practice Mean Performance Scores for Core Function–Related Performance Measures by Type of Local Health Department (*N* = 298), 1995. *Source:*

Exhibit 5–7 Assessment Protocol for Excellence in Public Health, Part I: Organizational Capacity Assessment Steps

Step 1   Prepare for Organizational Capacity Assessment
This step calls for preparing the organization for a self-assessment, including the agency's board, its leadership and employees. Ideally, all levels of the organization participate in teams after orientation and training in the process is provided. Information needed for the organizational self-assessment is identified and assembled.

Step 2   Score Indicators for Importance and Current Status
The teams determine which indicators will be reviewed. For each indicator, an assessment is made of its importance (high, medium, low, not relevant) for the agency's mission and role and its current status (fully met, partially met, not met, not relevant).

Step 3   Identify Strengths and Weaknesses
Based on the assessments of importance and status, indicators are sorted into those considered to be strengths or weaknesses as well as those in between. Generally, those indicators determined to be important and fully met are considered strengths while those considered to be important and not met are considered weaknesses. Debate and negotiation among those not found to be clearly strengths or weaknesses will determine how these are handled.

Step 4   Analyze and Report Strengths
Strengths are not to be overlooked or taken for granted in this process. Factors that contribute to strengths should be identified so that these can be used to address weaknesses. Strengths should also be identified so that they can be reported to boards, the media, and the public to enhance community support for the agency.

Step 5   Analyze Weaknesses
Weaknesses reflect problems that interfere with the agency's ability to effectively carry out its mission and role in the community. Factors that contribute to identified weaknesses should be explored, as these often contribute to weaknesses across several categories. Identification of these factors will serve to focus the strategies and activities of the capacity building plan.

Step 6   Rank Problems in Order of Priority
While many problems will be identified, limitations on resources will require that the most important ones be identified and targeted for resolution in the capacity building plan. Generally, only a limited number of priorities should be targeted; often this number is from 3 to 6. Various processes for coming to agreement around these priorities can be used.

continues

Exhibit 5–7 continued

Step 7   Develop and Implement Action Plans
          After selection and analysis of priorities to identify the factors that con-
          tribute to their importance, strategies and specific tasks to correct those
          problems are developed. Responsibility for accomplishing key tasks and
          time lines are clearly established in these action plans.

Step 8   Institutionalize the Assessment Process
          Organizational self-assessment is not a one-shot process; it is best viewed
          as a continuous improvement activity that will help even the best func-
          tioning organizations improve their performance. Using the evaluation
          strategy from the initial capacity building plan as a base, the process
          should be institutionalized within the agency and continue on an ongoing
          basis.

Source: Reprinted from National Association of County and City Health Officials and
Centers for Disease Control and Prevention, *An Assessment Protocol for Excellence in Public
Health,* 1991, Washington, D.C.

Planned Approach to Community Health

The Planned Approach to Community Health (PATCH) is a process for community organization and community needs assessment that emphasizes community mobilization and constituency building. PATCH focuses on orienting and
training community leaders and other community participants in all aspects of
the community needs assessment process and includes excellent documentation
and resource materials. While originally developed by CDC to focus on chronic
health conditions calling for health promotion and disease prevention interventions, PATCH is flexible enough to be used as in either broad or narrow needs
assessment activities.

Model Standards/Healthy Communities 2000

Another tool for addressing public health core functions and their associated
practices is the most recent edition of Model Standards, *Healthy Communities
2000.*[8] The steps outlined for implementation of the Model Standards process in
the community illustrates the linkages among various core function–related tools,
including the organizational self-assessment component of APEXPH; community needs assessment instruments available through APEXXPH, PATCH,
Healthy Cities, and other sources; Model Standards/Healthy Communities 2000;
and the national health objectives included in *Healthy People 2000.* The 11 steps
for implementing Model Standards[15] represent, in effect, a pathway for effectively

Exhibit 5–8 Assessment Protocol for Excellence in Public Health, Part I: Organizational Capacity Assessment; Examples of Indicators

I. Authority To Operate
- The health department has clear authority to act as a law enforcement office for public health problems.
- The health department has authority to develop and introduce local regulations when needed.
- The health department has the authority to delegate public health duties to municipalities within its jurisdiction.
- At least once every two years (biennially), the health department reviews its joint powers agreements, memoranda of understanding, and other agreements with units of government within its jurisdiction or in neighboring jurisdictions to identify problems, propose solutions, and look for areas for further development.
- At least biennially, the health department reviews and discusses its formal relationship with the state health authority to identify problems, propose solutions, and look for areas for further development.
- The health department is represented on a state public health committee or other body advisory to the state health authority.
- The health department has legal counsel sufficient to provide advice as needed on administrative practices; department powers, duties, policies and procedures; relevant laws and ordinances; contracts; and other legal matters.
- The health department maintains a current file or library of all relevant federal, state, and local statutes and regulations.

II. Community Relations
- The health department has a system that actively involves individuals and groups affected by its planning of services, its methods of service delivery, and its service results.
- At least every four years, the health department actively involves all key individuals and organizations within its jurisdiction that might be engaged in public health–related activities to determine their goals and their perceptions of their roles, authorities, and needs, including units of government, the general public, interest groups, health service providers, educational institutions, and other potential stakeholders.
- The health department has a documented plan for informing the public about the current health status of the community.
- The local media looks to the health department as a source of information about the health of the community.
- The health department maintains files documenting relations and communications with other organizations related to the public health.

continues

Exhibit 5–8 continued

- The health department maintains current information on the needs of health-related organizations.

III. Community Health Assessment
- The health department has a clear and concrete mission statement that all staff are capable of stating and explaining in relation to their duties.
- The health department has established a process for community health assessment and the development of a community health plan.
- At least every four years, the health department conducts a public review and discussion of its mission and role, its public health goals, its accomplishments, past activities, and plans in relation to community health.
- The health department maintains a database of existing health resources and community health status.
- The health department receives reports of communicable disease in the community on a daily basis.
- The health department has qualified professionals to review and analyze reported mortality and morbidity data.
- The health department has joint powers agreements with other units of government in neighboring jurisdictions or within its jurisdiction for the shared funding and operation of enforcement and service delivery programs where economies of scale and efficiency are possible.
- The health department participates in joint efforts to pool training needs with neighboring health agencies.
- The health department uses health data, including vital records, in its community health planning process.
- The health department has a standard, ongoing process to examine internal and external trends, to make forecasts, and to systematically develop long-term plans for its future.
- The health department monitors program impact indicators on a regular basis.
- The health department has community health objectives that are time limited and measurable.

IV. Public Policy Development
- The health department director assures and facilitates the completion of a community health assessment process.
- The health department and the community identify and set priorities for addressing health problems based on results of the community health assessment.
- The policy board obtains information from an established citizens' advisory group and from the health department regarding public policy issues affecting the public health.

continues

Exhibit 5–8 continued

> • The policy board establishes priorities and formulates strategies for action on high priority policy issues.
> • The local governmental unit collaborates with the policy board and the health department director in developing public policy that may impact public health.
>
> V. Assurance of Public Health Services
> • The policy board uses its authority to assure necessary services to reach agreed upon goals for its constituents.
> • The health department assures or provides direct services for priority health needs identified in the community health assessment.
> • The health department assures and implements legislative mandates and statutory responsibilities.
> • The health department monitors the availability of personal health services and assures an appropriate level of those health services in the community.
> • The health department identifies barriers to access to health care and develops plans to minimize them.
> • The policy board and health department director assure health protection and health promotion services utilizing community-based organizations.
>
> VI. Financial Management
> • A department budget is adopted annually by the policy board.
> • The budget accurately reflects the priorities established in the organizational action plan.
> • The health department has a predictable source of funds to allow the development and implementation of a long-range plan (minimum, 5 years).
> • The health department has a diverse funding base to lessen disruption of services caused by withdrawal of funds from any one source.
> • Expenditures follow the budget and financial plan of the health department.
> • A written standard budget development and review procedure is authorized by the policy board and is available to staff and the public.
>
> VII. Personnel Management
> • A written job description, including minimum qualifications, exists for each position in the health department.
> • Written personnel policies and procedures are developed and revised with staff input.
> • Written staff performance appraisals are conducted by supervisors with employees at established intervals.
> • Staffing patterns and levels match policy board authorized programs and services and current levels of demand for services.

continues

Exhibit 5–8 continued

- A periodic personnel administration audit is performed by a department team to determine if authorized personnel policies and procedures are being followed.
- There is a standard, written description of the health department personnel management system that is available to policy board members, department staff, and the public.

VIII. Program Management
- Operating programs are authorized by the policy board.
- The health department maintains emergency contact staff (on site or on call) to respond to local public health emergencies.
- The health department collects and regularly analyzes information describing program administration and funding, program activities, workload, client characteristics, and service costs needed to evaluate the process of program activities.
- The health department collects and regularly analyzes information that is needed to evaluate the impact and outcome of program activities on risk factors and health status.
- The health department has a management information system that allows the analysis of administrative, demographic, epidemiological, and utilization data to provide information for planning, administration, and evaluation.

IX. Policy Board Procedures
- Health department policy board members attend policy and committee meetings.
- New policy board members routinely receive orientation through an established and documented orientation program of the health department.
- Policy board meetings are scheduled on a regular basis, with sufficient frequency to ensure board control and direction of the health department.
- Policy board meetings deal primarily with policy determination, review of plans, making board authorizations, and evaluating the work of the health department.
- There are written board and administrative policies consistent with the mission statement.

Source: Reprinted from National Association of County and City Health Officials and Centers for Disease Control and Prevention, *An Assessment Protocol for Excellence in Public Health,* 1991, Washington, D.C.

Exhibit 5–9 Assessment Protocol for Excellence in Public Health, Part II: Community Process Steps

Step 1 Prepare for the Community Process
There are several important consideration before an agency should attempt to organize its community to identify and address critical health problems. Preparing the organization calls for orientation and training of staff, as well as enlisting the support and participation of agency boards, government leaders, and others. It is critical that an organizational self-assessment take place before a community needs assessment is attempted. If this is not possible, at the very least, the portion devoted to the capacity to carry out a community needs assessment should be completed.

Step 2 Collect and Analyze Health Data
While the community needs assessment will not be entirely driven by data, it is essential that a core of important information on community health status, needs, and resources be available for the process. This would ordinarily include mortality data from vital records as well as morbidity information from hospital discharges, disease reporting systems, school authorities, and employers, and behavioral risk factor information if available. Information on community resources is also vital.

Step 3 Form a Community Health Committee
The most critical step is the formulation of a group representative of the community stakeholders and interests to guide the process and its key decisions as to priorities and strategies. Various forms for community health committees are possible, as are the mechanics for how they complete their important tasks. The most important element is that this committee be the forum for key decisions.

Step 4 Identify Community Health Problems
Through the community health committee, information derived from data and indicators as well as insights and inputs not supported by hard data from community participants are blended to develop listings of problems to be considered by the committee.

Step 5 Prioritize Community Health Problems
After problems are identified, a limited number (generally 3–6) are selected as priorities by the community health committee. These become the focus of more intensive analysis to be directed by the committee.

Step 6 Analyze Community Health Problems
Risk factors and both direct and indirect contributing factors are identified for each priority health problem. These will serve as the basis for intervention strategies directed toward those contributing factors that contribute most heavily to the unacceptable levels of that problem in the community.

continues

Exhibit 5–9 continued

Step 7 Inventory Community Health Resources

For each priority health problem, resources available within and to the community that might be utilized to address the problem are identified and catalogued. Gaps in services are examined, and efforts are engendered to enlist these resources in expanded interventions.

Step 8 Develop a Community Health Plan

The final step calls for the completion of a community health plan with outcome objectives for each priority health problem and intervention strategies that target the most important contributing factors for each. As in any plan, tasks and time lines are clearly identified, and an evaluation strategy is put into place to track progress over time and make adjustments as needed.

Source: Reprinted from National Association of County and City Health Officials and Centers for Disease Control and Prevention, *An Assessment Protocol for Excellence in Public Health,* 1991, Washington, D.C.

executing the governmental presence in health responsibility (Exhibit 5–10 and Figure 5–3). These steps are generally described below, although Steps 8 through 11 will be examined in greater depth in Chapter 7.

1. *Assessment of Agency Role:* Communities are organized and structured differently. As a result, the specific roles of local public health agencies

Exhibit 5–10 Eleven Steps for Implementing the Model Standards

1. Assess and determine the role of one's health agency.
2. Assess the lead health agency's organizational capacity.
3. Develop an agency plan to build the necessary organizational capacity.
4. Assess the community's organizational and power structures.
5. Organize the community to build a stronger constituency for public health, and establish a partnership for public health.
6. Assess health needs and available community resources.
7. Determine local priorities.
8. Select outcome and process objectives that are compatible with local priorities and the Healthy People 2000 objectives.
9. Develop community-wide intervention strategies
10. Develop and implement a plan of action.
11. Monitor and evaluate the effort on an ongoing basis.

Source: Data from American Public Health Association and Centers for Disease Control and Prevention, *The Guide to Implementing Model Standards,* 1993, Washington, D.C.

Targeting the Year 2000

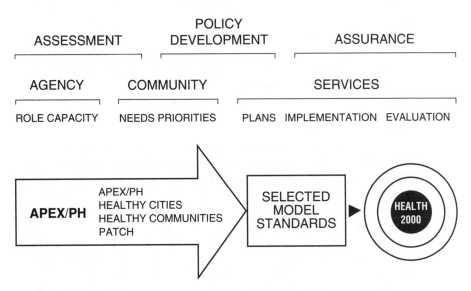

Figure 5–3 Targeting the Year 2000: Linkages among Core Functions and Available Tools for Community Public Health Practice. *Source:* Reprinted from W.W. Dyal, 1991, CDC Public Health Practice Program Office.

will vary from community to community. An essential first step is for an agency to reexamine its purpose and mission and develop a long-range vision through strategic planning involving its internal and external constituencies. The resulting mission statement and long-range vision serve to guide the organization (leadership and board as well as employees) and define it for its community partners. This critical step must be taken before the remaining steps can be successfully completed. Part I of APEXPH and other strategic planning processes are useful in accomplishing this task.

2. *Assessment of Agency Capacity:* After an agency's mission and role have been defined, it is necessary to determine its capacity to carry out its role in the community. This calls for the examination of the major operational elements of the agency, including its structure and performance for specific tasks. This type of organizational self-assessment is best carried out through the participation of all levels of an agency. Part I of APEXPH includes hundreds of indicators that can be used in this capacity assess-

ment. These indicators can be modified or eliminated if deemed not appropriate, and additional indicators can also be used. This step serves to identify strengths and weaknesses of the agency relative to its mission and role.

3. *Development of Agency Capacity-Building Plan:* The development of an agency capacity-building plan incorporates the agency's strengths and prioritizes the agency's weaknesses so that the most important are addressed first. As in any plan, specific objectives for addressing these weaknesses are developed, responsibilities are assigned, and a process for tracking progress over time is established. Again, APEXPH Part I is an invaluable tool for accomplishing this task.

4. *Assessment of Community Organizational Structure:* Having looked internally at the agency's capacity and ability to exercise its leadership role for identifying and addressing priority health needs in the community, the agency must assess the key stakeholders and necessary participants for a communitywide needs assessment and intervention initiative. This is often a long-term and continuous process in which the relationship of the health agency to community providers of health-related services, community organizations, community leaders, interest groups, the media, and the general public is assessed. This step determines how and under whose auspices community health planning will take place within the community. Both APEXPH and PATCH processes support the successful completion of this step.

5. *Organization of Community:* This step calls for organizing the community so that it represents a strong constituency for public health and will participate collaboratively in partnership with the health agency. Specific strategies and activities will vary from community to community but will generally include hearings, discussion forums, meetings, and collaborative planning sessions. The specific roles and authority of community participants should be clarified so that the process is not perceived as one driven largely by the health agency and so-called experts. Both APEXPH and PATCH are useful for completing this step.

6. *Assessment of Community Health Needs:* The actual process of identifying health problems of importance to the community is one that must titrate information derived from data sets with information derived from the community's perceptions of which problems are most important. Often community readiness to mitigate specific problems greatly increases the chances for success as well as support for the overall process within the community. In addition to generating information on possible health problems, this step gathers information on resources available within the community. This step serves to provide the information necessary for the com-

munity's most important health problems to be identified. The community needs assessment tools provided in both APEXPH and PATCH can be used to accomplish this step.

7. *Determination of Local Priorities and Community Health Resources:* After important health problems are identified, decisions must be made as to which are most important for community action. This step requires broad participation from community participants in the process so that priorities will be viewed as community rather than agency-specific priorities. Debate and negotiation are essential for this step, and there are many approaches to coming to consensus around specific priorities. Both APEXPH and PATCH support this step as well.

8. *Selection of Outcome Objectives:* After priorities are determined, the process must establish a target level to be achieved for each priority problem. For this step, the Model Standards process is especially useful in linking community priorities to national health objectives and establishing targets that are appropriate for the current status and improvement possible from a community intervention. This step also calls for negotiation within the community since deployment and reallocation of resources may be needed to achieve the target outcomes that are agreed upon. In addition to Model Standards, both APEXPH and PATCH can be useful in accomplishing this step.

9. *Development of Intervention Strategies:* This step is one of determining strategies and methods of achieving the outcome objectives established for each priority health problem. This can be quite difficult and at times contentious. For some problems, there may be few, or even no, effective interventions. For others, there may be widely divergent strategies available, some of which may be deemed unacceptable or not feasible. After agreement is reached as to strategies and methods, responsibilities for implementing and evaluating interventions will be assigned. With community-wide interventions, overall coordination of efforts may also need to be addressed as part of the intervention strategy.

10. *Implementation of Intervention Strategies:* After the establishment of goals, objectives, strategies, and methods, specific plans of action for the intervention are developed and specific tasks and work plans developed. Clear delineation of responsibilities and timelines are essential for this step.

11. *Continuous Monitoring and Evaluation of Effort:* The evaluation strategy for the intervention will track performance related to outcome objectives as well as process objectives and activity measures over time. If activity measures and process objectives are being accomplished, there should be progress toward achieving the desired outcome objectives. If this does not

occur, the selected intervention strategy needs to be reconsidered and revised.

Since 1990, LHDs have moved to utilize APEXPH, PATCH, Model Standards, and other tools for community public health practice (such as Healthy Cities and Healthy Communities, two similar community needs assessment processes).[13] Figure 5–4 identifies the status of the use of these tools by LHDs as of 1992 to 1993.

Capacity Building in Washington State

Extensive efforts at statewide capacity building have taken place in several states since 1990. The work of Washington State's Public Health Improvement Plan is a particularly noteworthy effort that has embraced the concepts embodied in the IOM core functions but has adapted these into comprehensive performance measures for local public health practice. The practice measures include both performance standards and performance indicators for four categories of public health capacities necessary to perform the functions of public health effectively (Table 5–1). Essential functions include assessment and policy development consistent with the framework in the IOM report, with the assurance function partitioned into three functions: administration, prevention, and access and quality. The key capacities for each function address questions of performance and improvement:[16]

- *Structure and Policies:* Does the public health jurisdiction have clear lines of authority, the organizational structure, and the procedures to carry out each function effectively and to improve its performance?
- *Skills and Resources:* Does the public health jurisdiction have the work force, financing, and equipment required to carry out each function effectively and to improve its performance?
- *Information and Communication:* Does the public health jurisdiction have the capability to receive, process, and communicate information, data, and reports to carry out each core function effectively and improve its performance?
- *Community Involvement:* Does the public health jurisdiction have processes in place to collaborate with the public it serves, the officials it represents, and the health providers with which it practices to carry out each core function effectively and improve its performance?

The statewide initiative to improve public health practice in Washington State resulted from the strong collaboration of state and local public health organizations, the school of public health and other academic institutions, and private-sector and community partners. The effort was stimulated by the inclusion of its framework

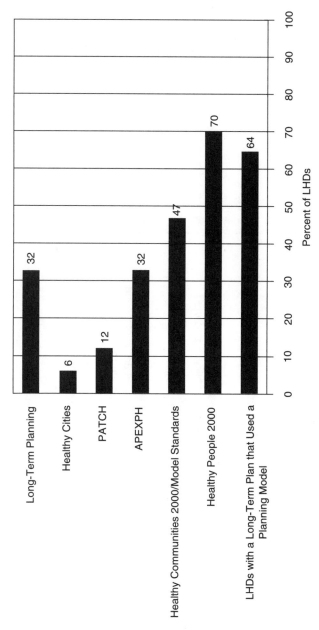

Figure 5–4 Use of Various Community Public Health Practice Processes and Tools by LHDs, 1992–1993. *Source:* Reprinted from National Association of County and City Health Officials and Centers for Disease Control and Prevention, *Profile of Local Health Departments, 1992-1993,* 1995, Washington, D.C.

Table 5–1 Performance Standards and Indicators for Washington State Public Health Improvement Plan, 1996

Core Function (Capacities)	Standards of Performance	Indicators of Performance
Assessment (structure and policies)	Policies, procedures, and legal authority guide the collection and use of data.	1. Local health jurisdiction (LHJ) has identified procedures for information collection from data sources, the organization and analysis of information, and the transmittal of findings to users.
		2. Local health jurisdiction (LHJ) has an established process to monitor and evaluate assessment activities to ensure their validity and accuracy.
Policy development (structure and policies)	Processes to develop public health policy are defined, applied, and consistent with legal authority.	3. LHJ has an identified process, which it uses, to develop policies that are presented to the Board of Health.
		4. LHJ has an established system for the ongoing evaluation of priority public health issues.
Administration (structure and policies)	Governance and management structures are in place that incorporate responsibilities and authorities of the Board of Health, Health Officer, and Administrator.	5. Legally constituted Board of Health meets at least quarterly in an open forum that facilitates community participation in the meetings.
		6. LHJ legal obligations, such as compensation plans and contracts for services, are approved by the Board of Health.
Prevention (structure and policies)	Community health services are based on the jurisdiction's explicit authority, Board of Health authorization, and internal policies.	7. LHJ prevention and protection programs are approved by the Health Officer, Administrator, and/or Board of Health.

continues

Access and quality
(structure and policies)

Policies, legal authority, and community action plans guide the assurance of access and quality of community health services.

Assessment activities are performed by equipped and competent personnel.

8. LHJ prevention and protection programs are reviewed annually to assure they meet the intent of the statutes, regulations, and contractual requirements.

9. LHJ has identified practices to assure community access to, and quality of, health services, including prevention and protection.

Assessment
(skills and resources)

10. LHJ has access to people technically skilled in carrying out assessment activities.

11. LHJ acts to assure the availability of resources required to effectively perform assessment activities.

12. LHJ provides opportunities for continuing education and peer support to staff involved in assessment activities.

Policy development
(skills and resources)

Policy options are developed by equipped and competent personnel.

13. LHJ has access to people technically skilled in carrying out policy development activities.

14. LHJ acts to assure the availability of resources required to effectively perform policy development activities.

15. LHJ provides opportunities for continuing education and peer support to staff involved in policy development activities.

continues

Table 5–1 continued

Core Function (Capacities)	Standards of Performance	Indicators of Performance
Administration (skills and resources)	Human resources, contracting, and procuring systems assure public health functions are performed by trained, equipped, and competent personnel in accord with contractual and legal obligations.	16. LHJ has access to people technically skilled in carrying out administration activities. 17. LHJ acts to assure the availability of resources required to effectively perform administration activities. 18. LHJ provides opportunities for continuing education and peer support to staff involved in administration activities. 19. LHJ has a written description of the personnel and financial management systems.
Prevention (skills and resources)	Prevention programs are managed by staff who are skilled and knowledgeable in community health services.	20. LHJ has access to people technically skilled in carrying out prevention programs. 21. LHJ acts to assure the availability of resources required to effectively perform prevention programs. 22. LHJ provides opportunities for continuing education and peer support to staff involved in the core function of prevention.

continues

Access and quality (skills and resources) LHJ uses skilled and knowledgeable staff to monitor and maintain the quality of community health services and to assure access and quality of care in the community.	23. LHJ has access to people technically skilled in carrying out the core function of access and quality. 24. LHJ acts to assure the availability of resources required to effectively perform the core function of access and quality. 25. LHJ provides opportunities for continuing education and peer support to staff involved in the core function of access and quality.
Assessment (information and communication) Information systems enable the collection, use, and communication of data.	26. LHJ systematically distributes public health data to the community, providers, boards, and organizations serving the community.
Policy development (information and communication) Public health policies are communicated within the public health community and to the community at large.	27. LHJ assures the provider community receives information on new, revised, and priority public health policies. 28. LHJ assures that Board of Health and staff members receive orientation to the role of LHJ in policy development.
Administration (information and communication) Information management enables oversight, planning, monitoring, and periodic evaluation of department policies and services.	29. LHJ management information systems track financial and service data. 30. Data from management information systems are analyzed, and information is developed for reporting to internal and external constituencies. 31. LHJs have the ability to communicate electronically with one another, the state health department, and CDC.

continues

Table 5–1 continued

Core Function (Capacities)	Standards of Performance	Indicators of Performance
Prevention (information and communication)	Prevention and protection services are consistent with community assessment and other data.	32. LHJ uses data acquired through the information systems in the development of health policy and the evaluation of prevention services.
Access and quality (information and communication)	LHJ and community providers collaborate on the collection and distribution of community health service data.	33. Local health providers are informed annually of programs to improve health priorities. 34. LHJ information system collects and distributes data on access to, and quality of, health services in the community.
Assessment (community involvement)	Community is involved in the assessment of health.	35. LHJ provides opportunities to involve the community in the development of methods used to determine the extent and magnitude of local public health problems.
Policy development (community involvement)	Community health priorities are established through a community-wide process.	36. LHJ assures that leaders in health care, government agencies, and the general public are involved in determining priority public health issues in the community.
Administration (community involvement)	Financial practices support community priorities and community involvement.	37. LHJ budget, reviewed and adopted by the Board of Health in a public process, reflects public health priorities.
Prevention (community involvement)	Public health promotion and protection activities are appropriate for the community.	38. LHJ identifies and collaborates with constituent groups to address priority health promotion and protection needs in the community.

continues

Access and quality
(community involvement)

The combined efforts of the LHJ and the community are effective in assuring access to, and quality of, local health services.

39. LHJ provides coordination, direction, and leadership within the community to improve the access to, and quality of, health services.

Source: Washington State Department of Health, *Assessment of Local Public Health Jurisdiction Performance Indicators,* 1996, Olympia, Washington.

in a health reform package enacted by the state legislature in 1994. Although several major provisions of that health reform package have since been repealed, there remains strong support, and additional resources, for the Public Health Improvement Plan. The efforts in Washington State, although more extensive and successful in many respects, parallel those in a handful of other states, including Minnesota, Missouri, Michigan, Illinois, and Ohio.

LESSONS OVER A CENTURY OF MEASURING PUBLIC HEALTH PRACTICE

Since the early part of the 20th century, an increasing body of information has been assembled on the structure of public health practice (LHDs, expenditures, health officers, boards of health, state-local relationship, size and type of jurisdiction, agency staff, professional disciplines of staff, organizational structure, etc.). At the same time, information on services provided to the community has become increasingly available for the Basic Six, as well as chronic disease prevention, medical care services, and a variety of optional and optimal services. Even with such information on the inputs and outputs of public health practice, the links between inputs (structure) and outputs (services), inputs and outcomes, and outputs and outcomes have remained somewhat unclear. Their relationship to an effective governmental presence has been even less clear.

Like earlier efforts, the more recent approaches of the post-IOM report period lacked comprehensiveness, resulting in neither a clear nor a complete picture of the status of public health practice at the end of the 20th century. The NACCHO profiles (conducted twice, in 1990 and again in 1992–1993, with a third to be available in 1997) provide considerable information on LHD characteristics, especially with respect to structure and services (inputs and outputs), and at least allow for a current estimate of full-time coverage. Although there is no nationally agreed-upon tool or instrument to assess whether LHDs are effectively carrying out the core functions (processes/practices), inferences from the NACCHO profiles, together with the practice performance studies stimulated by CDC, suggest that the current level of public health practice performance is 50 to 60 percent of what would be considered "fully" effective and that less than 40 percent of the U.S. population is served by an LHD effectively addressing public health's core functions within its jurisdiction.

These analyses are far from complete, but several common themes emerge. The first is that measurement of public health practice is a prerequisite for its improvement. The earliest available instruments, including the Appraisal Form and Evaluation Schedule, placed considerable emphasis on results, although generally these referred to the results of specific services rather than broader functions. In this light, they examined whether things were being done right rather than measuring whether the right things were being done.

Whereas the Appraisal Form of the 1920s and 1930s placed considerable emphasis on health department efforts such as "number of visits" and "number of inspections," the Evaluation Schedule of the 1940s and 1950s focused more on the resulting health protection of the community as a whole, recognizing contributions in effort from all sources—private practitioners, voluntary agencies, and others—as well as from the health department. This information was quite useful for the local jurisdictions that voluntarily participated in these assessments. Participation was far from universal, however, so the aggregated information could not adequately characterize the national effort. When efforts were undertaken to assess the national public health system (such as those described in Chapter 4), it was simpler to measure basic structural aspects such as number of LHDs and full-time coverage than either services or functions, which were not so well defined.

As would be expected, standards or performance expectations, when used prior to 1990, related primarily to inputs and outputs rather than to the processes necessary to carry out the public health core functions characterized in the IOM report. Standards, or performance expectations, for public health core functions developed after 1990 have proven to be useful for a variety of applications, including efforts at practice surveillance to track progress toward National Health Objective 8.14, agency self-assessment for capacity building, and the development of performance standards in state-local public health systems. Still, these standards appear to be in an early stage of development. Performance standards for other health organizations have become commonplace in recent decades, often involving the Joint Commission on the Accreditation of Healthcare Organizations (Joint Commission). The establishment of a national accreditation or certification initiative for LHDs through either the national public health organizations or the Joint Commission has not been given serious consideration. Absent a federal initiative to support and fund core function activities of LHDs through block grants to states, a voluntary national accreditation program for LHDs may be the most realistic approach to promoting widespread adoption of practice standards related to the core functions.

The somewhat interchangeable use of the terms *functions* and *services* before 1988 is revealing in that it suggests that the primary function of local public health was at least initially perceived as "to serve." The "Basic Six," though widely referred to as "functions," were essentially services—five clearly so (communicable disease, environmental sanitation, public health lab services, maternal and child health, health education), and the sixth (vital statistics) reflecting primarily the service elements of registering vital events. This confusion of services with functions is of more than passing interest, since measuring the performance of public health functions is essential to improve performance. If services are considered synonymous with functions, and services are measured, then the best that can be expected is that the performance of those services may be improved. Yet these may or may not be the right services in terms of community need and expectations. Operational definitions for the core functions (such as practice performance standards), to be measured along with inputs, outputs (including services), and outcomes, provide a more comprehensive framework for performance monitoring of the public health system. This type of comprehensive performance monitoring activity requires a performance database that regularly collects information on all four levels in a framework that allows for outcomes to be linked with specific inputs, practices, and outputs (Table 5–2). Without a comprehensive approach, measurement of outcomes will not provide information as to which inputs, practices, and outputs actually contribute to improved health status.

Revised LHD certification requirements in Illinois illustrate these issues. As part of an extensive reexamination and restructuring of state-local public health activities, the framework for rules governing state certification of Illinois LHDs was changed from one based on services provided to one based on carrying out public health's core functions within the community. Prior to 1993, to be certified

Table 5–2 Types of Measures Used in Activities Designed To Measure Public Health Practice

Activity	Inputs	Processes	Outputs	Outcomes
Appraisal Forms (1920s and 1930s)	X		X	
Evaluation Schedule (1940s)	X		X	
Public Health Reporting System (1970s through 1990s)	X		X	
NACCHO Profiles (1990s)	X	X	X	
Practice Performance Measures (1990s)		X		
Public Health Surveillance Activities				X

by the state health department, Illinois LHDs had to meet program requirements for 10 specific programs. After 1993, LHDs were required to meet performance expectations related to the core functions. This virtually changed the definition of an LHD from one based on its outputs to one based on its performance relative to its core functions (Table 5–3). Services that would result from each LHD's carrying out of its core functions would include three categories: those required by state public health laws (communicable disease control, food sanitation, sewage, water); those required by local laws or ordinances (varying from jurisdiction to jurisdiction); and those addressing priority community health needs established through a community needs assessment and planning process. Assessing programs and services alone without examining performance of the processes that generate such services leaves gaps in our understanding of LHDs' effectiveness in performing their core functions. Measuring inputs and outputs (i.e., services) without the core function–related processes is similarly inadequate.

The preceding examination raises the interesting question as to whether the functions of public health have changed over this century. One possibility is that it is not the functions that have changed but our ability to measure their performance due to the availability of a conceptual framework that allows for services to be distinguished from practices and new tools developed subsequent to the IOM report.

Table 5–3 Requirements for Certification of Local Health Departments in Illinois before and after July 1993

Before July 1993, To Be Certified as a Local Health Department in Illinois . . .	After July 1993, To Be Certified as a Local Health Department in Illinois . . .
A local health agency must carry out the following programs: 1. food sanitation 2. potable water 3. maternal health/family planning 4. child health 5. communicable disease control 6. private sewage 7. solid waste 8. nuisance control 9. chronic disease 10. administration	A local health agency must: 1. assess health needs of the community 2. investigate health effects and hazards 3. advocate and build community support 4. develop policies and plans to address needs 5. manage resources 6. implement programs 7. evaluate and provide quality assurance 8. inform and educate the public

An alternative or even additional explanation is that an understanding of the functions of public health has matured over time. The development and expansion of the public health infrastructure in the United States advanced rapidly between 1900 and 1950. It is conceivable that maturation of the functions of local public health was not possible until that infrastructure had been put into place. Although the IOM core functions are often conceptualized as a linear process (assessment → policy development → assurance), it appears that the assurance function, at least in terms of emphasis, developed without commensurate maturation of the other core functions. The limited studies to date consistently identify higher performance on assurance-related practices than on those related to either assessment or policy development. Improved local public health performance through implementation of APEXPH and its derivatives has been demonstrated. Greater promotion of these approaches will require new federal incentives to states and localities and greater commitment of the LHD community to performance improvement.

RISK ASSESSMENT AND RISK MANAGEMENT

Environmental health practitioners have devised methods for assessing and managing environmental risks that are grounded in the concepts embodied in the core functions and public health practices. These methods for risk assessment and risk management use different terms but accomplish the same aims in assessing, addressing, and ensuring responses to health risks in the community. A brief review of these methods provides another perspective as to how core functions and their associated practices are operationalized by public health practitioners.

Humans have always lived with risk, currently live with risk, and will continue forever to live with risk. Some risks are controllable through human behaviors and choices in daily life. Others risks, however, reside outside the realm of behavioral choices, such as those from environmental sources, including exposures to both naturally occurring and artificial toxicants. For these environmental health risks, the public health challenge is to make the public aware of the nature of risk in general as well as how to protect against specific risks. Unacceptable public health risks should be reduced or eliminated when feasible and, importantly, the means to accomplish this goal should not pose additional significant risks.

To translate this philosophy into practice, public health actions focus on hazard identification, exposure assessment, dose-response assessment, and risk characterization. Underlying these steps in the risk assessment and management process are specific activities important to public heath practice. These include

- identifying hazards that pose risks to public health and well-being
- acknowledging the essential participation of the public

- whenever possible, using information that makes it possible to arrive at an informed estimate of risk
- managing each significant risk through an approach that gives full consideration to alternative actions to control the hazard
- managing risks associated with the identified hazards in a manner that is prudent and in concert with the public's need
- communicating risks understandably to both experts and laypersons
- advancing the processes of risk assessment and risk management by research that reduces uncertainties

These actions closely parallel public health practices described previously. Terminology varies somewhat, but the concepts are the same. At the heart of risk assessment and risk management are epidemiological concepts concerned with the frequencies and kinds of illnesses and injuries in groups of people and with the factors that determine or otherwise influence their distribution.

Epidemiologic principles provide the tools for investigating the health effects of chemicals directly in humans under conditions of actual exposure, avoiding a need for extrapolation from animal models. However, epidemiologic observations can be made only after people have been exposed. Inferences can be made of the causal relationship between exposure and health effects if there is an adequate study design and an effective control of confounding factors. Many epidemiologic studies allow an evaluation of the relationship between the magnitude of exposure and the frequency or severity of health effects. The quality of exposure data is sometimes insufficient for an adequate quantitative dose-response assessment when data have to be obtained retrospectively.

Though identifying risk factors for an adverse health effect is highly desirable, full knowledge of etiology is not necessary for developing effective control measures. A typical example of this principle in practice is the lowering of blood lead levels by removal of leaded gasoline. The epidemiologic evidence supports a direct causal relationship between lead and a number of toxicological end points, although the precise toxic mechanisms are not fully understood.

Risk assessment and risk management are often described in terms of four steps, although all four are not necessarily involved in any given situation. A summary of each of these four steps follows.

Hazard identification attempts to determine, on the basis of the best information available, whether a risk under consideration either has the potential to produce or has actually produced adverse health effects. The classic example is Pott's description, in 1775, of cancer of the scrotum in chimney sweeps. This is often acknowledged as the first identification of a chemical as a carcinogen. More recent examples include lung cancer linked to cigarette smoke and asbestos dust, angiosarcoma of the liver traced to vinyl chloride, phocomelia (abnormally short limbs) traced to thalidomide, and adenocarcinoma of the vagina in women whose mothers were given DES. Hazard identification relies primarily on results generated from clinical and epidemiologic studies and from animal experiments.

Exposure assessment estimates the types, magnitudes, and durations of actual or anticipated exposures to hazardous agents; it is an extremely important component of the risk assessment process, especially with regard to the quantification of potential human risk. The lack of exposure data may significantly lessen the value of epidemiologic information. Such assessments are generally based on monitoring studies that directly measure exposures or utilize mathematical or animal models, or some combination of these approaches. Monitoring studies can target individuals (e.g., through dietary profiles, medication histories, or screening studies), the ambient environment, or specific locations (such as homes or workplaces). There are many possible limitations for exposure assessments. Multiple exposures may be additive, synergistic, or antagonistic depending on the number, duration, timing, and combination of agents. All potential sources and routes of exposure to a specific chemical should be considered with the relative significance and magnitude of each source.

Dose-response assessment is concerned with the evaluation and quantitative characterization of the relationship between the level of exposure and the response or responses that are elicited by such exposures. This is often accomplished through techniques that determine what is known as a *safety factor* (or the acceptable or allowable human intake level of a toxic agent). The no-observed-effect levels or, in some instances, lowest-observed-effect levels are determined and then divided by an appropriately chosen safety factor that reflects the outcomes under study as well as the quality of the available data. Margin-of-safety procedures are similar but use estimated no- or lowest-observed-effect levels and estimated human exposure levels. This provides some idea as to the proximity of an exposure level that may cause adverse health effects. Because it allows flexibility in regulating exposure in not stating a defined safety level, this approach is widely used in occupational health. Mathematical modeling is employed in risk estimation to describe the underlying dose-response relationship for the purpose of generating estimates and upper bounds on the unknown low-dose risk.

Risk characterization involves a multidisciplinary evaluation of all data relevant for hazard identification, exposure assessment, dose response, and species extrapolation to determine the overall risk posed by actual or anticipated exposures to a given agent. Differences in human exposure conditions and susceptibility argue for identification of high-risk subgroups in the population. Sources of uncertainty in the assessment are carefully considered and quantified to provide a more complete appreciation of the strengths and limitations of the process. It is important that distinctions be drawn among facts, consensus, assumptions, and science policy decisions in the risk assessment process and communicated to those involved in risk management.

In sum, risk assessment and risk management reflect a dynamic process in that great emphasis is placed on identifying and reducing uncertainties associated with the process. These practices parallel the more generic public health processes linked with public health's core functions—assessment, policy development, and assurance—but tailor these processes to more limited aims of quantifying risks so that appropriate interventions can be applied.

CONCLUSION

Public health's core functions call for identifying and addressing community health problems through activities related to assessment, policy development, and assurance. Several formulations that provide operational definitions for these concepts have appeared since 1988, and new tools that facilitate their successful implementation in community settings have been developed. Defining and measuring the operational aspects of these functions are necessary before initiatives to improve public health practice and its results can be efficiently and effectively targeted.

Efforts to measure the extent to which public health's functions are being successfully addressed have failed to document any improvement in core function–related performance since the appearance of the IOM report. Such efforts have suffered from both conceptual and methodological problems. The history of measuring public health practice prior to the IOM report lacked a conceptual framework that viewed services as an output of the public health system's functions. As needs and conditions changed, appropriate public health responses in the form of services changed. An initial set of six basic services may have represented an appropriate product of a functioning public health system in the 1920s, at least for LHDs serving large urban populations. But to measure various aspects of those services as a means of assessing performance of the underlying functions is incomplete at best.

Performance measurement in the public health system must be able to measure inputs, processes, outputs, and outcomes in ways that allow for changes in one to be linked with the others. Without such a comprehensive public health practice performance-monitoring system, we will not be able to make the changes necessary to improve the results we seek. After 80 years of trial and error, the essential ingredients are in place: a conceptual framework, useful instruments, a national objective for the public health system, and the means of tracking progress over time. With these processes, we can expect that interventions will change over time. These interventions, the outputs of the public health system, will be examined in a subsequent chapter.

DISCUSSION QUESTIONS AND EXERCISES

1. What are the three core functions of public health, and how are these operationalized by state and local public health agencies?
2. If asked to write a job description for an LHD, how would you characterize the duties and responsibilities?
3. The community outcomes for your program have been improving and now appear to be acceptable. Is there any need to evaluate your program?
4. Explain the relationships among inputs, public health practices, services, and outcomes in Figure 1–3 (Chapter 1).
5. What features are similar among APEXPH, PATCH, and the Model Standards? What features are different?
6. Exercise: determine whether your LHD has completed APEXPH. If it has, what were the results? If it has not, find out why and whether other approaches may have been taken.
7. Exercise: obtain the community health plan (or a summary) for your city or county, and review the process that developed it for consistency with the 10 public health practices and 11 steps of the Model Standards. In what ways did the process and plan differ from these frameworks?

REFERENCES

1. Institute of Medicine, Committee on the Future of Public Health. *The Future of Public Health.* Washington, DC: National Academy Press; 1988.
2. Vaughan HF. Local health services in the United States: the story of CAP. *Am J Public Health.* 1972;62:95–108.
3. American Public Health Association, Committee on Administrative Practice. Appraisal form for city health work. *Am J Public Health.* 1926;16(suppl):1–65.
4. American Public Health Association, Committee on Administrative Practice. *Evaluation Schedule for Use in the Study and Appraisal of Community Health Programs.* New York, NY: American Public Health Association; 1947.
5. Emerson H, Luginbuhl M. *Local Health Units for the Nation.* New York, NY: Commonwealth Fund; 1945.
6. Shonick W. *Government and Health Services: Government's Role in the Development of U.S. Health Services 1930–1980.* New York, NY: Oxford Press; 1995.
7. Hanlon JJ. Is there a future for local health departments? *Health Serv Rep.* 1973;88:898–901.
8. *Healthy Communities 2000: Model Standards.* Washington, DC: American Public Health Association; 1991.
9. Studnicki J, Steverson B, Blais HN, Goley E, Richards TB, Thornton JN. Analyzing organizational practices in local health departments. *Public Health Rep.* 1994;109:485–490.

10. Turnock BJ, Handler A, Hall W, Potsic S, Nalluri R, Vaughn E. Local health department effectiveness in addressing the core functions of public health. *Public Health Rep.* 1994;109:653–658.

11. Richards TB, Rogers JJ, Christenson GM, Miller CA, Gatewood DD, Taylor MS. Assessing public health practice: application of ten core function measures of community health in six states. *Am J Prev Med.* 1995;11(suppl 2):36–40.

12. Miller CA, Moore KS, Richards TS, Monk JD. A proposed method for assessing the performance of local public health functions and practices. *Am J Public Health.* 1994;84:1743–1749.

13. *Profile of Local Health Departments 1992–1993.* Washington, DC: National Association of County and City Health Officials; 1995.

14. *An Assessment Protocol for Excellence in Public Health.* Washington, DC: National Association of County and City Health Officials; 1991.

15. *The Guide to Implementing Model Standards.* Washington, DC: American Public Health Association and Centers for Disease Control; 1993.

16. *Assessment of Local Public Health Jurisdiction Performance Indicators.* Olympia, Wash: Washington State Department of Health; 1996.

CHAPTER 6

The Infrastructure of Public Health

After the violin virtuoso had finished his concert presentation and was attempting to slip out of the orchestra hall's delivery entrance, he was nonetheless mobbed by some adoring fans. One particularly aggressive young man pushed his way to the front of the throng and grabbed the musician's hand, shaking it furiously. "Maestro, you played those notes just brilliantly tonight," he said. Taken a little aback by these circumstances, the violinist replied, "Young man, anyone can play the notes correctly. It's the spaces between the notes that make the real difference."

In public health, as in the music of the classical masters, effectiveness depends on both the ingredients and how they are blended together. This chapter will examine the basic ingredients of public health and how these are integrated to carry out its work. This ground-level view of public health focuses on infrastructure, another concept that is more easily understood outside the field of public health. When we think of infrastructure, we routinely think of roads, bridges, sewers, and water supplies. It is not easy to see the similarities between these concrete and visible structures in our communities and their counterparts in public health. Further, there are different views as to what the concept of public health infrastructure actually represents.

Infrastructure can be described in terms of both static and dynamic attributes. In a static representation, public health infrastructure is the basic building block and the resulting foundation for public health activities. In a more dynamic representation, infrastructure is the capacity or capability of that foundation to carry out its main functions. Both of these views provide useful insights into the public health system and build on the concept of a governmental presence in health at the local level. Importantly, both also portray infrastructure as essential for carrying out all three public health core functions: assessment, policy development, and assurance.

This public health infrastructure represents a force more potent than one that merely addresses and monitors health problems and interventions continuously in reaction to changing circumstances. An infrastructure with only these roles would be composed of those resources that enabled the assessment and policy development functions of public health. Such a view of public health infrastructure, however, has one important shortcoming. It excludes a considerable share of the resources necessary to carry out the work of public health as not contributing to the infrastructure. This more limited view of public health infrastructure serves to emphasize some functions over others. Consequently, this discussion will address the public health infrastructure somewhat more broadly by including inputs and ingredients that support all three core functions.

The public health infrastructure serves as the nerve center of public health and represents the capacity necessary to carry out public health's core functions. It also represents a composite that can be broken down to reveal the ingredients or raw materials of the public health system. What makes the system's infrastructure or ingredients difficult to describe fully is that public health itself is not neatly partitioned within our complex society. Nonetheless, this chapter will present a broad description of the public health infrastructure as it exists in the 1990s. The key questions addressed are:

- What are the critical components of public health's infrastructure?
- What is the current status of these components?
- How can public health's infrastructure be enhanced?

INFRASTRUCTURE, INGREDIENTS, AND INPUTS

The public health infrastructure has been broadly characterized as the capacity required to carry out the core functions of governmental public health (assessment, policy development, and assurance).[1] The components of system capacity include a variety of relatively recognizable resources: human, informational, financial, and organizational, including an aspect of organization (governmental presence) that leads or facilitates responses to changing circumstances. These components are identified in Exhibit 6–1.

Exhibit 6-1 Components of Public Health Infrastructure

- Human Resources
- Organizational Resources
- Informational Resources
- Financial Resources

It is not always easy to separate the elements of the public health infrastructure into discrete categories. For example, drawing lines between the knowledge and skills of the work force and information resources and their use calls for an arbitrary distinction between what people are able to do and what they are able to do after accessing information that is readily available to them. Other distinctions between organizational relationships within a community and leadership roles also lack clear boundaries. Still, it is useful to characterize generally the elements of the public health infrastructure, realizing that these can be lumped or split in several different ways. The capacities for local public health practice developed as part of the Washington State Public Health Improvement Plan (see Chapter 5) represent a similar framework for characterizing the public health infrastructure.

Human resources include the work force of public health and their knowledge, skills, and abilities. Organizational resources are the relationships among the various system participants, public and private, and the mechanisms that manage the system practices, including their leadership components and collaborative strategies. Information resources include various data, information, and communication systems. Fiscal resources are the funding levels and sources for the work of public health. Each of these elements contributes to the system's capacity to perform, and each will be examined in turn. In this examination of resources, one might also consider physical resources, such as equipment and physical facilities necessary to carry out the work of public health. These are highly specific for the programs and services that are provided, however, and will not be examined in this chapter.

HUMAN RESOURCES IN PUBLIC HEALTH

The human resources involved in public health begin and end with the work force. Unfortunately, it has never been clear who is and who is not a public health professional. There has never been any specific academic degree or unique set of experiences that distinguishes a public health professional from professionals in other fields. Many, if not most, public health professionals have a primary professional discipline in addition to their attachment to public health. Physicians, nurses, dentists, social workers, nutritionists, health educators, anthropologists, psychologists, architects, sanitarians, economists, political scientists, engineers, epidemiologists, biostatisticians, managers, lawyers, and dozens of other professions and disciplines contribute to the field of public health. This multidisciplinary work force, with often-divided loyalties to multiple professions, blurs the distinctiveness of public health as a profession. At the same time, however, it facilitates interdisciplinary approaches to community problem identification and problem solving.

Also uncertain is the size of this work force, although it is admittedly small in comparison with the estimated 11 to 12 million workers in the entire health system as of 1996. The number of all health workers has doubled since 1975 and has increased by about 25 percent since 1990.[2] Estimates of the public health work force suggest that the current number is somewhere around 500,000. This number is compatible with Health Resources and Services Administration (HRSA) work force estimates from 1989 and the relatively stable level of funding for public health activities in terms of real dollars during the 1990s. The data on the public health work force presented in this section are derived from HRSA Bureau of Health Professions data.[3]

In the late 1980s, according to HRSA estimates, the public health work force was about equally divided among the three levels of government. Slightly more than one-third were employed by federal agencies, slightly less than one-third were employed in state agencies, and the remaining one-third worked in local public health agencies and other local settings spread among private, voluntary, community, and academic organizations.[3] Since that time, there has been relatively little change, although it is likely that the percentage employed by nongovernmental agencies has increased slightly, while the governmental share has declined. This diverse group represents the primary public health work force. The number, distribution, training, and competence of this work force are issues of public concern. Some of these issues have remained unaddressed for over 100 years as suggested by an editorial appearing in the *Journal of the American Medical Association* in 1893[4] (Exhibit 6–2).

Fewer than half of the 500,000 individuals in the public health work force have had formal training in public health. The major share of trained public health workers by category are environmental health practitioners (36 percent), public health nurses (23 percent), administrators (20 percent), and health educators (10 percent; Figure 6–1). Of these 500,000 professionals, the number with graduate degrees in public health from schools of public health or other graduate public health programs represents only a small fraction.

The relative lack of formal public health training in the public health work force is well illustrated in the environmental health work force, which numbered about 715,000 in the late 1980s. This work force included 480,000 technicians and operators and 235,000 professionals. Only about one-third of the professionals had received formal education in the environmental health sciences; the remaining 155,000 were engineers and chemists with relevant skills for the field but no formal environmental public health training (Figure 6–2). In view of the low numbers of master's-level graduates of schools of public health and other graduate-level public health degree programs, this is not surprising. For example, the nation's 27 accredited schools of public health in the mid-1990s had a total enrollment of about 14,000 students and were producing only about 4,000 master's-level graduates annually.

Exhibit 6-2 The Necessity for Trained and Educated Health Officials

There has probably been no time in the history of this country when trained, competent and efficient health officers were needed so much as they are now. The average health officer is appointed without any special training or qualification. . . . His tenure of office is so slight that very few feel warranted in qualifying themselves for such duties. . . . No one is eligible to such appointment in Great Britain without special training and his qualification having been established by examination; his position is then assured and he is not subject to removal with change in administration. It ought to be axiomatic that no health officer, no health commissioners, no executive officer of a board of health, should anywhere be appointed, until after thorough examination, or training in a subordinate capacity, and until he had evinced special aptitude for and interest in that line of work. A great misfortune in this country is that whenever a change of administration is brought about, it is considered necessary to change officers of health. . . . Instances frequently occur, involving great responsibility, where the appointee is wholly incompetent, and is dependent upon the subordinates in his office for information and advice; in short, is compelled to learn the duties incumbent upon him at the expense of the life and treasure of the public. . . .

In all civilized countries, except the United States, there are some special qualifications required for this office, and just in proportion as they are exacted, in the same proportion is the community protected from preventable diseases; from unnecessary panics with the suffering incident thereto, and from the economic loss caused thereby. . . . It is unfortunate that in the absence of epidemics or pestilence, too little attention is paid to the protection of the public health, and as a necessary consequence, to the selection of those whose duties require them to guard the public health. Laws should be passed in all the States defining the qualifications necessary for eligibility for appointment of health officers. This is the direction of a civil service reform much needed.

Source: Reprinted with permission from Editorial, The Necessity for Trained and Educated Health Officials, *Journal of the American Medical Association,* Vol. 20, p. 189, © 1893, American Medical Association.

Another glimpse of the public health work force is available through surveys of state health agency personnel.[5] The most recent data available reflect 130,000 full-time equivalent positions in state health agencies as of 1989. Excluding non-professional staff and professional caregiving staff working in state-operated institutions, state health agencies employed 63,000 professional, technical, and administrative staff. Of these, 22 percent were registered nurses, and 16 percent were environmental health professionals. Administrators and laboratory personnel each constituted 7 percent, and planners, public health physicians, nutritionists, social workers, health educators, and dentists each constituted 4 percent or less of the professional work force of state health agencies (Figure 6–3).

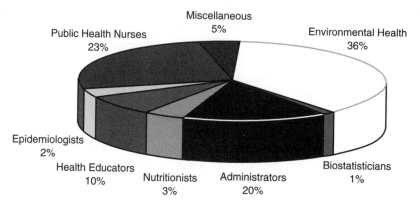

Figure 6–1 Public Health Trained Personnel in the United States by Professional Category, 1989. *Source:* Reprinted from *Health Personnel in the United States–Eighth Report to Congress,* 1992, Health Resources and Services Administration.

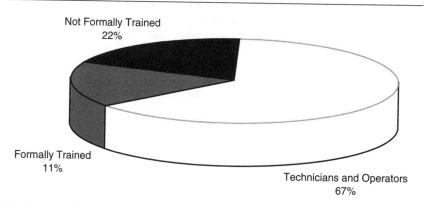

Figure 6–2 Public Health Training Levels for 235,000 Environmental Health Professionals, 1987. *Source:* Reprinted from *Health Personnel in the United States–Eighth Report to Congress,* 1992, Health Resources and Services Administration.

Changes in state agency staffing during the 1980s are presented in Table 6–1. During the 1980s, the number of nurses and sanitarians increased notably, although the largest percentage increases occurred among nutritionists, health educators, and planners. The substantial increase in the category of "other health care providers and other professional and technical employees" suggests that professional diversity within the public health work force is increasing.

Information on public health workers at the local and community level is even more scarce. The periodic profiles of local health departments (LHDs) completed

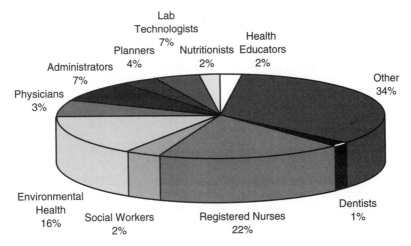

Figure 6–3 State Health Agency Professional, Technical, and Administrative Staff by Occupational Category, 1989. *Source:* Reprinted from Final Report of a Contract with DHHS-PHS-HRSA, *State Health Agency Staffs, 1989,* April 1992, Public Health Foundation.

by the National Association of County and City Health Officials (NACCHO) provide only general data on the proportion of responding agencies that employ specific public health job titles, either directly or through contracted services. This information does not distinguish between those who are public health trained and those who are not. Also the total numbers of public health workers in the various job categories cannot be determined. The NACCHO data do show that only 17 percent of the agency heads for LHDs surveyed held graduate degrees in public health.[6]

Due to the considerable limitations of these sources, HRSA commissioned a comprehensive evaluation of the training and education needs of the public health work force in 1995. The intent of this effort is to determine the size and composition of the public health professional work force in the United States, as well as its qualifications, staffing patterns, and distribution by public health core function. Pilot studies in five states beginning in 1996 will inform a national evaluation of these important questions. Defining the public health work force is necessary before assessment of its education, training, and career development needs can take place. Anecdotal information, historical as well as current, suggests that there are acute shortages of specific categories of public health workers, such as epidemiologists and public health nurses. There also appears to be increasing demand for graduate-level education in public health. But somehow these per-

Table 6-1 Trends in Staffing of State and Territorial Health Agencies by Occupational Category, 1979-1989

Occupational Category	1979	1989	% Change 1979–1989
Total	129,356	130,107	0.6%
Total institutional staff	52,759	35,871	−32.0%
Total noninstitutional staff	76,597	94,236	23.0%
Professional, technical, and administrative staff	49,199	63,226	28.5%
Physicians	1,974	1,939	−1.8%
Dentists	651	396	−39.2%
Registered nurses	11,663	13,884	19.0%
Nutritionists, dietitians	793	1,504	89.7%
Social workers	1,455	1,198	−17.7%
Health educators	701	978	39.5%
Laboratory technicians	5,156	4,255	−17.5%
Environmental and occupational health	7,951	9,914	24.7%
Planners, programmers, analysts, and statisticians	2,003	2,708	35.2%
Administrative and managerial	3,903	4,168	6.8%
Other health care providers and other professional and technical employees	12,949	22,282	72.1%

Source: Reprinted from Final Report of a Contact with DHHS-PHS-HRSA, *State Health Agency Staffs, 1989,* April 1992, Public Health Foundation.

ceptions do not appear to translate into an expanding professional public health work force. There has been frustratingly little progress toward clarifying and resolving these issues in recent years.

There has been considerably greater progress over recent years in delineating the competencies and skills necessary for public health practice. Many of these initiatives have their roots in the Institute of Medicine (IOM) report of 1988.[7] A key development was the convening of public health practitioners and academics through a Public Health Faculty-Agency Forum to outline a set of core competencies for public health professionals.[8] These competencies address analytical, communication, policy development and program planning, cultural, basic public health sciences, and financial planning and management skills (Exhibit 6–3). Additional competencies in specific public health disciplines were also established through this process for health administration, epidemiology/biostatistics, behavioral sciences, and environmental health (Exhibit 6–4).

Exhibit 6-3 Universal Competencies for Public Health Professionals

All public health professionals should be competent in:
- Analytical Skills
  - defining a problem
  - determining appropriate use of data and statistical methods for problem identification and resolution, and program planning, implementation, and evaluation
  - selecting and defining variables relevant to defined public health problems
  - evaluating the integrity and comparability of data and identifying gaps in data sources
  - understanding how the data illuminate ethical, political, scientific, economic, and overall public health issues
  - understanding basic research designs used in public health
  - making relevant inferences from data

- Communication Skills
  - communicating effectively both in writing and orally (unless a handicap precludes oral communication)
  - presenting accurately and effectively demographic, statistical, programmatic, and scientific information for professional and lay audiences
  - soliciting input from individuals and organizations
  - advocating for public health programs and resources
  - leading and participating in groups to address specific issues
  - using the media to communicate important public health information

- Policy Development and Program Planning Skills
  - collecting and summarizing data relevant to an issue
  - stating policy options
  - articulating the health, fiscal, administrative, legal, social, and political implications of each policy option
  - stating the feasibility and expected outcomes of each policy option
  - deciding on the appropriate course of action
  - writing a clear and concise policy statement
  - developing a plan to implement the policy, including goals, outcome and process objectives, and implementation steps
  - translating policy into organizational plans, structures, and programs
  - identifying public health laws, regulations, and policies related to specific programs
  - developing mechanisms to monitor and evaluate programs for their effectiveness and quality

continues

Exhibit 6–3 continued

- Cultural Skills
  - understanding the dynamic forces contributing to cultural diversity
  - interacting sensitively, effectively, and professionally with persons from diverse cultural, socioeconomic, educational, and professional backgrounds, and with persons of all ages and lifestyle preferences
  - identifying the role of cultural, social, and behavioral factors in determining disease, disease prevention, health promoting behavior, and medical service organization and delivery
  - developing and adapting approaches to problems that take into account cultural differences

- Basic Public Health Sciences Skills
  - defining, assessing, and understanding the health status of populations, determinants of health and illness, factors contributing to health promotion and disease prevention, and factors influencing the use of health services
  - understanding research methods in all basic public health sciences
  - applying the basic public health sciences, including behavioral and social sciences, biostatistics, epidemiology, environmental public health, and prevention of chronic and infectious diseases and injuries
  - understanding the historical development and structure of state, local, and federal public health agencies

- Financial Planning and Management Skills
  - developing and presenting a budget
  - managing programs within budgetary constraints
  - developing strategies for determining budget priorities
  - monitoring program performance
  - preparing proposals for funding from external sources
  - applying basic human relations skills to the management of organizations and the resolution of conflicts
  - managing personnel
  - understanding theory of organizational structure and in relation to professional practice

Source: Reprinted from Health Resources and Services Administration and Centers for Disease Control and Prevention.

The Public Health Faculty-Agency Forum also formulated strategies to facilitate the expansion of these competencies within the public health work force. Key recommendations called for

- strengthening relationships between the practice and academic sectors of the public health community

Exhibit 6-4 Professional Competencies for Selected Categories of Public Health Professionals

Public Health Administration
- Policy analysis/strategic planning
- Communication skills
- Team leadership
- Financial management
- Human resources management
- Program planning and administration
- Organizational management/positioning
- Cultural competence
- Basic health sciences
- Political analysis

Epidemiology and Biostatistics
Epidemiology
- Situation analysis
- Study design
- Study implementation
- Data management and analysis
- Presentation of health information

Biostatistics
- Data requirements
- Database management
- Descriptive statistics
- Statistical inference
- Statistical reporting

Behavioral Sciences
- Awareness and ability to implement behavior change strategies for primary, secondary, and tertiary health promotion/disease prevention activities in the public health setting
- Ability to disseminate knowledge of behavior and social concepts and methods
- Cultural sensitivity and understanding of how culture affects behavior and health status
- Ability to conduct an ongoing community and medical needs assessment, individually and as part of a team
- Knowledge of the public health system and policy and regulation development
- Evaluation skills
- Leadership skills
- Communication skills

continues

Exhibit 6–4 continued

Environmental Public Health
- Risk assessment skills
- Risk management skills
- Risk communication skills
- Epidemiology of acute and chronic diseases with environmental stresses
- Biostatistics
- Basic sciences
- Communicable/chronic disease
- Economic considerations in environmental public health
- Environmental law

Source: Reprinted from Health Resources and Services Administration and Centers for Disease Control and Prevention.

- improving the teaching, training, and practice of public health
- establishing firm practice links between schools of public health and public health agencies

In part, these strategies were a response to conclusions of the IOM report that the education of public health professionals had become isolated from the practice of public health. Both the delineation of competencies and the recommended implementation strategies have had a substantial impact on public health education and training since 1990. For example, most schools of public health have established public health practice offices to interface with practitioners and practice agencies and have developed ongoing affiliations agreements to cover faculty appointments, joint research agendas, technical assistance, and practica placements, among other activities.[9]

At the federal level both HRSA and the Centers for Disease Control and Prevention (CDC) have sought to strengthen the bonds between education and practice. Both agencies served as cosponsors of the Public Health Faculty-Agency Forum, and each has supported initiatives that would implement the forum's various recommendations. For example, CDC has spearheaded the development of a national training network and has sponsored leadership training activities at the national and state level. Educational resources contributing to this national network include 27 schools of public health (a number that has grown steadily over the past three decades), nearly 90 additional graduate training programs in public health, and as many as 300 other graduate-level training programs in areas related to public health, such as health administration, public health nursing, and environmental engineering.

A series of reports from the Pew Health Professions Commission have also generated discussion and debate as to approaches that would expand public health competencies among other health professions within the health sector. The commission concluded that current trends within the health system would result in substantial surpluses of physicians, nurses, and even pharmacists and that the proliferation of allied health professions would reverse itself with the growth of multiskilled professions as the health sector reengineered its service delivery activities. For public health, however, the commission projected a growth in demand for public health professionals also linked to the needs of an increasingly market-driven health system.[10] The expansion of public health skills within the health sector work force can be addressed through additional public health education programs in schools of public health and other sites, through the provision of public health education and training to other health professionals, or both. In any event, the universal competencies represent the educational products to be marketed and provided to new audiences of health professionals.

Large-scale assessments of the need for education and training toward these universal competencies are lacking. However, on the basis of assessments to date of the core function–related effectiveness of public health practice (such as those presented in Chapter 5), great need exists for enhancing competencies of the work force associated with each of the three public health core functions. For education and training of the public health work force to be taken seriously, both academic and practice interests must merge into state or regional alliances or consortia. Such efforts would serve to identify systematically the education, training, and career development needs of the public health work force and would apply existing resources to current needs.

ORGANIZATIONAL RESOURCES

Organizational resources in public health include the network of federal, state, and local public health agencies described in Chapter 4, as well as mechanisms for linking public, private, and voluntary organizations through community leadership and collaborative relationships. Before leadership and collaboration issues are addressed, several organizational aspects of public health agencies merit discussion.

Organizational Aspects of Public Health Agencies

Organizations are groups of individuals linked by common goals and objectives. This implies that each organization has a specific mission or purpose, resources appropriate to work toward that purpose, the ability to determine progress toward its goals and objectives, and a defined process for making decisions that change the direction or speed of the organization in pursuit of its goals. Each organization takes on a structure to delegate its activities to specific units or individuals and to coordinate the tasks among them. The specifics of these organizational arrangements are best left to texts in health administration and organizational behavior.

Public-sector organizations differ in many important respects from their private- and voluntary-sector counterparts. The most obvious, and perhaps most important, difference is apparent in their bottom lines. The bottom line of public health agencies is measured in health outcomes, with efficiency and effectiveness valued, but not nearly as much. For the private sector, the bottom line is often profits and customer satisfaction, and efficiency and effectiveness are viewed as means to those ends. Many community and voluntary organizations address missions that resemble those of public agencies. But public agencies often have political and bureaucratic environments that are unique among organizations. It should not be forgotten that employment itself is an important public objective, although the public sector lacks the ability to expand or contract its work force rapidly in response to market conditions. In fact, public-sector jobs and services become even more important during times of economic recession.

The presence of a civil service–based work force in many public health agencies is often cited as an impediment to getting things done, although the real problem may be more related to inadequate management practices than to institutionalized inertia. Civil service personnel systems were established in state and local governments in large part through personnel standards fostered by Maternal and Child Health (MCH) funding with the enactment of Title V of the Social Security Act in 1935. Although the initial intent was to provide added security for government workers, there has been long-standing discontent with the system and tension and conflict between government workers and elected officials ever since. Civil service employees generally lack to the power to strike, unlike their private-sector counterparts organized into unions.

For many years, public health agencies operated under a command-and-control approach to management. If a problem was assigned to the public health agency, the agency sought to acquire the resources needed to deal with that problem. Resources were deployed directly from the agency; this approach worked well when the major problems called for environmental engineering solutions or communicable disease control expertise. As problems became more complex, however, encroaching on the territory of other health and human service agencies, command-and-control approaches became problematic. To resolve delicate turf issues, cooperating with other agencies and collaborative approaches began to supplement more directly controlled strategies. These added to the challenges of public agency managers, which also included promoting workers' efficiency and effectiveness. Management training has never been well supported in the public sector, certainly not to the extent that it has been in the private sector. As a result, public health agencies often are poorly managed; this generates tensions and conflicts between professional staff and administrators brought into an agency to maximize efficiency and effectiveness, as well as between the agency and its community collaborators. For example, there has been a declining proportion of local health department agency heads with MD degrees. For larger health departments (especially those serving populations of 100,000 or more), this trend is partly explained by the employment of nonphysician agency heads to manage the increasingly complex array of clinical services. Clinical professionals in health departments have not always adjusted well to these changes, and the result has sometimes been management and morale problems.

Public health agencies at the state and local levels often have boards to guide their efforts. More than two-thirds of LHDs reported the presence of a local board of health in the 1992–1993 NACCHO profile.[6] Over the past century, boards have assumed roles less involved with direct agency operations than when initially established. Much of the direction of professional staff today has been assumed by agency leadership, and boards have retained roles of approving regulations, advising/approving agency budgets, and often hiring the agency director. The role of many local boards of health has become unclear and largely advisory to the agency, prompting debate as to their role in the modern practice of public health. In response to concerns over past and current roles, the IOM report[7] calls for public health councils so that historic baggage attached to boards of health will be minimized. Public health agencies often have a plethora of advisory boards and committees developed for specific programs or activities. Although the proliferation of these advisory bodies can be seen as unwieldy and sometimes conflicting with the roles of more formally established bodies, such as the board of health itself, these groups also serve to expand greatly participation and communication with professional constituencies. Superfluous from a management perspective, these are nevertheless often effective constituency-building activities. Boards of health and various forms of advisory committees provide a link between the agency and the community it serves. The agency's and community's interests are better served by fostering and utilizing these relationships than by limiting or controlling them.

Leadership

Within public health agencies, the leadership position carries several different responsibilities. The leader manages the agency, interacts with the major stakeholders and constituency groups, and carries out some largely ceremonial functions. The specific duties of the agency are vested in its director through statutes or ordinances; these are the only legal powers of that leader. Within state and local public health agencies, there has been a steady move away from physician directors of agencies, although about half of LHDs continue to hire a physician as the chief executive officer. An evolving literature on leadership is developing within the public health community. A national public health leadership institute has been developed by CDC, and at least a half-dozen state-based leadership development initiatives were in place by 1996. Leadership skills often revolve around concepts such as envisioning the future, inspiring others to act, and generally acting through others.

But leadership in public health involves more than individual leaders or individuals in leadership positions. Public health is intimately involved in leadership as an agent of social change by identifying health problems and risks and stimulating actions toward their elimination. Since the work of public health emphasizes collective as well as individual leadership, the battery of leadership principles and practices is pertinent throughout a public health organization. In many respects, tools like the Assessment Protocol for Excellence in Public Health (APEXPH) and Healthy Communities 2000 are tools of and for leadership.

Coalitions and Consortia

An increasingly important aspect of organizational resources is the ability to work through collaborative links with other agencies and organizations. Often these arrangements are described as coalitions or consortia, although other terms are frequently used, and distinctions are often blurred[11] (Table 6–2). Coalitions can be formed for short-term efforts or established to address ongoing problems on a long-term basis. They are most likely to be successful when they include representation from all groups affected by the problem and efforts to deal with that problem. In general, coalitions and consortia are formal partnerships involving two or more groups working together to achieve specific goals according to a common plan. The rationale for a consortia approach is that the goals are believed to be beyond the capacity of any one participating organizations. Goals can take various forms, from communication among members, to public and professional education, to advocating and lobbying for particular policy changes. It is essential that coalition members be in agreement that the problem is best addressed through a coalition approach and that they be comfortable with the scope of activities planned. Building on mutual interests allows a coalition to place expectations and demands on its member organizations. Most important, coalitions must do things that are important for their members; they must help their members as well as the group.

There are many advantages to working through coalitions and consortia. Collaborative efforts can function more efficiently than single organizations, as work plans are shared among collaborating organizations rather than carried out by a

Table 6-2 Characteristics of Collaborative Organizations

Organization	Characteristics
Advisory committees	Generally respond to organizations or programs by providing suggestions and technical assistance
Commissions	Usually consist of citizens appointed by official bodies
Consortia and alliances	Tend to be semiofficial, membership organizations; typically have broad policy-oriented goals and may span large geographic areas; usually consist of organizations and coalitions as opposed to individuals
Networks	Are generally loose-knit groups formed primarily for the purpose of resource and information sharing
Task forces	Most often come together to accomplish a specific series of activities, often at the request of an overseeing body

Source: Reprinted from Contra Costa County Health Services Department Prevention Program, *Developing Effective Coalitions: An Eight Step Guide,* 1994.

single group. This serves to conserve limited resources and also provides a pathway for reaching a larger part of the community. When organizations band together around specific goals, their efforts carry greater credibility than when only one or a few organizations are involved. Collaborative efforts are also excellent mechanisms for ensuring a broad range of inputs and perspectives into the policy development process and for facilitating communication and information across agencies and organizations. This has the added benefit of helping staff from one organization to view problems and possible solutions from a broader perspective than their usual vantage point. By building trust and personal relationships around one issue, collaborative approaches facilitate future collaborations around other issues.

There are no set rules for developing coalitions and consortia, but some general principles and approaches are useful after the decision is made to use a collaborative approach (Exhibit 6–5). That decision may come from a lead agency determining that a coalition would facilitate achievement of some goal or, in some instances, being required to establish one by a funding organization. On other occasions, an organization may be requested by community leaders or other agencies to organize a collaborative effort. Unmet community needs, scandals, and service breakdowns all serve to promote the development of coalitions, as do both informal and formal ties that exist among members.

Exhibit 6-5 Key Steps for Coalitions and Other Collaborative Organizations

Step 1: Analyze the program's objectives, and determine whether to form a coalition.
Step 2: Recruit the right people.
Step 3: Develop a set of preliminary objectives and activities.
Step 4: Convene the coalition.
Step 5: Anticipate the necessary resources.
Step 6: Define elements of a successful coalition structure.
Step 7: Maintain coalition vitality.
Step 8: Make improvements through evaluation.

Source: Reprinted from Contra Costa County Health Services Department Prevention Program, *Developing Effective Coalition: An Eight Step Guide,* 1994.

Most coalitions have an agency or organization that leads the effort. Lead agencies must have both the credibility and the resources necessary for a coalition to succeed.

If it is determined that a coalition is the best mechanism to address a particular goal, the resources needed from the lead agency and other coalition members should be assessed to determine if the coalition represents the best use of those resources to accomplish that goal. This requires examination of objectives and implementation strategies that might facilitate achievement of the coalition's goals. A range of implementation strategies are available to coalitions, including making advocacy efforts to influence policy and legislation, changing organizational behavior, promoting networks, educating providers, educating the community, and increasing individual knowledge and skills. One or more implementation strategies should be adopted by the coalition on the basis of how well these fit with the community's strengths and weaknesses.

After the decision is made to develop a coalition, recruitment of the appropriate members is necessary to advance the process. Questions to be addressed include whether membership will consist of individuals or organizations and, if the latter, who should represent a particular organization on the coalition. In some cases, it is desirable to have agency leaders; in others, lower level staff more familiar with the issues and programs may make better members. The size of the coalition also requires careful consideration. Once these issues are decided, preliminary objectives and work plans are developed, and the coalition is convened. At this point, the role of the lead agency in chairing or staffing the coalition should be determined, and resources needed to carry out the coalition's work plan should be identified and made available. Early decisions of the coalition should establish its expected life span, criteria for membership and decision making, and expectations for participation at and between meetings. Constant vigilance is necessary to identify problems internal to the coalition's operation. These can include loss of interest and participation from some members, tension and conflict over power and leadership of the coalition, lack of community representativeness, and turnover of coalition members. Frequently, coalition members perceive threats to their organizational autonomy or come to disagree about service priorities or, more specifically, about which members will provide specific services. Careful assessment of a coalition's strengths and weaknesses, together with a commitment to make a good process even better, are often necessary to maintain the vitality and momentum of even the best coalition.

Many of these steps and issues appear to be straightforward and noncontroversial until they are addressed within the context of an actual coalition experience. The Discussion Questions and Exercises include an opportunity to address these in the development of a statewide injury control coalition.

INFORMATION RESOURCES

In addition to human, organizational, leadership, and collaborative resources, information and access to information represent important elements of the public health infrastructure. The information resources that support public health practice include both the scientific basis of public health and the network of data and information needed to assess and address health problems. In large part, this knowledge base is outlined in the competencies for public health professionals presented in the discussion of the public health work force. It includes elements from the public health sciences consisting of epidemiology, biostatistiscs, environmental health sciences, health administration, and behavioral sciences. This knowledge base contributes to the development of competencies across a broad range of analytical, communication, policy development and planning, cultural, basic public health science, and management skills. Although this knowledge base is provided through graduate-level public health education, it can also be acquired through other educational, training, and experiential opportunities.

Information resources to carry out the activities of public health are increasingly abundant and accessible. Several important principles[12] that underlie the effective use of information sets in public health are highlighted in Exhibit 6–6. The need to ensure both flexibility and compatibility within information systems creates a tension that is not always readily resolved. In addition, two general categories of data sets are commonly encountered in public health practice. It is important to recognize their differences, although there is often great value in using both categories in efforts to identify and address health problems.

One category includes service- or encounter-based data, which are collected for a variety of purposes, such as reimbursement, eligibility, and evaluation of care. These data sets are common to programs that provide primary or episodic

Exhibit 6-6 Principles of Public Health Information

---

1. Recognize different types of data: encounter-based data on individuals as they encounter providers and universal data on populations from surveys and environmental monitoring systems.
2. Provide for integrated management to better meet individual needs and fully portray individual participation in multiple, categorical programs.
3. Maintain a service orientation to address the overriding concern of public health information systems.
4. Ensure flexibility so as to adapt to differences in data collection resources at the local level while accommodating data needs to support a broad range of public health programs and objectives.
5. Achieve system compatibility to allow data flow and functioning across systems in a fully compatible fashion.
6. Protect confidentiality to provide better service and preserve privacy.

Source: Reprinted from J.R. Lumpkin, Six Principles of Public Health Information, *Journal of Public Health Management and Practice,* Vol. 1, No. 1, pp. 40–42, © 1995, Aspen Publishers, Inc.

---

health care services, nutrition services for women, infants, and children (WIC), mental health and substance abuse treatment, and many other services. The information is collected for individual recipients of these services, which may include important clinical preventive services such as immunizations or cancer screening. Aggregate data from these service encounters provide useful information on health needs and the health status of a population, including program coverage and penetration rates. However, the population is limited to those seeking services and may not be representative of the larger population.

Another category of data sets describes populations rather than individuals. Examples include many of the federal surveys of health status and service utilization, as well as behavioral risk factor surveys of the population that collect information on population samples (composed of individual respondents) that are representative of the entire population. For these data sets, the population is described through the use of sampling techniques. Other data sets capture information on specific health events and outcomes for a defined population, such as cancer incidence registries and vital records systems. For these, data are collected on individuals and aggregated in comparison to a reference population often derived from census information (e.g., the rate of newly diagnosed lung cancers among women aged 45 to 64 in a state). Data sets that describe risks or hazards common to a population, such as environmental monitoring data, represent yet another form of population-based data.

The limitations of encounter-based information systems are apparent when individuals participate in more than one service program. A prenatal care program may have its own information system, the WIC program serving the same person may have another system and the lead screening program yet another. The communicable disease program may have separate systems for general communicable diseases, HIV infections, tuberculosis, and sexually transmitted diseases. Beyond these health information systems, an individual may also be receiving services from other agencies for mental health, substance abuse, spousal abuse, and Medicaid. The information systems are often problem specific, yet individuals generally have multiple problems. Integration of information systems across the entire spectrum of human services programs and needs is essential both to promote efficiency in programs and to characterize the health status and needs of individuals and populations.

Confidentiality issues can be especially difficult to address in information systems. A recently proposed model state law for the collection, sharing, and confidentiality of health statistics would make it impossible for individuals to be identified unless they consented. Disclosure of personal identifiers would be permitted only to a government entity or research project that had a written agreement to protect the confidentiality of the information or to a governmental entity for the purpose of conducting an audit, evaluation, or investigation of the agency.

Information and the Assessment Function of Public Health

Information drives the assessment function of public health in at least three ways. First, public health agencies commonly utilize surveillance data to monitor community health status and trends and to identify any new health risks or hazards. Second, once health needs and problems are identified, information is needed on the community's resources that are available to address those needs and problems and the effectiveness of those resources. Third, information from assessments of health needs and current efforts must be tailored to the needs of decision and policy makers to facilitate more effective interventions.[13] Data sources for these three facets of the assessment function are presented in Exhibit 6–7. This exhibit suggests that information is a resource widely utilized throughout public health practice in applications involving surveillance, planning processes, selection of scientifically based interventions, and health communications.

Information and Surveillance

Public health surveillance activities monitor health status and risk factors in the population. Although surveillance data sets have become both more sophisti-

Exhibit 6–7 Data Sets and Activities Associated with the Three Facets of the Assessment Process

---

I. Monitor health status and risk factors
  A. Health status
    1. Mortality
      a. vital statistics
      b. coroner and medical examiner reports
      c. infant mortality reviews
    2. Morbidity, injuries, and disabling conditions
      a. notifiable diseases
      b. hospital discharge records
      c. disease registries (e.g., cancer, trauma)
      d. health interview surveys
      e. newborn screening

  B. Risk factors
    1. Known risk factors
      a. health risk appraisals
      b. behavioral risk factor surveys
      c. knowledge and attitude surveys
      d. health care utilization surveys
      e. laboratory tests
      f. environmental measures
      g. family histories
      h. physical exams
    2. Unknown risk factors (research agenda)
      a. community studies
      b. clinical trials
      c. basic science research (e.g., gene mapping)

II. Identify and evaluate resources
  A. Types of resources
    1. Health resources
      a. health facilities
      b. health professionals
      c. medicines and vaccines
      d. emergency medical transportation systems
    2. Other resources
      a. sanitation programs
      b. educational programs
      c. disaster response plans
      d. counseling services

---

continues

Exhibit 6–7 continued

    B. Evaluation of resources
        1. Availability of resources
            a. proximity
            b. accessibility
            c. affordability
            d. acceptability
            e. appropriateness
        2. Effectiveness of resources
            a. size of population in need
            b. proportion of the population reached by programs
            c. effectiveness of current programs
            d. cost to provide the program
            e. cost for each unit outcome
            f. cost to meet some proportion of the unmet need
            g. evaluation of alternative ways to meet need
III. Inform and advise managers, policymakers, and the public
    A. Summarize the data simply and straightforwardly.
    B. Tailor the data to the audience.
    C. Provide information that answers questions.
    D. Educate those who ask the questions.

Source: Reprinted from Council on Linkages Between Academia and Public Health Practice, *Practice Guidelines for Public Health: Assessment of Scientific Evidence, Feasibility and Benefits,* October 1995, Council on Linkages, U.S. Public Health Services.

---

cated and more accessible in recent years, the most important consideration for their establishment relates to why and how they will be used. The very first collection of health statistics dates back to the work of John Graunt in England in the mid-17th century. Health data in the United States have had the benefit of national enumerations of the population every 10 years, although the decennial census was established to ensure fair representation in the Congress rather than to serve as a source of health or even demographic information on the population. Table 6–3 presents an overview of data sources for epidemiologic surveillance and demonstrates the numerous sources that can be tapped. These range from well-known data sets such as birth and death records to lesser known sources such as school and work absenteeism reports. A summary of the type of data included, availability and completeness, population coverage, value, and limitations is also provided.[14] Although this summary is illustrative of the range of available resources, it is far from exhaustive. For example, Table 6–4 identifies a

Table 6-3 Overview of Epidemiologic Data Sources

Data Source	Nature of Data	Availability	Population Coverage	Value and Limitations
Mortality statistics	Data from registration of vital events	Annually, from vital registration systems and political subdivisions	Complete	Useful for studying mortality
Medical data from birth records	Data on congenital anomalies, complications of pregnancy and childbirth, birthweight, etc.	Annually, from vital registration systems and political subdivisions	Complete	Routinely available; some aspects of morbidity may be incompletely reported (e.g., etiologic factors)
Reportable disease statistics	Statistics based on physician reports, new cases of communicable diseases	Weekly reports for the United States	Complete	Useful for detection of outbreaks of infectious diseases; some conditions not completely reported
Mass diagnostic and screening surveys	Data that result from diagnostic and screening tests for specified diseases	On an ad hoc basis	Variable	Unknown completeness
Disease registries	Statistics based on existing case registries of cancer, stroke, etc.	Continuous, from national, state, and local jurisdictions	Presumably complete for selected diagnosed diseases	Useful for studying the incidence of diseases such as cancer; used to select cases in case-control studies

continues

Morbidity surveys of the general population	From the US Health Examination (HES) Survey and the Household Interview Survey (HIS)	Continuous, data released on computer tapes	Complete for probability sample	Useful for epidemiologic research: some HIS data may not be accurate for self-reports; HES contains more precise diagnoses
Health insurance statistics	Cases given medical care under prepaid insurance coverage	Not generally available, although some agencies conduct research on their own insured	Covered population	Useful for health utilization studies; research on morbidity and mortality in selected populations
Life insurance statistics	Mortality data and results of physical examinations of those applying for coverage	Not generally available	Insurance policy holders	Data for selected population
Hospital inpatient statistics	Cases treated in hospital; dependent on type of hospital	Generally not available without special approval	Not determinable	Diagnostic information may be of higher quality than that from other sources; difficult to relate cases to a population denominator

continues

Table 6-3 continued

Data Source	Nature of Data	Availability	Population Coverage	Value and Limitations
Hospital outpatient statistics	Patients in clinics and outpatient divisions (OPD) of hospitals	Generally not available without special approval	Not deter-minable	OPDs provide a large volume of care; OPD hospital records are sometimes not well developed; diagnostic data may be incomplete
Data on diseases treated in special clinics and hospitals	Dependent on nature of clinic or hospital; essentially medical care data	Generally not available without special approval	Not deter-minable	Counts of patients treated; difficult to determine prevalence rates; population denominator unknown
Data from public health clinics	Data from physical exams of patients	Generally not available without special approval	Not deter-minable	Possible uses for identification of cases of disease and for study of health services; population denominator unknown
Data from records of physician practices	Medical care provided in physicians' offices	Generally not available without special approval	Not deter-minable	May be useful for identifi-cation of cases; records may vary in completeness and quality; duplication of cases for patients who see multiple providers

continues

Absenteeism data	Frequency of absenteeism from work or school	By special arrangements with school system or industry	Probably complete for selected population groups	Nonspecific indicator of disability in selected population; useful for assessing acute disease outbreaks
Data from school health programs	Findings of physical exams of school children	Generally not available	Elementary and secondary school population	Uneven quality and completeness of data
Statistics on morbidity in armed forces	Armed forces morbidity and hospitalization experience; results of selective service examinations	Generally available	Draftees and career military personnel	Comprehensive morbidity information on a selected population; important source for follow-up studies

continues

Table 6-3 continued

Data Source	Nature of Data	Availability	Population Coverage	Value and Limitations
Statistics on veterans	Veterans' hospitalization experience and deaths	Generally available	Hospital experience of those using VA system hospitals; may be incomplete for those who use other facilities	Useful for studying case mix, demography, and hospitalization experience
Social Security statistics	Disability benefit data and Medicare statistics	Data are released on computer-readable media	Nationwide	Useful for studying disability
Labor statistics	Injuries and illnesses in industry	Routinely reported by US Bureau of Labor Statistics	Workers in various occupations and industries in US	Useful data for studying accidents, injuries, and occupational diseases
Census data	Counts, enumerations, and characteristics of populations by geographic location in the US, including age, sex, race	Decennial census and annual estimates	Complete	Extremely useful for enumerating the population; some segments of the population may be undercounted

Source: Reprinted from R.H. Friis and T.A. Sellers, *Epidemiology for Public Health Practice,* © 1996, Aspen Publishers, Inc.

Table 6-4 Selected U.S. Data Sources That Support Environmental Public Health Surveillance

Title	Category[a]	Scope	Responsible Organization(s)	Source(s) of Data	Dates	Limitations of Data[b]
Aerometric Information Retrieval	H	National	Environmental Protection Agency	Air monitoring sites	1970–present	T
Ambulatory Sentinel Practice Network for North America	O	National[c]	Ambulatory Sentinel Practice Network	Family physicians	1981–present	T,I,R,N
Drug Abuse Warning Network	E,O	National	National Institute on Drug Abuse	Emergency rooms, medical examiners, and coroners	1972–present	I,R,Q
Hazardous Substances Emergency Events Surveillance System	H,O	5 states	Agency for Toxic Substances and Disease Registry	State agencies, hospitals, fire/police departments	1990–present	T,I,R,Q,N
Hazardous Materials Information System	H,O	National	Department of Transportation	Highway patrol	1971–present	I,R,N
Medical Examiner and Coroner Information Sharing System	E,O	National[c]	Centers for Disease Control and Prevention	Medical examiners and coroners	1990–present	T,R,Q
Medical Provider Analysis and Review	O	National	Health Care Financing Administration	Office-based medical practices, hospital discharge data	1992–present	T,I,R,Q,N

continues

Table 6-4 continued

Title	Category[a]	Scope	Responsible Organization(s)	Source(s) of Data	Dates	Limitations of Data[b]
McAuto	O	National[c]	McDonnell-Douglas Corp.	Hospital discharge abstracts	1982– present	T,I,R,Q,N
National Ambulatory Medical Care Survey	O	National	National Center for Health Statistics	Ambulatory care providers	1974– 1981, 1985, 1990	T,I,N
National Disease and Therapeutic Index	E,O	National	IMS Inc.	Office-based medical practice	1960– present	T,I,N
National Exposure Registry	H,E	National	Agency for Toxic Substances and Disease Registry	Personal interviews	1989– present	T,R,Q,N
National Health Assessment and Nutrition Examination Survey	E,O	National	National Center for Health Statistics	Population survey respondents	1971, 1976, 1982, 1988	T,N
National Health Interview Survey	H,O	National	National Center for Health Statistics	Household interview respondents	1957– present	T,I,N
National Hospital Discharge Survey	O	National	National Center for Health Statistics	Hospital discharge abstracts	1965– present	T,I,N
Professional Activities Study	O	National	Commission of Professional and Hospital Activities	Hospital discharge abstracts	1953– present	T,I,R,Q,N

continues

Surveillance, Epidemiology, and End Results Program	O	National[c]	National Cancer Institute, National Institutes of Health	Cancer registry	1973–present	T,R,N
Toxic Release Inventory	H	National	Environmental Protection Agency	Industry	1987–present	T,Q
Vital Records	O	National	National Center for Health Statistics, states	Death certificates, birth certificates	1925–present	I,Q
Water Data Storage and Retrieval System	H	National	Department of the Interior, US Geological Survey	Multiple soil and water sites	1880–present	T

Note: References to these systems are available from the original authors on request.

[a]H = hazard; E = exposure; O = outcome.

[b]T = not timely; I = incomplete data on outcomes; R = not representative; Q = poor-quality data; N = useful at national, regional, or state level only.

[c]Includes selected states or localities only.

Source: Adapted with permission from S.B. Thacker, D.F. Stroup, R.G. Parrish, and H.A. Anderson, Surveillance in Environmental Public Health: Issues, Systems and Sources, *American Journal of Public Health*, Vol. 86, pp. 633–638, © 1996.

number of sources of additional surveillance information primarily related to environmental health risks.[15] Several data sources are common to both summaries, notably those operated through CDC's National Center for Health Statistics, which maintains systems for

- Vital Statistics (births, deaths, fetal deaths, induced abortions, marriages, divorces, follow-back surveys to gather additional information)
- National Health Interview Survey (amount, distribution, and effects of illness and disability, using a multistage probability sample)
- National Medical Care, Utilization and Expenditure Survey (use of and expenditures for medical services, done in 1980 but not repeated since)
- National Ambulatory Medical Care Survey (location, setting, and frequency of ambulatory care encounters)
- National Health and Nutrition Examination Survey (direct physical, physiological, and biochemical data from national sample)
- National Hospital Discharge Survey (characteristics of patients, length of stay, diagnoses, procedures, patterns of patient use by type of hospital)

Surveillance is a multifaceted operation in that information is collected at a variety of levels. Surveillance information used in environmental public health applications illustrates this point. For any environmental agent that is considered a hazard, surveillance efforts can measure its effects at various steps in its chain of causation. For example, the agent's presence in the environment can be assessed, and its route of exposure can be measured through surveillance efforts that can be considered hazard surveillance. Beyond hazard surveillance, exposure surveillance can track actual exposures between the host and agent, the frequency in which the agent reaches its target tissue, and the early production of adverse effects. In addition, outcome surveillance can measure the actual adverse effects after these become clinically apparent. Together, these three levels of surveillance activities provide a more complete picture of the problem and allow for a more rational strategy for its control and for evaluating whether control strategies are working or not.

There is wide variability in the capacity of state and local health agencies to maintain and utilize surveillance information. More than two-thirds of the 50 states utilize surveillance systems for tracking lead poisoning, but fewer than 25 percent maintain surveillance systems for the other sentinel environmental diseases[16] included in Figure 6–4. LHDs also vary considerably in terms of maintaining surveillance data on common public health problems. More than 80 percent maintain surveillance data on communicable diseases, but less than half track water quality, air quality, chronic diseases, behavioral risk factors, or injuries[6] (Figure 6–5).

Most data sets are neither complete nor completely accurate. Each has problems and issues related to completeness, accuracy, and timeliness. For example, key denominator information provided through census enumerations undercounts important subpopulations and frequently groups at greater risk of adverse health effects. The data set often considered to be the most complete, birth and death records, includes some important data elements that are underreported or inaccurately recorded, including maternal behaviors, length of gestation, and congenital anomalies of newborn infants. Death records also suffer from variability in deter-

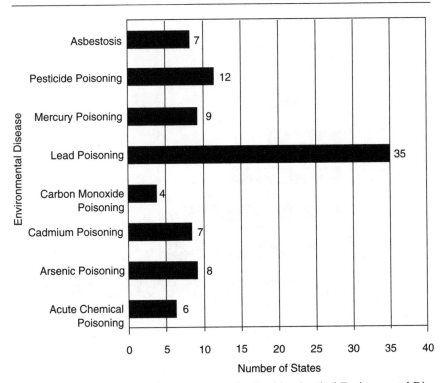

Figure 6–4 States with Surveillance Systems for Tracking Sentinel Environmental Diseases, 1993. *Source:* Reprinted from States Report Minimal Efforts to Track Environmental Diseases, *Public Health Macroview,* Vol. 7. No. 1, Public Health Foundation.

mining cause of death and specifically in identifying true underlying causes, such as tobacco or alcohol.

Vital records represent yet another example of an important federal health policy being operationalized through the states; there is no national mandate for uniform reporting of birth and deaths. Through a voluntary and cooperative effort with the states, a national model of these records is implemented by the states and localities, stimulated in part by federal grants for a national cooperative health statistics system.

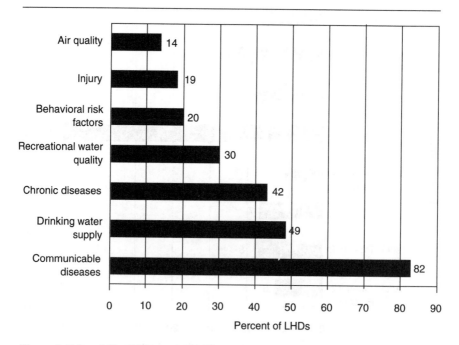

Figure 6–5 Local Health Departments That Maintain Surveillance Data by Selected Category, 1992–1993. *Source:* Reprinted from National Association of County and City Health Officials and Centers for Disease Control and Prevention, *Profile of Local Health Departments, 1992-1993,* 1995, Washington, D.C.

Access to information and data for surveillance purposes has improved steadily with improved technology for electronic management and transfer. As of 1996, reports including a mix of text, tables, and figures were available from an increasing number of federal and state sources through a variety of electronic modes: telephone, fax, CD-ROM and diskettes, modem, and the Internet. Tables 6–5 and 6–6 summarize electronic information resources available from CDC and the Agency for Toxic Substances Disease Registry (ATSDR) as of 1996.[17] In addition to these sources and modes of obtaining information and data, electronic systems are used in ongoing surveillance activities of federal, state, and local public health agencies. These include

- the National Electronic Telecommunications System for Surveillance (NETTS), which is used to collect, transmit, and analyze weekly reports of notifiable diseases from state and local health agencies; the system reports on a common set of diseases, using standard protocols for formatting and transmitting data, standard case definitions, a common record format, and designated individuals responsible for reporting from each agency
- the HIV/AIDS Reporting System, which collects detailed demographic, risk, and clinical information on persons diagnosed with either AIDS or HIV infection; since 1985, CDC has provided state and local health agencies with standardized case report forms and microcomputer-based software for managing HIV and AIDS surveillance in their areas
- the Public Health Laboratory Information System, which reports laboratory isolates to CDC to reduce the enormous paper burden in state laboratories, to facilitate cluster identification, to provide states with better access to data, and to reduce the lag time between identification and reporting to CDC
- CDC WONDER, which is also used as a vehicle for transmission of surveillance files by a number of CDC surveillance systems

Information and Planning

Although there are various forms of planning, each relies heavily on information resources. In public health, planning information is widely employed for purposes of community health planning, agency strategic and operational planning, and program planning and management.

The community health planning role is new for many local governmental public health agencies. From the mid-1960s through the mid-1980s, community health planning was carried out through a national program of state and local planning agencies. The Comprehensive Health Planning Act of 1966 and the National Health Planning and Resource Development Act of 1974 established the framework for these structures and activities. At the state level, state health departments generally coordinated the development of state health plans, in part through the generation of local health plans. These local plans were developed by

Table 6-5 CDC and ATSDR Electronic Resources for Obtaining Reports and Information

Resource	Description
CDC Voice Information System (available by fax or telephone)	The CDC Voice Information System (VIS) provides telephone access to hundreds of prerecorded messages on subjects such as AIDS, immunizations, hepatitis, chronic fatigue syndrome, Lyme disease, and injuries (just to name a few). There is a special section for information for travelers. The injury choice has a section on obtaining grants. Hundreds of documents can be faxed back to the caller (callers enter their fax number using a touch-tone telephone). Callers may request up to five documents at a time; certain documents can be mailed. Most of the documents are written for the public. There is often information on late-breaking news (e.g., outbreaks). Some choices offer the option of being transferred to a CDC professional who can answer more specific questions.
National Institute for Occupational Safety and Health (NIOSH) Information System (available by fax or telephone)	The NIOSH Information System provides telephone access to ordering information on NIOSH publications and databases (including the *Pocket Guide to Chemical Hazards, Manual of Analytical Methods,* NIOSHTIC®, and RTECS® [the databases are discussed separately in the text that follows]); prerecorded information on timely topics such as indoor air quality, carpal tunnel syndrome, homicide in the workplace, etc.; information about NIOSH training materials, including videos; information on obtaining NIOSH grants; and an explanation of how to request a NIOSH investigation of workplace hazards. There is also the option of being transferred to a CDC professional who can answer more specific questions. Unlike the CDC VIS described previously, much of this material is targeted at public health professionals, although some of the material is intended to provide the general public with access to NIOSH information.
Toxicological Profiles (available on CD-ROM)	ATSDR's Toxicological Profiles (on CD-ROM) consists of all final ATSDR toxicological profiles,

continues

Table 6-5 continued

Resource	Description
	which are extensively peer-reviewed, covering the toxicological effects of hazardous substances, chemicals, and compounds. It contains more than 14,000 pages worth of comprehensive, up-to-date data on the mitigation of health effects, all available health data, and data gaps. Each profile includes an examination, summary, and interpretation of available toxicological and epidemiological data evaluations of the hazardous substance, including environmental fate; and a determination of the levels of significant human exposure for the substance and associated acute, intermediate, and chronic health effects. It is fully indexed and can be searched easily (including across profiles).
CDC Prevention Guidelines Database (available on CD-ROM and diskettes)	The CDC Prevention Guidelines Database (PGDB; on diskettes and CD-ROM) contains all of CDC's officially cleared recommendations and guidelines for the prevention of disease, injury, and disability and many of CDC's guidelines for public health practice. The material for this database was assembled in a cooperative project by liaisons in all of CDC's centers, institutes, and offices under the guidance of a steering committee from the Public Health Practice Program Office, the Information Resources Management Office, and the Epidemiology Program Office. The PGDB contains over 400 prevention guideline documents. About two-thirds of these documents were originally published in the *MMWR;* the rest were published as CDC monographs, brochures, book chapters, and peer-reviewed articles. Most of the articles are relatively short; some (such as *Health Information for International Travel 1994* and *Youth Suicide Prevention Programs: A Resource Guide*) are book length. Although the main PGDB at CDC is updated weekly, the CD-ROM/diskettes version is published quarterly.
Chronic Disease Prevention File (available on CD-ROM)	The Chronic Disease Prevention (CDP) File (CD-ROM version) contains six comprehensive bibliographic datasets:

continues

Table 6-5 continued

Resource	Description
	1. The Health Promotion and Education Dataset, which contains over 25,000 bibliographic citations and abstracts focusing on disease prevention and health promotion, including program information;
	2. The Comprehensive School Health Dataset, which contains citations and abstracts focusing on various aspects of comprehensive school health programs. A core component of the dataset includes information on resources for HIV prevention education;
	3. The Cancer Prevention and Control Dataset, which contains entries emphasizing the application of effective breast, cervical, and skin cancer early detection and control program activities and risk reduction efforts;
	4. The Prenatal Smoking Cessation Dataset, which contains information on the application of effective prenatal smoking cessation program activities and risk reduction efforts;
	5. The Epilepsy Education and Prevention Activities Dataset, which contains entries emphasizing the application of effective epilepsy early detection and control program activities, education, and prevention efforts; and
	6. The Smoking and Health Dataset, which includes bibliographic references and abstracts of scientific and technical literature about smoking and tobacco use.
	A CDP directory listing key contacts and organizations in areas of chronic disease prevention (such as nutrition and cancer) is also included.
Health, United States (available on CD-ROM and diskettes)	Health, United States (on diskette) contains the annual report to the president and Congress on the health of the nation. There are data on mortality, morbidity, hospitalizations, etc., largely at the national and state levels. It is available as either spreadsheet files of the tables only, or a more enhanced version that uses a text viewer to provide access to text, charts, and tables.
NIOSHTIC® (available on CD-ROM and by modem)	NIOSHTIC® is the National Institute of Occupational Safety and Health's electronic,

continues

Table 6-5 continued

Resource	Description
	bibliographic database of literature in the field of occupational safety and health that is updated quarterly. About 160 current, English language technical journals provide approximately 35 percent of the additions to NIOSHTIC® annually. Retrospective information (some from the 19th century) is also acquired and entered. It includes information on behavioral sciences; biochemistry, physiology, and metabolism; toxicology; pathology and histology; chemistry; control technology; education and training; epidemiological studies of diseases and disorders; ergonomics; health physics; occupational medicine; safety; and hazardous waste.
Registry of Toxic Effects of Chemical Substances (available on CD-ROM and by modem)	The Registry of Toxic Effects of Chemical Substances (RTECS®) is a database of toxicological information compiled, maintained, and updated by NIOSH. It represents NIOSH's effort to list all known toxic substances and the concentrations at which toxicity is known to occur. It contains data on over 130,000 chemicals, abstracted from the open scientific literature.
CDC National AIDS Clearinghouse ONLINE (available by modem)	CDC NAC ONLINE is the computerized information network of the CDC National AIDS Clearinghouse (CDC NAC). It is designed for nonprofit AIDS-related organizations and other HIV/AIDS professionals. Users must be granted access by CDC NAC staff. Users include CDC and Public Health Service staff, other health administrators, universities, community-based organizations, health educators, and service providers. CDC NAC ONLINE contains the latest news and announcements about AIDS- and HIV-related issues, including prevention and education campaigns, treatment and clinical trials, legislation and regulation, and upcoming events.
CDC WONDER (available by modem and via the Internet)	CDC WONDER, an information and communication system developed by CDC specifically for public health, provides access to

continues

Table 6-5 continued

Resource	Description
	a wide variety of reports, including CDC publications (title, author, abstract) and other bibliographies; the Chronic Disease Prevention bibliographic files; the Healthy People 2000 objectives and associated data sources; all of CDC's official prevention guidelines; a calendar of public health training courses and resources at CDC and elsewhere; CDC's Emerging Infectious Diseases journal; and advisories for overseas travelers.
	The full text of MMWR (1982 to present) is searchable on-line. MMWR articles may be downloaded in full, and (for MMWR articles since September 1993) figures and tables are included in downloaded articles. There is also a listing of CDC experts by their area of specialization.
	CDC WONDER's Info Exchange is a special bulletin board–like database for posting and exchanging materials among CDC staff and the 16,000 registered CDC WONDER users in health departments, schools of public health and medicine, laboratories, clinicians' offices, and elsewhere. All requested documents are automatically downloaded for printing or inclusion in other materials.
CDC Home Page (available via the Internet)	The CDC Home Page on the Internet provides detailed information on CDC programs; access to CDC information resources such as CDC, WONDER, Emerging Infectious Diseases, HazDat, and the MMWR; and pointers to other public health resources on the Internet, including services at the Department of Health and Human Services, the National Institutes of Health, the National Library of Medicine, and the World Health Organization. There is also an FTP (file transfer protocol for the Internet) service for obtaining documents, including selections from Emerging Infectious Diseases, the MMWR, tuberculosis recommendations, and ratings of the inspection records of cruise ships; and for downloading Epi Info and related software.

continues

Table 6-5 continued

Resource	Description
CDC NAC Internet Services (available via the Internet)	The CDC NAC Internet Services provides access to the AIDS Daily Summary, AIDS-related *MMWR* articles; tables from CDC's HIV/AIDS Surveillance Reports and other CDC documents, as well as information about prevention, treatment, and living with HIV.
Emerging Infectious Diseases (available via Internet)	Emerging Infectious Diseases (EID) is a quarterly peer-reviewed journal distributed on the Internet. Its goals are to promote the recognition of new and re-emerging infectious diseases and to improve the understanding of factors involved in disease emergence, prevention, and elimination. EID has an international scope and is intended for professionals in infectious diseases and related sciences.
HazDat (available via Internet)	HazDat (Hazardous Substance Release/Health Effects Database) contains information on the release of hazardous substances from Superfund sites and emergency events, including information on site characteristics, contaminants found, impact on population, community health concerns, ATSDR recommendations, environmental fate of hazardous substances, exposure routes, and physical hazards at the site/event. HazDat also contains substance-specific information, such as the ATSDR Priority List of Hazardous Substances, health effects by route and duration of exposure, metabolites, interactions of substances, susceptible populations, and biomarkers of exposure and effects. There are hundreds of lengthy, detailed entries that can be searched by single words. Access to the Internet is required for use.
MMWR	The *MMWR* contains brief articles on timely issues and provisional notifiable disease data, based on weekly reports to CDC by state health departments. (The reporting week concludes at close of business on Friday; data compiled nationally are released to the public on the succeeding Friday.) Current issues and some back issues and selected associated publications (Reports and Recommendations,

continues

Table 6-5 continued

Resource	Description
	Surveillance Summaries) are available for downloading from a Web server. The files are in Adobe Acrobat format (the viewer is available for downloading). Typical issues are 250 to 400 Kb, but summaries are available on-line.

Source: Reprinted from A. Friede and P.W. O'Carroll, CDC and ATSDR Electronic Information Resources for Health Officers, *Journal of Public Health Management and Practice,* Vol. 2, No. 3, pp. 10–24, © 1996, Aspen Publishers, Inc.

agencies known as health systems agencies (HSAs), whose role was to organize community participation in the development and implementation of the local plans. Consumer majorities sat on planning boards at both the state and local levels. Largely due to their lack of focus, inability to make change happen, and widespread provider resentment of consumer-dominated processes, political support for this effort waned, and the federal program was repealed. Very soon thereafter, most of the local health planning agencies also disappeared, leaving a significant void. Local public health agencies, with a few exceptions, had not been very involved in community health planning and found it difficult to pick up the slack. LHDs often lacked staff with the skills and expertise in community health planning: many information sources resided at levels of government outside their direct control, and they simply did not see it as part of their job description at a time when demands for serving the uninsured and the AIDS epidemic were at their doorsteps. These factors contributed to the need for the development of tools such as APEXPH, the Planned Approach to Community Health (PATCH), and Model Standards, described in Chapter 5.

APEXPH and other community needs assessment processes call for a variety of mortality, morbidity, and risk factor information as well as data and information on available resources to address priority health problems. Information describing the health status and needs of the local population is often available from federal and state sources, but more often these sources must be supplemented with more locally developed information. The lessons from earlier attempts at consumer-directed local health planning demonstrate that community health planning is as much a political process as it is an objective process based on statistical data. Diversity in values and perspectives within a community cannot be homogenized through the use of what some consider objective data. These past failures make it all the more difficult for local public health agencies seeking to re-enter this minefield. Managerial planning improvements, however, have emerged, including planning-programming-budgeting-systems,

Table 6-6 CDC and ATSDR Electronic Resources for Obtaining Data

Resource	Description
AIDS Public Information Data Set (available via CD-ROM/diskettes)	The AIDS Public Information Data Set (on diskette) contains summary surveillance data on the AIDS epidemic in the U.S. The dataset has two components. The first is a file with one record per patient diagnosed and reported with AIDS. These records contain basic demographic, clinical, and HIV transmission risk information. This component is best used for analyzing trends and characteristics of the AIDS epidemic at the national level. The patient-level file can be exported in either ASHII or dBASE compatible format for analysis. The second component is a set of predefined tables that contains much of the information available on the patient-level dataset together with geographic identifiers (state and metropolitan statistical area). This component is most appropriate for analysis of data at state and local levels. Software for viewing, printing, and exporting the data and tables is included.
Behavioral Risk Factor Surveillance System (available via CD-ROM/diskettes)	Data from the Behavioral Risk Factor Surveillance System (BRFSS; 1984–1993; on CD-ROM) contains prevalence information on state level risk factors for chronic diseases, including smoking, drinking alcohol, seat belt usage, etc. Included software facilitates exploratory analysis and mapping. An updated CD-ROM with standardized geocoding and additional documentation is available.
National Center for Health Statistics (NCHS) Data Files (available via CD-ROM/diskettes)	NHS data files (on CD-ROM) are available for the National Health Interview Survey (1988–1992), the National Ambulatory Care Survey (1990), the National Hospital Discharge Survey (1990), the Longitudinal Study of Aging (1984–1990), and the Live Birth/Infant Death files (1985–1988). These data are accessed via the Statistical Export and Tabulation System (SETS), a software program written by NCHS to provide a query interface to national data and dataset documentation on CD-ROMs or diskettes that will allow public health practitioners to make wide use of the benefits of the information age.

continues

Table 6-6 continued

Resource	Description
CDC WONDER (available by modem and via the Internet)	CDC WONDER via modem provides access to data on mortality, natality, population, cancer incidence, motor vehicle and occupational injuries, hospitalizations, AIDS and other sexually transmitted diseases, and many other numeric datasets. Results are downloaded to the user's microcomputer, where, using integrated software supplied with the system, results can be viewed, tabulated, graphed, and printed; or exported for editing, inclusion in other documents, or analysis in specialized statistical software. Most queries take one to two minutes. Data are derived from standard public use files or data prepared especially for CDC WONDER from existing data. The databases and associated reports are developed cooperatively with data providers who add information to the system. Each dataset has on-line documentation (i.e., information on how the data were collected, the phrasing of the question on a questionnaire, sampling methods, known biases and errors, and references). New data are added regularly.
	CDC WONDER via the Internet provides access to much of the same data that are available in CDC WONDER via modem. Tabulating and graphing will require the user to download CDC WONDER Tables and Graphs, which is the no-cost, DOS-based software built into the CDC WONDER DOS client. Alternatively, users may use their own software for this purpose; CDC WONDER Tables and Graphs has an exporting module to facilitate conversions to any of 10 common formats.

Source: Reprinted from A. Friede and P.W. O'Carroll, CDC and ATSDR Electronic Information Resources for Health Officers, *Journal of Public Health Management and Practice,* Vol. 2, No. 3, pp. 10–24, © 1996, Aspen Publishers, Inc.

operations research, systems analysis, and program evaluation and review techniques.

Information resources also support the strategic and operational planning activities of an organization. Strategic planning seeks to identify external and internal trends that might influence the agency's ability to carry out its mission and role. Operational planning looks to maximize the use of available resources to achieve specific objectives that have been established for a specific period of time, generally one year.

Information and Scientifically Based Interventions

At the heart of public health interventions for improving the quality of life and reducing preventable mortality and morbidity are scientifically sound strategies and approaches. Although the scientific basis for public health interventions has always been highly valued, the formal application of rigorous assessments to the evidence for effectiveness is a relatively new undertaking for public health. To some extent, this process is modeled on the work of the U.S. Preventive Services Task Force, which has reviewed data and information related to the provision of clinical preventive services to assess what works and what does not. The clinical practice guidelines that emerged from that process have been widely accepted and have served to raise the standard of practice for clinical preventive services for specific age groups.

For preventive interventions, the job only begins with demonstrating efficacy: that an intervention works well under ideal circumstances. Although an intervention may be efficacious, it may not work somewhere else because of the particular conditions and circumstances that exist there. Such an intervention would not be considered effective: that is, it would not have the impact intended. Many different social, ethical, legal, and distributional factors may limit effectiveness in a particular setting.[18] Figure 6–6 illustrates the life cycle of a preventive intervention from its development through basic research to its eventual widespread intervention. In between, applied research activities and community demonstrations are necessary to provide a complete picture of its effectiveness in terms of its impact on outcomes, economic considerations, and safety.

Although these analyses have been applied to clinical preventive services, there has been little effort to apply them to community prevention activities. In 1995, the first steps were taken toward the development of practice guidelines for public health using these same principles.[19] An assessment of the feasibility of such an undertaking was completed through the Council on Linkages between Academia and Public Health Practice, which itself was established as a result of the recommendations of the Public Health Faculty-Agency Forum. The conclusions and recommendations of this assessment are presented in Exhibit 6–8 and indicate that there was strong support for developing population-based practice guidelines. Four specific community prevention interventions were examined: immunizations, tuberculosis treatment, cardiovascular disease prevention, and lead poisoning prevention. Organizing the volumes of information and data for each of the these areas was completed by the use of critical questions that assisted

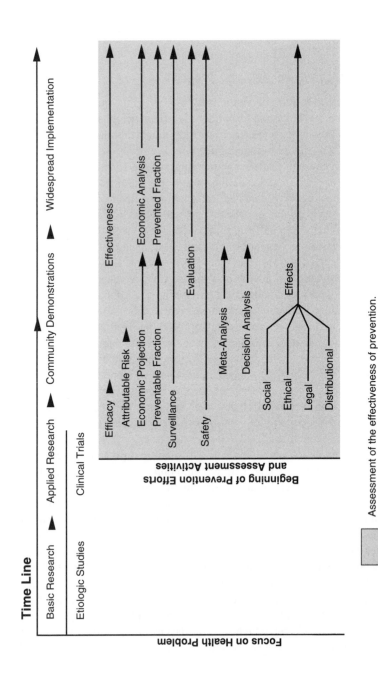

Figure 6–6 Natural History of the Development of an Effective Prevention Strategy and Temporal Relationship to the Types of Assessment Activities. *Source:* Reprinted from S. Teutsch, A Framework for Assessing the Effectiveness of Disease and Injury Prevention, *Morbidity and Mortality Weekly Report,* Vol. 41, p. RR-3, 1992, Centers for Disease Control and Prevention.

Exhibit 6-8 Practice Guidelines for Public Health: Recommendations for Assessment of Scientific Evidence, Feasibility, and Benefits

---

1. Public health practice guidelines are feasible, based upon scientific evidence and other empirical information.
2. The potential benefits of public health practice guidelines are immediate and far-reaching.
3. Each set of guidelines should have a carefully circumscribed scope.
4. Guidelines should be flexible rather than proscriptive.
5. Guidelines should be dynamic.
6. All major stakeholders should be involved as the guidelines are developed.
7. Critical questions are an efficient tool to structure the evidence-collection process.
8. A database search for scientific studies is a useful first step.
9. Additional sources of documentary evidence should be tapped and systematically evaluated.
10. Empiric evidence from state and local public health programs should be sought, evaluated, and incorporated into the guidelines.
11. Development of guidelines will stimulate needed research.
12. Guidelines should be pilot-tested before dissemination and then continuously evaluated.

Source: Reprinted from Council on Linkages Between Academia and Public Health Practice, *Practical Guidelines for Public Health: Assessment of Scientific Evidence, Feasibility and Benefits,* October 1995, Council on Linkages, U.S. Public Health Services.

---

the process to focus on key issues. Exhibit 6–9 identifies some critical questions related to lead poisoning prevention.

Information and Health Communications

One final aspect of information is its use in communication for public health purposes. As noted in Chapter 5, informing and educating the public is one of the important practices of public health. This practice is part and parcel of daily public health practice, as information about risks, healthy behaviors, appropriate use of preventive services, and health issues and needs within the community is conveyed in various forms to decision makers, the media, and the general public. It is commonplace for public health professionals to play important roles in assessing public health hazards and risks and in developing, recommending, advocating, and implementing approaches to their correction or amelioration. Most of the time, this process is quite simple and straightforward, as when there is a certain and noncontroversial remedy. However, the impact of a given problem often warrants action even though the evolving epidemiologic or other scientific evidence is not incontrovertible. In such instances, definitive action may be prevented, delayed, or otherwise compromised by true scientific doubts; concerns about costs, logistics, and the like; or special interest groups that may be adversely affected and may use scientific uncertainty to justify opposition. These factors, often coupled with a generalized poor understanding of scientific issues throughout our society, may impede regulatory action and enlistment of public cooperation and support. Problems in making public health decisions in the face of less than incontrovertible evidence have increased in recent decades, and solutions are often disproportionately driven by economic, political, and public relations considerations.

Although health statistics indicate that in many ways we have never had it so good or lived so long, we are bombarded as never before by communications proclaiming a multitude of hazards. To the extent that being conscious of risks helps us to confront and cope with them realistically, this bombardment is a blessing. But there are indications that it may also be having at least two negative effects. First, the very multiplicity of threats and the urgency with which they are presented make it difficult for most people to sort out major from minor, proven from suspect, and, most important, controllable from uncontrollable. Second, as a consequence, we are in danger of surrendering to feelings of helplessness and apathy that paralyze us in the act of coping even in situations where personal action can make a difference.

Exhibit 6-9 Sample of Critical Questions for Lead Poisoning Prevention

- What are effective secondary prevention efforts to combat lead poisoning that can be employed by the public health official in the community of interests? Specifically, should screening for lead poisoning be universal or targeted?
- What are effective environmental interventions and measures that can be employed by the public health official in the follow-up of children with elevated blood lead levels? How might these interventions differ on the basis of the level of lead toxicity?
- What recommendations should be made regarding residential lead and hazard reduction to families with children who have elevated blood lead levels?
- What are the primary prevention approaches to lead poisoning from residential lead-based paint, and what role should public health officials take in implementing such strategies? How should interdisciplinary approaches be developed?

Source: Adapted from *Translating Science into Practice, 1991,* CDC Case Study.

The challenge for those engaged in interpreting risks to the public is twofold. There is a need to convey a sense of relative risk and a need to accentuate the positive by communicating that it is well worth the effort for people to control the risks they can control. But there are major obstacles to be overcome.

One of the most serious and frustrating obstacles is a large and growing credibility gap. Some might call this the "Death of the Expert" in that there is growing skepticism, cynicism, and disbelief of the pronouncements of so-called experts, especially when these experts are associated with government. Often it appears that the public wants its worst fears to be confirmed. If public health professionals report that a perceived risk is indeed real, they tend to be believed. If they report that the perceived risk has been exaggerated, they face suspicion of "whitewash."

The simple way to deal with such situations is, of course, to tell the "the truth, the whole truth, and nothing but the truth" every time. But this is easier said than done, since in many instances the whole truth is not known. Still, communications can be effectively managed with appropriate use of the three-word sentence "I don't know." This can be quite difficult when the outside world thinks the expert does know but is not talking, and it can be disastrous when the expert begins to stray over the line between fact and opinion. More often than not, the opinions make the impressions on the public and the media, and the facts are quickly forgotten. Finally, as if "I don't know" were not difficult enough, saying "We blew it" is harder still. In what has become a suspicious and litigious society, such an acknowledgment of error has significant repercussions. But in many circumstances, evasion merely delays the inevitable, and candor in accepting responsibility for errors pays dividends in future credibility. In any event, information for effective communications around health issues is an important element of public health's infrastructure.

FISCAL RESOURCES

The fiscal resources available for public health activities can be viewed as both inputs and outputs of the system. They are clearly inputs in that they finance the human, organizational, and informational resources described above, as well as a variety of physical facilities, equipment, and other inputs that do not fit nicely into any of the other categories. But the fiscal resources provided for public health programs also represent the worthiness of these activities in comparison with other public policy goals. In this light, fiscal resources are a product of public health activities and an expression of their value in the eyes of society. Nonetheless, this section will primarily examine fiscal resources as inputs.

In previous chapters, it was noted that only about 1 percent of all health sector expenditures support population-based public health activities and that another 2 percent support clinical preventive health services. Here, some further description of the fiscal resources available for public health purposes will be presented.

The most difficult issue to be faced in analyzing public health fiscal resources is to determine what should be included and excluded. Although the 1 percent figure developed during the formulation of national health reform initiatives in 1994 appears to be a reasonable estimate of state and local public health expenditures for population-based services, it remains an estimate. In addition, this figure describes only expenditures of state and local public health agencies and excludes some important population-based activities in states if these are provided through agencies other than the official health agencies. For example, state environmental protection agencies, substance abuse prevention activities, and certain activities in the fields of mental health and developmental disabilities in some instances were not included in this estimate.

To provide a better estimate, efforts to capture all expenditures in states related to public health's core functions have been generated. A study in eight states in 1994 sought to identify expenditures of state and local public health agencies, as well as state environmental protection, mental health, and substance abuse agencies.[20] The findings from this sample were extrapolated to the nation as a whole, leading to the estimate that in 1993 about 1.3 percent of total health spending supported core function activities. This represents a per capita expenditure of about $44 per person (less than $1 per person per week) at a time when national per capita health expenditures were about $3,300 per person.

The categories of expenditures reflected spending in nine areas:

1   health-related data, surveillance, and outcomes monitoring
2. investigation and control of diseases, injuries, and response to natural disasters
3. immunizations, family planning, and STD and TB clinical services
4. protection of environment, housing, food, water, and the workplace
5. laboratory services
6. public information and education and community mobilization
7. accountability/quality assurance
8. training and education
9. leadership, planning, policy development, and administration

Expenditures for these public health responsibilities accounted for 27 percent of the total budgets of the state and local health, environmental protection, mental health, and substance abuse agencies in these eight states.[20] About 30 percent of this total was for the protection of environment, housing, food, water, and the workplace. Figure 4–10 from Chapter 4 presents the proportion spent in each of the nine areas of responsibility.

Public health agencies accounted for about 60 percent of these expenditures, and environmental health agencies expended 31 percent of the total (Figure 6–7). Substance abuse and mental health agencies accounted for the remaining 10 percent. However, as a percentage of total agency expenditures, environmental health agencies led the way, with 49 percent of their expenditures for core public health–related responsibilities. Forty-one percent of public health agencies' resources, 25 percent of substance abuse agencies' resources, and only 2 percent of mental health agencies' resources were expended for core function–related activities. Interestingly, nearly three-fourths of the core function–related expenditures were derived from nonfederal sources (Figure 6–8).

These figures are consistent with estimates from federal health reform work groups. In addition, they reinforce the observation that state and local governments bear the brunt of the burden for funding public health activities in the United States. In Chapter 4, it was noted that the federal government was the source of less than one-third of the expenditures of state and local health agencies in 1993. When the net is cast more widely to capture environmental and substance abuse activities outside of state health agencies, the federal share amounts to about one-fourth of such expenditures. Who currently pays the bills says much about the likelihood for expansion of public health efforts in the future. Tax bases of state and especially local governments and political opposition to tax increases

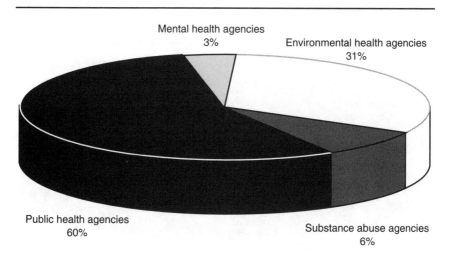

Figure 6–7 Estimated Expenditures for Public Health Functions by Type of Agency, 1993. *Source:* Reprinted from *Measuring State Expenditures for Core Public Health Functions,* 1994, Public Health Foundation, Washington, DC.

of any kind do not augur well for increased state and local public health resources in the future.

CONCLUSION

Public health infrastructure includes the inputs and ingredients of the public health system that are blended together to carry out public health's core functions of assessment, policy development, and assurance. Although these can be presented in various categories, several key elements are easily recognized. The first of these is the work force of public health, an army of individuals committed to improving the public health, although relatively few have had other than on-the-job training for their roles. The diversity of this work force in terms of educational and experiential backgrounds represents both a major strength and a potential weakness for efforts to focus and direct their collective efforts. Facilitating the contributions of the work force are the organizations in which they work. These organizations exist at all levels of government, as well as in all corners of the community. The relationships between and among the agencies, organizations, institutions, and individuals committed to this work are more often informal and collaborative than formalized and centrally directed. Leadership within and across organizations to assess and address health issues and needs in the community is essential to initiate the community problem identification and problem-solving activities that can foster the changes neces-

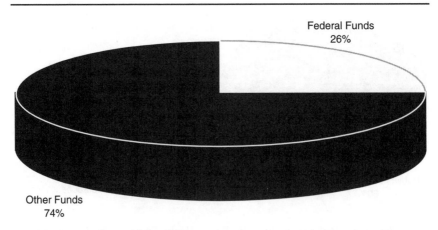

Figure 6–8 Public Health Function Expenditures, by Source of Funds, 1993. *Source:* Reprinted from *Measuring State Expenditures for Core Public Health Functions,* 1994, Public Health Foundation, Washington, DC.

sary for improved health outcomes. The work force, the organizations, and their leadership rely heavily on information for identifying problems, determining interventions, and tracking progress toward agreed-upon objectives. Together, these essential ingredients of the public system formulate the system's capacity to act in serving the public health. This infrastructure represents a small portion of the national economy and only about 1 percent of all health-related expenditures, but its contribution to improved health status and its potential for realizing further gains and closing current gaps suggest that it is worth its weight in gold.

DISCUSSION QUESTIONS AND EXERCISES

1. What characteristics distinguish a public health professional from a professional working for a public health organization?
2. Which strategy to expand public health skills within the health sector would be more effective: increasing the number of master's-degree graduates from schools of public health and other academic programs, providing more public health and prevention in the training of other health professionals, or providing non–degree-based training to health professionals now working in the health system?
3. Are public health organizations today viewed as change agents in their communities? Why or why not?
4. What factors determine the optimum size for a coalition?
5. How have the roles of local boards of health changed over the past century? What would be the most useful roles for such boards in the future?
6. What factors limit our ability to use the extensive amount of data and information that is currently available? How can these obstacles be overcome?
7. Is health planning at the community level necessary? If so, who should be responsible? How can duplication and replication of community health planning be averted?
8. Examine the data provided in Table 6–7, and, in small groups, prioritize the various injuries to determine which should be the target of a statewide injury reduction campaign focusing on sports and recreation equipment injuries. Which three should be targeted? Why?
9. Review the scenario described in Exhibit 6–10, and discuss the questions in small groups.

Table 6-7 Injuries Associated with Selected Sports and Recreation Equipment Treated in Emergency Departments, 1994

Estimated No. of Product-Related Injuries per 100,000 Population in the U.S. That Were Treated in Hospital Emergency Departments

Product Groupings	Estimated No. of Cases	All Ages	Age 0–4	Age 5–14	Age 15–24	Age 25–64	Age 65+	Disposition Treated and Released	Disposition Hospitalized or DOA
ATVs, mopeds, minibikes, etc.	125,136	48.1	14.5	111.7	116.8	27.0	6.5	45.1	3.0
Baseball, softball	404,364	155.3	45.0	410.7	294.4	100.1	3.3	153.4	1.7
Basketball	716,114	275.1	13.4	584.0	955.3	111.6	3.2	272.9	1.8
Bicycles and accessories	604,455	232.2	247.8	908.2	243.2	87.5	28.2	223.3	8.6
Exercise and exercise equipment	155,231	59.6	45.2	68.8	134.6	49.6	16.6	58.5	1.0
Football	424,622	163.1	5.0	484.7	557.1	30.4	1.3	160.8	2.2
Hockey	81,885	31.5	5.4	85.1	81.9	14.4	0.3	30.9	0.5
Horseback riding	71,162	27.3	7.9	38.7	41.0	29.4	3.0	25.1	2.2
Lacrosse, rugby, misc. ball games	90,252	34.7	18.4	126.4	63.4	11.9	1.1	34.2	0.3
Playground equipment	266,810	102.5	386.1	468.7	16.4	5.9	1.6	99.5	2.9
Skateboards	25,486	9.8	7.3	37.5	24.0	1.0	—	9.7	0.1
Skating (excludes in-line)	146,082	56.1	15.6	226.8	57.3	27.1	2.6	54.8	1.3
In-line skating	75,994	29.2	2.3	115.6	40.4	12.9	0.7	28.3	0.8
Soccer	162,115	62.3	2.7	190.6	180.7	18.5	0.6	61.4	0.8
Swimming, pools, equipment	115,139	44.2	62.4	128.8	63.3	21.1	10.1	42.5	1.7
Track and field activities, equipment	18,774	7.2	—	24.3	24.2	0.5	1.0	7.1	0.1
Trampolines	52,892	20.3	27.7	93.5	20.6	3.6	0.1	19.8	0.5
Volleyball	97,523	37.5	2.0	52.4	111.4	27.7	0.6	37.2	0.2

Source: Reprinted from National Electronic Injury Surveillance System, U.S. Consumer Product Safety Commission.

Exhibit 6-10 Coalition-Building Scenario

Scenario

You are the Director of the Center for Health Promotion, one of the units of the Office of Community Health within the Jordania State Department of Public Health (JDPH). Your office is within a few blocks of the state capitol building, which lies in the heart of the city of Jackson Springs, the capital of Jordania.

Data indicate that the number of deaths in the state attributable to injury continues to be a problem. The fourth leading cause of death in terms of numbers of deaths, injury accounts for more years of potential life lost before age 65 than any other cause among Illinois residents each year. Resources in state government are increasingly scarce. To maximize available resources, you convince your agency director that an Injury Coalition should be formed.

The Injury Coalition would be composed of organizational and individual representatives from throughout Jordania with an interest in injury control and an influence on potentially affected groups of people. Ideally, this broad participation would not only bring diversity of perspective but also ensure "buy-in" or commitment by involved organizations to project goals as these are developed. The role of the Injury Coalition would be to determine, on the basis of presentations of data concerning the burden of injury in Jordania, which populations in the state are at greatest risk of death from injuries and how these groups might best be reached with preventive services. The coalition would help develop a statewide injury control plan, set priorities in areas of greatest concern, and determine future interventions. The annual budget allocated to cover planning and other activities of the Injury Coalition is $100,000.

You and the state health department have had some experience setting up and working with coalitions on tobacco control and maternal and child issues in the past. Contact with legislators is not always easy in Jordania due to both political and geographic considerations.

Discussion Questions (Note: for these questions, respond as if Jordania were your home state!)

1. Why should an Injury Coalition be formed? What do you see as potential advantages and potential drawbacks of working with a coalition for this purpose?
2. How can you and the state health department build on prior successful involvement with coalitions?
3. What is the ideal size for such a coalition? What factors might help determine size?
4. Who might you invite to coalition meetings? How would you recruit members? What other facts should be considered when planning on coalition membership? Should members represent organizations or participate on the basis of individual leadership in their field? Should they be agency heads?

continues

Exhibit 6-10 continued

---

5. Are there organizations that you would not like to have represented on the Injury Coalition?
6. Assuming you decide on developing such a coalition, who should be in charge?
7. Would you choose JDPH staff to serve as coalition members? Why or why not? Should they be in charge of the coalition? Should they staff the coalition?
8. What powers and authorities should be given to the coalition? How might decision making within the coalition take place? What are the advantages and disadvantages of different styles of decision making?
9. What geographical factors particular to Jordania need to be considered when planning coalition meetings?
10. What can you expect to be the coalition's major expenses? How might these be reduced?
11. How would you evaluate the coalition's effectiveness?

Source Adapted from *Translating Science into Practice, 1991*, CDC Case Study.

REFERENCES

1. Roper WL, Baker EL, Dyal WW, Nicola RM. Strengthening the public health system. *Public Health Rep.* 1992;107:609–615.
2. *Health United States, 1995*. Washington, DC: National Center for Health Statistics; 1996.
3. Health Resources and Services Administration. *Health Personnel in the United States: Eighth Report to Congress*. Washington, DC: US Public Health Service; 1992.
4. The necessity for trained and educated health officials. *JAMA.* 1893;20:189. Editorial.
5. Public Health Foundation. *State Health Agency Staffs,1989*. Final report of a contract with DHHS-PHS-HRSA. Washington, DC: Public Health Foundation; April 1992.
6. *Profile of Local Health Departments, 1992–1993*. Washington, DC: National Association of County and City Health Officials; 1995.
7. Institute of Medicine. *The Future of Public Health*. Washington, DC: National Academy Press; 1988.
8. Sorenson AA, Bialek RG, eds. *The Public Health Faculty/Agency Forum*. Gainesville, Fla: University of Florida Press; 1992.
9. Schieve LA, Handler AH, Ippoliti P, Gordon AK, Turnock BJ. Building bridges between schools of public health and public health practice: results of a 1993 follow-up study. *J Public Health Manage Pract.* In press.
10. Pew Health Professions Commission. *Critical Challenges: Revitalizing the Health Professions for the Twenty-First Century*. San Francisco, Calif: University of California, San Francisco, Center for Health Professions; 1995.
11. *Developing Effective Coalitions: An Eight Step Guide*. Martinez, Calif: Contra Costa County Health Services Dept; 1994.

12. Lumpkin JR. Six principles of public health information. *J Public Health Manage Pract.* 1995;1(No. 1):40–42.

13. Keppel KG, Freiedman MA. What is assessment? *J Public Health Manage Pract.* 1995; 1(No. 2):1–7.

14. Friis RH, Sellers TA. *Epidemiology for Public Health Practice.* Gaithersburg, Md: Aspen Publishers, Inc; 1996.

15. Thacker SB, Stroup DF, Parrish RG, Anderson HA. Surveillance in environmental public health: issues, systems and sources. *Am J Public Health.* 1996;86:633–638.

16. Public Health Foundation. States report minimal efforts to track environmental diseases. *Public Health Macroview.* 1995;7(1):4–5.

17. Friede A, O'Carroll PW. CDC and ATSDR electronic information resources for health officers. *J Public Health Manage Pract.* 1996;2(No. 3):10–24.

18. Teutsch S. A framework for assessing the effectiveness of disease and injury prevention. *MMWR.* 1992;41:RR-3.

19. *Practice Guidelines for Public Health: Assessment of Scientific Evidence, Feasibility and Benefits.* Council on Linkages between Academia and Public Health Practice; 1995.

20. *Measuring State Expenditures for Core Public Health Functions.* Washington, DC: Public Health Foundation; 1994.

Chapter 7

Public Health Programs and Services

Public health services affect everyone in the community in one way or another. Still, the category of services most commonly associated with public health is the provision of medical—mostly medical treatment—services to low-income populations. Although this image is understandable, it is somewhat misleading.

It is understandable because public-sector agencies play an important safety-net role in providing medical services to individuals who otherwise lack access to such services. These vital safety-net services often overshadow preventive services targeted to both individuals and populations, fostering different perceptions as to which of these services represents the primary products of public health. In truth, both public and private sectors provide preventive as well as treatment services. The relative emphasis is different in that prevention represents a larger share of public-sector services. This is not to say that disease prevention and health promotion services are offered only through the public sector or that future shifts in the level and proportion of these services offered by public and private providers are not possible. The public simply understands, and values, the mix of services offered by private-sector providers more than those provided through the public sector.

Just as people wish to be known as much for their aspirations as for their deeds, public health seeks to be identified with the wide variety of services that promote, protect, and maintain health. These products, in the form of programs and services, represent the most tangible aspects of the public health system's functioning. This chapter will examine public health services and how these are provided through specific programs. In addition, the key steps in the planning, development, and evaluation of public health interventions will be described. Key questions addressed in this chapter include:

- What are the programs and services of public health?
- What distinguishes clinical preventive services from population-based services?
- How are public health interventions planned and evaluated?

PUBLIC HEALTH SERVICES AND PROGRAMS

The products of a system result from the system's inputs carrying out the system's processes. Carrying out public health's core function–related processes generates products intended to improve health status, the bottom line of the public health system. These products or outputs are identifiable as programs and services.

Programs consist of activities seeking to achieve common objectives. These activities can be considered services if some benefit is bestowed on the individual or groups targeted for those specific activities. Other activities of programs may be performed to support the provision of services. Some public health services can be classified as clinical services if directly aimed at improving individual well-being. Others can be considered population-based services if directed toward a group of individuals or the entire population.

Services represent a part of what programs do, although programs are often known for the services that are provided through them. For example, immunization programs are commonly thought of as vaccinations given to individuals, although the actual shots given represent only one activity of that program. Public education, provider education, outreach, compliance determination, recordkeeping, and follow-up are also activities of immunization programs. Together, these make up a program whose best known services are vaccinations. As we will see, the terms *programs* and *services* are often used interchangeably when public health activities are reported.

Because programs are collections of activities sharing the same objectives, they can be characterized differently by lumping and splitting of otherwise discrete programs. For example, an immunization program for measles and a measles surveillance and investigation program could be considered either as separate programs or as a single program, depending on the formulation of their program objectives. A separate measles immunization program might have an objective to achieve a 90 percent immunization rate among two- to three-year old children in a particular community. A separate measles surveillance program's objective might be to investigate newly reported cases of measles within 48 hours. Both of these could be considered as part of a more comprehensive measles prevention and control program whose objective might be stated as seeking a reduction in the incidence of measles by some percent from the current rate.

Programs and services also provide a framework for characterizing public health expenditures and for describing the scope and content of public health practice. Information on public health programs and services is available at a variety of levels, as described previously in both Chapters 4 and 6. Reporting systems that capture information on expenditures of state health agencies and local health departments (LHDs) provide a picture of general categories of programs and services offered through these official public health agencies. Recent estimates of core public health expenditures nationally also describe public health programs in terms of broad programs and services.

Figures 7–1 and 7–2 catalog activities of local health agencies in 1992 and 1993 for various personal health and environmental health services.[1] It should be noted that the activities reported here include a combination of programs and services, although they are reported as services. Several are provided by more than 75 percent of the nation's LHDs, including immunizations, tuberculosis services, well-child services, sewage, and private water supply safety. Among personal health services, 50 to 70 percent of LHDs provide prenatal care, sexually transmitted disease prevention and control services, HIV testing and counseling, family planning and health screening, and treatment for Medicaid-eligible children (EPSDT). For environmental health services, 50 to 70 percent of LHDs provide public water supply safety, surface water pollution, vector control, environmental emergency response, and groundwater pollution control services. Fewer than half of the nation's LHDs furnish case management, HIV/AIDS treatment, indoor air quality, hazardous waste management, animal control, and solid waste management services.

Inspection and licensing activities are another form of public health programs and services. Figure 7–3 presents the percentage of LHDs providing a variety of these activities. Food protection, swimming pool, water system, and recreational area inspections are more frequently provided by LHDs than by other organizations, including various health and other facilities. Still another category of public health services is presented in Figure 7–4. Community outreach and health education services are widely offered, and laboratory services are provided by 60 percent of LHDs. Together, these profiles describe a constellation of local public health services that are noteworthy for both their extensive scope and their local variability.

CATEGORIZING PROGRAMS AND SERVICES OF PUBLIC HEALTH

Aggregating these services into broader categories provides additional insights into the products of public health practice. The methodology used by the Public Health Foundation in its 1994 study of public health core function–related expend-

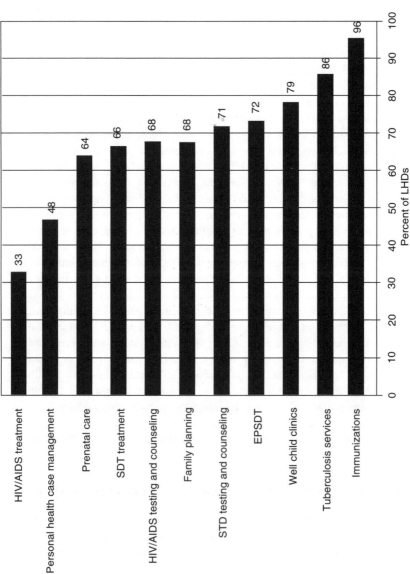

Figure 7–1 Local Health Departments Reporting Activity in Selected Personal Health Service Categories, 1992–1993. *Note:* EPSDT = early periodic screening, diagnosis, and treatment for Medicaid-eligible children; STD = sexually transmitted diseases. *Source:* Reprinted from National Association of County and City Health Officials and Centers for Disease Control and Prevention, *Profile of Local Health Departments, 1992-1993,* 1995, Washington, D.C.

itures is especially useful.[2] Table 7–1 identifies 10 broad categories of public health programs and services, with further breakdown of each category into activities, services, and programs that would fall within the broader groupings. This formulation allows for core function–related activities of health agencies to be distinguished from activities not linked with public health through core functions. It also provides a useful summary of public health programs and services in the public sector and the fiscal resources attached to them. The wide variety of

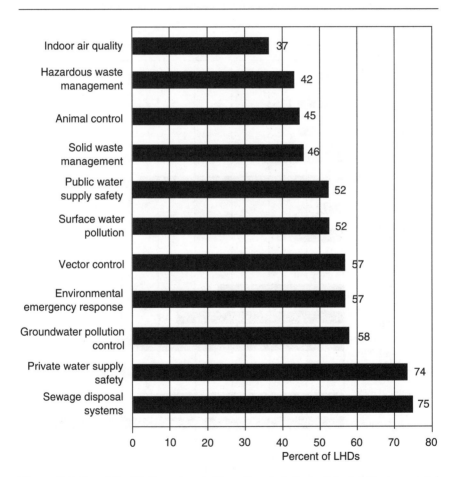

Figure 7–2 Local Health Departments Reporting Activity in Selected Environmental Health Service Categories, 1992–1993. *Source:* Reprinted from National Association of County and City Health Officials and Centers for Diesease Control and Prevention, *Profile of Local Health Departments, 1992-1993,* 1995, Washington, D.C.

community prevention and clinical preventive services is evident in this compendium:

- health-related data, surveillance, and outcomes monitoring
- investigation and control of diseases, injuries, and response to natural disasters (nonclinical services)
- investigation and control of diseases, injuries, and response to natural disasters (public health clinical services)
- protection of environment, housing, food, water, and the workplace
- laboratory services

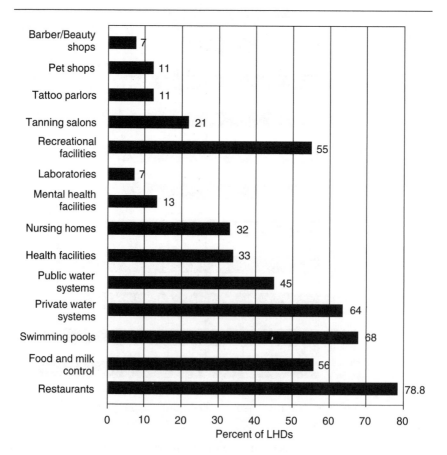

Figure 7–3 Local Health Departments That Provide Inspections and/or Licensing for Selected Activities, 1992–1993. *Source:* Reprinted from National Association of County and City Health Officials and Centers for Disease Control and Prevention, *Profile of Local Health Departments, 1992-1993,* 1995, Washington, D.C.

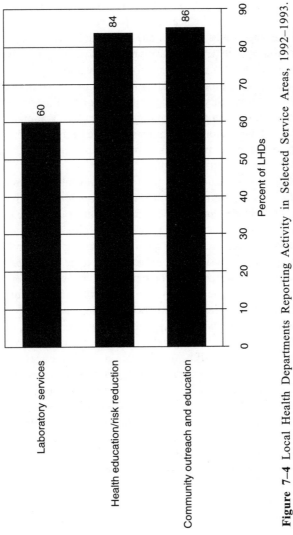

Figure 7–4 Local Health Departments Reporting Activity in Selected Service Areas, 1992–1993. *Source:* Reprinted from National Association of County and City Health Officials and Centers for Disease Control and Prevention, *Profile of Local Health Departments, 1992-1993,* 1995, Washington, D.C.

- public information and community mobilizations
- targeted outreach and linkage to personal services
- accountability and quality assurance
- training and education
- leadership, policy development, planning, and administration

Another understandable characterization of public health activities evolved from efforts to fashion public health provisions for the various national health reform proposals debated in 1994. Public health activities were recast by the Essential Services of Public Health Task Force (see Exhibit 1–5) into two groupings, one representing what public health does (6 categories intended for external audiences) and one representing how public health does what it does (10 categories for internal audiences).[3] These six categories of programs and services seek to prevent epidemics; protect the environment, workplaces, housing, food, and water; prevent injuries; promote healthy behaviors; respond to disasters; and ensure the quality, accessibility, and accountability of health services (Exhibit 7–1). Together, these furnish a clear and comprehensive summary of public health services. The formulation of 10 essential public health services (for internal audiences) parallels the 10 public health practices presented in Chapter 5 as a description of the important processes of public health.

These six categories often include a mixture of preventive services targeted both to populations and to individuals. *Preventing epidemics* includes efforts such as disease surveillance, disease investigation, contact tracing, case management, prophylactic treatment, laboratory services, and immunizations. *Environmental protection* includes air and water quality monitoring and permitting, food, housing and workplace safety standards enforcement, toxic waste permitting and hazardous conditions monitoring, environmental risk assessment services, toxicology evaluation services, laboratory services, and enforcement activities. *Injury prevention* includes injury surveillance, trauma network services, public education and awareness campaigns, child car seat loaner programs, and the like. *Promoting healthy behaviors* includes behavioral risk factor monitoring, fitness programs, comprehensive school health education, worksite health promotion, communitywide risk reduction programs, media involvement, health education, parenting education, and information clearinghouses and other referral sources. *Disaster response* includes disaster planning, emergency medical system maintenance, trauma networks, disaster management drills, and emergency information system establishment. *Assuring the quality, accessibility, and accountability of health services* can include health professions licensing and certification, medical facilities licensing and certification, laboratory services quality assurance, hospital outcomes monitoring, personal services outcomes monitoring, personal services availability assessment, patient satisfaction assessment, cost-effectiveness studies, and automated and linked database management.

Table 7–1 Guide To Estimating Core Function Expenditures

Function	Includes:	Does Not Include:
1. Health-related data, surveillance, and outcomes monitoring	• Disease and injury registries • Data systems related to service availability, utilization, cost, and outcome • Epidemiology (surveillance, disease reporting, sentinel events) • Vital statistics • Environmental epidemiology • Immunization status tracking • Injury epidemiology • Mental health epidemiology • Substance abuse epidemiology	• Client-based data systems

2. Investigation and control of diseases, injuries, and response to natural disasters (nonclinical services)	• Communicable disease detection
	• Chronic disease prevention and detection
	• Emergency response teams (e.g., disease outbreaks, toxic spills, product recalls, emergency systems, natural disasters)
	• HIV/AIDS prevention
	  • Counseling and testing
	  • HIV education/ information
	  • Partner notification
	• Outbreak investigation and control (including immunizations as part of outbreak control)
	• Screening activities
		• CD4+ testing
		• Dental health services (including topical flouride treatments in schools)
		• Treatment of diabetes, lupus, hemophilia, sickle-cell anemia, Alzheimer's disease, and other chronic diseases
		• Genetic disease services
		• Home health care
		• Hospitals
		• Purchase and provision of AZT/other drugs
		• Prenatal/perinatal care
		• Services for premature and newborn infants and preschool-aged children

continues

Table 7–1 continued

Function	Includes:	Does Not Include:

3. Investigation and control of diseases, injuries, and response to natural disasters (public health clinical services)	• Follow-up counseling (e.g., nutrition, exercise, smoking)
	• STD contact tracing
	• Selected public health clinic services
	  • Immunizations
	  • Family planning clinics
	  • STD clinical services
	  • TB clinical services
	• Management of client-based data systems that support the four types of services above
		• Services to children with special health care needs
		• WIC supplemental food program
		• Mental health clinical services
		• Mental retardation clinical services
		• Substance abuse clinical services
		• Personal health services other than those specified

4. Protection of environment, housing, food, water, and the workplace	• Air quality
	• Asbestos detection
	• Consumer protection and sanitation
	  • Food sanitation
	  • General sanitation
	  • Housing
	  • Public lodging
	  • Recreational sanitation
	  • Shellfish sanitation
	  • Substance control/ product safety
	  • Vector rodent control
	• Environmental risk assessment
	• Environmental sampling
	• Flouridation services
		• Construction of facilities and physical plants

continues

- Hazardous materials management (accidents, transportation, spills, etc.)
- Lead investigation
- Occupational health and safety
- Radiation control
- Radon detection
- Waste management—sewage, solid, and toxic
- Water quality control (public/private drinking water, groundwater protection, etc.)

5. Laboratory services
- Public health laboratory services (including newborn metabolic screening)
- Environmental health laboratory services
- Laboratory regulation and quality control services
- Medical examiner, toxicology, and other forensic medicine services
- Substance abuse laboratory services (DUI testing)
- Mental health laboratory services (therapeutic drug monitoring)

6. Public information and education and community mobilization
- Comprehensive school health education
- Populationwide health promotion/risk reduction programs
- School-based clinics
- Direct treatment services

continues

Table 7–1 continued

Function	Includes:	Does Not Include:
	• Injury prevention education and promotion • Nutrition education • Parenting education • Physical activity and fitness • Population-based risk reduction programs • Seat belts • Sexuality education • Tobacco use prevention and cessation • School campaigns such as "Say No to Drugs Day" • Substance abuse prevention • Public education campaigns • Worksite health promotion	
7. Targeted outreach and linkage to personal services	• Case management/ care coordination services • Information and referral hotlines • Outreach services (include services to school dropouts) • School health services • Transportation services	• School-based clinics • Direct treatment services
8. Accountability and quality assurance	• Enforcement of standards and laws • Facilities licensing • Health care systems monitoring • Health and environmental professionals licensing • Hospital outcomes data	• Capital outlay portion of certificate-of-need programs

continues

9. Training and education

- Personal health services monitoring (including analysis and use of client-based data)
- Program evaluation
- Regulation of EMS personnel/services
- Required continued education
- Professional training

10. Leadership, policy development, planning, and administration

- Advocacy
- Agency administration
- Agenda setting
- Coalition building
- Collaboration with outside agencies and organizations
- Development of policies and guidelines
- Legislative activities
- Management
- Planning (including certificate-of-need planning)
- Policy development
- Reporting requirements
- Development of primary care services in underserved communities
- Administration of primary care services

Source: Reprinted from Methodology, 1994, Public Health Foundation.

Exhibit 7–1 Six Public Health Service Categories

- Prevent epidemics
- Protect the environment, workplaces, housing, food, and water
- Prevent injuries
- Promote healthy behaviors
- Respond to disasters
- Assure the quality, accessibility, and accountability of health services

Source: Reprinted from Essential Public Health Services Working Group of the Core Public Health Functions Steering Committee, 1994, U.S. Public Health Services.

Using the framework presented earlier in Chapter 2, these programs and services can also be described in terms of intervention strategy, level of prevention, practice domain, and target population. *Intervention strategies* include health promotion, specific protection, early identification and treatment, disability limitation, and rehabilitation. By *level of prevention*, interventions can be classified as primary, secondary, or tertiary. By *practice domain*, interventions can be furnished by either public health or medical care practitioners. And last, interventions can be grouped by *target population*, either individuals or populations.

As demonstrated in Table 7–1, the activities available to carry out public health's core functions are extensive. Some are clinically oriented preventive services for individuals; others are population-based programs and services. The clinical preventive services emphasize early case finding and other aspects of primary care, whereas population-based programs and services largely involve a variety of health promotion and specific protection services. There is considerable overlap between the two, especially for specific protection and early case-finding services.

Clinical Preventive Services

Clinical preventive services include screening tests, counseling interventions, immunizations, and prophylactic regimens for individuals of all age groups and risk categories. Since the mid-1980s, the U.S. Preventive Services Task Force has reviewed information on the effectiveness of specific clinical preventive services. A rigorous evaluation has examined the evidence of effectiveness in order to establish a uniform set of recommendations for specific age and risk groups in the population. For screening tests, the criteria consider the accuracy and effectiveness of early detection. For counseling interventions, the criteria relate to the efficacy of risk reduction and the effectiveness of counseling. Efficacy of vaccines is the primary criterion for evaluating these interventions. For chemoprophylaxis, the criteria relate to efficacy as well as to the effectiveness of counseling. Recommendations for clinical preventive services were published in 1989 and revised in 1996[4] for the various age and risk status groups. These recommendations are presented in Table 7–2. They were not intended to serve as standards of care; rather, they were meant to be statements as to the quality of the evidence available to justify use of practices as effective preventive interventions.

The effectiveness of immunizations has been well established through reductions of more than 99 percent for diseases that include poliomyelitis, rubella, diphtheria, and pertussis. Several screening tests have also contributed to reductions in disease mortality and morbidity. For example, hypertension screening has contributed to the 67 percent reduction in stroke mortality since 1968, and newborn screening for both congenital hypothyroidism and phenylketonuria and cervical cancer screening through Pap tests have greatly reduced the burden of these diseases. Chemoprophylaxis, especially for diseases such as tuberculosis (TB), has also contributed to reductions in mortality and morbidity in recent decades. Despite the successes with these forms of clinical preventive services, the greatest potential lies in changing personal behaviors. In the clinical setting, counseling often supported with screening tests appears to be the clinical preventive service with the greatest potential.[4]

Notwithstanding the demonstrated effectiveness of many clinical preventive interventions, they remain underutilized, as demonstrated by the rates for specific clinical preventive interventions included in Figure 7–5. Reasons for the failure to provide clinical preventive interventions often relate to reimbursement practices, provider education and practice patterns, and the pluralistic and fragmented health system in the United States. In addition to these factors, the proliferation of recommendations as to appropriate use of these interventions has created confusion and uncertainty among many health providers as to exactly what should be done and when. Further complicating the picture are underlying suspicions and uncertainty among health providers as to whether interventions such as counseling are effective in the first place. The process developed by the U.S. Preventive Services Task Force sought to directly address these last two concerns.

The review of evidence leading to the age and risk group–specific recommendations of the task force was accompanied by several important findings. The task force concluded that interventions addressing patients' personal health practices are vitally important in view of the major health risks and problems currently facing the U.S. population. Providers must take on a greater role in assisting their patients to reduce risks in their daily lives. In short, personal health behaviors are a legitimate and important clinical concern, and both clinicians and patients should share decision making regarding possible interventions. In determining that many screening tests are effective, the task force also found that many are not. These unproved and ineffective services must be avoided and their costs averted as clinicians become more selective in ordering tests and providing

Table 7–2 Age-Specific Recommendations for Clinical Preventive Services, U.S. Preventive Services Task Force, 1996

Age Groups with Leading Causes of Death	Interventions for the General Population	Interventions for High-Risk Populations
Age: Birth to 10 years	Screening	• Hemoglobin/hematocrit for preterm or low birth weight
Leading causes of death:	• Height and weight	• HIV testing for infants of mothers at risk of HIV
• Conditions originating in perinatal period	• Blood pressure	• Hemoglobin/hematocrit for low-income and immigrants
• Congenital anomalies	• Vision screen (3–4 yr)	• PPD for TB contacts
• Sudden infant death syndrome	• Hemoglobinopathy screen (birth)	• Hemoglobin/ hematocrit; PPD; hepatitis A vaccine; pneumococcal vaccine for North American/Alaskan Natives
• Unintentional injuries (non–motor vehicle)	• Phenylalanine level (birth)	• Hepatitis A vaccine for travelers to developing countries
• Motor vehicle injuries	• T₄ and/or TSH (birth)	• PPD; hepatitis A vaccine; influenza vaccine for residents of long-term care facilities
	Counseling: Injury Prevention	• PPD; pneumococcal vaccine; influenza vaccine for certain chronic medical conditions
	• Child safety seats (age <5)	• Blood lead level for increased individual or community lead exposure
	• Lap-shoulder belts (age >5)	• Daily fluoride supplement for inadequate water fluoridation
	• Bicycle helmet; avoid bicycling near traffic	
	• Smoke detector, flame-retardant sleepwear	
	• Hot water heater temperature <120–130°F	
	• Window/stair guards, pool fence	
	• Safe storage of drugs, toxic substances, firearms, and matches	
	• Syrup of ipecac, poison control number	
	• CPR training for parents/caretakers	
	Counseling: Diet and Exercise	
	• Breast-feeding, iron-enriched formula and foods (infants and toddlers)	

continues

Ages:
11–24 years
Leading Causes of Death:
• Motor vehicle and other unintentional injuries

• Limit fat and cholesterol; maintain caloric balance; emphasize grains, fruits, vegetables (age <3)
• Regular physical activity
Counseling: Substance Abuse
• Effects of passive smoking
• Antitobacco message
Counseling: Dental Health
• Regular visits to dental care provider
• Floss, brush with fluoride toothpaste daily
• Advice about baby bottle tooth decay
Immunizations
• Diphtheria-tetanus-pertussis (DPT)
• Oral poliovirus (OPV)
• Measles-mumps-rubella (MMR)
• H. Influenza type b (Hib) conjugate
• Hepatitis B
• Varicella
Chemoprophylaxis
Occular prophylaxis (birth)
Screening
• Height and weight
• Blood pressure
• Pap test (females)

• Avoid excess/midday sun, use protective clothing for family history of skin cancer; nevi; fair skin, eyes, hair

• RPR/VDRL; screen for gonorrhea (female), chlamydia (female); hepatitis A vaccine for high-risk sexual behavior

continues

Table 7-2 continued

Age Groups with Leading Causes of Death	Interventions for the General Population	Interventions for High-Risk Populations
• Homicide • Suicide • Malignant neoplasms • Heart diseases	• Chlamydia screen (females <20 yr) • Rubella serology or vaccination history (females <12 yr) • Assess for problem drinking Counseling for Injury Prevention • Lap/shoulder belts • Bicycle/motorcycle/ ATV helmets • Smoke detector • Safe storage/removal of firearms Counseling for Substance Abuse • Avoid tobacco use • Avoid underage drinking and illicit drug use • Avoid alcohol/drug use while driving, swimming, boating, etc. Counseling for Sexual Behavior • STD prevention: abstinence; avoid high-risk behavior; condoms/female barrier with spermicide • Unintended pregnancy: contraception Counseling for Diet and Exercise • Limit fat and cholesterol; maintain caloric balance; emphasize grains, fruits, vegetables • Adequate calcium intake (females)	• RPR/VDRL; HIV screen; hepatitis A vaccine; PPD; advice to reduce infection risk for injection or street drug use • PPD for TB contacts, immigrants, low-income • Hepatitis A vaccine; PPD; pneumococcal vaccine for Native American/Alaskan Natives • Hepatitis A vaccine for travelers to developing countries • PPD, pneumococcal vaccine, influenza vaccine for certain chronic medical conditions • Second MMR for settings where adolescents and young adults congregate • Varicella vaccine; MMR for susceptible to Varicella, measles, mumps • HIV screen for blood transfusion between 1975 and 1985 • Hepatitis A; PPD; influenza vaccine for institutionalized persons and health care/lab workers

continues

- Regular physical activity
- Avoid excess/midday sun, use protective clothing for family history of skin cancer; nevi; fair skin, eyes, hair

Counseling for Dental Health
- Regular visits to dental care provider
- Floss, brush with fluoride toothpaste daily

- Folic acid 4.0 mg for prior pregnancy with neural tube defect
- Daily fluoride supplement for inadequate water fluoridation

Immunizations
- Tetanus-diphtheria (Td) boosters (11–16 yr)
- Hepatitis B
- MMWR (11–12 yr)
- Varicella (11–12 yr)
- Rubella (females >12 yr)

Chemoprophylaxis
- Multivitamin with folic acid (females planning/capable of pregnancy)

Screening
- Blood pressure
- Height and weight
- Total blood cholesterol (men age 35–64, women age 45–64)
- Pap test (women)
- Fecal occult blood test and/or sigmoidoscopy (>50 yr)
- Mammogram ± clinical breast exam (women 50–69 yr)

- RPR/VDRL; screen for gonorrhea (female), chlamydia (female); hepatitis B vaccine; hepatitis A vaccine for high-risk sexual behavior
- RPR/VDRL; HIV screen; hepatitis B vaccine; hepatitis A vaccine; PPD; advice to reduce infection risk for injection or street drug use

Ages 25–64 years
Leading Causes of Death:
- Malignant neoplasms
- Heart diseases
- Motor vehicle and other unintentional injuries
- HIV infection
- Suicide and homicide

continues

Table 7-2 continued

Age Groups with Leading Causes of Death	Interventions for the General Population	Interventions for High-Risk Populations
	• Assess for problem drinking • Rubella serology or vaccination history (women of childbearing age) Counseling on Substance Use • Tobacco cessation • Avoid alcohol/drug use while driving, swimming, boating, etc. Counseling for Diet and Exercise • Limit fat and cholesterol; maintain caloric balance; emphasize grains, fruits, vegetables • Adequate calcium intake (women) • Regular physical activity Counseling for Injury Prevention • Lap/shoulder belts • Motorcycle/bicycle/ATV helmets • Smoke detector • Safe storage/removal of firearms Counseling for Sexual Behavior • STD prevention: avoid high-risk behavior; condoms/female barrier with spermicide • Unintended pregnancy: contraception Counseling for Dental Health • Regular visits to dental care provider	• PPD for TB contacts, alcoholics, immigrants, low-income • Hepatitis A vaccine; PPD; pneumococcal vaccine for Native American/Alaskan Natives • Hepatitis B vaccine; hepatitis A vaccine for travelers to developing countries • PPD; pneumococcal vaccine; influenza vaccine for certain chronic medical conditions • Varicella vaccine; MMR for susceptible to Varicella, measles, mumps • HIV screen; hepatitis B vaccine for blood transfusion between 1975 and 1985 • Hepatitis B vaccine; hepatitis A vaccine; PPD; influenza vaccine for institutionalized persons and health care/lab workers • Avoid excess/midday sun, use protective clothing for family history of skin cancer; nevi; fair skin, eyes, hair • Folic acid 4.0 mg for prior pregnancy with neural tube defect

continues

Ages 65 and older
Leading Causes of Death:
- Heart diseases
- Malignant neoplasms (lung, colorectal, breast)
- Cerebrovascular disease
- Chronic obstructive pulmonary disease
- Pneumonia and influenza

- Floss, brush with fluoride toothpaste daily

Immunizations
- Tetanus-diphtheria (Td) boosters
- Rubella (women of childbearing age)

Chemoprophylaxis
- Multivitamin with folic acid (women planning or capable of pregnancy)
- Discuss hormone prophylaxis (peri- and postmenopausal women)

Screening
- Blood pressure
- Height and weight
- Fecal occult blood test and/or sigmoidoscopy
- Mammogram ± clinical breast exam (women <70 yr)
- Pap test (women)
- Vision screening
- Assess for hearing impairment
- Assess for drinking problem

Counseling for Substance Abuse
- Tobacco cessation

- PPD; hepatitis A; amanatadine/rimantadine for institutionalized persons
- PPD for chronic medical condition; TB contacts; low-income; immigrants; alcoholics
- Fall prevention intervention for persons >75 yr, or >70 yr with risk factors for falls
- Consider cholesterol screening for cardiovascular disease risk factors
- Avoid excess/midday sun, use protective clothing for family history of skin cancer; nevi; fair skin, eyes, hair
- PPD; hepatitis A vaccine for Native Americans/Alaskan Natives

continues

Table 7-2 continued

Age Groups with Leading Causes of Death	Interventions for the General Population	Interventions for High-Risk Populations
	• Avoid alcohol/drug use while driving, swimming, boating, etc.	• Hepatitis A vaccine; hepatitis B vaccine for travelers to developing countries
	Counseling for Diet and Exercise	• HIV screen; hepatitis B vaccine for blood product recipients
	• Limit fat and cholesterol; maintain caloric balance; emphasize grains, fruits, vegetables	• Hepatitis A vaccine; HIV screen; hepatitis B vaccine; RPR/VDRL for high-risk sexual behavior
	• Adequate calcium intake (women)	• PPD; hepatitis A vaccine; HIV screen;
	• Regular physical activity	hepatitis B vaccine; RPR/VDRL; advice to
	Counseling for Injury Prevention	reduce infection risk for injection or street
	• Lap/shoulder belts	drug use
	• Motorcycle and bicycle helmets	• PPD; hepatitis A vaccine;
	• Fall prevention	amantadine/rimantadine; hepatitis B
	• Safe storage/removal of firearms	vaccine for health care/lab workers
	• Smoke detector	• Varicella vaccine for persons susceptible
	• Set hot water heater to <120–130°F	to Varicella
	• CPR training for household members	
	Counseling for Dental Health	
	• Regular visits to dental care provider	
	• Floss, brush with fluoride toothpaste daily	
	Counseling for Sexual Behavior	
	• STD prevention: avoid high-risk sexual behavior; use condoms	

continues

Immunizations
- Pneumococcal vaccine
- Influenza
- Tetanus-diphtheria (Td) boosters

Chemoprophylaxis
- Discuss hormone prophylaxis (peri- and postmenopausal women)

Source: Reprinted from the U.S. Preventive Services Task Force, 1996.

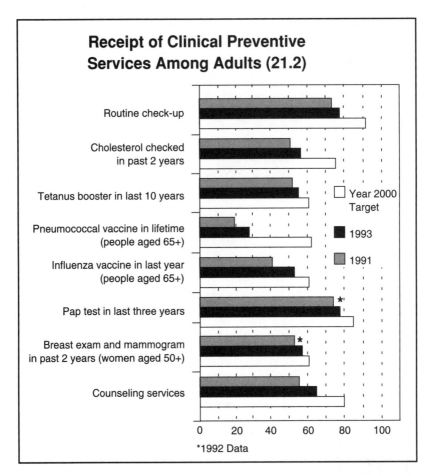

Figure 7–5 Receipt of Clinical Preventive Services among Adults. *Source:* Reprinted from CDC National Health Interview Survey, 1991–1993, NCHS.

preventive services. Most important, the task force concluded that many opportunities for delivering preventive services were being missed, especially for persons with limited access to care.

Another important conclusion of the U.S. Preventive Services Task Force was that for some health problems and risks, communitywide preventive interventions are more effective than clinical services. This does not diminish the role of clinical providers, however, as their standing in the community can do much to advance community interventions and link them more effectively with the provision of clinical services.

Additional insights into the scope and extent of public health services are provided through information on clinical preventive services. Until relatively recently, very little information on these services has been available. Through national surveys conducted by the National Center for Health Statistics of the Centers for Disease Control and Prevention (CDC; see Chapter 6), information on the general population has been generated. This information is less available at the local level, with just over one-half of local health agencies collecting information on clinical preventive services (Figure 7–6).

Community Preventive Services and Programs

Population-based community prevention focuses on assessing and addressing common as well as emergent health problems and needs. In terms of primary prevention, nutritional, environmental, and behavioral risks are targeted. Services include health information and education for the entire population or for specific high-risk groups, community health assessment, investigations of health hazards, enforcement of statutes and regulations, and clinical preventive services.

This category includes the two basic strategies for primary prevention, health promotion and specific prevention, as well as strategies for secondary prevention. These strategies are largely targeted to populations—the entire population or specific groups. These services should be considered public health practice regardless of whether they are provided by public- or private-sector organizations and providers. It is not essential that all these services be provided by the public sector, although some specific services can be organized and provided only through that route (e.g., fluoridation of water supplies).

The progress that has been made after 1950 in identifying risk factors associated with chronic diseases and injuries is sometimes called the second epidemiological revolution. With the importance of heart disease, stroke, cancer, diabetes, chronic lung diseases, and injuries as major contributors to morbidity and mortality, health promotion programs have grown in number and scope over the past two decades. Examples include injury risk reduction through seat belts, education to prevent tobacco use, drink and drive campaigns, nutrition education (fat intake), fitness campaigns, smokeless tobacco use, stress management, safe sex, abstinence, and risk reduction in general.

Although viewed as important for health purposes, and increasingly emphasized by public and voluntary organizations, these services have not been widely embraced by providers and organizations in the private sector. To some extent, this has been because these services are not viewed as valued by the public. As a result, providers have not sought to advertise or otherwise promote them. Instead,

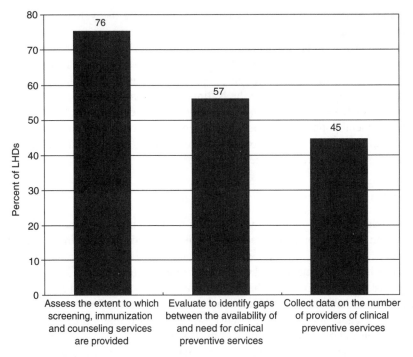

Figure 7–6 Local Health Department Activity in Assessing Clinical Preventive Services, 1992–1993. *Source:* Reprinted from National Association of County and City Health Officials and Centers for Disease Control and Prevention, *Profile of Local Health Departments, 1992-1993,* 1995, Washington, D.C.

disease-specific services emphasizing sophisticated, high-technology services, including screening tests, have been used to attract patients and market share.

It is likely, however, that as communitywide health needs assessments are completed across the United States, there will be greater recognition of the need for community prevention services geared toward injuries and chronic diseases. The community health priorities established as a result of all certified LHDs in Illinois completing a community needs assessment process and community health plan (an adaptation of the Assessment Protocol for Excellence in Public Health [APEXPH], described in Chapter 5) in 1993 and 1994 provide evidence of this direction.[5] More than 1,200 community participants across the state through 86 LHDs identified more than 300 health priorities in nine categories. Chronic diseases were the category most frequently selected as a public health priority, appearing in the priorities of 85 percent of the community health plans. Within the chronic disease category, cardiovascular disease and cancer were identified as priority concerns by 74 and 65 percent of the local planning processes. The second highest priority category was for maternal and child health, identified by 66 percent, with infant mortality reduction named as a priority within this category by 44 percent of the local processes. Figure 7–7 identifies the leading categories for priorities derived from these community needs assessment efforts.

Population-based services can be provided within the same program that offers clinical preventive services. As a result, it is sometimes difficult to view them as separate categories, and they are frequently reported on together. Immunization programs illustrate this point. Clinical preventive services in the form of individual doses of vaccine administered orally or by injection are carried out alongside population-based community prevention services such as community education, outreach, active and passive surveillance activities, and contact investigation.

PROGRAM MANAGEMENT IN PUBLIC HEALTH

Program management in public health includes the myriad activities involved with the development, implementation, and evaluation of interventions addressing public health problems. Effective program management is an organized response requiring a carefully designed problem statement, the availability of an appropriate intervention, and the capacity to deliver that intervention in a specific setting. Each of these is an essential component of an organized response. The task is to bring these elements together and direct them toward the solution of problems. Public health program management seeks to organize and direct public health workers, scientifically sound interventions, and appropriate strategies toward specific health problems.[6] The ultimate aim is to eliminate or reduce these problems to the maximum extent possible (effectiveness) and to achieve these results with the minimum resources necessary (efficiency). Effectiveness and efficiency are the primary criteria by which programs are judged or evaluated.

Management revolves around resource allocation and utilization. The resources of public health as described in Chapter 6 include the human, organizational, informational, fiscal, and other supportive resources. To utilize these resources both effectively and efficiently, there must be a process that carefully examines the problem for the pathways most likely to yield successful results. There are two cardinal sins of program management: failing to achieve program objectives when adequate resources are available and utilizing more resources than are necessary to achieve a program's objectives. The first situation is more commonly viewed as poor management than the second, although from a management point of view each results in resources being wasted. When program management is improperly or only partially applied, either resources and technology are underutilized and problems are not fully addressed or resources and technology are inefficiently utilized, resulting in excess resource consumption and opportunity costs.

Program management calls for the development of a program hypothesis. This is best understood when programs are considered at the level of their basic elements, namely the specific activities or tasks that are undertaken. The program hypothesis in its simplest form is that if the designated activities are successfully undertaken, then the program's goals and objectives will be successfully addressed. For health programs, we expect that these activities will change char-

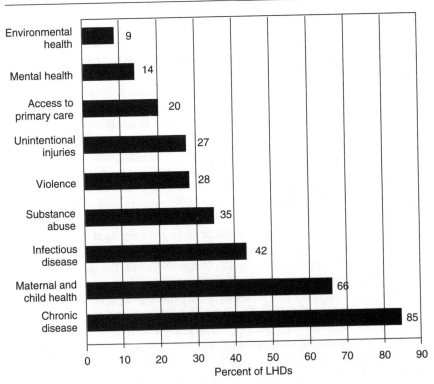

Figure 7–7 Categories of Health Problems Identified as Priority Community Health Problems through Community Needs Assessments, Illinois, 1993–1994. *Source:* Reprinted from Illinois Department of Public Health, IPLAN Objective Summary, 1996.

acteristics of individuals or populations such that factors contributing to the level of the health problem will improve. With improvements in these various factors affecting the health problem, we expect that the level of the health problem itself will also be improved. Depending on how many intervening levels of factors there might be, we expect that improvement at one level will result in improvements in higher levels. These terms will be defined and clarified below; the major point here is that rational programs directly address the chain of causation that creates the health problem being targeted by the program.

The management cycle is often described as consisting of three phases: planning (deciding what to do and how to do it), implementation (acting to accomplish what has been planned), and evaluation (comparing the results of what was accomplished with what was intended).[6] Very often, planning, implementation and evaluation have been viewed as linear processes. First we plan. Then we implement. Finally, we evaluate what has occurred. In this linear model, we stop planning when we begin implementing, and we do not evaluate until after we have implemented our program. This approach views planning and evaluation as discrete, independent functions carried out at different points in the life span of a program. There are few fallacies more dangerous to sound management than this one! It is critical that planning and evaluation be viewed as interrelated and interdependent processes working together at varying levels of emphasis throughout the life of a program. Rather than a linear process, program management should be viewed as a cyclical process in which one step logically leads to the next and feedback obtained at all steps is used to revise the directions established in preceding steps. Such a process is illustrated in Figure 7–8.

Program management centers on the development of objectives. Unfortunately, objectives are all too often viewed as the products of planners alone. Program management in public health and other areas is simply too important for objectives to be left to the planners! Objectives are more than abstract targets for achievement. Although they are often characterized as the blueprint of a program, they actually serve more as a road map than as a blueprint. Objectives point the program toward a specific destination and at the same time set its speed and its mile markers. Objectives guide program administration and establish the framework and strategy for program evaluation. Rather than serving primarily as a tool for program planning, they guide all aspects of program planning, administration, and evaluation (Exhibit 7–2).

Linking Planning and Evaluation

A practical definition of planning views it as the application of rational decision making to the commitment of future resources. Planning is as much an art as it is a science. Planners do not have any special abilities to predict or foresee the future, and planning does not result in certainty as to what will happen. Rational planning serves to reduce but not entirely eliminate risk. The management purpose behind planning must be kept in mind; it is to make the most efficient use of resources. As a result, planning should not be judged solely by the accuracy of its predictions or even by whether planning targets, such as objectives, are met. Instead, planning should be judged on the basis of whether it helps an organization achieve the best possible results in a changing environment. It is rare for programs to be carried out exactly as they were designed. Change occurs constantly among the external and internal factors that affect both the problem and programs designed to address the problem. Ongoing planning serves to recognize changes and modify implementation strategies accordingly. The ability of a program to evaluate itself continuously determines how quickly and effectively it can respond to changing conditions.

The key to the process of evaluation is the ability to ask the right questions. All too often, little thought is given to an evaluation strategy until the program is

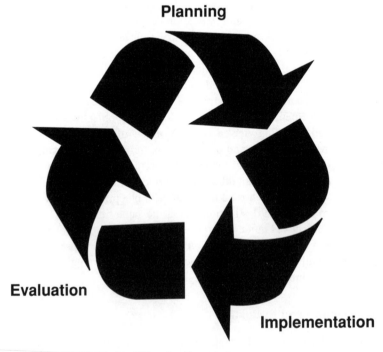

Figure 7–8 Steps in the Rational Planning Process.

already in place and decision makers or funders begin to ask for evidence of its benefit. In short, evaluation is an afterthought. As a result, programs scurry around, asking the question "What are we doing that we can measure?" Unfortunately, often very little can be done at this point. Evaluation strategies should be developed and agreed upon before programs are implemented, and they should be based on asking the quite different question "What do we need to measure in order to know what we are doing?" We will return to these issues in greater detail as we discuss planning and evaluation in subsequent sections of this chapter. The point here is that these are not to be considered as bookends for program implementation; rather, they are meant to be carried out concurrently and continuously. When this is done, planning and evaluation contribute substantially to a rational decision-making system in which managers are more likely to ask the right questions and direct resources toward the most promising intervention activities.

Key Questions for Managers

Five key questions guide the program management process:

1. Where am I?
2. Where do I want to be?
3. Should I do something?
4. What should I do?
5. How do I know I am getting there?[6]

These questions provide managers with much of the essential information needed to make better decisions. They focus attention on the essential components of any decision process: the starting point, the ending point, and the intermediate measurements. The logic and rational nature of this process can be tracked through decision models such as that developed by CDC for public health program managers. In Figure 7–9, the five questions serve as a road map of the program manager's major duties and tasks.

Exhibit 7–2 Uses of Objectives within Programs

- Road map for the program
- Basis for program administration
- Framework for program evaluation

Even with a road map, journeys require a destination or goal. For public health programs, goals are generalized statements expressing a program's intended effect on one or more health problems. Goals are often described as timeless statements of overall aspirations; these generally serve to establish boundaries for the program's operational activities, but they also serve as the philosophical justification for a program's existence. It is unusual for program managers to be

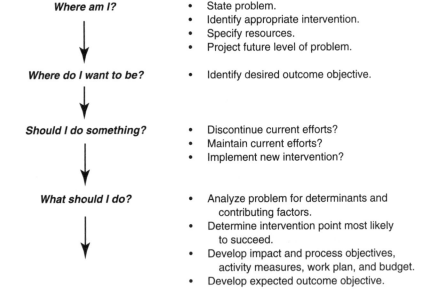

Where am I?
- State problem.
- Identify appropriate intervention.
- Specify resources.
- Project future level of problem.

Where do I want to be?
- Identify desired outcome objective.

Should I do something?
- Discontinue current efforts?
- Maintain current efforts?
- Implement new intervention?

What should I do?
- Analyze problem for determinants and contributing factors.
- Determine intervention point most likely to succeed.
- Develop impact and process objectives, activity measures, work plan, and budget.
- Develop expected outcome objective.

How do I know I am getting there?
- Track progress toward achieving activity measures and process objectives (doing things right).
- Track progress toward achieving impact and outcome objectives (doing the right things).

Figure 7–9 Key Questions for Managers of Public Health Programs. *Source:* Adapted from W.W. Dyal, *Program Management: A Guide for Improving Program Decisions*, 1990, USPHS-CDC-PHPPO, Atlanta, GA.

involved in the establishment of goals. These are usually established by higher authorities, such as boards, legislative bodies, or even funding sources. Despite being somewhat abstract and externally developed, goals serve a valuable purpose for public health programs. Goals need to be clearly stated, and they need to be understood by all program staff, if only to serve as a common bond and continuous reminder of the program's aspirations.

Where Am I?

The essence of decision making at any level is deciding either to do something or to do nothing. A rational decision to do or not do something calls for a thorough assessment of the current situation, or "Where am I?" Determining the current status of things assists the manager in several ways. It provides information that can be later used to decide whether action should be taken; it also serves to describe the dimensions of a potential problem in terms of which groups might be more affected, and it establishes a baseline for comparisons over time.

In examining where things stand, it is important to assess in detail the problem, the interventions capable of addressing the problem, and the resources available to deploy those interventions (Exhibit 7–3). Although these three elements need to be considered together in determining the current situation, the availability of an effective intervention is absolutely essential from the program management perspective. Without a potentially effective intervention, it makes little sense to plan and implement a program. The availability of an effective intervention refers to the current level of sophistication of the knowledge and techniques for its coordinated application. It is the science and knowledge base for developing and justifying a technical approach for accomplishing a goal. The specific intervention approach could be drawn from any of the categories of health interventions strategies described in Chapter 3 (health promotion, specific protection, early case finding and treatment, disability limitation, and rehabilitation). As a result, the intervention could be based on medical sciences, physical sciences, or social sciences. Sometimes referred to as "the state of the art," this knowledge or tech-

---

Exhibit 7–3 Key Considerations for Determining "Where Am I?"

- Health problem
- Effective intervention
- Available resources

Source: Adapted from W.W. Dyal, *Program Management: A Guide for Improving Program Decisions,* 1990, USPHS-CDC-PHPPO, Atlanta, GA.

nical information convinces program managers that a particular health problem can be addressed.

In addition to the capability to intervene, there are two other considerations in assessing where things currently stand. These are the level of a health problem and the capacity or resources to intervene. A health problem is defined here as a situation or condition of people (expressed in health outcome terms like mortality, morbidity, or disability) that is considered undesirable and is likely to exist in the future unless additional interventions are implemented. The heart of any intervention strategy lies in the definition of the problem. The development of objectives and intervention strategies flows naturally from a careful and precise statement of the problem. Problem statements come in all formats and lengths, and they vary significantly in their complexity. Still, all good problem statements present a clear, concise, and accurate description of the condition to be controlled or prevented. The more carefully a problem is stated, the more likely it is that it can be accurately measured.

Planning processes look to the future. Above all, planning is concerned with future resource allocation; therefore decisions will need to address the anticipated future level of problems rather than their current levels. It makes little sense to throw additional resources at a problem if that problem's level is declining and the level of the problem in the future may not be deemed unacceptable. This would constitute at least a partial waste of resources, something that is to be avoided with good management practices. Even a decreasing level of a problem may merit additional resource allocation if that level is judged to be unacceptable or if additional resources might accelerate the decrease.

Looking to both the past and the future is necessary to describe a problem adequately since its trends are an important aspect of its description. Tracking problems over time also helps to project their future levels through trend analysis techniques. Often, however, tracking the level of a problem provides only an incomplete picture of changes over time. It is also important to track changes and trends in the problem's major determinants. For example, changes in low birth weight (a major determinant of infant mortality) should be examined alongside infant mortality rates, and changes in tobacco use should be tracked alongside lung cancer rates. Projecting future levels of a problem on the basis of trends in the problem and its determinants is fraught with uncertainty and is imprecise at best. Nonetheless, it is both useful and rational in informing decisions that will allocate resources to achieve specific results.

In addition to trends and projections of levels, the process of problem specification calls for assessment of the size, scope, and distribution of a problem, beginning with a clear definition of the problem in terms of its nature and etiology, its magnitude and extent in terms of its incidence and prevalence, its affected populations in terms of specific populations at risk (by age, sex, race, occupation, or other risk factors), and its time and place of occurrence. In some respects, this reads like the major components of a news story in terms of who, what, when, where, and how much.

Just as problems need to be carefully specified in determining where we are, resources also need to be assessed for their trends over time in terms of financial resources as well as human resources (number, types, skills), organizational resources, information resources, facilities, equipment, and other materials. Tracking both the problem and resources over time allows for reasonable predictions to be made as to the effects (if any) of resources on the problem and what might be expected at various future resource levels. This information facilitates the development of realistic outcomes.

Where Do I Want To Be?

Determining where you are allows for a comparison with where you want to be. In answering this question, one makes an effort to identify the level at which a problem will be considered acceptable at some point in the future. This is the level at which a current problem will no longer be considered a problem, and it is very much dependent on how carefully and comprehensively the problem has been described. If a problem is well defined in terms of what, how much, who, when, and where, priorities can be established so that resources can be most efficiently utilized to achieve program results. Specific measurable objectives can also be established on the basis of these components of the problem description. The term *desired outcome objective* refers to the level to which a health problem should be reduced and or maintained within a specified time period. It is meant to be long-term (generally two or more years), realistic (achievable through the intervention strategies proposed), and measurable. Outcome objectives are designed to measure directly the level of the health problem; they include a statement of how much and when the health problem should be affected by the program. An outcome objective is a quantitative measurement of the health problem at some future date and is something that the manager feels the program can and should accomplish. To establish meaningful outcome objectives, the three key ingredients are the availability of effective interventions, the resources and capacity to implement these interventions, and projections for the future level of the health problem. By assessing the past and current relationships among capability, capacity, and outcomes, one can project realistic and measurable outcome objectives for various levels of program activity.

Should I Do Something?

The purpose of asking the first two questions ("Where am I?" and "Where do I want to be?") is to force a decision as to whether something additional needs to be done. When where you are (and are likely to be) differs from where you would like to be, change is indicated. Change can take one of two forms, doing more or doing less. As a result, there are three options in terms of resource allocation and deployment: reduce (or even eliminate) current efforts, maintain current efforts, or implement a new intervention (Exhibit 7–4).

Discontinuing current efforts may be called for if the health problem has already reached or is projected to reach desirable levels such that further resource allocation is unnecessary. From a manager's point of view, this represents an opportunity to save or redirect resources rather than waste them.

A second option is to continue to provide the same level of resources if that level will achieve the desired outcome level by the target achievement date. The decision for a maintenance level should never become automatic; it should be preceded by an active, analytical decision-making process. If the expected level of the problem falls within the acceptable range and resources are available, maintenance of the current level of effort is appropriate.

Interventions are called for when the projected level of the problem exceeds the desired outcome objective and when the capability and capacity to intervene are available. With the availability of technology and resources, the trick is to determine the best implementation strategy that will utilize these to achieve the desired outcome. How a program gets from where it is to where it wants to be requires that decisions be made as to which specific strategies and activities are to be used. There are generally at least several strategies for affecting the level or extent of a health problem. The decisions to be made are based on which options are likely to be most successful and how much of the program's resources should be devoted to each strategy. A program's intervention strategy determines how a program's resources are to be deployed to achieve the desired outcome objective. The logic behind this is simple: if the strategies and activities are carried out as planned, then the problem will be reduced to the expected level on schedule. Many uncertainties and unforeseen circumstances can prevent an intervention strategy from succeeding as planned. These can be viewed as analogous to the difference between efficacy (will it

---

Exhibit 7–4 Options for Determining What To Do

- Intervene
- Maintain current effort
- Reduce current effort

Source: Adapted from W.W. Dyal, *Program Management: A Guide for Improving Program Decisions*, 1990, USPHS-CDC-PHPPO, Atlanta, GA.

work?) and effectiveness (will it work here?). In any event, an intervention strategy is as much a hypothesis as it is a plan. It remains to be proven, and the likelihood of unforeseen problems and obstacles increases when the problem is inadequately defined and analyzed.

What Should I Do?

When the problem has been clearly and concisely stated, when the capability to intervene exists, and when the capacity to deploy the interventions is on hand, an intervention strategy can succeed. Success will further depend on how thoroughly the problem has been analyzed so that its major determinants and their contributing factors are identified. This analysis provides information as to which approaches are most likely to be effective and allows for matching of program resources with activities that will address key contributing factors.

Consistent with the health problems analysis model described in Chapter 2, measures of health problems should be stated in terms of health outcomes, such as mortality, morbidity, incidence, and prevalence. Determinants are risk factors that, on the basis of scientific evidence or theory, are thought to influence directly the level of a specific health problem. Contributing factors are those factors that directly or indirectly influence the level of determinants. Analysis should continue until all pertinent direct determinants and their associated contributing factors have been identified. The direct determinants are then examined to determine which offer the greatest chance of success in achieving the desired outcome. For some determinants, there are either no or only partly effective interventions. Those that offer the best chances for success are selected as points of intervention.

In addition to the expected outcome objective, other levels of objectives guide the intervention process. The outcome objective relates to the level of the health problem. Similarly, some objectives relate to determinants and still others relate to the contributing factors (Tables 7–3 and 7–4).

Impact objectives address the level to which a direct determinant is expected to be reduced within a specified time period. They are generally intermediate (one

---

Table 7–3 Levels of Program Management and Planning

Goal	Defines operational and philosophical parameters
Outcome objective	Projected future level of the health problem
Impact objective	Projected future level of a direct determinant
Process objective	Projected future level of a contributing factor
Activities	Actual tasks performed by program personnel

Source: Adapted from W.W. Dyal, *Program Management: A Guide for Improving Program Decisions*, 1990, USPHS-CDC-PHPPO, Atlanta, GA.

Table 7–4 Characteristics of Program Objectives

Term	Time Period	Description	Measurement
Outcome objective	Usually long-term	Related to health problem	Degree of accomplishment; addresses doing the right things
Impact objective	Intermediate	Related to direct determinants and risk factors	Degree of accomplishment; addresses doing the right things
Process objective	Short-term	Related to contributing factors	Degree of accomplishment; addresses doing things right
Activities	Usually short-term	Describes the use of program resources	Accomplishment (yes/no); addresses doing things right

Source: Adapted from W.W. Dyal, *Program Management: A Guide for Improving Program Decisions,* 1990, USPHS-CDC-PHPPO, Atlanta, GA.

to five years) in terms of time, and they are both realistic and measurable. An impact objective measures a determinant and states how much and when the determinant will be affected by the program. It is the quantitative measurement of the determinant at some future date.

Just as impact objectives measure determinants, process objectives measure contributing factors. For a program to function as planned, achieving process objectives will lead to achieving impact objectives, which, in turn, will result in achieving of the outcome objective. Process objectives are shorter term than outcome or impact objectives. They are short-term (usually one year), realistic, and measurable.

The establishment of process objectives initiates two activities, one focusing on developing a work plan for the activities necessary to address the process objectives, and one revisiting the outcome objective. The former activity is seldom overlooked, as it is essential to complete the program planning process. The latter activity, however, is often forgotten, resulting in programs operating with outcome objectives that cannot be achieved. The rationale for revisiting the outcome objective is that the intervention strategy selected, together with its process objectives and activity measures, is likely to be only partially successful in reducing the outcome objective to the desired level. Programs are seldom able to achieve the entire improvement called for in the desired outcome objective. As a result, an expected outcome objective is established by reassessing the probability of achieving the desired outcome objective within the estimated time frame for the program. The expected outcome objective represents an estimate of an important future event that can and should be accomplished through the program's efforts and within the resources available.

Completing the program-planning process requires the establishment of a work plan with specific activities and tasks that carry out the program's process objectives. Program resources are attached to these activities, and tasks and activity measures are used to track progress. Activity measures are generally very short-term (often expressed in weeks or months) but are also realistic and measurable. The program budget is expended in carrying out these activities and tasks. These work statements are short-term (less than one year), realistic, and measurable and describe what is to be done, by whom, when, and where. A budget is very much an operational plan for financial expenditures to support the actions agreed upon in the program plan.

As noted previously, the program plan is based on a set of theoretical linkages or assumptions involving the problem and its determinants, contributing factors, activities, and resources. Program resources are deployed through specific activities that serve to modify contributing factors, resulting in achievement of process objectives. Achievement of the process objectives affects the determinants, resulting in the achievement of impact objectives. Achievement of the impact objectives reduces the level of the health problem, resulting in the achievement of the expected outcome objective.

How Do I Know I Am Getting There?

To answer the last question, "How do I know I am getting there?", one examines the effectiveness of program design and implementation. Key to any evaluation strategy is the establishment of measurable checkpoints, or milestones, in both time and direction. These assist the manager in determining whether the program is moving in the right direction and whether it will arrive at its destination on time. Both the strategy and the importance of continuously assessing the effectiveness of a program are summed up in the well-known observation that it is more important to be doing the right things than it is to be doing things right. Evaluation focuses on both.

Evaluation was previously characterized as asking the right questions. With a well-analyzed problem statement and the selection of an appropriate intervention strategy, asking the right questions should be straightforward. The key questions are as simple as: "Was the outcome objective achieved?" "Were the impact objectives achieved?" "Were process objectives achieved?" and "Were program activities performed as planned?" Evaluation within this framework calls for measuring the actual result and comparing it with the intended result. Information on the intended result is derived from the program plan, whereas data and information on the actual result must be provided by the program's information system. Goals, objectives, activities, and other standards establish the level of the intended result for comparison.

The intervention strategy represents a causal hypothesis that must be continuously reassessed because circumstances and conditions may change in ways that affect the initial assumptions and linkages. Evaluation is essential before decisions are made as to whether efforts should be expanded, reduced, or even maintained.

Effectiveness represents the ability to produce an intended result and achieve expected outcomes. When a program fails to achieve its expected outcomes, the cause of that failure must be identified. Programs may not be effective for several reasons that relate to the various levels of the program's objectives and activities: its outcome objectives, its impact objectives, its process objectives, and its activity measures.

In reverse order, activity measures may not be achieved if resources are lacking or if personnel fail to carry out their tasks. This results in activity measures not being met. If the activity measures are closely linked to their associated process measures, these also will not be met. Failure to address a program's activity measures and process objectives successfully means that a program is not doing things right. Successfully carrying out activity measures and achieving process objectives, on the other hand, means that a program is doing things right. Even when a program is doing things right, however, it may not be doing the right things. Doing the right things means that program outcome and impact objectives are achieved. Four combinations of program effectiveness can occur:

1. Programs can be doing the right things and doing things right. These are well-designed and well-managed programs that merit emulation.
2. Programs can be doing the right things even though things are not being done right. The linkage between the program's process objectives and activity measures and the program's outcome and impact objectives has been poorly identified. These programs are neither well designed nor well managed. It is not possible to link program activities and resources to the outcomes achieved.
3. Programs can be neither doing the right things nor doing things right. These programs are poorly designed and executed on all accounts.
4. Programs can be doing things right but not doing the right things. Here, activity measures and process objectives are achieved but impact and outcome objectives are not. Although program staff may be satisfied with their performance, the program as a whole cannot be satisfactory. This situation occurs when a problem is inadequately analyzed. It can be argued that these programs, though poorly designed, are at least partly well managed.

As suggested in these alternatives, programs can suffer from invalid assumptions or incomplete strategies linking process objectives to impact objectives or linking impact objectives to an expected outcome objective. Pinpointing the location of a program's weaknesses in design or implementation calls for continuously assessing the validity, reliability, and completeness of the intervention strategy.

"Doing things right" refers to the performance of activities and the achievement of process objectives. It is measured through process evaluation. Process objectives can be unmet for two reasons: (1) lack of resources, which calls for reassessing the impact and process objectives in order to align them with the available resources (lower expectations or locate additional resources), or (2) lack of performance, which calls for reassessing the program personnel in terms of motivation, skills, and knowledge (hire, fire, train, or motivate). If process objectives are being met, then the program is doing things right.

"Doing the right things" refers to the achievement of impact and outcome objectives and measures the program's effectiveness. If the impact objectives are not being achieved but the process objectives are, then the manager must reexamine the assumed relationship between contributing factors and the determinants, revise the intervention strategy, and develop a new work plan. If the expected outcome objective is not being achieved but the impact objective is, the manager must reexamine the assumed linkage between the determinants and the health problem, revise the intervention strategy, and develop a new work plan. If a program is doing things right (activities and process objectives) but is not achieving its projected impact or outcome, the only conclusion is that the program is not doing the right things. If the expected outcome objective is being achieved, the manager must reassess the need for the program and begin the management cycle again.

The three-level objective and evaluation procedure (process, impact, and outcome) facilitates locating the source of problems when a program does not achieve its expected outcome[6] (Figure 7–10). Many programs start off with a focus on achieving outcomes but rapidly shift to a focus on accomplishing their activities and process measures. This is an example of outcome displacement in that outcomes are displaced as the driving force of programs by lower level activities. Since every program needs to succeed, a program defines its success by doing things right even if those things do not lead to the outcomes that the program was designed to produce. If a program cannot succeed in terms of outcome, it will shift its objectives to those it can achieve. Activities and processes then become the program's purpose and are accepted as surrogates for achieving the program's objectives. An analogous situation is apparent in the larger health system, where health outcomes have been displaced as objectives by processes such as access to medical care.

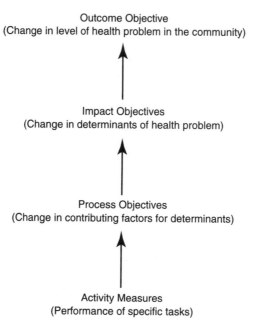

Outcome Objective
(Change in level of health problem in the community)

Impact Objectives
(Change in determinants of health problem)

Process Objectives
(Change in contributing factors for determinants)

Activity Measures
(Performance of specific tasks)

Figure 7–10 Multilevel Program Evaluation. *Source:* Adapted from W.W. Dyal, *Program Management: A Guide for Improving Program Decisions*, 1990, USPHS-CDC-PHPPO, Atlanta, GA.

This simple program management system works well in public health for many reasons. It is rational, flexible, and adaptable to most programs and allows for easily understood comparisons between programs. In addition, it fosters communications within an organization and serves to prevent outcome displacement. Most important, it provides a road map and mile markers for managers so that they can maintain a steady course along the road to achieving the program's stated outcome objectives.

CONCLUSION

"What have you done for me recently?" conveys the expectation for services that permeates society. Services and the programs that orchestrate their provision have become the hallmark of public health. Most people define public health in terms of the services they most frequently encounter. Because personal health services represent such a large share of public health expenditures and because

Exhibit 7–5 continued

> • Develop an evaluation plan for the program that will provide evidence that the
> program really works in the setting in which it is being implemented by
> • describing how each of the following will be assessed: activities, process
> objectives, impact objectives, and outcome objective. For each evaluation
> process, include information on items to be measured or counted, sources of
> information, flow or transfer of information, timeliness of data, how data and
> information will be analyzed, content of reports, and to whom and how often
> reports are to be made.
> • Assuming that you achieve all of your process objectives and that your outcome
> objective is 80 percent achieved, what actions would be appropriate? At 40 per-
> cent?
>
> *Source:* Adapted from *Translating Science Into Practice*, 1991, CDC Case Study.

REFERENCES

1. *Profile of Local Health Departments, 1992–1993*. Washington, DC: National Association of County and City Health Officials; 1995.
2. Public Health Foundation. Measuring state expenditures for core public health functions. *Am J Prevent Med*. 1995;11:58–73.
3. Essential Public Health Services Working Group of the Core Public Health Functions Steering Committee. Washington, DC: US Public Health Service; 1994.
4. US Preventive Services Task Force. *Guide to Clinical Preventive Services*. 2nd ed. Baltimore, Md: Williams & Wilkins; 1996.
5. Illinois Dept of Public Health, *Challenge and Opportunity: Public Health in an Era of Change*. Springfield, Ill: IDPH; 1996.
6. Dyal WW. *Program Management: A Guide for Improving Program Decisions*. Atlanta, Ga: US Public Health Service; 1990.

CHAPTER 8

Future Challenges for Public Health

Introductory texts emphasize the basic topics of a field and venture into more advanced issues only occasionally. That is not always possible with public health, since the basic topics can be quite complex and unfamiliar even to those who have worked in the field for many years. This text has approached public health from a simple conceptual framework of what public health is and how it works. The key components of that system have been examined, including its mission, functions, inputs, processes, outputs, and outcomes. Although this framework appears to be simple, many of the concepts addressed are anything but simple. As a result, much has been left unsaid, and many important issues and problems facing the public health system have been addressed only in passing. This may serve to whet the appetite of those eager to move beyond the basics and ready to tackle emerging and more complex issues in greater depth. It is hoped that the rational and simple concepts included in this text will facilitate that process. Diving into these other issues without the benefit of a broad understanding of the system and how it works, however, remains an occupational hazard in public health. Fighting off alligators every working day remains a major deterrent to studying swamps in order to plot better methods of alligator prevention and control.

The problems facing public health have changed over the past century due to several factors. Many past problems that were relatively easy to solve have already been addressed, as evidenced in the remarkable reductions in mortality and morbidity from the epidemic infectious disease problems of past centuries. More recent reductions in mortality and morbidity due to cardiovascular disease, stroke, and many forms of injuries also attest to the past successes of public health. Solving easy problems, however, leaves us with the more difficult and intractable ones. To these can be added emerging public health problems, those due either to the appearance of some new disease entity (like the AIDS/HIV pandemic) or to the reappearance of an old enemy that we had assumed was under control (tuberculosis [TB] is a good example here).

The ever-expanding social agenda of public health—the problems put onto the public policy agenda—adds another dimension to our current and future challenges. In recent decades, medical care issues, substance abuse, mental health, long-term care, and, today, violence have been categorized as public health problems and have taken their rightful place on the public health agenda.

Since persisting, emerging, reemerging, and newly assigned problems will forever challenge public health as a social enterprise, both the structure and the content of the public health response must be appropriate to the task. This chapter reviews the findings and recommendations of the Institute of Medicine (IOM) in its landmark 1988 study[1] of the American public health system and examines to what extent the failings identified in the IOM report represent opportunities and challenges for the future of public health. To provide a context for considering the current and future plight of public health in the United States, several different public health issues will be highlighted. These are the emergence and reemergence of infectious disease risks, the interfaces between public health and managed care, and the case for accrediting local public health agencies. Many other critical issues facing public health in the United States in the remaining years of the 20th century will not be addressed in this introductory text. Still, this sample of issues will demonstrate the scope of the problems and approaches that the public health system will be grappling with over the next decade. Key questions to be addressed in this chapter are:

- What are the challenges facing public health as it moves toward the twenty-first century?
- Will public health be up to the task of addressing these challenges?

EMERGING PATHOGENS

During the 1990s, several so-called emerging infections have received increasing attention from infectious disease experts, public health agencies, and the general public. *Emerging infections* generally refers to infectious conditions that are increasing in terms of their extent or impact on the population, although the term can also describe microorganisms that are appearing for the first time. Widespread media attention to these emerging pathogens has heightened public concern and caused increased demands on the public health system to detect and control their spread. For most infections classified as emerging problems, the level of public concern and fear is unwarranted. For some, however, this term describes public health problems that will challenge the public health system for years to come. HIV/AIDS infections certainly fall into this category, but some lesser known infectious conditions also deserve at least a brief mention.

Escherichia coli 0157:H7 (E. coli) and multi-drug–resistant pathogens are examples of current infectious diseases that are emerging as significant public health challenges.

Although many believe that infectious diseases no longer loom as major risks to the public, WHO data indicate that they remain the leading cause of death worldwide.[2] The Centers for Disease Control and Prevention (CDC) also shares this view:

> Infectious diseases remain the leading cause of death worldwide. Reduction in mortality from many infectious diseases has been described as the single most significant achievement of the past century. Unfortunately, historical successes in treating and controlling some of these diseases left many health policymakers with the false perception that the threat to public health from infectious agents had all but disappeared. The resulting public health complacency has been costly in both human and economic terms.[3(p9)]

The factors that contribute to the emergence or resurgence of infectious diseases are many and interrelated. The most important relate to population dynamics, environmental influences, or a combination of both. Improved identification and surveillance systems account for only a small share of recent increases in emerging pathogens. A more complete listing of factors responsible for emergent infections includes factors drawn from social, behavioral, environmental, and health system categories.[4] Social and demographic factors include population growth rates, poverty prevalence, immigration and especially urban migration, international travel, and social disruptions from civil conflict and natural disasters. Human behavioral factors include individual behaviors relating to diet, illicit drug use, sexual practices, travel, and outdoor recreation; collective behaviors such as changes in land management practices are also important. Environmental considerations include food production and potable water management factors; among these are pesticide and antibiotic use in crop and livestock management, changes in food processing, and inadequate water distribution and safety systems. Health system factors include antibiotic use, new technologies for transplantation, immunosuppression, medical devices, and inadequacies of ventilation and other mechanical systems of health facilities.

Infections due to *E. coli* 0157:H7 have emerged as a particularly frightening risk to the public (Exhibit 8–1). Initially identified as the cause of hemorrhagic conditions in the early 1980s, this pathogen has been increasingly associated with food-borne illness outbreaks in the 1990s, including a major outbreak in the Pacific Northwest related to *E. coli*–contaminated hamburgers distributed through a national fast food chain[5] (Figure 8-1). The source of the *E. coli* was cattle. Other outbreaks of this pathogen involved swimmers in lake water contami-

Exhibit 8–1 Assuring Food Safety

"It was a difficult situation. We kept seeing these children come through the hospital door, many with complications for which we had no cure; we could only give them supportive care. We relied on the state epidemiologists to stop this outbreak, and they came through for us."—Phillip Tarr, M.D., Pediatrician, Children's Hospital and Medical Center, Seattle, Washington

As many as 6.5 million cases of foodborne disease occur each year in the United States. This estimate is based on data from states and may represent substantial underreporting because of differences in monitoring and reporting requirements. Approximately 500 outbreaks of foodborne illness are reported by state and local health departments each year, with an average of 50 cases per outbreak. In 1993, a multi-state outbreak of *Escherichia coli*, strain 0157:H7, emphasized the importance of the complex infrastructure needed for an adequate public health response.

In January 1993, a physician in a Seattle hospital noted that more children were admitted with hemolytic uremic syndrome (HUS). This serious health problem may involve renal failure, stroke, or other grave consequences. When the physician coupled the unusual number of children seen in the emergency room for bloody diarrhea with the unusual number of children already hospitalized with HUS, he suspected an outbreak and reported his suspicions to the local health department, which immediately launched an investigation to find the source. Two days later, public health laboratories identified the causative agent as *E. coli* 0157:H7.

An investigation conducted by state public health epidemiologists implicated hamburgers from a chain of fast-food restaurants as the source of the infection. While state and local laboratories were confirming new cases of infection, federal laboratories using newly developed techniques documented that the *E. coli* from hamburger samples from the fast-food restaurant chain was the same type isolated from samples from ill persons. Five days after the initial report, the state health department announced that hamburgers were the probable source of infection, and 250,000 hamburger patties were recalled. A media campaign providing health education and information to an alarmed public helped identify additional infected individuals. Ultimately, more than 600 people were affected, including 45 with acute kidney failure. Three children died. With an effective surveillance system, which included appropriate diagnostic testing for *E. coli*, Washington state's public health agencies could respond rapidly and appropriately to control the outbreak and prevent many more cases of illness and death from occurring.

Nevada had recently had an outbreak of *E. coli* 0157:H7, but it was only recognized after the publicity associated with the Washington outbreak. At least one major difference between the two situations was that Nevada's clinical laboratories were not routinely screening for *E. coli* 0157:H7 despite an earlier outbreak in a day-care center. Without local reporting, the state had no surveillance information, and private physicians were not alerted about a possible outbreak. Of the 58 cases of *E. coli* identified in Nevada, none was accurately diagnosed originally or reported to local health departments.

continues

Exhibit 8–1 continued

It is estimated that medical care and losses in productivity due to *E. coli* infections cost between $200 million and $600 million each year. The estimated direct medical care costs for the Washington state outbreak alone total $1 million. If the surveillance system had not identified the outbreak for 10 more days, direct costs could have exceeded $2 million.

The outbreak of *E. coli* infection and public health's subsequent response led to increased regulations to decease these organisms in animals and to improve slaughtering and meat-handling procedures and enforcement of cooking temperatures for meat sold to the public. The Food and Drug Administration raised its recommended cooking temperatures for hamburgers. Although Washington state already had a regulation requiring that hamburgers be cooked at a temperature high enough to kill the organism, not all counties were able to regularly inspect restaurants.

Surveillance for this deadly bacterial infection is being strengthened. Recently the Council of State and Territorial Epidemiologists approved a position statement requiring notification of *E. coli* 0157:H7 infection in all states. Many more state public health laboratories are now able to confirm *E. coli* 0157:H7 isolates they receive from clinical laboratories—up from 78% in 1989 to nearly 100% in 1993. In addition, the federal government developed training materials to educate microbiologists at the local level about the types of organisms they should identify and report to public health departments. This collaboration of national, state, and local public health officials continues to provide the basis for successful public health practice. Such partnerships help ease the economic burden of foodborne infection and other health problems in the United States.

Source: Reprinted from *For a Healthy Nation: Return on Investment in Public Health*, 1995, U.S. Public Health Service, Washington, DC.

nated by bathers infected with the organism. Because many of the illnesses are minor and because both medical and public health practitioners fail to perform the tests necessary to diagnose *E. coli* infections properly, current surveillance efforts greatly underreport the extent of this condition.

Multi-drug–resistant pathogens represent another emerging infectious disease problem for the public health system. The widespread and, at times, indiscriminate use of antibiotics in agricultural and health care settings produces strains of bacteria that are resistant to these drugs. Antimicrobial agents have been increasingly deployed throughout the second half of the 20th century. Slowly, over this period, the consequences of these "miracle drugs" have been experienced in the community as well as in health facilities. The emergence of drug-resistant strains has reduced the effectiveness of treatment for several common infections, including tuberculosis, gonorrhea, pneumococcal infections, and hospital-acquired

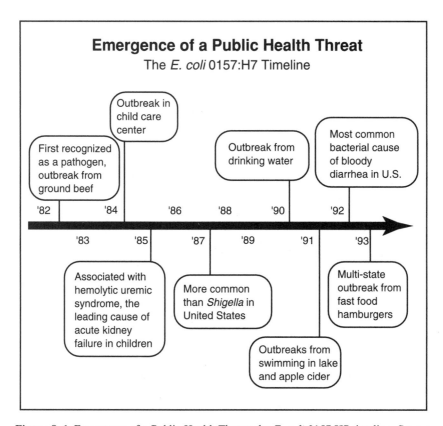

Figure 8–1 Emergence of a Public Health Threat: the *E. coli* 0157:H7 timeline. *Source:* Reprinted from *Addressing Emerging Infectious Disease Threats: A Prevention Strategy for the United States*, 1994, U.S. Centers for Disease Control and Prevention, Atlanta, GA.

staphylococcal and enterococcal infections. For tuberculosis, drug resistance is but one of the issues responsible for its resurgence.

TUBERCULOSIS: THE RETURN OF AN OLD ENEMY

TB remains a leading contender for the dubious distinction of being the most important plague in the history of mankind. The World Health Organization estimated that in the mid-1990s, over 1.7 billion people worldwide had been infected with mycobacterium tuberculosis, with projections for another 500 million infections in the next 50 years. Each year, about 8 million people develop TB in a recognizable form, and nearly 3 million die from the disease. More deaths were attributed to TB in 1995 than in the year 1900, when an estimated 2.1 million persons globally died from the disease. In fact, there were more deaths from TB in 1995 than in any year in history.[6] Even these large numbers fail to describe the impact of TB fully, due to its concentration among young adults throughout most of the developing world. The indelible imprint the disease has left on many families when the disease was commonplace only a few generations ago and the fear invoked by a disease that is spread from person to person through an airborne route, especially to household members, make TB a uniquely feared disease in America.

The Rise and Fall and Rise of TB

TB's history is lengthy and ancient; the disease may be as old as the history of humans. It apparently existed in ancient Egypt and is mentioned in the earliest writing of Greek, Roman, and Chinese physicians. Its absence from the written history of some cultures may be due more to the limited urbanization of those societies than the actual absence of the disease itself. Hammurabi's Code, the oldest code of laws in the world, makes reference to a chronic disease in Babylonia before 1900 BC that was very probably TB. Hippocrates was one of the first to describe TB's clinical features, in about 400 BC. The condition became known as *phthisis* (pronounced TIZ-I-sis), a term that initially was used to describe conditions resulting in wasting. Later, the term came to connote pulmonary disease. Although the disease probably changed little over history, only in modern times has a consistent set of signs, symptoms, and effects been recognized. The most important advances in the clinical and pathological aspects of TB occurred in the 17th and 18th centuries, culminating with the work of Robert Koch.

Although TB has been an important disease for centuries, it was the crowding and expansion of international commerce associated with the Industrial Revolution that raised the disease to the level of a major global health problem. There had never been much that could be provided in terms of treatment, but the massive increases of TB in crowded urban settings made the problem so visible it could not be ignored. TB continued to be of less public concern than more immediately life-threatening diseases such as cholera, typhoid, and yellow fever, but it was emerging as a major health problem in Europe and America. The development of specialized treatment facilities, sometimes called *sanatoria*, reflect efforts to deal with disease and its victims.

In the United States, a remarkable approach to TB was developed in the late 19th and early 20th centuries, the so-called tuberculosis movement. This movement was unique in that it believed that a wide range of social policy changes were needed to address TB. The disease was depicted as both preventable and curable if addressed not only from a scientific and medical perspective but through wider public health approaches, social policy changes, and improved economic conditions.

The scientific and medical advances were drawn from the rapidly expanding field of bacteriology and the more traditional public health strategies based on sanitation and hygiene. One of the earliest comprehensive TB prevention and control programs was established by the New York City Department of Health in the 1890s. This program included education of the public, precautionary measures against the spread of infection, separation and isolation of TB patients, assignment of inspectors to visit and disinfect the apartments of patients, sputum exams for disease detection, and the reporting of all cases of TB. Other large cities soon followed suit, although these early efforts clearly recognized the need for collaborative approaches involving health providers, voluntary associations, public agencies, and the public. The growth of volunteer efforts and voluntary organizations around TB prevention and control was unique. Volunteers were enthusiastically welcomed, and many small voluntary organizations appeared on the scene. Eventually, these small and sometimes competing voluntary groups coalesced into the larger and more powerful units that ultimately became the American Lung Association.

The active involvement of volunteers and the adoption of a broad view of the health and social factors that contribute to the TB problem resulted in a new attitude and approach to disease control. The underlying theme was positive. TB could be controlled, and even infected persons could lead normal, productive lives. The disease was portrayed as a threat to national prosperity and vitality. Public and community education approaches never before seen became commonplace as health messages were posted in store windows, hotel rooms, schools, community facilities, and public transportation vehicles. Common to these information and education efforts was the campaign's symbol, the double-barred cross. Innovative fund-raising strategies were developed, including an annual Christmas Seal campaign that has continued on to the present day. Still, the TB movement reflected the predominant values of the day, as evidenced in the near-complete failure to address TB among the nation's black population.

These initial activities were bolstered by the development of effective drug therapies during the middle decades of the 20th century. As a result of these combined weapons, TB mortality rates plummeted. Because of these successes, the prevailing opinion, especially during the 1960s and 1970s, was that TB could be controlled with the tools available. Both the scientific tools and the methods necessary for their application were thought to be well understood. A concerted effort to utilize these tools and methods on a broad scale was all that would be needed to eliminate TB, just as smallpox had been wiped off the face of the globe. Although it is understandable how this optimism developed, it subsequently proved to be unjustified.

The persistence of TB through the 1970s and early 1980s suggested that elimination would require both greater commitment and new strategies. CDC sponsored a national conference in 1985 to identify and address the needed technologies. The timing of this conference was ironic in that 1985 was the year in which the steady downward trend in TB cases in the United States reversed itself and became a steady upward trend into the 1990s. From 1985 through 1992, the United States saw a 20 percent increase in reported cases, as illustrated in Figure 8–2. It is now apparent that the HIV epidemic was one cause of these increases, and its effect on TB morbidity in the United States is likely to persist for some time.[7] Furthermore, TB has increasingly become a disease of the poor and the socioeconomically disenfranchised, and, alarmingly, cases have begun to increase among children (Table 8–1). Outbreaks of drug-resistant TB have become common, especially among persons with HIV infection. Patient noncompliance with screening programs and with therapy and preventive therapy recommendations continues to thwart control efforts. Cutbacks in health department resources for

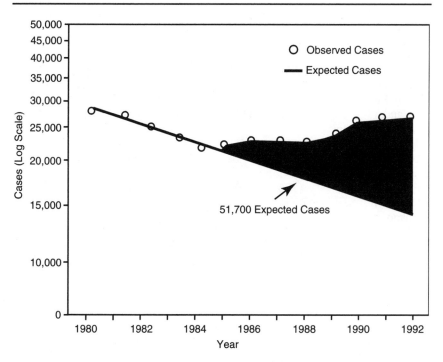

Figure 8-2 Expected and Observed Number of Tuberculosis Cases, United States, 1980–1992. *Source:* Reprinted from Tuberculosis Morbidity–United States, 1992, *MMWR*, Vol. 42, pp. 696–703, 1993, Centers for Disease Control and Prevention.

Table 8–1 Reported Cases and Rates of Tuberculosis, by Sex, Age Group, Race/Ethnicity, and Country of Origin—United States, 1985 and 1992

Characteristic	No. Cases 1985	No. Cases 1992	% Change	Rate[a] 1985	Rate[a] 1992	% Change
Sex						
Male	14,496	17,433	+20.3	12.5	14.0	+12.0
Female	7,704	9,236	+19.9	6.3	7.1	+12.7
Unknown	1	4	—[b]	NA[c]	NA	
Age group (yrs)						
0–4	789	1,074	+36.1	4.4	5.5	+25.0
5–14	472	633	+34.1	1.4	1.7	+21.4
15–24	1,672	1,974	+18.1	4.2	5.5	+31.0
25–44	6,758	10,444	+54.5	9.2	12.7	+38.0
45–64	6,138	6,487	+5.7	13.7	13.4	−2.1
≥65	6,356	6,025	−5.2	22.3	18.7	−16.1
Unknown	16	36	—	NA	NA	
Race/ethnicity						
White, non-Hispanic	8,453	7,618	−9.9	4.5	4.0	−11.1
Black, non-Hispanic	7,592	9,623	+26.8	23.0	31.7	+37.8
Hispanic[d]	3,092	5,397	+74.5	21.4	22.4	+4.7
Asian/Pacific Islander	2,530	3,698	+46.2	41.6	46.6	+12.0
American Indian/ Alaskan Native	397	305	−23.2	18.9	16.3	−13.8
Unknown/other[e]	137	32	—	NA	NA	
Country of origin[f]						
Foreign-born[g]	4,925	7,270	+47.6	NA	NA	
U.S.-born	17,712	19,225	+8.5	NA	NA	
Unknown	131	178	—	NA	NA	
Total	22,201	26,673	+20.1	9.3	10.5	+12.9

[a]Per 100,000 population. Populations by race/ethnicity are projections obtained from the Bureau of Census (Source: Bureau of Census, Current population reports; series P-25, no. 1092, November 1992).

[b]Not calculated.

[c]Denominator data not available.

[d]Persons of Hispanic origin may be of any race.

[e]Includes blacks and whites of unknown ethnicity.

[f]Cases reported for 1986, the first year with uniform national reporting of country of origin for persons with tuberculosis.

[g]Persons born outside the United States and its territories.

Source: Reprinted from Tuberculosis Morbidity–United States, 1992, *MMWR*, Vol. 42, pp. 696–703, 1993, Centers for Disease Control and Prevention.

TB control, or level funding in the face of increasing morbidity, complicate matters, as have shortages of anti-TB drugs.

A number of the key issues related to the reemergence of TB can be readily appreciated from Table 8–1. This reemergence of TB as an important public health problem challenges us to revisit the strategies and approaches used to prevent and control infectious diseases in general and TB in particular. In many ways, the reemergence of TB represents a case study of the U.S. public health system and its response to major health problems. It is also a review of what public health is and how it works.

TB and Infectious Disease Control

As we have seen, the functions of public health have matured over the past century, evolving from two general roles that themselves have different roots in political and social values. These duties call for preventing the consequences of disease and injury and providing health care for those "not otherwise provided for." These roles derive from quite different duties of government. Protecting the public from infectious disease hazards is an exercise of government's police power duty, whereas serving the indigent derives from government's role in promoting the general welfare. TB is noteworthy for the importance of both preventive and treatment strategies. In that respect, it differs from public-sector prevention and control programs aimed at many other infectious diseases, such as polio, measles, mumps, and hepatitis. A similar balance, however, is found in programs addressing HIV and sexually transmitted diseases.

The modern infectious disease program arsenal has many weapons for prevention and treatment. Various combinations and emphases characterize programs aimed at different infectious diseases. Among the available weapons to identify infectious diseases in the community are reporting requirements (generally for providers and laboratories), surveillance efforts in state and local health agencies, investigations of contacts of infected persons, and diagnostic laboratory capabilities. Weapons for controlling the spread of infectious diseases include monitoring of treatment to ensure compliance with treatment plans, immunization and chemoprophylaxis for specific diseases, and the use of isolation and quarantine practices. Investigation of the source and extent of infectious diseases is another weapon with both disease identification and control capabilities.

The authority for activities such as isolation and quarantine derives from the police power of the state, somewhat tempered in recent decades by the need to use the least restrictive means available. This concept calls for the use of measures that are the least restrictive on individual rights and liberties as possible in achieving a program's objective.

Prevention and control programs may include any or all of these activities organized through strategies of primary or secondary prevention. The actual interventions may be clinical, environmental, behavioral, or some combination of these three. For example, TB programs heavily emphasize secondary prevention through early case finding and rapid contact investigation, even though there is a primary prevention tool (BCG vaccine) available. TB, as noted earlier, also extensively deploys clinical, as well as environmental and behavioral, strategies for prevention and control. Critical components of modern TB prevention and control programs include

- mandatory reporting (with confidentiality)
- capabilities for examination, treatment, and monitoring of compliance with treatment regimens until treatment is completed
- diagnostic laboratory capability
- identification of and prophylactic treatment for close contacts
- assurance of financial access to treatment services

Several facets of the resurgence of TB in the United States underscore its importance to public health. The increase in cases between the mid-1980s and early 1990s was largely confined to persons born outside the United States and those with HIV infection. The risk to much of the population did not grow at all. In addition, the emergence of drug-resistant strains of TB necessitated the development of increased monitoring of treatment regimens and improved communitywide surveillance efforts. The linkage between case finding and treatment, especially for those with little access to the private health system, suggests that TB can never really be conquered until public health and medical care components of the health system are better integrated than they have ever been. Certainly, the same lesson is evident in the first 15 years of the HIV/AIDS epidemic in the United States. With ultimate success dependent on greater integration between public health and medical care, the expansion of managed-care strategies in the health system becomes very significant for the public health system.

MANAGED CARE AND PUBLIC HEALTH: STRANGE BEDFELLOWS?

The forces of reform have buffeted the U.S. health system during much of the 1990s, resulting in significant change in the organization, provision, and financing of health services. These changes certainly constitute reform, although this reform is likely to take decades rather than years or months. Central to these changes are managed-care plans and the competitive purchase of health services from large health systems. The links with public health have not always been clear, but what is clear is that public health practitioners need to better understand managed care and how it works. The most important reason is that effective partnerships with managed care will be critical to solving many public health problems. In addition, public health surveillance will depend, in part, on the nature and quality of information available from managed-care plans. Finally, the mix and match of public health programs and services will depend upon what the medical-care system does and does not do. For these reasons, the basic concepts and practices of managed-care organizations are presented in the following section.

Managed Care in the 1990s

Managed-care organizations exist for two related purposes, to insure plan members and to furnish and manage the care they receive. There are many different variations on this theme, but definitions of managed care characterize a system that is under the management of a single entity that insures its members and then furnishes benefits to those members through a defined network of participating providers. Services may be furnished either directly or through intermediaries. In any event, the system strives to manage the health care practices of its participating providers. Still, it is the providers who manage the patients. Since it is provider decisions, certainly more than the decisions of patients, that influence service utilization and costs, modern managed-care organizations must manage providers.

In the United States, managed-care organizations are generally corporations. Although some of these were established by insurance companies, more recent managed-care organizations are investor owned. Generally, the largest investors are health care providers themselves, so the principal stakeholders are hospitals, physicians, and specialized entities that offer a single-service product line, such as behavioral health benefits. The common denominator among managed-care organizations is their assumption of risk on a complete or partial basis. Profits are derived from the difference between premium payments and costs of providing services to patients.

The rapid growth of health maintenance organizations (HMOs) and other forms of managed care in the 1990s was described in Chapter 3. In the mid-1990s, more than 90 million privately insured individuals were covered by managed-care plans.[8] Managed care has also begun to penetrate governmentally financed health services, with more than a quarter of Medicaid beneficiaries and 1 in 10 Medicare recipients receiving services through managed-care operations. These numbers will grow rapidly over the next decade.

Many forces are at work to promote the growth of managed-care arrangements in the United States. First and foremost has been the rising costs associated with health care services. As costs escalated, and because the majority of Americans are covered through employers, businesses moved to control costs. Many businesses had already moved to self-insure their workers and dependents in an effort to better control decisions affecting costs. They soon began to treat health services as they would other costs of doing business and looked for insurance products that would allow them to control costs through controlling providers. Managed care was an attractive product. Managed care also afforded an opportunity for government to control its costs in a manner that would overcome at least some of the obstacles that had traditionally discouraged providers from serving Medicaid recipients (such as delayed payments and extensive paperwork). With predictable reimbursement levels and lower utilization of services, at least in comparison with their greater risk and need, the opportunity for profit margins has attracted interest from managed-care organizations in virtually every state. Managed care for Medicare beneficiaries has proceeded less rapidly than for the private sector and Medicaid. Official predictions of inadequate resources to serve baby boomers when they reach senior citizenship, however, suggest that managed care will eventually penetrate the Medicare program.

The jargon and terminology of modern managed care confuses all but a few knowledgeable individuals. More important than understanding the jargon, however, is understanding how these plans work. In general, there are both open and closed variations of managed-care plans. *Open* and *closed* refer to the relationship between the managed-care plan and its patients in terms of freedom to choose providers other than those controlled by the managed-care organization. Closed plans often have tighter control over providers, and enrolled plan members have little ability to secure covered services outside these panels of providers. Some of the traditional staff-model HMOs are examples of closed plans. Open panels are looser arrangements that allow members to obtain services from a wider (and less tightly controlled) network of providers. Preferred provider organizations and physician/hospital networks are examples of open panels. In this form of managed care, enrolled members can obtain services at very little additional cost out of pocket unless that service is received outside the plan. When that occurs, members pay more, although they generally remain partially covered by the plan.

A hybrid arrangement is the point-of-service model. Here services provided by plan providers are tightly controlled, but services can also be obtained outside the plan through a looser network of providers for an added fee. This allows for greater consumer choice as to providers but still provides for some control of costs for basic benefits.

Naturally, the more interested the purchaser is in controlling costs, the less open the plan will be. Medicaid managed-care plans, and even private plans less concerned over patient freedom to choose among providers, find the closed panels more amenable to aggressive cost-control strategies. Decisions to go the closed-panel route require that an assessment has been made of the capacity of the managed-care organization to provide covered services, including both primary and specialized care services. Unfortunately, methods and tools for such assessments are seldom afforded the same priority as controlling costs.

Methods for controlling costs are straightforward, with utilization control serving as a primary approach. The services and procedures that cannot be quickly and cheaply provided during a provider visit are reviewed for appropriateness in terms of whether such services are actually needed and, if needed, from whom and in what settings they will be provided. In short, the plan determines whether the service is covered and where the member can get it. Denial of approval can be tantamount to denial of care for those who lack the ability to secure the services using their own resources.

Sharing of costs between the plan and the enrollee is used as another approach for controlling costs. When costs are shared, the plan ends up paying less. Such cost sharing also serves to discourage the member from actually receiving the service, another savings for the managed-care plan. Other cost-control measures relate to member selection. Marketing to potential members from healthier age groups and populations also serves to control costs down the road. Some marketing efforts are even more explicit in terms of more actively enrolling (even door to door) the healthier members of an eligible group, a practice that has been identified especially with the development of Medicaid managed-care programs.

In addition to risk-profiling potential members, similar profiles can be done on providers in order to identify those whose practice patterns and decisions result in "unnecessary" costs for the plan. Patterns for use of screening tests, performance of office procedures, return visits, and hospital admissions are examined to identify providers whose practice patterns might be modified or even whose participation might be excluded. There is some scientific merit to these reviews in the face of numerous studies describing greatly varying rates of medical procedures across the United States, often with no apparent differences in health outcomes.

These approaches to economic credentialing often do not consider differences in the risk mix of populations served. Asthma management of a white teenage male in the suburbs may not be the same as for an inner-city, African American teenager. Identification and consideration of different risk mixes and contributing factors is a public health skill that is not widely available in managed-care operations.

Opportunities for Improving Public Health

Despite the tensions and conflicts that have emerged between managed-care organizations and both providers and consumers, aspects of managed care hold opportunity for improving public health. Fragmentation and lack of coordination of health services have long been a hallmark of the American health system. Managed care imposes some semblance of a structure on this pluralistic "nonsystem" and affords a framework for effective health services that can reach more individuals. In the past, this could only be done on a provider-by-provider basis. There are now access and leverage points for networks of providers to provide clinical preventive services more extensively and to integrate their activities with community prevention efforts. There are even financial incentives for these to occur. Diseases and conditions prevented today will mean lower expenditures and greater profits tomorrow. Although managed-care organizations with a long-term view and a stable base of enrollees recognize this opportunity, many newly established managed-care operations focus on shorter-term financial viability concerns, such as expanding enrollment and rapid generation of profits.

But profit orientations can cut both ways, and public health agencies may find themselves cut out of the picture for many services they have been providing in recent decades. Some services, such as primary and even treatment care services, may shift to managed-care organizations for individuals covered by Medicaid or other third-party insurers. Other services are specialized public health services, such as treatment services for TB, HIV infections, and sexually transmitted diseases. The future for these services is very much an open question. Managed-care plans would prefer not to enroll individuals who need specialized, often high-cost services. Providers of specialized services are also worrisome to managed-care plans, as these might serve to attract more individuals with high-cost needs. Yet these needs will exist, and it is unclear how and by whom they will be addressed.

One approach is to require that managed-care plans include specialized public health providers in their networks. Needless to say, this approach is not very popular among managed-care organizations. Another option is to tax a portion of the revenues of managed-care plans to support specialized public health providers through grants or contracts. The public health agencies would not be formally part of the managed-care networks, but they would share information on individuals as referrals were made back and forth. Another approach is to carve out certain services from the managed-care plans and let individuals seek out these services on an as-needed basis. This approach, however, fosters fragmentation and lack of continuity of care. The advantages of defining and carving out specific services as public health rather than components of a comprehensive benefit package have not been well established to date.

Another opportunity is afforded by the information systems necessary to manage networks of providers and services. Traditionally, public health surveillance has been not been able to access and utilize information on health status and health conditions of living persons captured in the ambulatory care system. Combining this information with other data sources can greatly benefit public health surveillance efforts, as well as inform the needs of managed-care plans and providers. But public health interests are not the only ones likely to be seeking access to health plan data and information. The very same stakeholders whose priorities promoted the expansion of managed care will be looking for information that proves that their resources are being used effectively and efficiently. Businesses and the government will be demanding information that demonstrates the value that their health dollars are realizing and that allows them and their employees to evaluate and compare health plan performance. Ideally, health outcome concerns should drive these developments, but financial concerns are more likely to dictate what information is collected and how it is used.

The managed-care industry has developed a data set for use in evaluating and comparing health plan performance, the Health Plan Employer Data and Information Set (HEDIS). Recent revisions of HEDIS have sought to incorporate community and public health performance measures; the public health community is actively seeking to build on HEDIS so that public health data needs might be better addressed. At least three categories of data may have applications for public health purposes:

1. Managed-care plans maintain administrative data sets such as provider names and payments.
2. Managed-care plans have enrollment data such as the neighborhoods and communities where enrollees are located. Enrollment data might also include details such as the sex, age, race, and national origin of enrollees. From a public health perspective, these enrollment data are useful in identifying high-risk communities.[8]
3. Managed-care plans can obtain patient encounter data. At least some managed-care plans currently use encounter data to profile what their providers order and the frequency of hospital admissions. Encounter data, however, tend to be limited because these are the most expensive form of data to obtain, especially if on-site inspection and abstracting information from medical records are required. Also, managed-care plans do not rely on encounter data for reimbursement, as is common with fee-for-service systems.

There has been little agreement to date as to which information from encounter data would be most useful for public health purposes and would be appropriate for managed-care plans to provide. The many issues surrounding data questions are only beginning to be explored. It is likely that additional opportunities will surface as they are discussed and developed.

For example, school health may represent another opportunity for forging closer working relationships between managed-care plans and public health organizations. In many parts of the country, school health programs are being dismantled because of financial pressures on state and local government. School health nurses have long been the linchpin of school health programs. These too, are declining in numbers even while new mandates and expectations are being established in areas such as compliance with immunization requirements, vision and hearing screenings, medical assessments for special education students, medication administration, and crisis intervention services. With these duties, their involvement in health curriculum issues is greatly diluted. But as Medicaid managed-care conversions develop and as managed care penetrates further into the private sector, school health may represent an opportunity to integrate managed-care plans with public health objectives. For example, children at a single school may be served by 10 to 20 managed-care plans currently, and in the future perhaps only 5 to 10. These plans could contribute proportionately to the funding of school nurses and support staff to carry out the duties described above in ways that would be less expensive than either providing them at plan provider sites or not providing them and dealing with preventable disease outbreaks or asthma attacks requiring hospitalization.

The many opportunities afforded by the expansion of managed care call for new thinking and new roles,[9] as suggested in Exhibit 8–2. Both managed-care plans and public health agencies must approach these challenges with common objectives. Still, there remains one role that is likely to be aggravated by the expansion of managed-care plans: the role of providing medical services for those who have no coverage. This number has been estimated to include about 40 million Americans at any one time. The expansion of managed care, with its heavy emphasis on price competition and financial bottom lines, will serve to reduce the amount of so-called charity care previously furnished by private-sector providers. This is already apparent in communities where managed care has captured large segments of the market, and it is likely to occur in many, if not most, U.S. communities. These circumstances suggest once again that reform of the medical care system must be accompanied by reform within the public health system.

THE CASE FOR ACCREDITING PUBLIC HEALTH AGENCIES[10]

"Chicago ain't ready for reform!" is an observation first attributed to Paddy Bauler, one of the city's most infamous aldermen during its heyday of political bossism. To some observers, the rejection of comprehensive national health reform in 1994 reflects a similar failing—the U.S. health system simply "ain't ready for reform." Others, however, argue that reform of our health system is alive and well in the steady advancement of managed-care approaches to the organization, financing, and provision of personal health care services. In contrast to proactive strategies seeking insurance and medical care reform, reform of governmental public health activities has been largely reactive, despite considerable impetus since 1988 provided by the IOM report. Among the actual and perceived threats buffeting the public health community have been political shifts, funding reductions, and territorial encroachment by managed-care entities, in addition to public health's self-inflicted characterization as being in disarray.

Exhibit 8–2 Managed Care and Public Health Issues for the Future

Public health goals and Medicaid services	How these can be merged • to increase the focus on health • to simplify and increase access for Medicaid recipients • to incorporate health services (broadly defined) essential for good health outcomes
Case management and enabling services	How to ensure • inclusion of these services in view of evidence that they improve access and yield better health outcomes for enrollees than systems that only coordinate medical treatment
System capacity and the roles of providers	How these can be clearly articulated • to clarify the sometimes conflicting case management roles of both patient advocates and cost containment agents
Fluctuations in enrollment	How these will • complicate efforts to supply case management to Medicaid populations • affect provider accountability for continuity of care • increase the likelihood that public health agencies will maintain a significant role in delivering services as "providers of last resort"
Assurance of quality	How to deal with issues of quality so that • quality will not be compromised • quality will be monitored by government • there is a public health focus on access and clinical care as well as a financial focus on solvency and enrollment composition • there is a careful analysis of broad outcome data • encounter data will facilitate consumer choice and identify problems in the shift from fee-for-service care delivery to managed care with capitated payments • the appropriate roles of government, employers, and consumers are identified

continues

Exhibit 8–2 continued

Data	How to address
	• the need for data essential for a successful "outcome-oriented" approach to continuing quality processes within managed-care systems
	• integration in systems that collect, make meaningful, and disseminate data to facilitate decision making
Provider and consumer acceptance	How to resolve
	• dependence on the degree to which provider concerns regarding practice autonomy and consumer perceptions of diminished choice are addressed
	• the need for a consumer-oriented approach to quality, requiring consumer support, and independent access to medical advice such as second opinions

Source: Adapted from Illinois Department of Public Health, *Challenge and Opportunity: Public Health in an Era of Change,* 1996, Springfield, Illinois.

A case in point has been the inability of the public health community to capitalize on the first-ever national health objective to ensure that Americans are adequately served by the governmental presence in health characterized as essential in the IOM report. Objective 8.14 of the year 2000 national health objectives calls for 90 percent of the U.S. population to be served by local health departments (LHDs) that are effectively addressing public health's three core functions: assessment, policy development, and assurance. When this objective, the first and only one addressing the performance of state and local public health agencies with regard to public health's core functions, was unveiled in 1990, several key elements were not in place. Notably lacking were benchmark data, methods of ascertainment, and operational definitions for the concepts to be measured. In mid-1995, these elements are still not in place, despite some important efforts in this direction, largely due to the overwhelming challenges and threats that have intervened since 1990. This is unfortunate in view of evidence from the limited assessments performed to date suggesting that the nation is less than halfway to achieving this important year 2000 objective.

Still, there may be one significant initiative, a national program for accrediting local health departments, that the public health community can marshal to address Objective 8.14. A voluntary national accreditation program could build on the framework provided by the Assessment Protocol for Excellence in Public

Health (APEXPH), complement current statewide certification and standard-setting initiatives, and facilitate the effective implementation of any new federal block grants established for the purpose of promoting core functions and essential services. Several factors argue for and would promote the success of such an accreditation initiative. These factors are best understood in the context of five important, yet basic, questions that underpin a national accreditation program.

What Is a Local Health Department? Current definitions of *local health department* inadequately characterize the purpose and functions of these important agencies. They define LHDs by describing aspects of their general structure, such as their relationship to local or state government, minimum number of full-time employees, and general concern or responsibility for health within a defined jurisdiction. As a result, agencies that are unable to carry out public health core functions or provide essential community public health services are viewed as LHDs under these criteria. Evidence for this assertion is apparent in the low performance levels of many small agencies qualifying as LHDs under these definitions in recent studies of local public health performance based on performance measures related to public health's three core functions. Long-standing recommendations that LHDs should serve populations of at least 50,000 conflict with the national experience, which has witnessed the greatest growth among those LHDs serving populations of under 50,000. An essential component of any new definition of LHD must be that the agency be in the business of addressing public health core functions. Accreditation could be used to differentiate LHDs that are effectively addressing the core functions from those that are not. In this process, small agencies that constitute a local public health presence rather than a local health "department" could be distinguished, and their role and performance capacity could be appropriately clarified and supported. Recent approaches to defining public health practice in terms consistent with public health core functions have spawned methods to measure and assess local public health practice and to certify LHDs on the basis of practice standards (either performance expectations or capacity to perform) for statewide public health systems. Through these approaches, the capability to define LHDs based on public health's core functions now exists.

Why Accredit Local Health Departments? The self-flagellation of public health since the appearance of the IOM report has been apparent at all levels of public health activity. Campaigns and initiatives to improve the marketing of public health have been developed by the national public health organizations and associations to complement and supplement similar efforts developed by state and local counterparts of these national organizations. These efforts respond to the realization that many important community constituencies view public health agencies primarily as providers of medical care to indigent populations. Enhancement of public understanding and appreciation of public health among legislative, political, community, and health provider partners is not an unrealistic expectation from a national accreditation program. Beyond the value for external audiences, accreditation has the potential to clarify the content of the public health mission (the collective practice of public health) for public health's diverse internal constituencies. Lack of consensus as to the content of public health practice is perhaps the most important barrier to effective public health action identified in the IOM report. This peer recognition of common function and minimal performance would foster the development of a new standard of LHD practice linking agencies from all states through a common conceptual framework. In sum, accreditation status could well serve LHDs with respect to both internal and external constituencies.

Are Core Function–Based Approaches a Rational and Acceptable Basis for Accrediting LHDs? In less than three years after its formal introduction, one-third of U.S. LHDs have utilized the APEXPH. Among LHDs that had not used APEXPH at the time of the survey conducted by the National Association of County and City Health Officials (NACCHO), 35 percent indicated their intent to implement the organizational self-assessment component with its extensive catalog of organizational indicators (Part I), and 43 percent reported intent to implement the community health assessment component (Part II).[11] NACCHO's recent *Blueprint for Healthy Communities,*[12] CDC's 10 public health practices,[13] and the list of 10 essential public health services[14] by the U.S. Public Health Service all serve to further characterize local public health practice in terms that are understood and valued by public health professionals. Summarized in Exhibit 8–3, together with tools to measure public health practice performance, these provide a rational, understandable, and acceptable basis for the development of accreditation criteria.

Two states, Washington and Illinois, have already introduced core function–based approaches as the basis for local public health practice. Washington State has developed an extensive catalog of capacity indicators for LHDs to be phased in as the basis for performance-based contracts between the state and its local health districts. The Washington Public Health Improvement Plan explicitly attempts to redirect the statewide public health system back to the core functions of assessment, policy development, and assurance. Illinois also adopted a Public Health Improvement Plan and revamped its certification standards for LHDs to incorporate performance expectations grounded in the three core functions rather than categorical program performance standards. Certification enables LHDs to receive a share of the Local Health Protection Block Grant and funding preference for other grant programs offered by state agencies. In both states, LHDs have affirmed approaches grounded in public health core functions as both rational and acceptable. In effect, LHDs are volunteering to be measured against rational standards.

Exhibit 8–3 Rational Public Health Framework

Public health delivers these services:	By performing these practices:
• Prevents epidemics and the spread of disease • Protects against environmental hazards • Prevents injuries • Promotes and encourages healthy behaviors • Responds to disasters and assists communities in recovery • Ensures the quality and accessibility of health services	• Assessing community health needs • Investigating hazards within the community • Analyzing identified health needs for their determinants • Advocating and building constituencies for public health • Prioritizing among identified community health needs • Developing comprehensive policies and plans to respond to priority needs • Managing resources and organizational structures • Implementing programs and services to respond to priority needs • Evaluating programs and services • Informing and educating the community

Source: Data from W.L. Roper et al., Strengthening the Public Health System, *Public Health Reports,* Vol. 107, pp. 609–615, 1992; and *Public Health in the U.S.,* 1994, Essential Public Health Services Working Group of the Core Public Health Functions Steering Committee.

Are There Better Approaches to Improving LHD Practice Performance? The proof as to whether accreditation will improve LHD practice performance is likely to be in the pudding, but early results from the implementation of APEXPH and its adaptations across the United States are promising. As yet, there has been no examination of this question for LHDs that have implemented APEXPH in comparison to LHDs that have not, but there has been an assessment of LHD practice performance before and after the statewide implementation of an APEXPH derivative in Illinois. That study documented substantial improvements in practice measures related to the assessment, policy development, and assurance functions over a two-year period and linked increased practice performance to the use of APEXPH and the establishment of certification criteria.

One alternative to a national accreditation program would be continued promotion of APEXPH and other capacity-building tools. Experience to date demonstrates that many LHDs are voluntarily using APEXPH and other available tools as part of continuous quality management (CQM) initiatives and that even greater LHD use can be anticipated. Nonetheless, it is unlikely that these tools will be used by all LHDs, and additional incentives will be necessary.

Another alternative would be to leave the accreditation process to the states. Yet few states currently set operational or performance standards for their LHDs, and the capabilities for statewide capacity building vary considerably from state to state. Many of these differences are related to variations in statutory authority, historical relationships, funding streams, and other factors that may not be easily amenable to change. Nonetheless, states could still set standards equal to or greater than any national accreditation standards where such authority exists or could be established. States might also choose to accept national accreditation in lieu of separate state standards. Given these possibilities, state innovation in this area need not be stifled by a national accreditation program; in fact, an accreditation initiative would be likely to be informed and enhanced by the experience of statewide capacity-building initiatives in innovative states. Some direction for these efforts is anticipated from the IOM's Committee on Public Health Performance Monitoring when its report is issued in late 1996.

In an era when state control is being promoted, it is noteworthy that accreditation of many other health organizations such as hospitals remains a national function coordinated through the Joint Commission on Accreditation of Healthcare Organizations (Joint Commission). A similar process for LHDs would elevate these agencies as well as the role of public health.

Who Should Accredit Local Health Departments? It would seem logical for NACCHO, the Association of State and Territorial Health Officials (ASTHO), and the American Public Health Association to play leading roles in a national accreditation program. The merger of city and county officials into one organization representing LHDs certainly facilitates this possibility. Other participants might include CDC's Public Health Practice Program Office, the Public Health Foundation, and the Association of Schools of Public Health (ASPH). Schools of public health have considerable experience with accreditation processes and could provide valued service to the practice community as part of such an effort. The possibility of collaboration with the Joint Commission is also intriguing. The Joint Commission has already established standards for provider networks and is currently working to develop community health and prevention standards for hospitals and other health organizations.

These questions are by no means the only ones that arise in considering the notion of a national accreditation system for LHDs. They are, however, among those that must be raised early in its consideration. LHD accreditation would represent reform in the purest sense of the word by taking the basic building blocks of our governmental public health system and reshaping (or re-forming) them through common definitions and operational measures related to function. In this light, accreditation is entirely consistent with recent calls for the reinvention and reengineering of public health. With an accreditation program in place and supported by the public health community, progress toward attainment of Objective 8.14 can be tracked and remedial capacity-building strategies targeted more effectively. Although this approach may appear threatening to many small public health units, an overarching objective must be to incorporate these units into strengthened state-local public health networks. A strong argument can also be made that accreditation of LHDs would be synergized if state health agencies would also submit to accreditation based on core function–based approaches.

Perhaps these aims could be accomplished through other approaches, such as a nationally funded core functions block grant to state and local health departments. Although such a program appears (at times) politically feasible, the likelihood of its success will rise or fall with the development of a stable, secure, and adequate funding stream. A "bottom-up" approach embracing voluntary accreditation would certainly complement such a core function block grant program. However, in the absence of such a national funding program, national accreditation is even more essential. Ultimately, accreditation only makes sense if there is consensus that LHDs should and must have a strong role no matter what a reformed health care system for the United States may look like in the future. Reforming public health agencies would also address some of the shortcomings of the U.S. public health system cited in the well-known indictment of the system described in the section that follows.

PUBLIC HEALTH: A SYSTEM IN "DISARRAY"?

The findings and clarion call of the IOM report set the stage for improvement of the public health system. This landmark report, completed in 1988, found much of value and importance in the nation's public health efforts, but it also found an even longer list of problems. The most serious problem of all was that Americans were taking their public health system for granted. The nation had come to believe that epidemics of communicable diseases were a thing of the past and that food and water would forever be free of infectious and toxic agents. Americans assumed that workplaces, restaurants, and homes were safe and that everyone had access to the information and skills needed to lead healthy lives. They also assumed that all this could occur even while public health agencies were being increasingly called upon to provide health services to nearly 40 million Americans who had no health insurance or were underinsured. But across the nation, states and localities were failing to provide the resources that would allow both the traditional public health and more recent health service roles to be carried out successfully. When future benefits compete with immediate needs, the results are predictable.

These results fostered the image of a public health system in disarray. Within this system, neither the public nor even those involved in the work of public health have a clear vision of the scope and content of public health in modern America. A consensus as to which levels of government should be carrying out various aspects of those responsibilities is an even more remote possibility.

Previous chapters demonstrate that several formulations in the IOM report have been widely embraced by the public health community. These include statements of the mission, substance, and core functions of public health. The mission has been described simply as assuring conditions in which people can be healthy. The substance consists largely of organized community efforts to promote health and prevent disease. The IOM report identifies an essential role for government in public health in organizing and assuring that the mission gets addressed. An expanded view of the fundamental functions of governmental public health was articulated in the three core functions of assessment, policy development, and assurance. These represent a more comprehensive view of public health efforts than that conveyed by earlier views that public health primarily furnished services and enforced statutes. The new public health differed in its emphasis on problem identification and resolution as the basis of rational interventions (that would still include service provision and enforcement activities).

These broad strokes serve virtually to define the public health enterprise with three components: mission statement (common goals/values); substance (areas of concern for public health); and organizational framework (how is public health different from what public health agencies do). The essential role of government in public health in terms of its special authority, obligations, and duties is also elucidated through the three core functions of public health frequently addressed in earlier chapters.

Perhaps the most well-known feature of the report is its characterization of the disarray of public health and the significance of that disarray. The IOM report painted a picture of disjointed efforts in the 1980s to deal with immediate crises, such as the epidemic of HIV infections and an increasing lack of access to health services, and enduring problems with significant social impacts, such as injuries, teen pregnancy, hypertension, and tobacco and drug use. With impending crises on the horizon in the form of toxic substances, Alzheimer's disease, and public health capacity, the IOM report found the situation to be grimmer still.

The IOM report found a wide gap between the capabilities of the current public health system and those of a public health system capable of rising to modern challenges. Therefore it charted some initial directions that would move us closer to an optimal system. Several enabling steps[1] were also identified:

- improving the statutory base of public health
- strengthening the structural and organizational framework

- improving the capacity for action, including technical, political, management, programmatic, and fiscal competencies of public health professionals
- strengthening linkages between academia and practice

Working through a multitude of society's institutions rather than only through traditional public health organizations is the key to improving the public health system. It is also a daunting task. It calls for challenging the concept of control by entering into partnerships with sectors like corrections, education, law enforcement, and business and by fostering change through leadership and influence rather than through command and control. The barriers to effecting these collaborations are also the major obstacles to achieving the aspirations outlined in the year 2000 national health objectives. These barriers come in all sizes and shapes and from many different sources. Some are perceived as external barriers; others appear to be more internal.

The IOM report sought to identify some key barriers inhibiting effective public health action. Ten such barriers were identified:[1]

1. lack of consensus on the content of the public health mission
2. inadequate capacity to carry out the essential public health functions of assessment, policy development, and assurance of services
3. disjointed decision making without necessary data and knowledge
4. inequities in the distribution of services and the benefits of public health
5. limits on effective leadership, including poor interaction among the technical and political aspects of decisions, rapid turnover of leaders, and inadequate relationships with the medical profession
6. organizational fragmentation or submersion
7. problems in relationships among the several levels of government
8. inadequate development of necessary knowledge across the full array of public health needs
9. poor public image of public health, inhibiting necessary support
10. special problems that limit unduly the financial resources available to public health

Though not as spellbinding as one of David Letterman's top-10 lists, these 10 barriers are both imposing and important. There are several themes common to this collection. Foremost among the barriers affecting public health are the prevailing values of the American public, and in particular, those restricting the ability of government to identify and address factors that influence health. Social values determine the extent to which government can regulate human behavior, such as through controlling the production and use of tobacco products or requiring bicycle or motorcycle helmet use. These values also determine whether and to what extent family planning or school-based clinic services are provided in a community and determine the content of school health education curricula. Some of these social values find strange bedfellows. For example, many Americans oppose control of firearms on the basis of principles of self-protection embodied in the U.S. Constitution; gun companies also oppose control, although on the basis of more direct economic considerations.

Economic and resource considerations are common themes as well. One obvious issue is that most public health activities remain funded from the discretionary budgets of local, state, and federal government. At all levels, discretionary programs have been squeezed by true entitlement programs such as Medicaid and Medicare, as well as by some governmental responsibilities that have become near-entitlements, such as public safety, law enforcement, corrections, and education. Funding one set of health-related services from governmental discretionary funds while other health services are financed through a competitive marketplace will only continue to increase the imbalance between treatment and prevention as investment strategies for improved health status. There are powerful economic interests among health sector industries, as well as among industries whose products affect health, such as the tobacco, alcohol, pesticide, and firearms industries. One could only dream that equally powerful lobbies might develop for hepatitis or drug-resistant TB.

All too often, the complex problems and issues of public health, with causes and contributing factors perceived to lie outside its boundaries, lead public health professionals to believe that they should not be held accountable for failure or success. But many facets of public health practice itself could be further improved. These include relationships with the private sector and medical practice and some internal reengineering of public health processes. Fear and suspicion of the private sector can lead to many missed opportunities. Just as the three most important factors determining real estate values are location, location, and location, it can be argued that the three most important factors for health are jobs, jobs, and jobs. If this is anywhere near true, suspicions of the private sector need to be put to rest. There is little question that employment is a powerful preventive health intervention in terms of both individual and community health status. Community development activities that bring new businesses and jobs to a community will affect health status more positively than a public health clinic on every corner. Further, businesses have been major forces behind the growth of managed-care systems in the United States. Their partnership with public health interests will be essential to secure new resources or shift the balance between treatment and prevention strategies. Increased partnerships with medical care interests will also be necessary. Unfortunately, there is widespread ignorance of the medical care sector among public health workers.

Among barriers internal to public health agencies is one that often goes unnoticed: the widespread use of categorical approaches to program management, which often fragments and isolates individual programs one from another. In addition to the unnecessary proliferation of information, management, and other administrative processes, each program tends to develop its own assortment of interest and constituency groups, including those involving program staff, who often work to oppose meaningful consolidation and integration of programs.

Another limiting factor is the generalized inability to prioritize and focus public health efforts, despite the wealth of information as to which factors most affect health at the national, state, or even local levels. Time and time again, tobacco, alcohol, diet, and violence have been shown to lie at the root of most preventable mortality and years of potential life lost. Ideally, resource allocation decisions would be made on the basis of the most important attributable risks rather than being spread around to address, ineffectively, risks both large and small. With scores of priorities, there are really none, and without clear priorities, accountability is seldom expected. Public health has always operated at the confluence of science and politics, so political issues and some compromises to clear priorities are natural. Still, inconsistencies between stated public health priorities through goals and actual program priorities as demonstrated through funding are themselves barriers to public understanding and support for public health work.

Other factors that influence public understanding and support for public health relate to the transition from conditions caused by microorganisms to those caused by human behaviors. It is more difficult for the public to appreciate the scientific basis for public health interventions when social rather than physical sciences guide strategies. This occurs at a time when government is increasingly portrayed as both incompetent and overly intrusive. Largely because governmental processes are considered by the public to be intensely political, the public view of public health processes, including programs and regulations, is that of highly politicized and partly scientific exercises.

There has been considerable debate as to whether the IOM report accurately captures the problems and needs of the American public health system. In many respects, the report restated the fundamental values and concepts underlying public health in terms of its emphasis on prevention, professional diversity, collaborative nature, community problem solving, loosely attached constituencies, assurance functions, need to draw other sectors into the solution of public health problems, and lack of an identifiable constituency. Taken together, these features certainly appear to represent disarray. But the cause of this disarray may not lie with public health but rather with our social and governmental institutions more generally. Posing solutions that restructure the system's components may do little more than rearranging the deck chairs on the Titanic.

It may be necessary to restructure more broadly the tasks and functions of public health to deal with modern public health problems. The larger work of public health is to get the prevention job done right rather than to get it done through a traditional structuring of roles and responsibilities. Preventing disease and promoting health must be embraced throughout society and its health institutions rather than existing in a parallel subsystem. There is no evidence to support the contention that public health activities are best organized through public health agencies of government. It is the mission and the effort that are important and not necessarily the organization from which those efforts are generated.

CONCLUSION: WHY WE NEED A MORE EFFECTIVE PUBLIC HEALTH SYSTEM

The key issues and challenges facing the future of public health defy simple summarization. This chapter has examined several, including those offered by the IOM report, and earlier chapters presented many more. Which of these are most important remains a point of contention. It would be useful to have an official list that represented the consensus of policy makers and the public alike. But since an official list is lacking, several general conclusions as to the critical challenges and obstacles facing the future of public health in the United States are presented. They summarize some of the important themes of this text in describing why we need more effective public health efforts.

All the Easy Problems Have Already Been Solved! Major successes have been achieved through public health efforts over the past 150 years, largely related to massive reductions in infectious diseases but also involving substantial declines in death rates for injuries and several major chronic diseases since about 1960. The list of current problems for public health includes the more difficult chronic diseases, new and emerging conditions (such as AIDS and Alzheimer's), and broader social problems with health effects (teen pregnancy and violence are good examples) that have identifiable risk and contributing factors that can only be addressed through collective action. The days of command-and-control approaches to relatively simple infectious risks are behind us. In the past, environmental sanitation and engineering could collaborate with communicable disease control expertise to address important public health problems. The collaborations needed for violence prevention or reduction of tobacco use require much different skills and relationships.

When You're a Hammer, the Whole World Looks Like a Nail. Behind this proverb is the perception that common education and work experiences foster common professional perspectives. The danger lies in believing that one's own professional tools are adequate to the task of dealing with all of the problems and needs that are served by the profession. Each profession has its own scientific base and jargon. Problems are given labels or diagnoses using the profession's specialized language so that the tools of the profession can be brought to bear on those problems. All too often, however, the problems come to be considered as the domain of that profession so that the potential contributions of other professions and disciplines may not be appreciated. Although public health professionals are diverse in terms of their educational and experiential backgrounds, they also can fall into this trap. When they do, bridges to other partners are not built, and collaborations do not take place. As a result, problems that can only be addressed through collaborative intersectoral approaches flourish unabated.

A Friend in Need Is a Friend . . . until Someone Better Comes along. Finding means to build such bridges can be difficult, but some key collaborations appear to be absolutely essential for the work of public health to succeed. Certainly, links between public health and medical care must be improved for both to prosper in a reforming health system. Links with businesses also represent another avenue for mutually successful collaborations. The key is to find major areas of common purpose. For medical care interests, the common denominator is that prevention saves money and rewards those who use it as an investment strategy. For business interests, the bottom line has to be improved, and businesses must accept the premise that improving health status in the community serves their bottom line through healthier, more productive workers and healthier and wealthier consumers.

You Get What You Pay for. There is much reason to question the current national investment strategy as it relates to health services. The excess capacity that has been established is becoming increasingly unaffordable, and the results are nothing to write home about. Still, the competition for additional dollars is intense among the major interests that dominate the health industry, and there is little movement to alter the current balance between treatment and prevention strategies. With only 3 percent of all health expenditures supporting all forms of prevention and only 1 percent supporting population-based prevention, even small shifts could reap substantial rewards. The argument that resources are limited and that there simply are not adequate resources to meet both treatment as well as prevention purposes is uniquely American and is quite inimical to the public's health.

Nobody Told Me/It Ain't My Job! The job description of public health has never been clear. As a result, public health has become quite proficient in delivering specific services, with less attention paid to mobilizing action toward those factors that most seriously affect community health status. Among traditional health-related factors, tobacco, alcohol, and diet are factors responsible for much of modern America's mortality and morbidity. Nonetheless, the resources supporting interventions directed toward these factors are minuscule. Similarly, the primary cause of America's relatively poor health outcomes in comparison to other developed nations as well as the most likely source for further health gains in the United States resides in the huge, and increasing, gaps between racial and ethnic groups. The public health system, from national to state and local levels, must recognize these circumstances and move beyond capably providing services to aggressively advocating and building constituencies for efforts that target the most important of the traditional health risk factors and that promote social policies that both minimize and equalize risks throughout the population. These represent a new job description for public health in the United States, but one that is both necessary and feasible.

DISCUSSION QUESTIONS AND EXERCISES

1. Do you think that the history and future of public health can be told through the saga of TB? Or of HIV/AIDS or other emerging diseases?
2. How are methods of primary, secondary, and tertiary prevention applied to TB control? Or to the HIV/AIDS epidemic?
3. What effects have managed-care approaches had on costs, quality, access, and health outcomes? What additional approaches may be necessary?
4. What current roles of public health should be carried out in a reformed health care system? By whom?
5. Would public health efforts be better served if local and state health agencies were accredited in accordance with national standards?
6. What do you see as the most important new or expanded roles for public health in the future?
7. Do you agree with the IOM assertion that public health is in disarray, or with the counterassertion that it is government, not public health, that is in disarray?

REFERENCES

1. Institute of Medicine. *The Future of Public Health.* Washington, DC: National Academy Press; 1988.
2. WHO warns of inadequate noncommunicable disease prevention. *Public Health Rep.* 1996;111: 296–297.
3. Centers for Disease Control and Prevention. *Addressing Emerging Infectious Disease Threats: A Prevention Strategy for the United States.* Atlanta, Ga: US Public Health Service; 1994.
4. Malloy CD, Gallo RJ, Leib HB, Marr JS. Emerging pathogens: the white horse of the Apocalypse. *J Public Health Manage Pract.* 1995;1(No. 2):48–61.
5. *For a Healthy Nation: Return on Investment in Public Health.* Washington, DC: US Public Health Service; 1995.
6. TB deaths reach historic levels. *Public Health Rep.* 1996;111:292.
7. Centers for Disease Control and Prevention. Tuberculosis morbidity: United States, 1992. *MMWR.* 1993;42:696–703.

8. Rosenbaum S, Richards TB. Medicaid managed care and public health policy. *J Public Health Manage Pract.* 1996;2(No. 3):76–82.

9. *Challenge and Opportunity: Public Health in an Era of Change.* Springfield, Ill: Illinois Dept of Public Health; 1996.

10. Turnock BJ, Handler AS. Is public health ready for reform? The case for accrediting local health departments. *J Public Health Manage Pract.* 1996;2(No. 3):41–45.

11. National Association of County and City Health Officials. *1992–1993 Profile of Local Health Departments.* Washington, DC: NACCHO; 1995.

12. National Association of County and City Health Officials. *Blueprint for Healthy Communities.* Washington, DC: NACCHO; 1994.

13. Roper WL, Baker EL, Dyal WW, Nicola RM. Strengthening the public health system. *Public Health Rep.* 1992;107:609–615.

14. Essential Public Health Services Working Group of the Core Public Health Functions Steering Committee. *Public Health in the U.S.* Washington, DC: US Public Health Service; 1994.

Glossary of Terms

ACCESS

The potential for or actual entry of a population into the health system. Entry is dependent upon the wants, resources, and needs that individuals bring to the care-seeking process. Ability to obtain wanted or needed services may be influenced by many factors, including travel distance, waiting time, available financial resources, and availability of a regular source of care.

ACTIVITIES

Specific tasks that must be completed for a program's processes to achieve their targets.

ACTIVITY MEASURES

Indicators of whether a program's activities are successfully completed.

ACTUAL CAUSE OF DEATH

A primary determinant or risk factor associated with a pathologic or diagnosed cause of death. For example, tobacco use would be the actual cause for deaths from many lung cancers.

ADJUSTED RATE

The adjustment or standardization of rates is a statistical procedure that removes the effect of differences in the composition of populations. Because of its marked effect on mortality and morbidity, age is the variable for adjustment used most commonly. For example, an age-adjusted death rate for any cause permits a better comparison between different populations and at different times because it accounts for differences in the distribution of age.

ADMINISTRATIVE LAW

Rules and regulations promulgated by administrative agencies within the executive branch of government that carry the force of law. Administrative law represents a unique situation in which legislative, executive, and judicial power are carried out by one agency in the development, implementation, and enforcement of rules and regulations.

AGE-ADJUSTED MORTALITY RATE

The expected number of deaths that would occur if a population had the same age distribution as a standard population, expressed in terms of deaths per 1,000 or 100,000 persons.

APPROPRIATENESS

Health interventions for which the expected health benefit exceeds the expected negative consequences by a wide enough margin to justify the intervention.

ASSESSMENT

One of public health's three core functions. Assessment calls for regularly and systematically collecting, analyzing, and making available information on the health of a community, including statistics on health status, community health needs, and epidemiologic and other studies of health problems.

ASSESSMENT PROTOCOL FOR EXCELLENCE IN PUBLIC HEALTH (APEXPH)

A voluntary process for organizational and community self-assessment, planned improvements, and continuing evaluation and reassessment. It focuses on a health department's administrative capacity, its basic structure and role in its community, and the community's actual and perceived problems. It offers an opportunity for the local health department to assess its relationships with local government agencies and with community, state, and federal health agencies. Finally, it provides a protocol through which a health department, by working with the community to assess health needs, sets priorities, develops policy, and ensures that health needs are met, will become recognized within the community as having a major role in the health of its citizens.

ASSOCIATION

The relationship between two or more events or variables. Events are said to be associated when they occur more frequently together than one would expect by chance. Association does not necessarily imply a causal relationship.

ASSURANCE

One of public health's three core functions. It involves assuring constituents that services necessary to achieve agreed-upon goals are provided by encouraging actions on the part of others, by requiring action through regulation, or by providing services directly.

ATTRIBUTABLE RISK

The theoretical reduction in the rate or number of cases of an adverse outcome that can be achieved by elimination of a risk factor. For example, if tobacco use is responsible for 75 percent of all lung cancers, the elimination of tobacco use will reduce lung cancer mortality rates by 75 percent in a population over time.

BEHAVIORAL RISK FACTORS SURVEILLANCE SYSTEM

A national data collection system funded by the Centers for Disease Control and Prevention (CDC) to assess the prevalence of behaviors that affect health status. Through individual state efforts, CDC staff coordinate the collection, analysis, and distribution of survey data on seat belt use, hypertension, physical activity, smoking, weight control, alcohol use, mammography screening, cervical cancer screening, and AIDS, as well as other health-related information.

CAPACITY

The capability to carry out the core functions of public health. Also see **Infrastructure**.

CAPITATION

A method of payment for health services in which a provider is paid a fixed amount for each person served, without regard to the actual number or nature of services provided to each person in a set period of time. Capitation is the characteristic payment method in health maintenance organizations.

CASE MANAGEMENT

The monitoring and coordinating of services rendered to individuals with specific problems or who require high-cost or extensive services.

CAUSALITY

The relationship of causes to the effects they produce; several types of causes can be distinguished. A cause is termed *necessary* when a particular variable must always precede an effect. This effect need not be the sole result of the one variable. A cause is termed *sufficient* when a particular variable inevitably initiates or produces an effect. Any given cause may be necessary, sufficient, neither, or both.

CENTERS FOR DISEASE CONTROL AND PREVENTION (CDC)

The Centers for Disease Control and Prevention, based in Atlanta, Georgia, is the federal agency charged with protecting the nation's public health by providing direction in the prevention and control of communicable and other diseases and responding to public health emergencies. CDC's responsibilities as the nation's prevention agency have expanded over the years and will continue to evolve as the agency addresses contemporary threats to health such as injury, environmental and occupational hazards, behavioral risks, chronic diseases, and emerging communicable diseases such as the Ebola virus.

CHRONIC DISEASE

A disease that has one or more of the following characteristics: it is permanent, leaves residual disability, is caused by a nonreversible pathological alternation, requires special training of the patient for rehabilitation, or may be expected to require a long period of supervision, observation, or care.

CLINICAL PRACTICE GUIDELINES

Systematically developed statements that assist practitioner and patient decisions about appropriate health services for specific clinical conditions.

CLINICAL PREVENTIVE SERVICES

Clinical services provided to patients to reduce or prevent disease, injury, or disability. These are preventive measures (including screening tests, immunizations, counseling, and periodic physical examinations) provided by a health professional to an individual patient.

COMMUNITY

A group of people who have common characteristics; communities can be defined by location, race, ethnicity, age, occupation, interest in particular problems or outcomes, or other common bonds. Ideally, there should be collective discussion, decision making, and action.

CONTRIBUTING FACTOR

A risk factor (causative factor) that is associated with the level of a determinant. Direct contributing factors are linked with the level of determinants; indirect contributing factors are linked with the level of direct contributing factors.

CORE FUNCTIONS

Three basic roles for public health for assuring conditions in which people can be healthy. As identified in the Institute of Medicine's landmark report *The Future of Public Health*; these are assessment, policy development, and assurance.

COST BENEFIT ANALYSIS

An economic analysis in which all cost and benefits are converted into monetary (dollar) values and results are expressed as dollars of benefit per dollars expended.

COST-EFFECTIVENESS ANALYSIS

An economic analysis assessed as a health outcome per cost expended.

COST UTILITY ANALYSIS

An economic analysis assessed as a quality-adjusted outcome per net cost expended.

CRUDE MORTALITY RATE

The total number of deaths per unit of population reported during a given time interval, often expressed as the number of deaths per 1,000 or 100,000 persons.

DECISION ANALYSIS

An analytic technique in which probability theory is used to obtain a quantitative approach to decision making.

DEMOGRAPHICS

Characteristic data, such as size, growth, density, distribution, and vital statistics, that are used to study human populations.

DEMONSTRATION SETTINGS

A population- or clinic-based environment in which prevention strategies are field-tested.

DETERMINANT

A primary risk factor (causative factor) associated with the level of health problem: i.e., the level of the determinant influences the level of the health problem.

DISABILITY LIMITATION

An intervention strategy that seeks to arrest or eradicate disease and/or limit disability and prevent death.

DISCOUNTING

A method for adjusting the value of future costs and benefits. Expressed as a present dollar value, discounting is based on the time value of money (i.e., a dollar today is worth more than it will be a year from now even if inflation is not considered).

DISTRIBUTIONAL EFFECTS

The manner in which the costs and benefits of a strategy affect different groups of people in terms of demographics, geographic location, and other descriptive factors.

EARLY CASE FINDING AND TREATMENT

An intervention strategy that seeks to identify disease or illness at an early stage so that prompt treatment will reduce the effects of the process.

EFFECTIVENESS

The improvement in health outcome that a strategy can produce in typical community-based settings. Also, the degree to which objectives are achieved.

EFFICACY

The improvement in health outcome effect that a strategy can produce in expert hands under ideal circumstances.

EPIDEMIC

The occurrence of a disease or condition at higher than normal levels in a population.

EPIDEMIOLOGY

The study of the distribution of determinants and antecedents of health and disease in human populations; the ultimate goal is to identify the underlying causes of a disease and then apply findings to disease prevention and health promotion.

ESCHERICHIA COLI (E. COLI) 0157:H7

A bacterial pathogen that can infect humans and cause severe bloody diarrhea (hemorrhagic colitis) and serious renal disease (hemolytic uremic syndrome).

ESSENTIAL PUBLIC HEALTH SERVICES

A formulation of the processes used in public health to prevent epidemics and injuries, protect against environmental hazards, promote healthy behaviors, respond to disasters, and ensure quality and accessibility of health services; 10 essential services have been identified:

- monitoring health status to identify community health problems
- diagnosing and investigating health problems and health hazards in the community
- informing, educating, and empowering people about health issues

- mobilizing community partnerships to identify and solve health problems
- developing policies and plans that support individual and community health efforts
- enforcing laws and regulations that protect health and ensure safety
- linking people to needed personal health services and ensuring the provision of health care when otherwise unavailable
- ensuring a competent public health and personal health care work force
- evaluating effectiveness, accessibility, and quality of personal and population-based health services
- research for new insights and innovative solutions to health problems

FEDERALLY FUNDED COMMUNITY HEALTH CENTERS

An ambulatory health care program (defined under Section 330 of the Public Health Service Act), usually serving a catchment area that has scarce or nonexistent health services or a population with special health needs; sometimes known as a "neighborhood health center." Community health centers attempt to coordinate federal, state, and local resources in a single organization capable of delivering both health and related social services to a defined population. Although such a center may not directly provide all types of health care, it usually takes responsibility to arrange all medical services for its patient population.

FIELD MODEL

A framework for identifying factors that influence health status in populations. Initially, four fields were identified: biology, lifestyle, environment, and health services. Extensions of this approach have also identified genetic, social, and cultural factors and have related these factors to a variety of outcomes, including disease, normal functioning, well-being, and prosperity.

FOOD-BORNE ILLNESS

Illness caused by the transfer of disease organisms or toxins from food to humans.

GENERAL WELFARE PROVISIONS

Specific language in the Constitution of the United States that empowers the federal government to provide for the general welfare of the population. Over time, these provisions have been used as a basis for federal health policies and programs.

GOALS

For public health programs, goals are general statements expressing a program's aspirations or intended effect on one or more health problems, often stated without time limits.

GOVERNMENTAL PRESENCE IN HEALTH AT THE LOCAL LEVEL

A concept that calls for the assurance that necessary services and minimum standards are provided to address priority community health problems; this responsibility ultimately falls to local government, which may utilize local public health agencies or other means for its execution.

HEALTH

The state of complete physical, mental, and social well-being and not merely the absence of disease or infirmity. It is recognized, however, that health has many dimensions (anatomical, physiological, and mental) and is largely culturally defined. The relative importance of various disabilities will differ depending on the cultural milieu and on the role of the affected individual in that culture. Most attempts at measurement have been assessed in terms of morbidity and mortality.

HEALTH CARE FINANCING ADMINISTRATION

The government agency within the U.S. Department of Health and Human Services that directs the Medicare and Medicaid programs (Titles XVIII and XIX of the Social Security Act) and conducts the research to support those programs.

HEALTH EDUCATION

Any combination of learning opportunities designed to facilitate voluntary adaptations of behavior (in individuals, groups, or communities) conducive to good health. Health education encourages positive health behavior.

HEALTH MAINTENANCE ORGANIZATIONS

Entities that manage both the financing and provision of health services to enrolled members; fees are generally based on capitation, and health providers are managed in order to reduce costs through controls on utilization of covered services.

HEALTH PLANNING

Planning concerned with improving health, whether undertaken comprehensively for a whole community or for a particular population, type of health services, institution, or health program. The components of health planning include data assembly and analysis, goal determination, action recommendation, and implementation strategy.

HEALTH POLICY

Social policy concerned with the process whereby public health agencies evaluate and determine health needs and the best ways to address them, including the identification of appropriate resources and funding mechanisms.

HEALTH PROBLEM

A situation or condition of people (expressed in health outcome measures such as mortality, morbidity, or disability) that is considered undesirable and is likely to exist in the future.

HEALTH PROBLEM ANALYSIS

A framework for analyzing health problems to identify their determinants and contributing factors so that interventions can be targeted rationally toward those factors most likely to reduce the level of the health problem.

HEALTH PROMOTION

An intervention strategy that seeks to eliminate or reduce exposures to harmful factors by modifying human behaviors. Any combination of health education and related organizational, political, and economic interventions designed to facilitate behavioral and environmental adaptations that will improve or protect health. This process enables individuals and communities to control and improve their own health. Health promotion approaches provide opportunities for people to identify problems, develop solutions, and work in partnerships that build on existing skills and strengths.

HEALTH PROTECTION

An intervention strategy that seeks to provide individuals with resistance to harmful factors, often by modifying the environment to decrease potentially harmful interactions. Those population-based services and programs control and reduce the exposure of the population to environmental or personal hazards, conditions, or factors that may cause disease, disability, injury, or death. Health protection also includes programs that ensure that public health services are available on a 24-hour basis to respond to public health emergencies and coordinate responses of local, state, and federal organizations.

HEALTH REGULATION

Monitoring and maintaining the quality of public health services through licensing and discipline of health professionals, licensing of health facilities, and enforcement of standards and regulations.

HEALTH STATUS INDICATORS

Measurements of the state of health of a specified individual, group, or population. Health status may be measured by proxies such as people's subjective assessments of their health; by one or more indicators of mortality and morbidity in the population, such as longevity or maternal and infant mortality; or by the incidence or prevalence of major diseases (communicable, chronic, or nutritional). Conceptually, health status is the proper outcome measure for the effectiveness of a specific population's health system, although attempts to relate effects of available medical care to variations in health status have proved difficult.

HEALTH SYSTEM

As used in this text, the health system is the sum total of the strategies designed to prevent or treat disease, injury, and other health problems. The health system includes population-based preventive services, clinical preventive and other primary medical care services, and all levels of more sophisticated treatment and chronic care services.

HEALTHY COMMUNITIES 2000

A framework for developing and tailoring community health objectives so that these can be tracked as part of the initiative to achieve the year 2000 national health objectives included in *Healthy People 2000*.

HEALTHY PEOPLE 2000

The national disease prevention and health promotion agenda that includes some 300 national health objectives to be achieved by the year 2000, addressing improved health status, risk reduction, and utilization of preventive health services.

IMPACT OBJECTIVE

The level of a determinant to be achieved through the processes and activities of an intervention strategy. Impact objectives are generally intermediate in term (two to five years) and must be measurable and realistic.

INCIDENCE

A measure of the disease or injury in the population, generally the number of new cases occurring during a specified time period.

INDICATOR

A measure of health status or a health outcome.

INFANT MORTALITY RATE

The number of live-born infants who die before their first birthday per 1,000 live births; often broken into two components, neonatal mortality (deaths before 28 days per 1,000 live births) and postneonatal mortality (deaths from 28 days through the rest of the first year of life per 1,000 live births).

INFECTIOUS DISEASE

A disease caused by the entrance into the body of organisms (such as bacteria, protozoans, fungi, or viruses) that then grow and multiply there; often used synonymously with *communicable disease.*

INFRASTRUCTURE

The human, organizational, informational, and fiscal resources of the public health system that provide the capacity for the system to carry out its core functions.

INPUTS

Sometimes referred to as *capacities*, human resources, fiscal and physical resources, information resources, and system organizational resources necessary to carry out the core functions of public health.

INTERVENTION

A generic term used in public health to describe a program or policy designed to have an impact on a health problem. For example, a mandatory seat belt law is an intervention designed to reduce the incidence of automobile-related fatalities. Five categories of heath interventions are health promotion, specific protection, early case finding and prompt treatment, disability limitation, and rehabilitation.

LEADING CAUSES OF DEATH

Those diagnostic classifications of disease that are most frequently responsible for deaths; often used in conjunction with the top 10 causes of death.

LIFE EXPECTANCY

The number of additional years of life expected at a specified point in time, such as at birth or at age 45.

LOCAL HEALTH DEPARTMENTS (LHDs)

Functionally, a local (county, multicounty, municipal, town, other) health agency, operated by local government, often with oversight and direction from a local board of health, that carries out public health's core functions throughout a defined geographic area. A more traditional definition is an agency serving less than an entire state that carries some responsibility for health and has at least one full-time employee and a specific budget.

MANAGED CARE

A system of administrative controls intended to reduce costs through managing the utilization of services. Managed care can also mean an integrated system of health insurance, financing, and service delivery that focuses on the appropriate and cost-effective use of health services delivered through defined networks of providers and with allocation of financial risk.

MEASURE

An indicator of health status or a health outcome, used synonymously with **Indicator** in this text.

MEDICAID

A federally aided, state-operated and administered program that provides basic medical services to eligible low-income populations; established through amendments as Title XIX of the Social Security Act in 1965. It does not cover all the poor, however, but only persons who meet specified eligibility criteria. Subject to broad federal guidelines, states determine the benefits covered, program eligibility, rates of payment for providers, and methods of administering the program.

MEDICARE

A national health insurance program for elderly persons established through amendments to the Social Security Act in 1965 that were included in Title XVIII of that act.

META-ANALYSIS

A systematic, quantitative method for combining information from multiple studies to derive the most meaningful answer to a specific question. Assessment of different methods or outcome measures can increase power and account for bias and other effects.

MIDLEVEL PRACTITIONERS

Nonphysician health care providers such as nurse practitioners and physician assistants.

MISSION

For public health, assuring conditions in which people can be healthy.

MORBIDITY

A measure of disease incidence or prevalence in a given population, location, or other grouping of interest.

MORTALITY

Expresses the number of deaths in a population within a prescribed time. Mortality rates may be expressed as crude death rates (total deaths in relation to total population during a year) or as death rates specific for diseases and sometimes for age, sex, or other attributes (e.g., the number of deaths from cancer in white males in relation to the white male population during a given year).

OBJECTIVES

Targets for achievement through interventions. Objectives are time limited and measurable in all cases. Various levels of objectives for an intervention include outcome, impact, and process objectives.

OUTCOMES

Sometimes referred to as results of the health system; these are indicators of health status, risk reduction, and quality-of-life enhancement. Outcomes are long-term objectives that define optimal, measurable future levels of health status; maximum acceptable levels of disease, injury or dysfunction; or prevalence of risk factors.

OUTCOME OBJECTIVE

The level to which a health problem is to be reduced as a result of an intervention. Outcome objectives are often long-term (two to five years), measurable, and realistic.

OUTPUTS

Health programs and services intended to prevent death, disease, and disability and to promote quality of life.

POLICE POWER

A basic power of government that allows for restriction of individual rights in order to protect the safety and interests of the entire population.

POLICY DEVELOPMENT

One of public health's three core functions. Policy development involves serving the public interest in the development of comprehensive public health policies by promoting the use of the scientific knowledge base in decision making and by leading in developing public health policy.

POPULATION-BASED PUBLIC HEALTH SERVICES

Interventions aimed at disease prevention and health promotion that affect an entire population and extend beyond medical treatment by targeting underlying risks, such as tobacco, drug, and alcohol use; diet and sedentary lifestyles; and environmental factors.

POSTPONEMENT

A form of prevention in which the time of onset of a disease or injury is delayed to reduce the prevalence of a condition in the population.

PREVALENCE

A measure of the burden of disease or injury in a population, generally the number of cases of a disease or injury at a particular point in time or during a specified time period. Prevalence is affected by both the incidence and the duration of disease in a population.

PREVENTED FRACTION

The proportion of an adverse health outcome that has been eliminated as a result of a prevention strategy.

PREVENTION

Anticipatory action taken to prevent the occurrence of an event or to minimize its effects after it has occurred. Prevention aims to minimize the occurrence of disease or its consequences. It includes actions that reduce susceptibility or exposure to health threats (primary prevention), detect and treat disease in early stages (secondary prevention), and alleviate the effects of disease and injury (tertiary prevention). Examples of prevention include immunizations, emergency response to epidemics, health education, modification of risk-prone behavior and physical hazards, safety training, workplace hazard elimination, and industrial process change.

PREVENTIVE STRATEGIES

Frameworks for categorizing prevention programs based on how the prevention technology is delivered—provider to patient (clinical preventive services), individual responsibility (behavioral prevention), or alteration in an individual's surroundings (environmental prevention)—or on the stage of the natural history of a disease or injury (primary, secondary, tertiary).

PRIMARY MEDICAL CARE

Clinical preventive services, first-contact treatment services, and ongoing care for commonly encountered medical conditions. Basic or general health care focuses on the point at which a patient ideally seeks assistance from the medical care system. Primary care is considered comprehensive when the primary provider takes responsibility for the overall coordination of the care of the patient's health problems, whether these are medical, behavioral, or social. The appropriate use of consultants and community resources is an important part of effective primary health care. Such care is generally provided by physicians but can also be provided by other personnel such as nurse practitioners or physician assistants.

PRIMARY PREVENTION

Prevention strategies that seek to prevent the occurrence of disease or injury, generally through reducing exposure or risk factor levels. These strategies can reduce or eliminate causative risk factors (risk reduction).

PROCESS MEASURES

Steps in a program logically required for the program to be successful.

PROCESS OBJECTIVE

The level to which a contributing factor is to be reduced as a result of successfully carrying out a program's activities.

PUBLIC HEALTH

Activities that society undertakes to assure the conditions in which people can be healthy. This includes organized community efforts to prevent, identify, and counter threats to the health of the public.

PUBLIC HEALTH PRACTICE GUIDELINES

Systematically developed statements that assist public health practitioner decisions about interventions at the community level.

PUBLIC HEALTH PRACTICES

Those organizational practices or processes that are necessary and sufficient to assure that the core functions of public health are being carried out effectively. Ten public health practices have been identified:

1. Assess the health needs of the community.
2. Investigate the occurrence of health risks and hazards in the community.
3. Analyze identified health needs for their determinants and contributing factors.
4. Advocate and build support for public health.
5. Establish priorities from among identified health needs.
6. Develop comprehensive policies and plans for priority health needs.
7. Manage resources efficiently.
8. Ensure that priority health needs are addressed in the community.
9. Evaluate the effects of programs and services.
10. Inform and educate the public.

PUBLIC HEALTH SERVICE

U.S. Public Health Service as reorganized in 1996; now includes the Office of Public Health and Science (which is headed by the Assistant Secretary for Health and includes the Office of the Surgeon General), eight operating agencies (Health Resources and Service Administration, Indian Health Service, Centers for Disease Control and Prevention, National Institutes of Health, Food and Drug Administration, Substance Abuse and Mental Health Services Administration, Agency for Toxic Substances and Disease Registry, and Agency for Health Care Policy and Research), and the Regional Health Administrators for the 10 federal regions of the country.

PUBLIC HEALTH SYSTEM

That part of the larger health system that seeks to assure conditions in which people can be healthy by carrying out public health's three core functions. The system can be further described by its inputs, practices, outputs, and outcomes.

QUALITY OF CARE

The degree to which health services for individuals increase the likelihood of desired health outcomes and are consistent with established professional standards and judgments of value to the consumer. Quality also may be seen as the degree to which actions taken or not taken maximize the probability of beneficial health outcomes and minimize risk and other undesired outcomes, given the existing state of medical science and art.

QUALITY-ADJUSTED LIFE YEARS (QALYS)

A measure of health status that assigns to each period of time a weight, ranging from 0 to 1, corresponding to the health-related quality of life during that period; these are then summed across time periods to calculate quality-adjusted life years (QALYs). For each period, a weight of 1 corresponds to optimal health, and a weight of 0 corresponds to a health state equivalent to death.

RATE

A mathematical expression for the relation between the numerator (number of deaths, diseases, disabilities, services, etc.) and denominator (population at risk), together with specification of time. Rates make possible a comparison of the number of events between populations and at different times. Rates may be crude, specific, or adjusted.

REHABILITATION

An intervention strategy that seeks to return individuals to the maximum level of functioning possible.

RISK FACTOR

A behavior or condition that, on the basis of scientific evidence or theory, is thought to influence susceptibility to a specific health problem.

RISK RATIO/RELATIVE RISK

The ratio of the risk or likelihood of the occurrence of specific health outcomes or events in one group to that of another; risk ratios provide a measure of the relative difference in risk between the two groups. Relative risk is an example of a risk ratio in which the incidence of disease in the exposed group is divided by the incidence of disease in an unexposed group.

SCREENING

The use of technology and procedures to differentiate those individuals with signs or symptoms of disease from those less likely to have the disease. Then, if necessary, further diagnosis and, if indicated, early intervention and treatment can be provided.

SECONDARY MEDICAL CARE

Specialized attention and ongoing management for common and less frequently encountered medical conditions, including support services for people with special challenges due to chronic or long-term conditions. Services provided by medical specialists who generally do not have their first contact with patients (e.g., cardiologists, urologists, dermatologists). In the United States, however, there has been a trend toward self-referral by patients for these services rather than referral by primary care providers.

SECONDARY PREVENTION

Prevention strategies that seek to identify and control disease processes in their early stages before signs and symptoms develop (screening and treatment).

SPAN OF HEALTHY LIFE

A measure of health status that combines life expectancy with self-reported health status and functional disabilities to calculate the number of years in which an individual is likely to function normally.

SPECIFIC RATE

Rates vary greatly by race, sex, and age. A rate can be made specific for sex, age, race, cause of death, or a combination of these.

STATE HEALTH AGENCY

The unit of state government that has leading responsibility for identifying and meeting the health needs of the state's citizens. State health agencies can be free-standing or units of multipurpose health and human service agencies.

SURVEILLANCE

Systematic monitoring of the health status of a population.

TERTIARY MEDICAL CARE

Subspecialty referral care requiring highly specialized personnel and facilities. Services provided by highly specialized providers (e.g., neurologists, neurosurgeons, thoracic surgeons, intensive care units). Such services frequently require highly sophisticated equipment and support facilities. The development of these services has largely been a function of diagnostic and therapeutic advances attained through basic and clinical biomedical research.

TERTIARY PREVENTION

Prevention strategies that prevent disability by restoring individuals to their optimal level of functioning after a disease or injury is established and damage is done.

WAIVER

States must obtain waivers of current federal Medicaid law provisions from the Health Care Financing Administration to enroll their Medicaid population in managed-care plans or otherwise deviate from law.

YEARS OF POTENTIAL LIFE LOST (YPLL)

A measure of the impact of disease or injury in a population that calculates years of life lost before a specific age (often age 65 or age 75). This approach places additional value on deaths that occur at earlier ages.

Index